HIGH ABOVE
COURTSIDE

THE LOST MEMOIRS
OF JOHNNY MOST

BY
MIKE CAREY

WITH
JAMIE MOST

www.sportspublishingllc.com

Director of production: Susan M. Moyer
Developmental editor: Kipp Wilfong
Book design: Jennifer L. Polson
Project manager: Jim Henehan
Dust jacket design and insert: Christine F. Mohrbacher
Copy editors: Cynthia L. McNew and Holly Birch

ISBN: 1-58261-740-6

Printed in the United States.

This book is dedicated to
my children. The loves of my life.

ACKNOWLEDGMENTS

Mike Carey and Jamie Most would like to especially thank Red Auerbach and Larry Bird for their contributions to *High Above Courtside*. We'd also like to thank all the Celtics players for their cooperation. Special thanks to: Jeff Twiss, who never failed to give his time to provide answers to hundreds of questions; Jan Volk, an adviser and friend; Rick and Donna Carlisle; Dr. Stu and Sonia Freedman; Mrs. Jim Pansullo; Marv Albert; Steve Holman; Ellen Jones, who spent weeks of her own time editing this book; KC Jones; Tommy and Helen Heinsohn; Bob Cousy; Bill Walton; Ed Gillooly; *Herald* reporters Rich Thompson and Steve Bulpett; Bill Fitch, who graciously took the time to read and edit the manuscript; former Celtics owner Harry Mangurian; Derek and Renni Vogel; Ashley Sollima; *Globe* executive sports editor Don Skwar; *Globe* librarian Elizabeth Tuite; *Herald* columnist Joe Fitzgerald; Mrs. Al Grenert; Scott Grenert; Bob Fish; Jimmy Myers; Glenn Ordway; Ted Serandis; Dave Gavitt; referees Norm Drucker, Darrel Garretson, Kenny Mauer, and Wally Rooney; attorneys Valerie Pawson and George Hailer; attorney Al Kafka; NBA commissioner David Stern; NBA Entertainment; Zelda Spoelstra; Tom Carelli; Doug Lane; Harvey Pollack; Don Ainge; Dan Ainge; NBA Properties; Jim Tuberosa, who provided invaluable help; Mike Newlin; *Patriot Ledger* reporter Mike Fine; *Herald* librarian John Cronin; the Celtics organization; Ron Burton; Joe DeNucci; Tony DeMarco; Adam Silver; Gregg Winik; Charlie Rosenzweig; Dan Opallo; Howie Sylvester; Eddie Andelman; Paula Silas; Nancy O'Brien; Dr. Allan Ropper; Dr. Arnie Scheller; Wayne Lebeaux; Mark Vancil; and most importantly, Margery, Rob, and Andrea Most and the late Mrs. Joseph Carey.

CONTENTS

PREFACE

When Johnny Most asked me to co-write his autobiography in June of 1984, I believed his memories of his broadcasting career, including his years as Celtics play-by-play man for the 16-championship team, would be a fascinating subject.

A well-known publisher agreed with my assessment, and in 1985 Johnny and I began to write this book. Unfortunately, Johnny's health began to decline two years later. Although he continued to broadcast Celtics games, he was beginning to experience blood circulation problems and could not devote sufficient time to finishing the project. At the same time, my mother was battling terminal cancer, and I had to temporarily delay writing the final chapters.

Before long, a representative of the publisher called Johnny and me and told us *High Above Courtside* was "being shelved" because, in his opinion, the book would not be profitable because Johnny would not be able to promote the book due to his health issues.

Johnny was crushed. He desperately wanted to complete the project and see his autobiography in print. He told me, "I don't care about the money end of it. I wanted this book to be a tribute to the Celtics players, coaches, Red Auerbach, and Walter Brown. I wanted it to be dedicated to my children. Now it's not going to happen."

As his health continued to decline, he said to me, "Keep knocking on doors, babe. Just don't give up on this. Promise me that."

When Johnny passed away on January 3, 1993, I vowed to complete the book and eventually find a publisher. Throughout the past 14 years, I continued interviewing Celtics players, from Arnie Risen to Kevin Stacom, to "High Henry" Finkel and "Tall Paul" Silas. Each had specific, fond, often humorous memories of Johnny, a man they considered both a "teammate" and a friend.

For 16 years, the incomplete manuscript was kept in a file cabinet, with anecdotes and new information added periodically.

Thanks in large part to the NBA and ESPN Classics, Johnny's most famous calls lived on. In 2002, I sent three sample chapters of *High Above Courtside* to Mike Pearson, an acquisitions editor at Sports Publishing. Within days, he called me and said, "We want to publish Johnny's book. As far as we're concerned, the book is timeless."

The main body of the book was completed in 1988. Unfortunately, since that time, some of the players, coaches, broadcasters and opponents quoted or mentioned in the book have passed away. Among them: Marty Glickman, Earl Strom, Wilt Chamberlain, Chick Hearn, Chuck Connors, Bob Davies, Jack Nichols, Andy Phillip, Don Barksdale, Jim Pansullo, Al Grenert, Earl Strom and Richie Powers.

Obviously, Johnny's chapter entitled "My All-Opponents Team" is somewhat outdated since Michael Jordan was only in his fourth year and had yet to win a championship or an MVP Award.

This work is not intended to be a history of the Boston Celtics' successes and failures. Rather, it is a collection of Johnny's memories about the characters and character of the Celtics teams he covered as well as a self-portrait of one of sports' most fascinating, controversial, and opinionated figures.

—Mike Carey

INTRODUCTION

By Red Auerbach

I was delighted when author Mike Carey invited me to provide the introduction for this book on the life and career of Johnny Most, because no one served the Celtics with greater devotion or distinction and it would be a shame if that legacy were to get lost with the passage of time.

Johnny was our play-by-play man for 37 seasons, and I completely agreed with his philosophy. He told me, late in his career, "Red, the way I look at it, the most important game I'll ever broadcast is tonight's."

Even then, with physical ailments slowing him down, there was no resting on his laurels, no coasting on his reputation, no "false hustle," to use one of my own pet terms. Until his final wrap-up at the microphone, Johnny approached each game exactly the way I wanted our players approaching them, as if the game they were about to play was the only one that mattered, the one they had to win.

There was no such thing as a meaningless game to Johnny, not even in the lean years, and we had a few of those, too. For all his theatrics and eccentricities, which were many and legendary, he was, above all, a consummate pro who never lost that enthusiasm for his job or the great pride he took in his performance of it.

In all our years of winning championships, it was a source of great comfort to me to know that our roster also included a champion "high above courtside," as he used to say, connecting us to our fans.

I used to laugh at the very predictable knock he'd receive as each new wave of critics arrived, rushing to inform me, "He's a homer!" They'd tell me that as if I didn't know; I'd answer, "You're damn right he is, and that's just the way we want him!"

He was funny and entertaining, but don't misunderstand, Johnny Most was no clown. He understood the intricacies and theories of the game, and sure, he loved the Celtics, just as they loved him, and he made no secret of it. Only a phony would have denied that, and Johnny was no phony.

From his great friendship with Don Barksdale, who joined us in 1953, to the friendships he developed with Larry Bird, Kevin McHale, Danny Ainge and Robert Parish, Johnny shared a bond with every player who wore the Celtics jersey, spending time in serious conversation, getting to know them, making them aware of the players we had before them and the legacies they left. He was a wonderful link from generation to generation.

Johnny could get along with just about everyone, and he did.

He was a Jewish guy from New York who knew a thing or two about hatred and bigotry, which enabled him to relate to many players' personal backgrounds, sympathetically and helpfully. In that respect, he reminded me a lot of Bill Reinhart, my own coach at George Washington University, an American of German descent who taught me that if you treat a man with respect, regardless of his race or nationality, you will get that man's respect in return.

Johnny believed that, too, proving it over and over.

He was also a World War II Army Air Corps veteran who earned seven battle stars as an aerial gunner on a B-24, which meant he had credentials of his own when it came to character, bravery and coolness under fire.

It wasn't something he talked about openly, because heroes don't go around taking bows for being heroes, but for those of us who knew his background, it was just one more reason to hold him in highest regard.

He was a poet, an exceptionally keen observer of individuals, someone you could safely confide in, and a raconteur who could hold court all night long in hotel coffee shops, which he often did.

Johnny Most was, in a word, an original.

And I am proud to say he was my friend.

In his memory, I hope you will enjoy this book.

He would have loved it, and so do I.

Boston, Massachusetts
April 30, 2003

1

FROM THE BRONX
TO BOSTON

"Havlicek Stole the Ball"—four words that were to
become my signature call. I screamed them out as
the Celtics edged the Philadelphia 76ers, 110-109,
to win the Eastern Division on April 15, 1965. Little did I realize at
that time that my gravel-voiced, near-hysterical call would be the
pinnacle of my career. I certainly had no idea that my description
would be aired countless times on radio and TV throughout the
ensuing years, with announcers labeling the play and call as one of
the NBA's most unforgettable moments.

Yet it is but one of thousands of wonderful memories I treasure
when I recall my experiences in broadcasting, which all began with
the nighttime fantasies of a sports-crazed little boy.

Many kids would dream of becoming cops, firemen, pilots or
football players. Me? I would sit up at night in my bed and envision
myself as a big-time sportscaster. I'd pull the blankets over my head
and pretend I was broadcasting a Dodgers-Yankees World Series game
from the press box at old Ebbets Field. For my "microphone," I'd use
an empty glass or maybe a hollow flashlight. Then I'd be all set to
create some of the most exciting games in baseball history. Or so I
firmly believed.

I had memorized all the rosters—by name, by number, by position. I knew batting averages, earned run averages. I knew every player's nickname. I knew whether they were righty or southpaw. I could even tell you their hat and shoe sizes. Knew 'em by heart. I mean, how could a kid not know that Frankie Frisch, the Fordham Flash, was a switch hitter with a lifetime batting average well above .320? Or anyone worth his salt would never dream of calling "Rabbit" Maranville, one of the game's greatest base stealers, by his given name, Walter. That would be like referring to Yogi Berra as "Lawrence."

Yes, even in my imaginary, under-the-covers games, I devised my own nicknames for both the good and bad guys. My "productions" had to be thrilling, nail-biting and "edgy." Other elements of my play-by-play gave me the opportunity to create nonstop controversy and tense, unpredictable endings.

There might be an unassisted triple play by Yankee second baseman Tony Lazzeri or a steal of home by Dodger speedster Billy Herman, maybe an inside-the-park grand slammer by Babe Ruth, a no-hitter by Dodger righty Van Lingle Mungo, or even a perfect game thrown by Yankee star Lefty Gomez, my favorite player.

Nothing short of sensational was the essence of my broadcasts. And, of course, I supplied my own crowd noise—which I had down pat, from the sound of vendors selling i-i-i-i-c-e cold Ballantine be-ee-ers and red-hot franks to the fans' cries of "ya bum" or "down in front."

The same applied to the football season. When autumn arrived, I moved over to announcing college gridiron games, where the highlight of my season was imitating my hero, broadcaster Bill Stern, calling the always rousing Army-Navy contest.

My 10-year-old audience of one loved every exciting minute of it. My parents, John and Rose Most, who could overhear my "broadcasts" from the living room, must have thought I was eccentric, to say the least. Yet they tolerated it—perhaps because they derived as much enjoyment from hearing my imagination at work as I did from "immortalizing" the feats of my sports idols as I sat in my bed.

My nightly "productions" were just a case of a 10-year-old boy entertaining himself for an hour or so. One might have thought mine was simply a childhood fantasy that sooner or later would run its course. Yet here I am almost 60 years later, still experiencing the same passions and thrills as that small boy from the Bronx.

Let me tell you just how much I loved sports and athletes. Each day when the Yankees were playing an afternoon home game, I'd walk the four miles to arrive at the stadium just as the game was ending. Then I'd wait outside the players' exit for the privilege of meeting the great Lou Gehrig and escorting him to his car. I never asked him for an autograph. All I wanted was a handshake and the chance to ask as many questions as he could tolerate answering. And Lou Gehrig had the patience of a saint. He'd open his car door and then stand for five, sometimes 10 minutes, answering each and every question from this wide-eyed, inquisitive boy with dreams of a future in the world of sports.

Born June 15, 1923 in Tenafly, New Jersey, I was an only child raised by two exceptionally caring, patient, and unselfish parents. Several years later our family moved to the Bronx, where my dad, a struggling young dentist, often treated his patients for free because they almost all were poor, especially during the Depression years. My family lived near Van Cortland Park, a neighborhood above my father's means, in order to ensure the best education for me and a healthy environment of fine libraries, parks, stores, etc.

My grandfather, Johann Most, was a political dissident in Bavaria, a region in southwestern Germany. He was a rather well-known radical whose philosophy was to speak out against bigotry and corruption. Even though he was an activist long before Adolf Hitler rose to power, Johann Most was an outspoken critic of the German government, with its openly anti-Semitic views and authoritarian ways. Although not a Jew, he married a Jewish woman.

In 1882 he emigrated to the United States because his public statements concerning the social problems in Germany made him an enemy of the state. Once he was settled in the United States, my grandfather continued, with perhaps even greater fervor, to crusade against social injustices and bigotry.

My father's political views mirrored those of my grandfather. He not only refused to tolerate bigotry and injustice, he did everything in his power to speak out against these wrongs. He encountered anti-Semitism on a daily basis in New York City. His method of combating it as an individual was simply to lead an exemplary life as a devoted family man openly proud of his Jewish heritage. As a child, I remember how my father would talk with me about how he dealt with incidents of ethnic prejudice. He wanted me to understand that I, too, would inevitably face such intolerance and bigotry. More importantly, his goal was to teach me to be strong, independent and unafraid to stand up for my principles and heritage.

My father fought against all forms of bigotry. His patient list included people of all races and creeds. Not too many medical professionals do business on a "pay-me-when-you-can" basis, but my father did.

And in the early forties when African-Americans first began to organize protests to fight back against centuries of prejudice, my father joined the NAACP. He attended rallies, marched, and even wrote articles for the Bronx chapter of the NAACP.

"In Germany," he would tell me, "Jews were treated as second-class citizens even when I was a youngster. Many Jews, I am ashamed to say, accepted their status as merely a fact of life. Those who were brave enough to speak out against their unfair treatment—such as your grandfather—were harassed, berated, and punished economically. The Negroes [as blacks were called by whites in the '40s] face the same problems, and I want to do what I can to stop this hatred and prejudice."

My mother, a Russian immigrant, was proud of my father's views and his political activism. On many occasions, she would join him when he attended a political event or a protest. However, her role in my family as a homemaker was equally important, because we had a household budget of less than $20 a week and it was up to her to keep us well fed and well dressed.

All of our clothes came from second-hand shops. Nearly all of the shirts and pants she bought needed altering or mending, which she would do herself on an ancient Singer sewing machine. When it came to cooking, she was a genius. She would buy a huge chicken, cut it into sections, and then use different recipes to make a variety of dinners for three days. Our breakfast consisted of a bowl of cereal, sometimes topped with evaporated milk and sometimes eaten dry. Our lunch usually consisted of a baloney and egg sandwich.

It may sound like we struggled, but I never felt that way. The love in that house made me feel like a king.

Some of my enthusiasm for sports came from my father, who played semipro baseball, ran cross-country and boxed for NYU. He played against Frisch, who was known for his roughhouse tactics. Yet it was Frisch who described my dad as "the dirtiest guy I ever played against." I guess that was Frankie's way of delivering a compliment.

Even though my father didn't have a lot of spare time or pocket money, he'd usually take me to three or four baseball or football games a year. I'd notice he would always root for the Yankee or Brooklyn players who hustled but never cheered for anyone on the visiting team. The only time he would get upset was when an outfielder misplayed a fly ball or when a base runner didn't slide on a close play.

"Johnny, everyone out there is going to make fielding errors," he'd explain to me. "Can't be helped. But the really good players never make mental mistakes. They're always thinking about what they're going to do in different situations. I want you to remember that, no matter what sport you're playing."

At Dewitt Clinton High School, I made the football, soccer and basketball teams, as well as taking and giving some lumps in Police Athletic League boxing. Whenever possible, my father would be in the stands, watching my every move. Never once, no matter how poorly I might have played, did he criticize me. Instead he'd find a couple of things I did well, and he would make some offhand, positive comment to me, just for encouragement.

Dewitt Clinton, an all-boys school, has produced a long list of famous athletes and celebrities, such as actor Burt Lancaster, comedians Jan Murray and Larry Storch, Yankee pitcher Eddie Lopat, Syracuse Nats forward-center Dolph Schayes and boxer Sugar Ray Robinson, all classmates or teammates of mine. Later, such outstanding basketball players as Lou Bender, Tiny Archibald, Tom Henderson, Butch Lee, Steve Shephard, Ron Behagen and Ricky Sobers also began their careers playing for Clinton.

My cousin, Stuart Friedman, now a retired veterinarian in California, was my best friend throughout high school. We were two "rebels" and would do anything for a laugh. For example, all 1,200 graduates were supposed to wear the same outfits—a blue blazer, a white shirt, a tie and white pants. Stu and I decided we'd do things a little differently. At my class's ceremony there were 1,198 boys dressed in the proper attire, and then there was Stu and me, wearing identical white jackets, blue shirts with ascots, and blue slacks. We drew a lot of stares from the faculty and fellow students, but for the most part, the teachers and kids got a kick out of our little gag.

After graduating from Clinton, I enrolled at Alabama but eventually decided to transfer to Brooklyn College, where I majored in liberal arts. In sports, I concentrated on football, playing quarterback in the same backfield as Allie Sherman, who went on to become the successful head coach of the New York Football Giants. (Later, when I was inducted into Brooklyn College's Sports Hall of Fame in 1986, the emcee for the night was none other than Allie, which made the honor even greater than I anticipated.) I was a good all-around athlete but certainly not pro material, so I focused my ambitions on the next best thing, sports broadcasting.

However, before I could venture into the business, I was drafted into the army in November of 1942, a month into my senior year at Brooklyn College. I spent a year in the tank corps, working in the mobile artillery as a member of the tank destroyer division before transferring to the Army Air Corps. For the next three years, I was to experience the most emotional and disturbing times of my life as the realities of World War II took a devastating toll on me.

My duties were as waist gunner and radio operator on a B-24 bomber. In all, I flew 28 raids in Europe, including missions over Vienna, Brenner Pass, Munich, Lintz, Ragenburgh, Milan and Trieste.

I was awarded seven major battle stars, a Purple Heart, a Distinguished Flying Cross, the Air Medal and two Presidential Citations. On one mission our plane was hit, and my legs were burned when an electrical wire singed them badly. After we managed to make it back to the base, I refused to go to the hospital for treatment, because the army would automatically send a telegram home to inform your family of your injury. I didn't want to worry my parents, so I had a couple of buddies bandage the wound. The doctors were so angry that I wouldn't be examined that I was arrested and confined to quarters.

As any veteran will tell you, medals never ease the memories of the horrors of war. Returning from one mission over Austria, I looked down at a small, leveled town, which had no signs of life. When I got back to my barracks, I wrote down my feelings:

THE BOMBED VILLAGE
Dark streets
like dead snakes
lie unblessed
in bleak wake.

Near the end of my tour, I visited an Allied cemetery in France. I was the only visitor on that particular day, and I slowly walked toward the center of what must have been 40 rows of graves, many without markers. A million thoughts crossed my mind as I unsteadily walked past grave after grave. What were these soldiers' lives like? How did they die? Did they have families? Why did they die, while I survived? I had a million questions and no answers.

So, again, in the only way I could express myself, I sat down near a cement shack that "guarded" the dead and wrote this poem:

THE WAR DEAD
I stood among the graves today
and swept the scene with sight
and the corps of men who lay beneath
looked up to say goodnight.
The thunder still, the battle done
the fray has passed them by
but as they rest forever more
they must be asking why.

When I returned home from Europe in 1945, I visited the parents of a good friend of mine, Howard Wolheim, who had been killed on a bombing mission over Japan on his 21st birthday. He had been a gunner on my crew for a year before being transferred to the Pacific.

One day I had been sitting in my barracks when a letter arrived from Howard's parents informing me that his plane had been shot down and that there were no survivors. The letter ended, "I know you would want to know. God bless you and keep you safe."

For three hours I stared at the letter as memories flooded my mind and anger filled my soul. The loss of life, the helplessness, the unfair reality of war all hit me at once.

When I returned to the U.S., I thought I could ease Howard's family's pain a little by visiting their home in Trenton, New Jersey. I recall meeting his mother and being invited into the living room. The first thing I saw was Howard's photo on the fireplace mantle. And next to it was a letter from his commanding officer and a silver case containing the medal Howard had been awarded posthumously.

She handed me the silver case, and I opened it gently. As tears streamed down my face, I closed the case, patted it, handed it back to her and gave her a hug. She thanked me for coming, and then I left without saying another word. That night, as I recalled all of the times I shared with my brave, deceased friend, I wrote down my thoughts about my final visit with him:

THE MEDAL
I went to see my friend today
but he glitters in a case
bright, shiny, mute
with no more tomorrows.

Several months after returning from the war, I reentered Brooklyn College to complete my degree. While there, I mustered enough nerve to audition for some bit parts in (believe it or not) soap operas. I never did land a part larger than a one-liner, but I did get to appear in a few of the most popular radio shows of the day, such as *Dick Tracy, Young Widow Brown,* and *Portia Faces Life.*

I was eager, ambitious, and broke, so I gladly worked for peanuts. If a job paid enough to buy a little dinner and my fare home on the subway, I'd take it. On many occasions I worked for less than the price of a meal and a token, but I knew the value of gaining experience and making contacts.

For a while, I worked on a radio program called *The House We Live In*, which was devoted to publicizing the virtues of the newly established United Nations. At the same time I served as an announcer-actor-script writer for *FM Playhouse*, a show created by two Brooklyn College friends, Frank and Doris Jacoby. The "soap opera" scripts were a bit on the schmaltzy side, but the public was listening and enjoying this sort of melodrama. Some famous people, including actress Jean Stapleton and newsman Marvin Kaplan, began their careers on this show.

To earn a few extra dollars, I found employment on the CBS Television Network's quiz shows, which were just gaining popularity with audiences. In rehearsals, I would stand under hot lights pretending to be a contestant, answering a few questions about what kind of job I held, where I lived, how I planned to spend all my winnings. Then I would be quizzed. All of my responses were timed so that the producer could judge how many contestants might be needed for the actual show.

Now, I don't want to brag and call myself a quiz whiz, but I did manage to come up with the correct answers more than 75 percent of the time. Which inevitably enticed me to try out and be selected to appear on *The $64,000 Question*. I made it to the $32,000 level when I lost to a mailman who was later named in the quiz game scandals as one of the contestants who was provided with the answers in advance by the producers. I had no idea the shows were rigged. It was a secret that somehow went undetected for more than eight years.

All of my early jobs shared two things: The hours were ridiculously long and the pay was ridiculously short. You could wait days or weeks for a part to come along. You could log hundreds of miles walking from audition to audition. But I was still having a hell of a time searching for my one big lucky break.

Shortly after graduating from Brooklyn College in '46, I landed my first full-time position at a radio station in Oil City, Pennsylvania, located about 80 miles north of Pittsburgh. The job was offered to me by the Jacobys, my *FM Playhouse* bosses, who now had become program directors for Oil City's only radio station. They warned me that the town was nothing more than one large, filthy mine pit; they also cautioned me about terrible working conditions. But the chance to work with the Jacobys again made the offer too good to resist. Within 24 hours, I was packed and on a bus bound for the Pennsylvania mountains.

Working for the princely sum of $41.62 a week, I put in 58 hours over the course of seven days (there was no such thing as a day off back then). For this, I was given the title of "assistant program director." Perhaps that lofty job description sounds impressive, but I had to do every job at the station except spit-shine the boss's shoes. In the morning I was the newscaster; in the afternoon I switched into the DJ's seat; then at night I'd get to the fun part of the job, my own sports show.

After that, I'd head to the nearest bar, have a couple beers, and then go home to rest up for the next day's work marathon.

The three of us did have a blast. We created a show called *Bedtime Bash*, which was what you might call a radio version of *Saturday Night Live*. We did spoofs on commercials, ad-lib comedy and man-in-the-street interviews. We even caused a near riot one night when we voted to break every copy of our most hated record, a top 10 tune called "Near You" by Frances Craig. Within an hour after we had gone on the air and cracked that god-awful piece of music into tiny pieces, 100 irate teenagers stormed the station in protest. Finally we calmed them down by managing to dig up the station's one remaining copy of "Near You."

Unfortunately our fun lasted only two months in "good old Oil City" before all three of us were abruptly fired—after I tried to remold the station owner's round nose into a flat one with a right-handed hook. No sir, no one has ever accused me of excelling in the traditional game known as "office politics."

Here are the details of how I managed to get canned so quickly from my first full-time gig in radio. The owner, a guy named Gene Gosch, whom I shall always refer to as a first-class jackass, was being his usual obnoxious self one night when he made a remark that insulted Doris. I took offense and exchanged words with this self-proclaimed "King of Oil City," who also owned both of the town's newspapers. He didn't like my choice of descriptive adjectives regarding his character and made the mistake of shoving me. That gave me my opportunity to vent all my hostility by clocking him.

Easy come, easy go. All three of us were immediately canned.

"Johnny," said Doris, as we left the station that night, "thanks for sticking up for me. I hope we can work together again. I've had so much fun. You've taught me so much, including every curse word I know. And with Gosch for a boss, I got a chance to use every bad word I learned from you to put him in his place."

After collecting our paychecks, the Jacobys and I headed back to New York City. Less than a month later, I traveled north to Norwich, Connecticut, where I found a job at WNOC that gave me my first taste of broadcasting live sporting events, the Norwich Free Academy basketball games. Call it my internship. I discovered my strengths and weaknesses and worked on developing my own signature style.

In the fall of '47, I moved on to a larger and better-paying station, WVOS in New York's Catskill Mountain region, to do the basketball play-by-play for Liberty High School. As luck would have it, Marty Glickman, who was broadcasting the New York Football Giants and the New York Knickerbockers, happened to be vacationing at nearby Grossinger's and was listening to one of my broadcasts while enjoying a beer at a neighborhood tavern.

"That kid's good," he remarked to the bartender. "Any chance I could meet him?"

Well, because the bartender and I had spent many a night talking and arguing about sports, he immediately called my station engineer and left this message for me: "Get your butt down here fast. Marty Glickman wants to meet you."

The message was relayed to me, and as soon as the game ended, I broke all land speed records. Five minutes from the gym to my house, two minutes to spruce up a little by putting on the least wrinkled tie I could find, one minute to dash up to Grossinger's. Here I was, a complete unknown, a squeaky-voiced kid, being given the honor of meeting a legend like Glickman. How much of a legend? Well, if someone had given me the choice of meeting Marty Glickman or Marilyn Monroe, Marilyn would have had to wait her turn.

Not only was Marty an accomplished broadcaster, but he had also been a world-class athlete. At James Madison High in Brooklyn, he had broken numerous school and league track records while also starring in basketball and football. He went on to Syracuse University, where he became an explosive halfback and a strong All-America candidate.

In track, he was virtually unbeatable as a sprinter. In fact, he was considered a cinch to win a medal in the '36 Olympics. To no one's surprise, Marty earned a berth on the U.S. 400-meter relay squad, which consisted of Foy Draper, Mack Robinson (the older brother of baseball star Jackie) and Sam Stoller, who, like Marty, was Jewish.

Marty never did receive the chance to fulfill his dream of winning a gold medal, however. Instead, he was victimized by the politics of 1936, the bigotry of Adolf Hitler and the stupidity and cowardice of Avery Brundage, the head of the U.S. Olympic Committee.

The site of the games was Berlin. During the first few days of the games, the renowned Jessie Owens embarrassed Hitler and the entire German government by winning three medals. Now, with the 400-meter relays approaching, Hitler maneuvered, pressured, and begged Brundage to let Germany save face—at the expense of two fine Jewish men who were about to be cheated out of the greatest achievement in sports.

To the shock of everyone, the spineless and, in my opinion, bigoted Brundage bowed to the pressure exerted by Hitler. Moments before the race was to have begun, Brundage replaced Glickman and

Stoller with Owens and another black sprinter, Ralph Metcalf, who would later become a Chicago congressman. Although the U.S. team won by a full 15 yards and Germany finished a distant fourth, Brundage's lack of courage turned what could have been a magnificent moment in sports into a disgrace.

Each day since, Marty Glickman has had to live with the bitter memories. As the years pass, he prefers to talk about any subject other than the injustices he and Stoller suffered on that summer day. Just once, he shared his thoughts with me about the consequences of Brundage's disregard for human feeling. It occurred shortly after Marty revisited Berlin in 1985 for the first time since the '36 Olympics.

As he told me of his stay in Berlin, all the rage he had suppressed for decades came flowing out.

"I was near the area where the Olympic Stadium had stood. Suddenly I found myself cursing and yelling out to no one but myself," he told me. "I let all my emotions come out, feelings I didn't even know I had been carrying with me all these years. 'How could such evil people plot to take a teenager's dream away because of bigotry and politics? How could they just crush my dream, a dream I had worked so hard to achieve?' When I regained my composure, I turned, left the area, and caught the first plane out of Berlin.

"I was just 18 when I earned my spot on the U.S. Olympic team. I was filled with pride that I was fortunate enough to be representing my country. And then, without any warning, Brundage made his absurd decision. He didn't have the guts to inform me personally. Instead he had one of his flunkies give me the bad news. I was shattered, numb. How could politics and prejudice infiltrate their way into athletics? And why did it have to occur at this particular moment in time? I'll think about what happened every day for the rest of my life. It hurts me to know I will never have that gold medal to show my grandchildren."

For you and me, those events might have been enough to make us bitter about sports, politics, and life in general. Yet Marty never has allowed the heartache of those days in Berlin to affect his love and enthusiasm for athletic competition. All of which is why I, as a young broadcaster, felt so honored that a person of Marty Glickman's character had asked to meet me.

And I'll never forget the manner in which he spoke to me. There wasn't a trace of "know-it-all" in his voice. There wasn't any pointed criticism. In fact, what he offered was praise and fatherly advice. Sitting in Grossinger's bar, he talked of how I would have to make my own breaks.

"This business is funny. Just having a decent voice and good grasp of the facts doesn't guarantee success," he noted. "You have to meet the right people. If you're going to move up the ladder, you're going to need a boost every now and then. Stay as close to New York City as possible and try to get into the Sportscasters' Association. The contacts you make there can help you throughout your whole career."

It was largely through Marty's efforts that I was eventually able to join this elite broadcasters' "fraternity," which had New York Yankee play-by-play man Mel Allen as its president and Glickman as its vice president. Once I got in, I never missed a meeting. In fact, I'd be the first to arrive and the last to leave. This was, after all, a chance to be among my idols and listen to them exchange classic stories about athletes and sportscasters.

Despite my new status, I didn't kid myself into thinking I was "one of the boys" just yet. Their balding heads, deep voices, strong opinions, experience, and, in some cases, their ability to drink for hours at a time were constant reminders to me that I still had a long way to go before I would be anything more than an apprentice in this trade. Still, there was a great feeling of pride and excitement just to be sitting in the same room as these "old pros."

My broadcasting style was influenced principally by four legends: Ted Husing, Bill Stern, Mel Allen, and, above all, Marty Glickman.

Husing had a great vocabulary and a gift for painting vivid pictures with his phrases. For example, when Yale crushed Harvard in an Ivy League title game, Husing concluded his broadcast by stating, "The men from Yale were magnificent; the boys from Harvard were putrid."

Sometimes, though, Husing would go overboard to showcase his use of language. I remember one particular night when he was broadcasting boxing from the Eastern Parkway Arena. One fighter was covered with blood as he sat in his corner after being pummeled by his opponent. Husing got a little fancy with his description: "The poor fellow is expectorating claret into a receptacle."

Now, even I didn't know the meaning of the word "claret," so I looked it up in a dictionary and discovered it meant a deep red wine. All Husing had to say was that the boxer was spitting up blood, but Ted always wanted his descriptions to be unique.

While I didn't care for Husing's use of rarely used words and phrases, I did admire his effort to sound unique. That became one of my goals.

There were many reasons why I admired Stern. He was the Howard Cosell of his time—a brash, loud, cocky know-it-all who earned a reputation of being controversial long before Cosell entered the field of sports broadcasting. I'm positive Cosell copied Stern's style. However, Stern was far more imaginative and creative than Cosell. If Bill didn't know the background of a player or a coach, he would just make up stories about the guy. He believed good fiction could be more entertaining than dull facts.

And Bill had a way with words. To give you an illustration, Stern covered the 1940 Tennessee-USC Rose Bowl game in which the Vols were soundly beaten, 14-0. A year earlier, the Vols had beaten Oklahoma 17-0 in the Orange Bowl. Stern used one sentence to wrap up his broadcast of Tennessee's loss to Southern Cal: "A garland of roses to the '39 Tennessee team; onions and garlic to this year's edition."

My habit of inventing nicknames for players, coaches and referees was largely due to the influence of Mel Allen's play-by-play. The "Voice of the Yankees" was one of my idols when I was a kid. He referred to a home run as a "Ballantine Blast." In calling a game, DiMaggio was always "Joltin' Joe." Phil Rizzuto was "The Little Scooter." Mantle was "The Mick." And whenever there was a spectacular play, Mel would emphasize its greatness by exclaiming, "How 'bout that!"

From Marty, I learned that to be an effective play-by-play man, you had to be hard-hitting, expressive, quick, accurate but concise. "If you try to describe every little thing that goes on in a basketball game, you'll always be 10 seconds behind the action. You can't waste words," he told me. "For instance, you can't say that a player 'dribbles right, then dribbles left, looks for someone to get open, now he picks up his dribble and is in trouble.' You've got to put fast-paced action into every sentence. "I knew exactly what he meant, which is why, decades later, I came up with the phrase "fiddlin' and diddlin'."

Another example: When I first started broadcasting basketball, I would say something like, "Ed Macauley drives into the pivot. Now he turns, now he holds the ball high and takes a shot. It's good." Soon I found a better, quicker way of saying the exact same thing: "Macauley in the pivot, turns, shoots. Bang!"

Perhaps my most famous phrase was invented out of necessity. The Lakers' Jerry West had the quickest release I've ever seen. I simply was always two seconds behind with my play-by-play when he shot the ball because he was so quick with his pull-up move and shot. In order to keep pace, I decided to use the phrase, "West stops and pops." It worked, and my audience understood exactly what was taking place.

If I had to label my style, it would be "speaking in short machine-gun rapid-fire sentences," which, not coincidentally, also happened to be the same delivery Glickman used.

Marty also gave great advice on career moves. "Kid," he said to me, "the more job hopping you do, the closer you'll get towards reaching your goal of being a play-by-play man on the big-league level." His words of wisdom paid off for me. A short stay as an announcer at WGNR in New Rochelle, New York, was followed by a job in New York City at WFDR, where Kevin Kennedy—a real pro who would go on to become an award-winning newscaster for WPIX-TV—and I co-hosted a nightly sports talk show.

The format was basic: We staged heated arguments between ourselves on various subjects. We'd try to make our conversation sound as lively and controversial as possible. We'd compile a list of subjects before each show and then randomly choose sides and debate, with all the passion and bluster our imaginations could generate. The fan mail poured in. Many people thought I was a loud-mouthed jerk; the rest accused Kevin of being an egotistical bully. It was obvious that all our listeners thought Kevin and I were bitter enemies. In actuality, we had a tough time not breaking into laughter as we "berated" each other's knowledge of sports.

Kevin and I also weren't above playing pranks on our audience. For instance, when we'd report the scores and highlights of games, we'd invent names just to see if our audience would catch us. For instance, I'd say, "The Indians beat the White Sox, 3-2," and Kevin would add, "on a 450-foot ninth-inning homer by rookie sensation George Fink." We both knew there was no such player as George Fink. But we were impish enough to see if we could sneak it by our listeners. Take my word for it, we usually succeeded. Kevin and I shared a lot of funny moments during our brief partnership, but both of us had far more ambitious goals. He was determined to be a newscaster, following in the footsteps of his idol, Edward R. Morrow. I was praying for my chance to be in a big-time press box radio booth.

When the Giants' baseball club asked me in the spring of '48 if I wanted to co-host a Saturday pregame show with one of their star players, Johnny Mize, I jumped at the chance. The show, which was named *Johnny on the Spot*, only aired when the Giants were playing at home in the Polo Grounds, but I was thrilled at the prospect of working side by side with a certain future Hall of Famer.

To my shock, Mize, who finished his career with a .312 batting average and 359 homers, turned out to be a full-fledged redneck and an anti-Semite. From the start, Mize treated me like dirt and refused to say a word to me before or after each show. After the show had been airing for a month, I asked him if I had done anything wrong to cause his obvious hostility toward me. Mize told me point-blank, "Yeah, you're a Jew, and I don't like Jews."

"Well, if that's how you feel," I replied, "then go and fuck yourself. You don't know me as a person and yet you hate me, huh?"

Somehow I managed to finish the season as Mize's co-host before quitting. The day I resigned I told two Giants executives that their star outfielder was a bigot and a redneck. I knew full well that as a relatively new broadcaster, I might be hurting my career by voicing my opinion, but I felt compelled to make sure the club's management knew Mize was a bigot. I can honestly say he was the only broadcasting partner I ever worked with whom I despised.

In the summer of 1949 I applied for a job as the play-by-play man for the North Carolina State football and basketball teams. The first question the station manager at WNAO in Raleigh asked me was whether I had ever done play-by-play for football. "Sure, for a couple seasons," I told him, without showing any signs that I was answering with an out-and-out lie. Seeing that he believed me, I stretched the fib a little bit more. "Actually, football is my strength. If you liked the recording disc [there was no such thing as audio tape back in those days] I sent you of my basketball play-by-play, you'll be crazy about how I handle football."

He bought that fib and offered me the job on the spot. Before that first NC State football game, I took out a little insurance, memorizing both teams' rosters, reading the rule book backwards and forwards, and making sure I knew how to pronounce every name

on the program, including the refs and both coaching staffs. Then I
prayed for the best.

My first game was NC State versus powerful North Carolina.
Not only was it the biggest rivalry in the South, but this particular
UNC squad featured three-time All-America halfback Charlie "Choo-
Choo" Justice, a 5'9", 165-pound bolt of lightning who was also a
magician at hiding the ball.

On the first two kickoff returns, Justice faked a reverse handoff
and headed upfield for huge gains. On the third kickoff, it sure looked
like a real reverse. Justice went through his routine and then suddenly
stopped completely and turned as if to watch his running mate carry
the ball. Everyone in the stadium turned their eyes away from Justice
to watch the play develop. Just one small problem: Justice still had
the ball tucked behind his hip.

While all 11 NC State players pursued the wrong guy, Justice
ran all alone down the sidelines for a touchdown. Fortunately for
me, my call was so far behind the action (three or four seconds late)
that I was able to give my audience the correct play-by-play call. It
was dumb luck, because like everyone else who witnessed the game,
I initially fell for Justice's fake handoff.

After that first game, I was prepared for anything. I enjoyed the
fast pace of football and the challenge of making instant identifications
of receivers, ball carriers and tacklers. Football play-by-play, in my
opinion, may just be the toughest job in sports because, with all the
fakery, your eyes can play tricks on you.

Even Bill Stern was capable of being totally deceived. One of
his greatest mistakes occurred while he was doing the radio play-by-
play for the Army-Navy game in 1945 when West Point's offense
featured Doc Blanchard and Glenn Davis, Mr. Inside and Mr. Outside
respectively. Blanchard was the tough-yardage ball carrier. If Army
needed two yards on fourth down, Doc plunged up the middle to get
the first down; Davis was the breakaway threat. If he could get loose
around the corner, it was an automatic TD.

Stern was so accustomed to the Army's patterned offense that he was able to call the plays even before the handoffs were completed. But one day, the West Point coaches surprised him. Blanchard took a handoff, banged toward the line and then went to the outside. Stern, seeing that the Army runner had gone around end and had broken free at midfield, presumed it was the speedy Davis. As soon as it was apparent that the play was going for a touchdown, Stern broke into his emphatic description: "Davis has some room. He dekes out three Navy defenders. He's in the clear."

Stern's spotter, however, realized the error and managed to slip a piece of paper to Stern which read, "Blanchard carrying, not Davis." Stern looked up and, with some quick thinking, came up with a call that would remedy his error. "Davis is at the 30, the 20," he said. "Now he's at the 10. He laterals the ball to Blanchard, who takes it in the rest of the way."

The phantom lateral had bailed him out without his audience being any the wiser—although the true story of Blanchard's TD made the rounds in broadcasting circles within hours.

Two years later, the country's top horse race announcer, Clem McCarthy, a true gentleman who was loved and respected by his colleagues, mistakenly identified the wrong horse as the winner of the 1947 Preakness. McCarthy's error came when a group of closely bunched three-year-olds battled for position around the final turn. He called out on the public address system that Jet Pilot (who actually finished fourth) had taken command. In fact, the horse that had broken away from the pack was Faultless. Realizing his mistake after Faultless had crossed the finish line, McCarthy apologized to the crowd, "Ladies and gentleman, I have made a terrible error. The winner of the '47 Preakness is Faultless, not Jet Pilot as I had mistakenly called it."

Shortly thereafter, at a meeting of our broadcasting group, Stern was giving poor Clem the business about his error in calling the wrong winning horse in the Preakness. "Hey, Clem," Stern said, "I wonder how many fans tore up winning tickets when you confused Jet Pilot with Faultless?" Finally, Ted Husing decided it was time to give Stern a bit of his own medicine.

"You know, Clem," Ted said as loudly as possible to McCarthy, "it's just too bad that in racing an announcer can't invent a fake lateral of a horse when he makes a bad call." For one of the few times I can remember, Stern was left speechless.

Following a season covering NC State football, I remained in Raleigh, where I had been hired to handle the broadcasts of the Raleigh Caps, a minor league baseball club. In the off season, I had married my first wife, Eleanor, a graduate of Cooper Union, a prestigious arts and science college in New York City's East Village. I did so against the advice of my cousin Stu, who told me that Eleanor seemed very self-centered and arrogant.

As I soon found out, Stu was 100 percent correct. Eleanor loved spending my money, and when we divorced shortly after our first anniversary, she took me to the cleaners. It was a lesson learned the hard way.

A month before the Caps' training camp was scheduled to begin, I spotted an ad in the *Radio Daily* that announced that the Brooklyn Dodgers were forming their own network. It said they would be seeking a play-by-play man to do their home games live and to "recreate" their away games from a New York studio.

I sent in an application, along with some discs of my broadcasts, on the first day the ad appeared. But I was not alone. In their response to my letter, the Dodgers informed me that more than 300 applications for the job had been received. The screening process, they cautioned, would take months.

Although I immediately all but dismissed my chances of working for the Dodgers, Glickman, as always, gave me a sense of optimism. "You never know. They might want someone who's relatively new," he said. "They might not give a damn about experience. You've got the talent to handle the job. I see it. Maybe they will too." Just the fact that Marty would say that to me was the ultimate compliment. But I couldn't make myself believe there was any prayer of me, at 26 years old, becoming a Dodgers broadcaster—not with 300 applications standing in my way.

While I was waiting to hear, I went down to Florida to do some 15-minute Caps training camp reports. Since I had so much free time on my hands, I became the team's batting practice pitcher. I confess that because I had a halfway decent arm, I pictured myself making it all the way to the majors. I'll even admit I daydreamed about standing on the mound while Stan Musial stood in the batter's box, shaking in his spikes.

But these Walter Mitty fantasies ended abruptly when I was given an opportunity to make two short relief appearances in exhibition games against the Washington Senators. On both occasions, I was lucky to escape with my life as player after player teed off on my not-so-fast fastballs.

Several days after my pitching career suffered irreparable damage, I received a call from a man named Jim Stevenson, who was in charge of establishing the Dodger radio network. "Our team owner, Branch Rickey, listened to all the discs, and yours was the best by far," he said. "Mr. Rickey says the job is yours if you want it." Then he paused, waiting for my response.

"You're kidding, right?" I eventually said. "I know this is a joke. Which wise-ass put you up to this?"

"Well," replied Stevenson, "the wise-ass is Branch Rickey, and the job is really yours if you want it."

"Oh, you're serious," I said, with a definite tone of embarrassment. "Tell me when you need me, because I'm packing my bags right this minute."

"Before you get too excited, I have to apologize because we can only pay you $550 a month for the first year. I hope that's satisfactory," said Stevenson. Considering I was only making $70 a week at the time, the offer was downright staggering. But I didn't want to sound too anxious. In the calmest voice I could manage under the circumstances, I answered, "I guess $550 will be all right—at least to start with."

One month later, in April of 1950, I began my duties as the radio network play-by-play man for the "Boys of Summer." It was truly a dream come true for me, not just because I was covering the Dodgers, but because I would get to know some of the great characters who made up this team whose essence was later so perfectly captured in Roger Kahn's classic book.

Because I didn't travel with the Dodgers, there were some players whom I really didn't get to know on a personal level. But just by broadcasting the Ebbets Field games and handling a postgame show, I did manage to establish good working relationships with quite a few of the Brooklyn legends.

Pitcher Don Newcombe was one of the first players to strike up a friendship with me. He was the major leagues' first outstanding black pitcher, a guy with unlimited potential who, in the end, just couldn't handle the pressure of making good in the majors. Without exaggeration, Newcombe was the Roger Clemens of his time. His fastball was both scary and accurate. His size (6'4", 220 pounds) was intimidating. In 1949 he was voted Rookie of the Year when he won 17 and lost only eight. In 1955, he not only went 20-5 but also batted .359, with seven home runs. His best year came in '56 when "Newk" was both the Cy Young Award winner with a 27-7 record and the National League MVP. After that, however, fame, money and racism became too much for him to handle.

Soon Newcombe began to drink every off day, then simply every day. In a matter of two years, he was a classic alcoholic whose immense talent was being completely drowned by booze. After leaving baseball prematurely, Newcombe, with the support of the Dodgers organization, recovered from his alcoholic problems. Today he devotes his life to helping young men, both in pro sports and in the community, avoid going through the nightmare he experienced. The war against drugs and alcohol has no more dedicated foot soldier than Don Newcombe.

Quiet, very observant, and with a good sense of humor, Newk would always say hello when I first became a steady visitor in the clubhouse. After I had interviewed him a couple of times, Newk began calling me over to his locker. "Hey, Johnny Most, make me sound good today," he'd kid me before almost every one of his starts. Before long, we'd talk for a few minutes every time I walked into the clubhouse. Maybe because I was quiet and almost shy (yes, I really was back in those days), Newk decided he could trust me and, on some occasions, even confide in me.

Branch Rickey could have brought Newcombe to the Dodgers at the same time as Jackie Robinson. Rickey, however, was smart enough to realize that Robby had the benefit of a college education, while Newk had come into pro baseball directly from the ghetto. So he, along with catcher Roy Campanella, was assigned to the Nashua (New Hampshire) Dodgers. It wasn't because they didn't have major league talent; it was because Rickey wanted to test their reactions to racism in the minors.

"Campy was more relaxed and mature than I was," Newcombe told me. "I remember playing against the Lynn [Massachusetts] Red Sox when this guy, who was only standing 10 feet away from Campy and myself, yelled out, 'Get the niggers off the field.' I started to charge him, but Campy put me in a bear hug and wouldn't let go until the guy, realizing I was going to kill him if I caught him, sprinted away.

"There were many other times that we were tested by racist comments. Looking back, and knowing my own personality, it's a miracle I kept my temper in check. There were times Campy and I couldn't get served in diners or restaurants. It was difficult to ignore how we were being treated by not only the fans but other ballplayers and even some coaches and managers. Still, as Mr. Rickey had told us, if we wanted to get to the majors and stay there, we had to keep our emotions under control, both on and off the field. After going through what we did in the minors, I think both Campy and I realized things really weren't going to be a heck of a lot better for us when and if we made it to Brooklyn."

And Newcombe was correct. The Dodgers' black players were the victims of racism, even at Ebbets Field. The cheers for black players were not as loud nor as long as those for the white players. And every so often some jerk in the stands would yell a racist taunt that could be heard even up in the press box. Outwardly, Newk seemed to handle the indignities well. Inside, however, it ripped at the heart of this giant of a man.

In my opinion, Newcombe, who finished his career in 1960 with a 149-90 lifetime record, could have won 250 games and played another five years had it not been for the deadly combination of the racism he faced daily and the alcohol he turned to as a way of numbing his feelings.

Another member of the Dodger staff whom I got to know well was Clem Labine, who began his career as a starter but became one of the top relievers in the game. I used to get a kick out of Clem because he was a tough guy with a cocky attitude, someone I would call an original macho man. Yet he made all of his own clothes— either by hand sewing or with a machine. Here was this rugged six-footer who would rather spend a night stitching a sweater than going out for a beer. When he finally retired in 1962, he turned his hobby into a very profitable full-time career. Today he's a successful clothes designer in Rhode Island.

Of all the Dodgers, I'd have to say pitcher Billy Loes was the craziest. When I first met him, Billy was a 24-year-old with loads of talent and wild enough to come up with the nuttiest quotes imaginable.

Just to give you a hint of Billy's unique thought processes, here's how he responded when a newspaper reporter asked him who would win the '52 World Series between Brooklyn and the Yankees.

"All things considered, I'll take the Yanks in six," he said without hesitating. And the right-hander was not joking.

"I guess Billy doesn't have much faith in us," said Dodger captain Pee Wee Reese. "I just hope he isn't pitching the sixth game for us. Then I'll know we're really in trouble."

Another Loes gem: It was July of '52, and Billy was really on a roll. He had just thrown a shutout to boost his record to 12-7. As he was walking into the clubhouse following his brilliant outing, Billy threw his glove into a trash can and proclaimed loudly, "That's all for me this season." Everyone stood open-mouthed for a moment. "Billy," said Duke Snider, "what the hell are you talking about? You've got an outside chance to win 20 this year."

"Look, when I signed my contract, they told me they wanted me to win a dozen games. And that's what I did," Billy replied. "If I win 20 games this year, they'll expect me to win 20 every year. I don't need that kind of pressure. They don't pay me enough money to expect me to pitch that good."

One final Loes story: In the ninth inning of a tie game, Billy bounded off the mound to field a squibber eight feet from home plate that never got off the infield grass. The ball went through his legs, and his error eventually cost the Dodgers the game. Afterward, a reporter asked Loes what happened. "I had good position on it, but I lost it in the sun."

With that, fellow Brooklyn pitcher Carl Erskine doubled over with laughter and yelled out, "I'll have to remember that one next time I bobble a bunt."

Of course, I'd be remiss if I didn't mention the most famous, or infamous, of the early '50s Dodger pitchers, Ralph "Number 13" Branca. Unfortunately for me, the game was being broadcast nationally, so I didn't get to actually call Ralph's home run pitch to Giants outfielder Bobby Thompson that cost Brooklyn the pennant.

I was, however, in the Polo Grounds press box that day and still can hear play-by-play man Russ Hodges' frantic call of the most dramatic hit of the decade: "The Giants win the pennant! The Giants win the pennant! The Giants win the pennant!" Branca never did recover from the stigma. A 21-game winner in '47 and a 47-35 pitcher from '48 to '51, Ralph won only 12 more games in his career, which ended in 1956.

Many times I've seen Branca interviewed about the "shot heard 'round the world." Each time he talks about it, I can sense that the pain from making one bad pitch still hasn't diminished. Still, he always displays tremendous class by granting those interviews.

The Dodger catchers back in 1951 were Campy, a young, pudgy good-humored youngster, and a veteran backup named Bruce Edwards, who happened to have been my teammate on an army ball club back in 1944.

Campy, despite his soft-spoken, smiling nature, was a fierce competitor. No matter what the score, I don't think he ever thought there was a game his team couldn't win during his 10-year career. He possessed a strong arm and amazing quickness for a 5'9" 200-pounder; he could hit with power, as his 242 lifetime homers proved. And Campy could come through in the clutch, as his league-leading 142 RBIs in 1953 demonstrated.

What I admired most about Campy was that he was very down to earth. He wasn't one of these guys who said, "You're a nobody. I don't have to talk to you." He didn't view himself as a star. I'd walk through the locker room and see him talking to a baby-faced cub reporter or a batboy. An hour and a half later I'd return, and Campy would still be at his locker carrying on the same conversations. He appreciated everyone as a human being, which is why this Hall of Famer was perhaps the most beloved of all Dodgers.

Edwards was a character. By the time I joined the Dodger network, he had a chronic sore right arm and just couldn't make a strong throw to second. However, he was a solid backup who worked well with Brooklyn's young pitching staff and kept the team loose with his sense of humor.

I recall one day when Edwards was behind the plate and Branca was on the mound. The Dodgers had a one-run lead with two outs in the ninth against St. Louis. The Cardinals, however, had the bases loaded with Stan Musial coming to bat. Suddenly, Edwards asked for time and ran out to the mound for a discussion with Branca and the Dodger infielders.

The discussion hadn't lasted more than 10 seconds when all the players on the mound started laughing as Edwards headed back toward home. As things turned out, Branca was able to strike out Musial and save the win. Out of curiosity, I later asked Edwards what he had said that was so funny. "Well, I could see Ralph was extremely tense," Bruce told me. "I had to do something to loosen him up. So I just handed him the ball, looked him in the eyes, and said, 'Ralph, what a fucking mess you're in.' Then I left."

The Dodgers' infield in the early '50s was as spectacular as any in history. There was Gil Hodges, who was not only a power hitter but also the best-fielding first baseman in the league. Hodges, who had 370 lifetime homers, was a bull. I once asked Yogi Berra who was the strongest human being in baseball. "Gil Hodges," he said.

While I was well aware of Gil's strength, I was shocked by Yogi's answer, because it was almost universally accepted that the strongest player in the majors was Cincinnati Reds first baseman Ted Kluszewski, whose cutoff sleeves showed off biceps as big as thighs. In fact, I was so startled by Berra's response that I felt obliged to remind him about Kluszewski. "Who ever said Kluszewski was human?" replied Berra.

At second was Jackie Robinson, Mr. Everything, the first black in organized baseball. What he couldn't field cleanly, he would dig out with his teeth if he had to. When Jackie first came up to the Dodgers from the team's Montreal farm club, he was a first baseman because Brooklyn had Eddie Stanky at second. One interesting reason the Dodgers didn't make use of his outstanding speed in the outfield was that he would have had to play next to Dixie Walker, a southerner who wanted no part of being in the same outfield as a black player.

When Jackie broke into the majors in '47, he knew the problems he would encounter because of racial prejudice. He'd been explicitly warned by Rickey of the indignities he would suffer. "I'll bring you up, give you your chance, but you'll have to stand there and take all the garbage they'll throw at you. And that garbage will absolutely flow down," Rickey told Jackie. The abuse Robby took went far beyond name calling. He'd be playing first and get spiked intentionally by runners who'd slide into his legs on routine grounders. When he'd be batting, his head, not the catcher's mitt, was often the pitcher's target. Yet Robinson knew he couldn't strike back. He knew he couldn't afford to be labeled a troublemaker.

Jackie made a commitment to Rickey to avoid problems whatever the cost, even though by nature he was a fighter, a person who didn't take guff from anyone. Fortunately, Robinson was probably the finest selection of the total human being to fill the role of the first black in baseball. Above all, he had the education and the intelligence to handle any situation, having attended UCLA for three years before leaving school to support his mother. He also was "streetwise" and experienced, having served in the army for three years as a lieutenant in World War II and having played pro football with the Los Angeles Bulldogs of the Pacific Coast League in 1941.

Next to Jim Thorpe, I regard Robinson as the best all-around athlete in history. He was an All-America football player, he held the NCAA record for the broad jump, and he was the leading scorer in PAC-Eight basketball. And then, among his many achievements with the Dodgers, he led the National League in hitting twice and was the league's MVP in 1949.

Jackie had strength, athletic grace and unstoppable speed. It was his base-running ability that immediately established him as a star. After Ty Cobb retired in 1928, base stealing became a lost art. Jackie restored it into a major offensive weapon. Later, others such as the Giants' Willie Mays and the Dodgers' Maury Wills, followed Robinson's example.

Jackie kept his promise to Rickey to remain calm, cool and silent for his rookie year. After that, Rickey gave Jackie the go-ahead to speak his mind. And Jackie was not one to mince words. On national TV in 1954 he was asked if there was still prejudice in baseball. His response was, "Do you want me to answer that diplomatically or do you want the truth? If you want the truth, yes, there's prejudice in baseball."

Because of that frank and correct statement, Robinson was criticized by the media. But Jackie could not have cared less, because he had his self-respect and his honesty, which is why I admired him as a person. If he liked you, you knew it. If you were his enemy, you knew that, too.

He never refused me, a young and often nervous newcomer, an interview. I believe in my heart it was because Jackie and I had several off-the-record conversations concerning prejudice when we were first introduced. I'm not trying to claim any credit for the manner in which Robby handled the pressure of being the first black in the majors, but I have always hoped that the talks the two of us had concerning the anti-Semitic incidents I had faced helped him in some small way to handle the prejudice he encountered.

Most of Jackie's teammates liked and admired him. Typical was Brooklyn's gutsy and respected shortstop Pee Wee Reese. My fondest memory of Reese took place in the final week of the 1951 spring training. The Dodgers were working their way back north and had an exhibition game in Louisville, Reese's hometown. At the time, Louisville fans were still very much of the opinion that baseball was a whites-only sport. So when Robinson stepped onto the field from the dugout before the game, the crowd booed him. Reese reacted immediately, running over to Jackie and putting an arm around Robby's shoulder for all the crowd to see. Without saying a word, Pee

Wee had made his statement. That's an example of why he was the heart and soul of this team.

Billy Cox was the club's joker—and the greatest-fielding third baseman of his day. My booth was located right above third base, and after every infield practice, he would toss a ball up to me. It became a ritual. By the end of the season, I had a booth full of baseballs that I was able to give to the kids who would wait for autographs outside Ebbets. I remember interviewing Reese once and asking him to name the best gloveman at each infield position. Pee Wee's answer: "Billy Cox. He can play them all better than anyone else."

The Dodgers had some excellent outfielders. The right fielder, Carl Furillo, had the best arm I've ever seen, better than Roberto Clemente, better than any of today's players. I recall the day he threw out Pirate pitcher Mel Queen at first base on a one-hop "single." Furillo's favorite trick was to catch a liner on a bounce, look toward second, and then throw behind the runner to nail him before he could scramble back to first. He'd pull it off once a month.

Another player who had my complete respect was Andy Pafko, the toughest guy I've known in sports. In one game he ran into the left field fence trying to chase down a line drive and continued to play for four more innings despite suffering a broken arm on the play. Today, guys take themselves out of the lineup when they have a hangnail. (That's why, unlike many Boston fans, I admire Red Sox first baseman Bill Buckner so much, because he was a guy who was completely crippled up yet was willing to sacrifice his body in order to compete. By the time he came to Boston, Buckner had a bad back, bad knees, bad elbows and arthritis in his arms. But he refused to give in to the chronic pain. One play in which a slow grounder went through his legs marred what I consider to be an outstanding career. Given all his health problems, I didn't criticize him; I sympathized with him.)

Without a doubt, the highlight of my stay with the Dodgers came in the final month of the '51 season when an injured rookie infielder named Dick Williams, the same Dick Williams who would become one of baseball's most successful and controversial managers, was asked to join me in the booth as my color commentator. Dick and I hit it off right from the beginning, probably because he was as much of a ham as I was. He loved to talk, he had a good sense of humor, and he was both knowledgeable and well-spoken.

After Dick and I had broadcast a few games together, he decided to liven up my play-by-play by supplying me with a little "inside information." "Johnny, here's what we're gonna do," he said to me one morning as we arrived at the ballpark. "I'm going to go down for the team meeting and find out which signs our coaches are going to be using today. Then when the game is going on, I'll slip you a piece of paper now and then that'll tell you what's gonna happen on the next pitch. All you have to do is take it from there."

Naturally I was more than mildly concerned about the possibility of the plan somehow backfiring. Despite my nervousness, the more I thought about it, the more I was ready to give it a try.

To my surprise, things went off without a hitch. Dick would slip me a scrap of paper that read "steal," and I'd tell the audience, "Well, the count is 2-1. If ever there was a perfect time for Jackie Robinson to steal second, it definitely has to be right now."

Presto. The pitcher would go into his wind-up, and before he'd release the ball, Robinson would take off for second. Dick and I worked this routine for the remainder of the season. I'd "speculate" that the Dodgers would try a hit-and-run play, and, like clockwork, they'd do exactly what I suggested. I'd call for a bunt, and, sure enough, the Brooklyn batter would plunk one down the third base line. I mean, Williams made me sound like an absolute genius.

I'm just glad Brooklyn manager Walter Alston couldn't listen to the broadcasts. I don't think he would have had too much trouble figuring out that my broadcasting partner was leaking a few team secrets to me.

I guess Dick will always be most famous for his postgame comments after his Montreal Expos lost to the Phillies back in the late '70s. With runners on second and third, one out and the game tied in the bottom of the ninth, Williams had ordered an intentional walk to Bake McBride. Philadelphia's Mike Schmidt then laced a single to win the game for the Phils.

Afterward, Dick attempted to defend his strategy. "I don't care if Jesus Christ was coming up to bat, I would have walked McBride," he said. "What if Babe Ruth was coming up?" asked a reporter, trying to be more realistic. Williams paused and then answered, "Well, I'm not sure about the Babe."

As I have mentioned, I didn't travel with the Dodgers. Instead I recreated live broadcasts of the away games off the Western Union ticker tape, which gave a short description of each hit, steal, out, and personnel change. As an example, if Duke Snider hit a fly ball to Willie Mays, the tape would read: "SNIDER FLIES TO CENTER ON 3-2 COUNT, TWO OUTS, NOBODY ON BASE, DODGERS SIXTH."

Obviously, it would sound dull if I just gave the basic facts, so I would do my best to make the "at bat" sound exciting. I'd "recreate" each pitch, telling the listeners whether the pitch was a fastball or a curve, whether it was outside or a brushback. Then when I had brought the count to 3-2, I'd have Duke line a shot to short center. In my description of the play, Mays would race in, dive, and amazingly come up with the acrobatic grab.

To make my broadcast sound like I was really at the ballpark rather than in a studio, I would play sound-effect records to provide different background noises. My collection included the national anthem played on an organ, beer vendor shouts, boo records, cheer records, umpire calls, even rain and thunder. It was a complete theatrical production—all done from within a small, dirty studio in New York City.

My biggest problems occurred when the ticker tape would break down or when the guy who operated the ticker tape suddenly had to make a trip to the men's room. When that happened, I had to stall for time. I would immediately call to get an assessment from Western Union as to how long the ticker would be out of service. If it was going to be a long time, I would invent fights, arguments, or even rain delays. If it would buy me some time, I'd have the umpires change second base because it was crooked.

My "old reliable" was having Robinson get into an argument with an ump. Jackie frequently disputed calls, so my audience had no trouble believing it when I made up a story about how Robby and some umpire were hotly debating a call. Or I'd have Furillo run into the Giants' dugout to fight New York manager Leo Durocher. That, too, was plausible, because Durocher and Furillo hated one another. The feud was so intense that if Giant pitcher Sal "The Barber" Maglie threw at Furillo's head, Carl would go after Durocher rather than Maglie.

If the ticker tape broke down just when there was a pitching change, I was lucky. All I had to do was have the reliever warm up for five or six minutes instead of the usual three or four minutes. If the tape was still not working after that, I'd just have to invent another delay, such as a sneak rainstorm. All I can say is that those recreations were an adventure. Each time I came into the studio, I never knew what to expect. I might have a nice quick game, or if I ran into technical difficulties, I might have a marathon work day. No matter how smooth or rough, I loved every minute of it.

Unfortunately, the Dodger radio network temporarily suspended operations after the '51 season due to financial problems. Having picked up such valuable major league experience, I thought it would be relatively easy to find another full-time job. I was wrong. I pounded the pavement, checked out every rumor of a possible opening, and, most importantly, continued to attend the Sports Broadcasting Association meetings.

At one of these sessions I learned that Bill Stern, who had broadcast the NBC radio college football game of the week for decades, was moving over to TV, leaving his radio job open. NBC had given Stern a say in choosing his successor, so I called him at his office the next morning, made an appointment, and rushed over to talk with him. More than 400 broadcasters sought the position. Eventually Stern narrowed the field to four candidates, including me. At that point, he decided to hold a final audition, with each applicant handling the play-by-play for one quarter of the Yale-Bates football game.

Before the game, each of us drew a number out of a hat to determine which quarter we'd broadcast. I happened to pick the fourth quarter. By the time my turn came behind the mic, Yale had left Bates for dead, leading 41-0. Needless to say, I felt like the deck was stacked against me. How was I going to make this meaningless final quarter sound exciting? Worse yet, Yale coach Herman Hickman had taken out his varsity players and put in the junior varsity scrubs. No one had even bothered to deliver the JV roster to the press box. That shook me up a little. All I knew for certain was that I couldn't spend the next half hour talking about the spectacular plays made by "Number 12, Number 44, Number 63 and Number 82."

Then I remembered what a member of the Sports Broadcasters Association had once said about Stern: "Bill never lets the truth stand in the way of a lively broadcast." So, taking my cue from that remark, I decided to make up 11 names and use them in the broadcast. For better or worse, that was my strategy.

I wasn't sure what the reaction would be until Stern walked up to me after the game had ended. "That's the kind of alert thinking I want," he said, flashing a huge grin. "I don't know whether you'll win this audition or not, because I'm not on the program committee that makes that decision. But I guarantee there will be a job for you with me."

Stern invited me to lunch the next day. Since I wasn't sure whether I'd have to pay for my own meal or not, I went scrambling around my room for money. All I had was a bagful of pennies, so I rolled up a couple of dollars' worth and headed out of the house. When I got to the restaurant and still wasn't sure whether I'd have to pay my share of the bill, I ordered the cheapest thing on the menu, a cream cheese and jelly sandwich. While Stern and I were eating, a member of the NBC staff came in and told me that I had won the job. Ever since that day, my two good luck charms have been a roll of pennies and a cream cheese and jelly sandwich.

My first on-air game, California versus Pennsylvania, proved to be comical, although I didn't think so at the time. Penn had provided me with a spotter named Skippy Mennessi, who also scouted for the team. With California totally dominating, Mennessi, who was sitting inches away from me, became more and more frustrated. Finally, late in the game, a Penn runner broke loose for a long gain. In the middle of my play-by-play, Mennessi suddenly couldn't contain himself. To my shock, he jumped out of his chair, which was located right next to my microphone, and began to scream, "Go, you son of a bitch. Keep moving, you son of a bitch." I was mortified and somewhat worried about what the NBC executives might think of the colorful background language heard on my broadcast. To my surprise, not a word was ever said to me about Skippy's on-air remarks.

Actually I guess you could say I got my introduction to big-time broadcasting hours before the Cal-Penn kickoff. The night before, Jack Lightcap, my producer and roommate, called room service and left our order for breakfast. He asked me what I wanted, and I told him to get me some bacon and eggs. When the waiter knocked on our door the next morning, I found myself staring at my bacon and eggs, along with Jack's breakfast—a bucket of ice-cold bottles of beer. That's when I first realized that members of the media have the strangest eating and drinking habits in the universe.

Several weeks later, Lightcap and I were in Chicago getting ready to do the Navy-Northwestern game. I was going out for dinner with ex-welterweight champion Barney Ross, an old friend of mine who had sort of adopted me seven years previously when he was training at Grossinger's for his title fight against Ceferino Garcia. Lightcap wanted to meet Barney, so I invited him along.

While I waited for him to get dressed, I picked up a copy of a book Bill Stern had written. One particular chapter intrigued me. It was a story about the Montana Tech football team of 1941. It seemed that when the Japanese attacked Pearl Harbor, all 11 of Montana Tech's starters enlisted in the service. Four went into the army, four signed up with the marines, and three joined the navy. One by one, each of the 11 was killed in the war.

"This Montana Tech story is almost too amazing to be true," I said to Jack, who had already read the book.

"It isn't true," Lightcap replied. "Bill just made up the name of a school and a tale to go with it. There is no Montana Tech." As Stern always said, "Never let the truth stand in the way of a good story."

Shortly before the football season ended, I received word that WNGM, my station, would be taking over the Dodger network for the 1953 season and that I would be rehired to do the play-by-play.

Even though I had only missed one year of broadcasting the Dodgers, my first day back at Ebbets Field was like visiting paradise. That one season away from Ebbets made me aware of just how much character the ballpark possessed.

The park was surrounded by tall apartment houses, which made it look even smaller than it actually was (405 feet to straightaway center). Ebbets was "intimate," a little like Fenway Park, except the handball wall was in right field, not left. Near the right field foul pole was a steep incline that led to the screen. Many times Furillo would run up the incline, take off in the air and come down with what everyone else in the park thought was a sure home run.

The people who came to see the Dodgers were strange, different, fun-loving. Only at Ebbets could there be an organist, Gladys Gooding, who was more well known than some of the players. Only at Ebbets was there a three-member "Dodger Bums Band," which consisted of fans who just enjoyed going around the park playing music and getting the crowd revved up. The team even had a mascot, a scruffy-looking woman in her late fifties who never missed a game. She became such good luck charm to the Dodger players that they actually chipped in to pay for her to accompany them on all their road trips.

New Yorkers at that time were great fans, whether they rooted for Brooklyn, the Giants or the Yankees. They yelled, they screamed, they booed, but they behaved themselves. Today the New York crowds have changed a lot. I truly object to their obscene signs and their vulgarisms. And it's the adults and older teenagers, not young kids, who are responsible.

Maybe something about the nature of the New York crowds changed when the Dodgers and Giants moved out to the West Coast in 1957. Even though my days as a Dodger broadcaster had already ended, as a former New Yorker, I was indignant at the decision by Dodger owner Walter O'Malley. I could understand the Giants' move, because that team did have financial problems. In fact, only the Dodgers-Giants rivalry and the amazing all-around abilities of a young player by the name of Willie Mays, whom I consider to be baseball's version of Larry Bird, enabled the Giants to draw enough fans to stay afloat at the Polo Grounds.

But the Dodgers were making money and had been supported by loyal fans for years. O'Malley wanted New York City to build him a bigger stadium, so he sold Ebbets Field to a real estate developer in order to force the city to come up with funds for a new ballpark. It was a form of blackmail, and city officials quite properly stood their ground. O'Malley then turned around and left the people of Brooklyn high and dry by taking his team to Los Angeles. The league never should have allowed it. What they should have done was to create an expansion team for L.A. and order O'Malley and the Dodgers to stay put in Brooklyn.

Thus ended my baseball broadcasting stint.

2

BREAKING INTO
PRO BASKETBALL

My first experience calling play-by-play pro basketball came in December of 1951. I received a phone call from an engineer at WNGM, which carried the Knickerbockers. It seemed that Marty Glickman and his color commentator, Bert Lee Jr., had been stranded by a blizzard in Kentucky and would not be able to make it back to New York in time for that night's Knicks game. "Marty recommended you. Can you fill in for him?" said the voice at the other end of the phone. Without even asking whom the Knicks were playing, I accepted the offer.

Within minutes, I was on my way over to the old Madison Square Garden on Eighth Avenue to broadcast my first NBA game, New York versus the Minneapolis Lakers. I thought the show was going smoothly enough until my engineer tapped me on the shoulder at halftime and whispered, "Call [station manager] Bert Lee Sr. first thing in the morning." For the rest of the evening, I nervously wondered what I had done wrong.

When I got up the next day, I summoned up enough courage to call Lee, expecting to get an earful of criticism. Instead he greeted me with, "You did a great job, kid. I want to talk to you about doing some more work for us, because my son's going into the marines in five days. Starting tomorrow, you'll be working with Glickman if you want to."

If I wanted to? Being Marty's partner had been my ambition since the day I introduced myself to him at Grossinger's some eight years earlier. I'd have worked for nothing for this opportunity. Glickman and I teamed up for the remainder of that season and all of the next.

During my stay with the Knicks, I developed close friendships with many of the Knicks players. Guards Dick McGuire and Max Zaslofsky and center Sweetwater Clifton were my favorites. They were New York's version of the "Gashouse Gang," always laughing, playing poker, hitting all the nightspots, never getting any sleep.

Zaslofsky was, in my opinion, the best defender in the game even though he was barely 6'2" and 170 pounds, because he had long arms and quick hands. Had the NBA kept track of steals during Max's playing days, he would have led the league. Whenever Max would enter the game, I'd tell the audience, "In comes New York City's greatest pickpocket."

McGuire, who had earned the nickname "Tricky Dick" from Glickman, was a good playmaker and shooter. He and Bob Cousy were among the best passers in the league, and they knew it. It was their battles against each other that really sparked the Knicks-Celtics rivalry. The big difference between the two was that Cousy was more creative and a much more effective decision maker when it came to directing the fast break, which greatly irritated Dick, a guy whose temper wasn't always under control.

"What I don't like about Cousy is that he always tries to make you look bad," McGuire would complain to me. "God forbid the Celtics have a big lead, because that's when he really likes to add insult to injury." McGuire would never admit it, but he would do the exact same thing to an opponent.

As for Sweetwater, he was as nice a person as his nickname indicated. In a game, however, Clifton had a mean streak. At 6'8", 240 pounds, he was the Knicks' enforcer and one of the league's top rebounders. McGuire was Nat's biggest fan. "The biggest thrill I can get when I'm playing is running my defender into one of Sweetwater's picks," he'd tell me. "If the defender isn't smart enough to see what's coming, there's just that look of panic in his eyes a second before impact."

Because of racial barriers, Nat was held back from playing in the NBA until he was 28 years old. He never complained about it, though. Like my future roommate, Don Barksdale, whom I'll talk about later, Clifton didn't live in the past; instead he chose to savor the present.

Another character I had met while broadcasting the Knicks was Bones McKinney, who was then with the Celtics. He was a quiet guy who, because of his size (6'6" and 180 pounds), used to take a nightly pounding. Frequently the Celtics would play the Knicks in New York, and then both teams would take a sleeper-car train to Boston for a game at the Garden the next day. That's how I got to know a little about Red Auerbach, Bones, Cousy and Bill Sharman.

On one of those train rides, Cousy told me about the time the Celtics were taking a plane trip from Boston to Minneapolis when, all of sudden, there was a great deal of air turbulence. Bones began to shake visibly. Cousy tried to calm him down. "Bones, relax. There's nothing you can do," Cousy said. "When your number's up, your number's up." Replied Bones, "It ain't my number I'm worried about; it's the pilot's number that worries me."

Just when I felt totally at ease working with Marty on the Knicks' broadcasts, there was a major problem. Bert Lee Jr. had returned from the marines and was looking to get his old job back. However, the Knicks' owner, Ned Irish, wanted me to stay right where I was.

"I know there's people back at your station who are trying to push you out the door because they figure you were just Bert Lee Jr.'s fill-in. Now that he's back, I guess everyone thinks he deserves to just move right back into his old slot, right?" Irish said to me. "Well, from my viewpoint, I've got the greatest broadcast team in the league, and I'm not going to give it up. The audience determines who's best for the job, not the station staffers."

I was grateful, proud. And yet I just couldn't stomach walking into the radio station every day and being snubbed by co-workers who thought I was stealing someone else's job. I kept on telling myself this was Ned's idea, not mine. But in the end, I couldn't take the harassment. In September of '53, I phoned Irish, thanked him for his backing, and informed him that I was quitting.

3

BECOMING A MEMBER OF THE CELTICS FAMILY

Within a week after I had left my Knicks job, I received a call from a friend of mine to let me know that he had heard that Curt Gowdy was leaving as play-by-play man with the Celtics to broadcast the Red Sox, as well as doing some national TV. I figured there was no harm in checking it out, so I called Boston's general manager, Red Auerbach, whom I had gotten to know a little bit through Marty Glickman. Auerbach wasn't in his office when I called, but he did call me back the next day.

"Hello, Johnny," Red said. "You're interested in the job, aren't you? Well, I like your broadcasting, but the decision will ultimately be made by our owner, Walter Brown."

"Yeah, I'd like to compete for the position. What are my chances?" I replied. Auerbach said the auditions were already under way, with only five broadcasters still in the running. "But we can just as easily make it six," he said. "I'll call the radio station tomorrow at 11 to set it up. You just make sure you're at the station when I call." With that, Red hung up without even saying goodbye or good luck.

I called WCOP, which was handling the Celtics games, and managed to make an appointment with the program manager, Elly Dierdoff. In fact, I was sitting in Dierdorff's office when Auerbach called him and got me the audition. Since the Celtics were playing

12 exhibition games, the audition schedule called for each candidate to get two turns at handling the play-by-play. I was sixth in line and happened to get my first crack at it when Boston faced the Knicks in New Haven, Connecticut.

I made a couple of mistakes here and there in my broadcast. Overall, I was satisfied with my performance, figuring I could make an even better impression when I got my next chance. After the New Haven game, Red and I walked back to the hotel, where he called Boston owner Walter Brown, who had listened to the broadcast back in Boston.

Turning to me and winking, Auerbach asked Brown, "Well, what did you think of that Most guy we tried out tonight?"

"I loved him," said Brown. "But will a Boston audience accept a New Yorker as the team's play-by-play man?"

"Why wouldn't they?" said Auerbach. "They haven't run me out of town yet, and I'm a New Yorker, aren't I?"

"Red," said Brown, "if you honestly think they will, then Most has got the job 'cause he's the guy I want. You might as well just cancel the rest of the auditions and let him finish out what's left of the exhibition schedule."

Auerbach hung up the phone, turned to me, and said, "Well, that's all set. Walter talked me into it. You've got the job." That was my official welcome into the Celtics family. I was on my way to Boston Garden.

I didn't have any intention of making Boston my permanent home when I accepted Red's offer. My grand scheme was to be the Celtics' play-by-play man for two or three years and then make a triumphant return to New York, where I had really always played second banana to Marty Glickman.

The first year in Boston was rough for me. The pay was decent ($5,500 a season, plus $8 a day for meals when we were on the road), but I really didn't have a strong feeling that I belonged or that I was accepted. I suppose the fact that I lived in the less-than-luxurious

Lenox Hotel my first year didn't give me much of a "home life," as you'd call it. But I was satisfied with the job as a stepping stone, and I believed I was doing a reasonably good job of describing the games accurately and briskly.

The '53-'54 Celtics had three excellent players—Ed Macauley, Bob Cousy, and Bill Sharman—but the team lacked a real rebounder. They'd win three or four and then lose a couple. In those days, basketball in Boston was struggling to gain popularity. The Garden crowds were sparse. Spectators back then may have been curious to see the Celtics, but I would hardly describe them as enthusiastic, diehard fans.

In fact, about the only times the Celtics would come close to drawing a sellout crowd was when the Harlem Globetrotters, with Goose Tatum as their star, came to town. The Globetrotters would put on a show against the Washington Generals in the first game of a doubleheader and then the Celts would play their NBA game. It wasn't at all unusual to see 25 or 30 percent of Boston fans leave the Garden just as soon as the 'Trotters had finished putting on their always entertaining show.

The lack of fan support for the Celtics had an effect on my broadcasts. While I thought I was doing a "professional" job, I wasn't showing much emotion in the play-by-play. My vocabulary was above average, my knowledge of the game was more than adequate, my interviewing skills seemed OK. But I knew I was boring the listeners to death.

About two months into the season, the sports editor of the *Boston Record American*, the late Sam Cohen, who became one of my best friends, approached me and offered some very wise advice. "Look, kid, I listen to you at my office and at home all the time. I think everything you're doing is great," Sam told me, in a fatherly manner. "But just remember this: Boston is a big small town. Everybody is family to everybody else. You've got to become a fan yourself if you're going to be appreciated by the fans in this town. You can't be a robot.

Show your emotion. Let your audience know that you want to see the Celtics win as much as they do.

"Don't wait for the Garden crowd to get you fired up. You're the one who's supposed to generate the excitement. If the team's own play-by-play man isn't emotional about how the team is doing, how can you expect the average fan to become revved up about the Celtics?"

It was Sam's advice that made me realize that all the restrictions about being objective were inhibiting my broadcasts. He made me understand that if I was truly going to put my heart and soul into the broadcasts, then I had to let my true emotions come across on the air.

For the first time, I saw that there was nothing wrong with rooting for the team you're covering. And from that point on, I've never felt I had to defend myself to anyone, including the holier-than-thou media critics. Hey, how can you *not* root for guys whom you're around 24 hours a day, guys you travel with, eat with, socialize with? I quickly realized that all the high and mighty preaching about being totally objective was not only baloney, it was an impossibility if I was going to be an honest broadcaster.

If you do the play-by-play for a team year after year and game after game, there's no way you can avoid making friendships and caring about how your friends perform. I know there are broadcasters who would like their audience to believe they are totally objective. Believe me, there's not one of them who doesn't have certain players they root for because of personal relationships they have formed.

During the first half-dozen years of the Celtics' existence, Boston was anything but a pro basketball hotbed. The local press was extremely critical and often outright hostile. Few writers actually believed basketball, as a pro sport, was going to last, so they seized every chance they got to blast the Celtics as being "minor league in every way." In this city, hockey was king during the winter and the Red Sox were idolized from spring to fall. There was no room for the Celtics to be loved. To be honest, even horse racing was far more popular than the Celtics. After all, Bostonians have always loved the excitement of gambling.

The small Garden crowds were a major disappointment to Red. "Johnny," he told me, "we're a damned good team, a winning team. We hustle more than any other club, and there's no doubt in my mind we pass the ball better than anyone. My guys put on a great show, and yet nobody seems to give them a fucking bit of credit. It burns my ass that people here just don't care about how we do. Hell, we're leading the league in offense, but nobody ever mentions that."

What made it even tougher for the Celtics to receive any publicity was the fact that the PR directors of the Bruins, Red Sox and the race tracks all had close friends in the media. It was a typical case of one hand washing the other. A writer would do a favorable story, and in return, he'd receive free tickets and a free lunch. It was standard policy.

In order to combat the Celtics' negative image in town, Walter Brown had hired Howie McHugh, an All-America hockey goalie at Dartmouth, to handle the team's PR chores. He was perfect for the job. Friendly and cooperative, he gradually won over the media. "Considering that I don't know much about basketball, I guess I'm doing OK," he said to me one day in his tiny office located below the Garden. "But I still don't know if this team's going to make it financially. We're friends, so you know I'm not bragging about myself when I tell you I know there are writers who come to our games, not to cover the Boston Celtics, but just because they want to say hello to me and bullshit a little."

Howie, who passed away in 1983, was correct. Most of the writers who came to see the Celtics were doing so as a favor to Howie. They wanted him to be successful, so every once in a while they'd do a story on the Celtics just to make him look good to Walter and Red.

Inviting athletes like Ted Williams, Bobby Doerr, Bruins legend Milt Schmidt, and undefeated heavyweight champ Rocky Marciano to attend Celtics games was a tactic Howie frequently employed to fill more seats at the Garden and get media attention. He made sure that every sports figure or celebrity had front row seats and he made sure the Celtics players all stopped by their seats, for some friendly chat. Young fans, in particular, enjoyed the opportunity to get an autograph from these "big-name" sports figures. Knowing Howie, he would have even brought in Roy Rogers and Trigger or Rin Tin Tin if he thought they would help sell tickets.

In order to drum up increased fan support, Red and his players would occasionally conduct free clinics for kids. During the basketball season these events would usually be held at the Garden. When the summer came around, Red and Walter Brown would schedule autograph sessions and clinics that would blanket the entire metropolitan area. I'd handle the introductions at many of these events.

The players didn't mind showing up for these clinics even though they received little more than expense money for their time and work. "Red doesn't have to convince us to show up," Sharman told me. "If we can sell the kids on the Celtics, then the kids will sell their parents on NBA basketball. Besides, it's fun. It's also the only time Red wears a smile all the time."

At one clinic held at the Garden in November of '53, I witnessed an amazing one-on-one match. While Red was instructing a group of youngsters at one basket, Sharman began playing against a young-looking guy dressed in street clothes and wearing shoes, not sneakers, at the other end of the court. I could tell this was not a casual game at all. Bill would shoot and make a jumper, and then this rugged fellow would take Bill to the basket and score. Time after time. The guy couldn't match Bill's shot-making ability, but he certainly was stronger. After a 20-minute battle, Bill managed to win, but only by a couple of points. I couldn't resist asking Sharman what was going on.

"Johnny, I want you to meet a friend of mine, Harry Agganis. He's about to sign a contract with the Red Sox," Bill said.

"Good to meet you, Mr. Most," Harry said, extending his huge right hand out to me. "I really enjoy listening to your broadcasts." Although flattered by Harry's greeting, I was also embarrassed that I hadn't recognized him. "Please don't call me 'Mr. Most.' I'm Johnny, and I'm a big fan of yours. I've read a thousand stories about you."

And that wasn't an exaggeration. At age 23, Agganis was already a legend in New England. And rightly so. At Lynn Classical, Harry had been All-Everything in both baseball and football. It wasn't unusual for 20,000 fans to show up at Lynn's Manning Bowl to watch Harry, a quarterback and defensive back, demonstrate why he was a man among boys on the gridiron. In his two years as starting quarterback (as well as starting defensive back), Harry led Lynn Classical to a 21-1-1 record. He passed for 48 touchdowns and scored 24 himself.

Rejecting more than 160 scholarship offers, including ones from such powerhouses as Notre Dame, Southern Cal and Boston College, Harry surprisingly chose perennial doormat Boston University.

He then single-handedly turned BU's pitiful football program into a major national force. All he did for BU was start at quarterback, start at defensive back and handle all the punting and place-kicking duties. In his three varsity years he set virtually every offensive record for rushing, passing, interceptions and punting average. Following his junior year, Cleveland Browns coach Paul Brown drafted him in the first round. Harry turned him down because he wanted to complete his education and then become a pro baseball player.

"I think I've already proved myself in football," he said when he announced he would be signing with the Red Sox instead of going to the NFL. "I don't know if I can be successful in baseball, but I have the confidence that I can."

To give you an idea of his popularity and talent as a football player, I'll just point out that BU's student body was a little more than 6,000, yet when the Terriers played their home games at Braves

Field, they drew an average of 28,000 fans. So naturally it came as a shock to everyone when Harry chose to gamble on achieving his goal to be a major leaguer over the opportunity to be almost a guaranteed MVP candidate in the NFL.

There's no doubt in my mind that Agganis would have been a Hall of Fame-caliber football player. But knowing Harry as I did, I'm sure he wanted a challenge more than glory. After he signed with the Red Sox, he spent 1953 in the minors, where he finished second in the MVP voting to a scrappy infielder by the name of Don Zimmer.

The next year Harry earned a spot with the Red Sox. For most of the season, he started at first base. But he didn't enjoy the success most fans expected from him. While Agganis did manage to lead the Red Sox with eight triples, he batted a disappointing .251, with just 11 homers and 57 RBIs.

Still, Harry was optimistic about his baseball future. One night when he sat next to me at a Celtics game, he explained why he believed he would succeed with the Sox. "I made too many rookie mistakes. I know how to fix those mistakes," he told me. "I'm ready to prove I can play at a much higher level."

I should point out that Harry didn't like being in the limelight. As a matter of fact, when he attended a Celtics game, he wouldn't let me interview him because, as he told me, "I don't want people to think I look at myself as a big shot."

Harry got off to a great start with the Sox in 1955. By early May, he was batting over .300 and had the fewest errors in the club. Then tragedy struck. Harry began complaining of tremendous pain on his right side. He also had a high fever. He was treated at a local hospital for pneumonia and was released 10 days later. When he returned to the team, he had lost 20 pounds and looked pale. On a trip to Kansas City, Harry's condition grew worse and he was sent back to Boston. He re-entered the hospital for more tests. By this time he was coughing blood and had developed a bad case of phlebitis in his right leg. Within days, Harry began to complain of severe pain in his chest and lungs. Twenty minutes after he told the doctors of his symptoms, Agganis was pronounced dead. Doctors later concluded that he had suffered a fatal pulmonary embolism.

I, along with every Boston sports fan, was devastated. It seemed so unfair. Here was this 25-year-old man, a true gentleman, who was loved by so many friends who now would never fulfill his dreams. I had rooted for Harry probably as hard as I have rooted for any member of the Celtics. A great number of fans today think Bo Jackson, Jackie Robinson or Jim Thorpe was the best all-around athlete in history. No one can convince me that Harry couldn't have ranked right up there with them.

I attended a memorial service for Harry, and I don't think one teammate from the Red Sox, from BU or from Lynn Classical missed the ceremony. Like all those in attendance, I was proud to have known him, not as an athlete but as a person. At that memorial I sat next to Walter Brown. "Did you know Harry well?" I asked him. "No," replied Walter. "But I met him several times. You couldn't help but like the man. He was so modest, so courteous. Just from the little time I spent with him, I admired his character."

Walter's description of Harry mirrored my opinion of Walter. From my first meeting with Walter, I knew he was a class act. He desperately wanted success for himself and his team, but he never wanted to sacrifice honesty for the sake of achieving his goals. By no means was Walter the perfect human being, but he did possess many great traits. He worked hard and expected his players and office staff to work equally hard. He could be very critical, very stubborn, very loud. Yet Walter was loyal, caring, down to earth, and above all, passionate about his team.

The only way you could describe the Celtics organization in those first five years of Red's era was that it was a "fly by the seat of your pants" operation. The offices were small and crowded with staff, secretaries, players, players' wives, writers and even fans that Brown and Auerbach used to hold their two-man executive board meetings in the men's room because it was the only place where they could get some privacy. In fact, if something really important had to be discussed, Howie McHugh would hang an "out of order" sign on the bathroom door and then stand guard so that Walter and Red would not be interrupted. Still, anyone could hear the two of them loudly arguing with each other from 50 feet away.

The relationship between Walter and Red was an interesting, often volatile one. By the time I arrived, they had developed great respect for one another. That didn't mean they didn't still have their share of heated disagreements. Red had complete charge over all basketball decisions; Walter handled all the business matters.

I'm sure you've heard stories about what a pleasure it was to work for Walter. Take my word, all the stories are true. Walter was a humble gentleman, a person without prejudice, a person who had absolutely no tolerance for prejudice.

Here's a perfect example of Walter's character:

On the Sunday after Brown had hired Red, a man came up to Walter outside a church in Hopkinton where Walter was a parishoner.

"How come you hired Auerbach?" the man asked.

"Well, I believe he's the best coach available," replied Walter. "He's the best coach [part-owner] Lou Pieri and I could possibly hope to get."

"But Walter, Auerbach's a Jew," the man said.

Without any hesitation, Walter looked up at the image of Christ on the church steeple and answered, "So was He."

And that indeed was how Walter Brown lived his life. He didn't have a prejudicial bone in his body. If you were an achiever, Walter wanted you. He didn't care what you were. It was your work ethic, your talent, that solely mattered. And I can be personally sure of that because he hired me, a New York Jew, as his broadcaster. The factor that helped most to make this ball club into what it became was Walter's kindness to the guys—the fact that he (along with Howie McHugh) would always find housing for new players, that he would always be concerned about the happiness of players' families, that he would go out of his way to make sure players who needed an off-season job found work.

As a result, when the time came for Walter's back to be against the wall, like when he couldn't pay his players their playoff shares, they understood the situation. That happened in 1955. At the start of the next season, Walter paid each player his playoff share (plus interest) and also thanked everyone for the support he had received. Anyone who did business with Walter became his friend. There was a major airline that gave the Celtics credit for three years simply because the airline executives knew that Walter Brown was a man of his word. If he said the bills would be paid eventually, it was as good as done. Today, such practice in big business is unheard of. In fact, it doesn't exist.

The airline wasn't the only company to have faith in Walter. When the Celtics needed a hotel to stay in in New York City, we went to the Summit, because its owner allowed the team to defer paying even a penny for more than three years. And when Walter finally was able to pay off the hotel bill, he and Red didn't forget the hotel owner's generosity. For more than 30 years, the Celtics have continued to stay at the Summit out of loyalty and gratitude, even though there are hundreds of far more luxurious places to stay.

No owner in the history of sports ever had a better relationship with his players than Walter Brown. Deep down, they respected the man, because he always dealt with them fairly and was strictly above board. One time "Fat Freddy" Scolari, a reserve guard, asked Walter for a raise because he needed money to help pay for an operation for his mother. "Freddy, I can't give you a raise, because it wouldn't be fair to some other guys who are playing better than you are. See me tomorrow, though." When Freddy bumped into Walter the next day, Walter handed him $200 and a note that read, "This isn't a loan or a raise. It's a gift. Tell your mom I hope she's feeling better."

Those were the kinds of things that were the foundation of the
club. Those feelings were what created the family atmosphere. And it
started at the top, because Red and Walter never had a contract
between them. Just a handshake agreement.

However, there could be real warfare between Auerbach and
Brown when Walter's idea of sound business conflicted with Red's
view of solid basketball decisions, as happened with Red's first draft
as Celtics coach in 1950. Because Walter had put himself in hock to
keep the Celtics franchise going, he was willing to do almost anything
to put people in the stands. The opportunity to draft a young hotshot
playmaker by the name of Bob Cousy, a kid who had led Holy Cross
to the '50 NCAA title, was almost irresistible to Walter. In Cousy,
Walter saw a way to dramatically increase attendance while also
making the Celtics a better club. But Red, who had signed on to
coach the Celtics only a month before the draft, vehemently opposed
the idea. From what I was told by Walter, the decision of whether or
not to draft Cousy was, without question, the biggest argument he
and Red ever had.

"I was totally surprised when Red told me to 'drop dead' when
I suggested we select Cousy. He didn't like Bob's game one bit," Walter
recalled when I interviewed him during my first year in Boston. "In
fact, he absolutely hated Cousy's style of play. He thought Bob's no-
look behind-the-back passes would absolutely ruin the concept of
teamwork he was trying to establish.

"'Walter, I've seen this kid play and there's nothing to like. His
defense stinks. On offense, he wants to be the star and he tries to
show off by always attempting to make the spectacular play. He's
undisciplined, and he thinks he's a hell of a lot smarter than he really
is. He's uncoachable, and I don't need to start off my career in Boston
by drafting a guy like that,' Red yelled at me. 'In the end, he'll drive
people away because he'll hurt us with all of his mistakes. If we don't
win, people won't want to come no matter how many local kids we

have on this team. And we sure as hell won't win if Cousy's playing for us.'

"What could I say to all of that?" Walter said. "Since Red and I had an agreement that he would have total control of the team's personnel, I eventually backed off. But it wasn't without a fight."

That was putting it mildly. Howie McHugh told me that when Walter kept pressuring Red to draft Cousy, Red finally lost his temper. According to Howie, Red almost quit two days before the '50 draft when he stormed out of the office and yelled over his shoulder, "If that little showoff is coming here, then I'm leaving." It took Walter an entire day to convince Red to come back.

"You win," Walter told Red. "We won't take Cousy if you don't want him. But I'm still not happy about it."

"I'm not asking you to be fucking happy, Walter," Red replied. "Just trust my opinion."

Red made no apologies for his decision not to select the Holy Cross whiz kid. "Am I supposed to win or am I supposed to worry about some local yokel?" he told the press. Instead Red drafted 6'11" Charlie Share from Bowling Green, who, by the way, would never play a single game for Boston, with his first pick. Then, in the second round, the Celtics chose Duquesne guard Chuck Cooper, the first black player ever drafted by the NBA.

When Walter announced to his fellow owners that "Boston takes Charles Cooper of Duquesne," one of them piped up, "Do you realize that Cooper is a Negro?"

Walter's response was quick and firm: "I don't care if he's plaid. All I know is this kid can play basketball and we want him." That shut up everybody. If you asked Walter a question, you got a straightforward answer.

When the Chicago Stags unexpectedly folded three weeks before the '50-'51 season was to start, the Celtics ended up acquiring Cousy's rights in a dispersal draft involving three players—Max Zaslofsky, Andy Phillip and Cousy. The three names were written down on pieces of paper and put in a hat. The first player chosen was by the Knicks, who drew Zaslofsky's name; the second piece of paper chosen was by the Philadelphia Warriors, who drew Phillip's name. The only name left in the hat for the Celtics was Cousy's—and Brown didn't even bother to pull out the paper. Like it or not, Red was going to coach Cousy.

Still, Auerbach made it crystal clear that Cooz was not exactly a welcome addition to the Celtics roster. "I wanted Zaslofsky [who had been a four-time All-NBA first-team player] or I would have settled for Phillip [a proven point guard]. Cousy was the only guy left," Red told the press. "Now I have to figure out what to do with him. To me, he's just another rookie who has to show me that he can play professionally."

And Bob did indeed prove himself in his first two years, averaging 18.6 points and almost 5.8 assists a game over that span. Still, Red has always insisted that he didn't make a mistake in not drafting Cousy instead of Share in the first place. "I KNOW I made the right decision," Red lectured me in one of my first interviews with him. "The thing fans don't understand is that Cousy is 10 times the player he was coming out of Holy Cross. He worked hard to improve and to earn my respect."

So Cousy ended up being the answer to both Red's and Walter's prayers. Red ended up with a perennial All-Star playmaker, and Walter got himself a legitimate local hero to help increase attendance. Although Bob seldom engaged in physical confrontations, he was involved in one of the first brawls I broadcasted. He had driven to the basket, and Philadelphia's huge center Neil Johnston, who stood 6'8" and weighed 220 pounds, just tackled him at chest level. Cousy, after dropping to the floor and lying still for about a half-minute, finally bounced up and started flailing his arms in anger. The next thing I saw was Johnston being pummeled by the entire Celtics team.

Red had a knack of out-thinking the other coaches and GMs in the league when it came to drafting players—although no one fully realized it until after he had "stolen" Bill Russell from two other franchises, a story I'll explain later.

His first coup, which really set the stage for building a dynasty, came in the 1953 draft. It was five months before I came aboard. National powerhouse Kentucky had been on a year's probation in 1952 and had decided to redshirt three of its top players—6'4" Frank Ramsey, 6'5" Cliff Hagan, and 6'5" Lou Tsioropoulos—that season. Although their original graduating class was '53, they each had an additional year of eligibility. At that time, NBA rules allowed teams to draft players if they were in their graduating year. Even though the Celtics desperately needed help immediately to contend for a division title, Red made the bold move of drafting all three Kentucky stars, knowing full well he would have to wait a full year to get them into Celtics green.

Following that draft, the owners immediately voted to ban teams from drafting players who still had college eligibility remaining, but Red could have cared less. "They were bullshit. They didn't expect me, as coach of a team which hadn't won even a division title, to use draft picks on three guys who I wouldn't be able to sign right away," Red told me. "I didn't care, though. I had just gotten three of the country's top 10 players, and there was nothing anyone could do about it."

(Ironically, the rules eventually changed back, and in 1978 Red again outfoxed the entire league by choosing a guy with a year of eligibility left named Larry Bird, who had already told the world he was staying at Indiana State for another season.)

But back to the memories of my early days in Boston.

During my first year I developed what would turn out to be a great and lifelong friendship with Don Barksdale, a 6'6" forward who was obtained from the Baltimore Bullets in the summer of '53.

Don was the fourth black to enter the league, following in the footsteps of Chuck Cooper, Sweetwater Clifton and Earl Lloyd, and he was probably the best athlete of the group. He was the first black ever to play for a U.S. Olympic basketball team when he made the squad in 1948. His speed, strength, quickness and jumping ability impressed the U.S. track coaches so much that they almost entered Barksdale in the decathlon when one of the U.S. team members suddenly became ill the night before the start of the events. I can assure you that Barksdale would not have embarrassed himself. In fact, at the 1947 San Francisco Relays, a major college invitational, Don won the high point totals trophy for winning three gold medals in running events along with a bronze in the high jump.

His athletic achievements on the college level and in the NBA, where he became the first black to play in the league's annual All-Star Game, were so impressive that in 1980 Paramount bought the rights for a made-for-TV movie. "If they do it, then you're going to be in it. I've got to let people know the kind of person I hung around with back then. I can't let them picture me as a saint," he always kids me.

In 1954 I left the Lenox and rented an apartment with Barksdale in the Kenmore Square area. Despite our different backgrounds, we enjoyed many of the same things. We liked the same type of music, so we'd hit all the jazz clubs; we liked the same kind of food, so we'd make a habit of going to Symphony Sid's for ribs once a week; we both liked the night life and the city itself. Those were nothing but good times.

While Don had incredible athletic ability, he did not possess extraordinary basketball skills. He was neither a great shooter nor a superior passer. He made the Celtics strictly on raw talent, hustle, and aggressiveness. His favorite move in practice was one that everyone on the team, with the exception of our muscle man, Bob Brannum, enjoyed tremendously. If Brannum was standing between Don and the basket, trying to box him out, Barksdale would simply leapfrog straight over Bob's head. Brannum would be infuriated; the rest of us literally would be rolling on the court with laughter.

Barksdale was a real night owl, a guy who would stay up and party until seven in the morning almost daily. To this day, he credits me with keeping him in the league. "Put it this way," he said to me, "I always had trouble going to sleep early. I didn't drink, but I loved going to clubs and listening to music for as long as the band wanted to play. I'd never get home before the sun had risen. Then, two or three hours later, I'd hear this unmistakable voice: 'Don, get up or you'll be fined again. You've got 15 minutes to make practice.'

"Johnny," he told me years later, "you saved a career, whether you know it or not."

I wasn't comfortable being in Boston. I didn't have a lot of friends. In my own mind, I wasn't doing a great job broadcasting the Celtics, and I liked baseball a lot more than basketball. My dream was that I could return to a job in New York doing the play-by-play for one of its major league teams.

Boston's star, "Easy Ed" Macauley, a guy who wanted to get into broadcasting after he retired, also knew me well. In fact, he would regularly just pull up a chair and join me for the first three or four minutes of my pregame shows when Boston was playing on the road. Ed was damn good, too. He has a great sense of humor and a crisp voice, and he loved being behind a microphone. Because Macauley was a natural communicator, it didn't come as a surprise to me that he eventually became the St. Louis Hawks' color commentator in the early '60s.

One night on a train ride from New York to Boston, Ed sat down next to me and struck up a conversation. "I don't mean this as criticism, but I don't quite understand why you accepted the Celtics job in the first place," he said very seriously. "All you ever talk about in your spare time is baseball. If not baseball, then football. You hardly ever bring up the subject of basketball. I just wonder if you have the same passion for basketball as you do for other sports." And he was 100 percent correct, although I didn't admit it to him.

My conversation with Ed only reinforced my own self-doubts. So I decided to seek the advice of Sammy Cohen, who by this time had become my unofficial mentor. "Johnny, do you know how many fans in New England would love to have your job?" he said. "Just think of yourself as the one lucky fan who gets to tell all the thousands of other fans about how great the Celtics are doing."

Sammy's phrase, "the one lucky fan," became my motto for my entire career. If I didn't talk about any game with a sense of intensity and urgency, then in effect, I was letting down those "thousands of other fans" who were at home rooting for the Celtics to come through for them.

I also talked with Curt Gowdy, my predecessor as the voice of the Celtics and another broadcaster I have always admired greatly. Gowdy has developed his own unique style. When he broadcasts a game, listeners feel almost as if Curt is sitting in their living room just casually discussing each play. "I listen to your broadcasts and I love the way you let your emotions come through. It's very effective," he told me. "Johnny, you're giving the fans a good idea of the flow of the game. If I were you, I wouldn't change a thing." Getting that kind of reassurance from a great play-by-play man like Gowdy was a big psychological boost.

Within a week of my conversations with Sammy and Curt, the Celtics visited the Knicks. New York was absolutely crushing Boston, and Red was starting to lose his temper. I was sitting at courtside and began to take my cue from Auerbach. When Sid Borgia, a legendary referee who had a habit of overdramatizing his calls, signaled a charge on Macauley, I yelled into the microphone: "He's going blind. Borgia just made his third straight bad call against Boston. Macauley got attacked, mauled. And this official is pretending he didn't see Ed crumble to the floor."

Borgia, who was standing 10 feet away, couldn't help but overhear my criticism and walked up to me. "Say another word and I'll throw you out of here even before I toss Auerbach," he warned me. I was actually thrilled that he had reacted to my play-by-play, and I could see that the Celtics players were all staring at me and Borgia. I wasn't quite sure if Borgia had the power to throw me out, so I kept quiet. Instead of making a wise comment, I took a big puff on my cigarette and blew the smoke right in Borgia's face. He just turned and sort of strutted away. After the game, Red came up to me and simply said, "Nice going. That's exactly how I would have handled it."

I respected Borgia because he hustled, and truthfully, he seldom missed a call. On the rare occasions when he did make a mistake, he'd go over to Red and say, "My fault. I blew it and I know it." Because of Borgia's point-blank honesty, he was the one official who could leave Red speechless. If Borgia admitted he missed a call, Auerbach would nod and quietly say, "Glad to hear it, Sid, but now you owe us one. Right?"

For a man who stood about 5'7" and weighed maybe 160 pounds, Sid was a tough SOB. One night in Syracuse a fan who made his living as a meat packer and looked like a fullback came charging out onto the court to give Borgia a piece of his mind. Sid greeted the guy with two quick punches to the face. The unruly fan staggered backwards, lost his balance and ended up breaking a leg. An unsympathetic Borgia just motioned for the security guards to carry the guy away. "C'mon, get this moron off the court," he told them. "I've got a game to officiate. Throw him out and let him limp to the hospital. I don't want the team to have to pay for the expense of an ambulance just to give this jerk a ride."

I had one other notable incident involving Borgia. The Celtics were playing the Hawks in a playoff game at St. Louis. There were three seconds left in the game, with Boston ahead by a point. St. Louis inbounded the ball to Pettit near halfcourt. The clock, however, didn't move. Pettit took three dribbles and hit a jumper as the buzzer sounded. The play took at least five seconds. As Borgia walked past me, I made a loud comment concerning the St. Louis timekeeper.

"That official is either blind, incompetent or crooked," I screamed. Sid mistakenly thought I was referring to him.

When I returned to Boston, I was met by a battery of lawyers representing Borgia. They told me that Sid was prepared to sue me. It took me about a half-hour to convince them that the target of my remarks was the timekeeper, not Sid. Fortunately for me, the attorneys accepted my explanation and asked only that I talk to Sid about my comments. When I approached Sid a couple days later, he began to laugh. "Johnny, don't say a word. You're a royal pain in the ass," he said. Then he shook my hand and walked away.

Throughout my career, I've been involved in a number of altercations. In fact, my first fistfight in 1954 was a classic. It occurred in Saint Louis following a game against the Hawks which ended in a 20-minute brawl. I was broadcasting from the balcony and had to pack up my radio equipment into two suitcases and carry everything down to the Celtics' locker room. By the time I made my way down all the steps to the hallway leading to the teams' locker rooms, Red and the players had left the arena to catch a train to Fort Wayne. As I was walking towards the exit, the Hawks' owner, Ben Kerner, approached me. "You're broadcasting for a bunch of assholes, starting with Auerbach," he screamed in my face. That's all I needed to hear. I dropped the equipment and whacked Kerner in the puss. Got him good, too. For the next couple minutes, he and I exchanged roundhouse punches before wrestling each other to the ground. After a security guard pulled me away, I scrambled to catch up with the Celtics team at the train terminal. When I walked onto the train, my left eye was swollen shut and my shirt was torn.

"Damn, Johnny, who jumped you?" said Barksdale as the entire team gathered around me.

"No one. I just beat the hell out of Kerner," I proudly replied. "He started in on how we were bush league, so I popped him a couple of times."

Just when I was starting to enjoy describing how I had waged a fearless battle against Kerner, I spotted Red, who had overheard my conversation with the players, staring at me. Leaning back in his seat, he threw the butt of his cigar on the floor, crushed it, and then yelled out for everybody to hear: "Looks to me like you got in one lucky punch and then Kerner kicked the crap out of you."

His remark made me feel more than a little embarrassed. Even though I really did get in my share of shots at Kerner, once Red made his comment, the players, with the lone exception of Barksdale, all began to rib me about my fighting abilities.

My biggest fan was always Don, who would constantly tell me how Boston fans were enjoying my work. He would relate conversations he had with people he met about how they would say I was so enjoyable to listen to on the radio. I suspected these stories were a product of his imagination, simply a way for him to ensure he didn't lose a roommate.

Racism really affected Barksdale's career. He didn't even get a chance to get into the NBA until he was 28 years old because blacks were not given the opportunity when he graduated from UCLA in 1947. "I knew Jackie Robinson and a few of the other finest black athletes. We'd sit and talk about all the crap that was going on," Barksdale explained to me. "We'd talk about a guy named Johnny Allen who was probably the best athlete in the Bay Area. He could have been an All-Star shortstop. He could have played pro basketball or football. He was that good."

But Johnny Allen never got past San Jose State, where he was an honorable mention All-America halfback in 1939 and 1940 and was a three-time division MVP in baseball, because he was born too soon to get an opportunity to play in the major leagues or in the NBA.

"It's a shame," Don said. "Johnny Allen was a combination of Jackie Robinson, Bill Russell and Jim Brown. He was that good, and yet he never had a chance."

If you were black, it was difficult to get a scholarship. You had to be among the top one or two percent of black athletes to even have a shot at playing sports in college. As Don would say, "You had to be so good, they [the coaches and the school administrations] had to ignore the color of your skin because they knew what your talent could mean to their athletic programs. UCLA opened the door. First Jackie Robinson, then Kenny Washington, Woody Strode [who later became a successful Hollywood actor, with starring roles in such pictures as *Spartacus*, *The Man Who Shot Liberty Valance*, and *Sergeant Rutledge*], Tom Berkley and Tom Bradley, who set several track records for the Bruins before entering politics and eventually becoming mayor of Los Angeles. If you wanted to go to a place where you had a chance to play sports, you went to UCLA."

Despite tremendous basketball achievements at UCLA, Don was not welcome in the NBA. "After the '48 Olympics, I got one feeler, a letter from [St. Louis owner] Ben Kerner saying that if 'they ever allowed colored ballplayers,' he 'sure as hell' would want me. It was what is commonly known as the brush-off," Don told me. "Finally, after Cooper and Sweetwater Clifton got into the league, I was selected by Baltimore, where I played for two years. Then Red traded for me. I never did hear back from Kerner, which was no great surprise."

Don instantly found Auerbach to be a great coach and an even better person, as he told me one day after practice. "Red gave us a pep talk this morning. It impressed the hell out of me. He just stood up in front of us real calm and said, "This is my team. I don't trade a lot and I don't deal a lot unless you're not giving me a hundred percent.' It was the way he said it. You knew that if you go all out, you wouldn't have to worry. You work your butt off for 10, 20, 30 minutes and there's no problem."

Auerbach's ability to judge character was another quality Barksdale admired. "He's so damn astute at picking up players, guys whom other coaches thought were nothing more than a pain in the ass. Just look at me. I'm the perfect example." But Don's admiration for Red went further. "One night we went to a diner in Baltimore and the owners wouldn't serve me," Barksdale recalled. "Red stood up and said, 'Screw it, the food looks like garbage anyhow.' Red wanted his team to be united in every way. If a hotel down South wouldn't allow blacks, the white players on the team might be forced to stay one night, but Red would never go back."

Don was a gentleman, a guy who not only played fair and hard but also played hurt. He had a condition on the soles of his feet that would cause the skin to actually split open and then bleed. There was no remedy for it at the time. As a result, Barksdale played game after game with considerable pain, as evidenced by the fact that his sweat socks were completely soaked with blood at the end of each game. Yet he never complained, never asked to be taken out. He'd sooner limp and be in the lineup than sit on the bench.

Following the '54-'55 season, Barksdale, with age against him, decided to retire, having failed in his quest to win an NBA championship. "I'll tell you, it would have been nice to have gone to the pros straight out of college," he still says to me. "I've actually figured it out. The money Moses Malone makes for playing five games is more than I made in my whole career. It's a bitch to think about. I don't know how else to say it."

When Don retired from the game, he certainly didn't go back home and sit in a rocking chair. First he became the owner of a nightclub called The Showcase, which featured such acts as Lou Rawls (his first regular gig), Laverne Baker, Redd Foxx, Marvin Gaye, B.B. King, Richard Pryor and Dinah Washington. "All those people whom I booked, who started out with me, they have gotten big. I never had a contract with one of them. Never needed one. I was in heaven listening to great music every night and actually helping to build careers of people who would go on to be superstars. A few years later, though, the dope scene became too heavy," he told me. "People were getting a little nuts. That's when I decided to get out of the business."

From there, Don became a disc jockey, working at KROW and KWBR, where Sly Stone was also spinning records. He became good friends with saxophonist Gerry Mulligan, who wrote a tune called "Bark for Barkhouse" in Don's honor. At age 64, Don quit his full-time job to devote time to help youngsters, organizing "Save High School Sports," a non-profit organization that raises funds to keep programs alive in the Bay Area. He puts in 12-hour days, runs fundraisers, and makes any sacrifice necessary to see his project succeed. His goal isn't to gain credit for himself but to help inner-city youth increase their chances of success in life. He is the living definition of a team player in all aspects of life.

Following my second season in Boston, I received a call from Marty Glickman. "Hey, Johnny, how would you like to team up with me again?" he said. "The [New York football] Giants just hired me to do the play-by-play on radio because [future four-time National Sportscaster of the Year] Chris Schenkel is moving over to handle the television job. I know you won't be able to be with me for all the games because of the Celtics job, but just do the ones you can make and I'll get someone else to fill in for you. What do you say?"

"You're on," I replied, without even inquiring about my salary. Being teamed with Marty again, making some extra cash, and getting to spend a little more time with my parents all appealed to me. "Just tell me when you're going to need me."

Truth be told, Marty's offer couldn't have been more timely, because I was flat broke. My Celtics salary, supplemented by some unsolicited generous financial support that my parents regularly provided, barely enabled me to pay the bills. Occasionally I did manage to get some baseball fill-in work during the summers, but the extra income didn't amount to much.

The Giants' exhibition season went smoothly. Fortunately, I already was a friend of New York's starting offensive right end, Ken McAfee, who was a diehard Celtics fan from Brockton, Massachusetts. He was kind enough to introduce me to every single player, including

Emlen Tunnell, whom I consider the greatest safety of all time, and a smart and very tough defensive back named Tom Landry, who eventually went on to coach the Cowboys for 29 years and win two Super Bowls.

By the time the Giants' regular season began, I felt very much at ease, especially with Marty guiding me along in the broadcasting booth. However, I ran into some trouble when the Cleveland Browns visited New York in the opener. Marty had sent me to the locker rooms to get the starting lineups for both teams. I had never met Cleveland's legendary coach Paul Brown, so I walked up to him and cheerfully introduced myself, "Coach, my name is Johnny Most and I'm part of the Giants' broadcasting team. Can I get the starting defensive unit from you?"

Well, Paul Brown proceeded to reel off 11 names—all of which were dead wrong. As soon as the teams took the field for the first play from scrimmage, I realized Brown had fed me a totally false lineup. As I was scrambling frantically to write down a corrected version of the Cleveland defensive starters for Marty's play-by-play, he began chuckling to himself. During the game's first timeout, Marty eased my mind and conscience by explaining why Brown had out-and-out lied to me.

"Don't worry about it," he said. "What you have to realize is that Paul Brown is football's version of Red Auerbach. Once Brown knew you were a Giants broadcaster, he wasn't about to give you his real starting lineup. He didn't want to take the chance that you might show his real lineup to the Giant coaches, so he lied to you. He just would never do anything that might give the opposition the slightest edge. It wasn't personal."

Still, I was embarrassed. As soon as Brown gave me that phony lineup, I should have been smart enough to realize it was completely bogus. I have to confess it took me more than a few years to stop hating the guy.

It was only after witnessing how Red would constantly pull little tricks on the Celtics' opponents and their broadcasters that I was able to laugh about the whole episode. If I ever had told Auerbach about what Paul Brown did, I know he would have understood, even admired, Brown's actions.

My days of partnering with Marty came to an end following the 1955 Giants season. The New York station decided it needed to have a color commentator who could be available for every game. Because of conflicts with my Celtics schedule, there was no way I could make that commitment. Besides, by that time I finally felt that Boston was where I belonged. I was comfortable, my circle of friends was growing, I was making decent money, and I was establishing a loyal following. I'd love to walk down the street and hear people say, "Hey, isn't that Johnny Most, the Celtics' announcer?"

I felt like I was developing my own style of broadcasting and learning more about the subtleties of basketball. The players respected and trusted me. I finally believed I had become a part of the Celtics family.

And, speaking of families, I had met a young woman from Brookline named Sandra Schultz, who was both beautiful and intelligent. We shared many interests, including music and poetry. After dating only six months, we decided to get married.

I'd have to say that my favorite character on the pre-dynasty Celtics teams was Togo Palazzi. A 6'4" guard out of Holy Cross, Togo was very superstitious. For instance, he always insisted on being the last player to leave the locker room at the start of a game. Then, on the day Red had decided to give Togo his first pro start, the inevitable happened. Fellow rookie Frank Ramsey saw the perfect opportunity to play a joke on Togo.

First, Ramsey lingered in the locker room, just to make Togo nervous. When Ramsey finally headed out the door, Palazzi, relieved that he would not break his superstition of being the last man to step onto the court, said a little prayer while holding his rosary beads and headed for the door. But Ramsey had already told a security guard to lock and bolt the room from the outside. It wasn't until a minute before the tipoff that Red realized Togo was nowhere to be found. He sent a ballboy back to the locker room where Togo was pounding on the door from the inside with his fists and a basketball shoe. As the two teams were lining up for the tip, Togo, already in a full sweat, sprinted onto the court. Normally Red would have yanked any player who was so late right out of the lineup. However, when Red saw that Togo's hands were purple and red from banging on the locker room door, he figured Togo had learned his lesson.

"As soon as I realized the locker room door wasn't budging, I knew Ramsey had gotten me good. That didn't bother me. It was worrying about whether Red was going to pull me from the starting lineup, which really made me a wreck," Togo told me afterward. "As things turned out, I played really well that game, probably because I was so darned mad at Ramsey."

Another of Togo's superstitions was that he had to wear his lucky purple Holy Cross T-shirt underneath his Celtics practice jersey. Rumor was that Togo never washed it. So one day while Togo was taking a shower, the entire team conducted a T-shirt burning ceremony. Then they deposited its remains in front of Togo's locker and waited to see his reaction. When he saw what had been done, Togo wanted to kill whoever was responsible, but he never could narrow down the field of suspects.

Probably the most gullible Celtic in history, Togo was a quiet, very respectful kid. The fact that he was somewhat naive and so polite and easy-going off the court made him a favorite target of numerous other practical jokes.

At the Minneapolis Airport while waiting for a plane to take the Lakers and our team to an exhibition game in Hibbing, Minnesota, Ramsey asked Minneapolis center Clyde Lovellette to page Palazzi. When Togo picked up the paging phone, Lovellette pretended to be a county sheriff. "Is this Togo A. Palazzi?" he asked, in a deep voice. "Yes sir, it is," replied Palazzi.

"Well, this is Sheriff Smith, and we have an arrest warrant out for you. You've being charged with bothering a female patron at a hotel bar," Lovellette said firmly. Togo adamantly denied that he had done anything wrong and became upset.

At the same time Ramsey had persuaded the ticket agent to announce: "Will Mr. Palazzi please report to the ticket desk because a law officer would like to talk to you."

Togo became scared and bolted for the plane. Once the plane took off, Togo thought he was in the clear. But Ramsey had gone so far as to clue in the pilot, who announced over the loudspeaker that the Hibbing chief of police would be waiting when the plane landed to question "Mr. Palazzi about his alleged misconduct in Minneapolis."

By now Togo was sweating bullets. Auerbach, who was in on the gag, finally decided to show some mercy and told Togo that he was a victim of a practical joke. Togo vowed revenge against Ramsey but was too nice a guy to ever carry out his threat.

Another interesting character with the Celtics was forward Bob "Gabby" Harris, a strong, lean, silent cowboy type. In all my years as a broadcaster, Bob was the most difficult guy I ever interviewed. One night I invited him over to do a short interview. It was a major goof on my part. Every time I would ask a question, Gabby would just nod, not saying a word. During the first commercial break, I tried to loosen him up. "Please don't just nod at me. The people listening to their radio can't hear anything but dead silence if all you do is nod," I said. "You can take your time but try to think of this interview as simply one friend chatting with another."

"OK," Gabby replied.

When I came back on the air, I asked Gabby six or seven more questions. Each time he responded with either a "yup," "nope" or "sure."

Finally, I gave up. "Well, Gabby, thanks for taking time to share your thoughts with us," I said. "You're welcome, Johnny. It's been my pleasure," Gabby replied. His goodbye sentence was longer than all of his previous responses combined. Needless to say, I crossed Gabby off my interview list.

The Celtics' "big man" in the pre-Russell years was the ultra-skinny 6'8" Macauley, who was awarded to Boston in 1950 when the St. Louis Bombers folded and the league decided Walter Brown's franchise needed a major boost to survive. A two-time All-American at the University of St. Louis, Ed had a smooth shot, quick moves, smarts and guts. However, because he weighed no more than 185 pounds, he took a physical pounding every night. Picture Danny Ainge going up against Charles Barkley, Maurice Lucas, Bill Laimbeer or Rick Mahorn on a nightly basis, and you have an idea what life was like for Macauley.

"Easy Ed" was tough on the court but a bit of a joker off the court. If he was late for practice, he always had a very creative excuse. One time he and reserve forward Jack Nichols, who later became a dentist in Seattle, missed a train from Rochester to New York City because they were having a few beers in the station's bar and lost track of the time. Red was furious, but Macauley, who arrived eight hours late, came up with an excuse that left Auerbach speechless.

"Red," said Macauley, "Nichols and myself stopped into the bar for just one beer. A minute after we sat down, two guys came in and robbed the place. They told everyone not to move, so we had to stand there until they left. We ran to the train but, because of the robbery, we missed the train."

In my opinion, it was Ed's determination that was most responsible for Auerbach's early Celtics teams developing a winning attitude. Every opposing center he faced outweighed him by a minimum of 40 pounds, yet Macauley used his speed and finesse to make bigger men look not only clumsy but often stupid.

The obvious strategy against Ed was to beat him up and wear him down. As Cousy would say, "Some night Ed's going to get murdered out there and the officials are going to miss the call." In fact, he took such a beating that Red would use 6'5", 220-pound Bob Brannum as Ed's personal bodyguard, which Macauley appreciated. "I needed the protection," Ed told me once in an interview. "In college, I thought I was a pretty tough kid, despite being so skinny. Here in the pros, though, these big guys toss me 10 feet up in the air every time they throw an elbow."

Brannum, the first in a long line of Celtics enforcers, feared no one in the league, including 6'11", 255-pound center George Mikan of the Minneapolis Lakers. Mikan was slow but incredibly strong. Plus, he loved to stick out his huge elbows whenever he set a pick. One night he was just bouncing Macauley around as if he were a human pinball. Brannum warned him to knock off the roughhousing, but Mikan just kept whacking Macauley in the back every chance he got.

Then Brannum evened the score. When big George went up in the air for a rebound, Bob lowered his head and rammed him in the stomach. Mikan's glasses went flying as he flew through the air before landing on the court. "George, cut the crap with Macauley," Brannum yelled as Mikan, with a glazed look in his eyes, stared up at him. "Each time I have to hit you, it'll be just a little bit harder than the last time." Not surprisingly, Macauley wasn't so much as touched for the rest of the night.

Brannum's reputation as a brawler was well known around the league. Before one game at Syracuse's Onondaga War Memorial Auditorium in 1954, the Nats handed out 5,000 cardboard hatchets to their fans. The inscription on the hatchets read: "BOSTON BUTCHER BOY BOB BRANNUM." Just as the tipoff was about to take place, the majority of those 5,000 hatchets were thrown onto the court. Brannum, who relished his reputation as an enforcer, scrambled around the court collecting as many of them as he could.

"They'll make great souvenirs," he said. "I'm going to give them to my friends and put one on top of my locker. I guess this shows that I'm doing my job. My thanks to the good people of Syracuse for honoring me."

The Nats' fans were the wildest in the league. They felt that buying a ticket to the game entitled them to be actual participants. It was not at all unusual for Syracuse fans to actually come out onto the court and attack a visiting player, nor was it out of the norm for a fan to challenge a player on the bench to a fight in the stands during a game.

Just to give you an idea of how wild the fans would become in the "snake pit," I even became a part of a brawl in 1958. I was at courtside next to the Boston bench when a Syracuse fan ran into the Celtics huddle and started throwing punches at several of the players. As the entire Celtics team, including Red, pummeled the uninvited guest, another fan sitting a row behind me tossed a roundhouse punch toward the back of Cousy's head. The punch missed Cousy and then glanced off my shoulder.

"Excuse the interruption," I said on the air, "but I have to restrain an unruly, overweight, sloppy, pathetic drunk." I then stood up, turned around and shoved the obnoxious heckler back into his seat. But this pest wasn't through yet. He started to charge me but suddenly stopped dead in his tracks and scurried back to his seat. I felt very proud of how I had backed down the guy, until I happened to look over my shoulder and saw Brannum cocking his fist and motioning to the fan to sit down and shut up.

In those days it was an unusual game when there *weren't* at least one or two minor fights. Referees adopted a "boys will be boys" attitude about one-on-one altercations. Unless blood was flowing and punches were exchanged, players seldom were ejected for tossing elbows or sharp jabs to an opponent's stomach. Brannum knew just where to draw the line.

For instance, one night Brannum went after Fort Wayne forward Fred Schaus, who was a tough cheap-shot artist. Schaus instigated the incident by throwing an elbow to the back of Macauley's head. The elbow landed with full force, and Red immediately signaled for Brannum to enter the game. When play continued, Schaus made a huge mistake by attempting to throw yet another elbow, this time in Bob's direction. Brannum ducked and threw a beauty of a right-hand uppercut to Schaus' chest. Schaus crumbled to the court and was immediately taken to the hospital, where he was treated for a broken rib.

On the air, I was having some fun. "Oh, look at Fearless Freddie. He's practically in tears," I said. "One quick punch and Brannum has turned a bully into a bawling baby. Will somebody please give little Freddie a hanky?"

There was one occasion, however, when Brannum decided that discretion was the better part of valor. It took place against the Knicks after Gabby Harris had been bumping New York's tower of strength, Sweetwater Clifton, who spent his off seasons as a sparring partner for heavyweight champ Jersey Joe Walcott. Sweetwater decided he had taken one too many elbows from Harris and simply KOed him with a single punch. The Boston bench, led by Brannum, charged out onto the court, only to see Sweetwater smiling, ready and waiting for round two to begin. Brannum and the rest of Boston's reserves stopped so quickly that you could see the skid marks on the court as they halted their advance and headed back to the relative safety of the Celtics bench.

The classic "Butcher Boy" story occurred in '55 when the Celtics were again playing at Syracuse. We had beaten the Nats easily, and the last guy off the court was Brannum, who was walking just behind Red. A fan decided to take a sneak punch at Auerbach. The punch glanced off Red's head, but before the fan could get away, Brannum picked the guy up with one hand and carried him into the Celtics' locker room. "Now things are even," said Brannum as he deposited the fan directly in front of Red. Auerbach just nodded approvingly, smacked the fan and literally kicked him out into the hallway.

Even today, Bob Brannum is one tough guy. He was riding a horse on a street near his home when the animal became frightened by a speeding car. The horse started to buck and then bolted toward the middle of the street. Bob tried desperately to control the horse, but he just couldn't calm him down. Finally, out of desperation, he threw a punch at the horse's nose. Down went the horse, with Bob still in the saddle. The horse then rolled over Brannum, breaking Bob's pelvis. When I called Bob at the hospital to see how he was doing, Brannum refused to admit the horse got the best of him. "I'll be fine," he told me. "But that horse is going to have a very sore nose for the rest of his life."

Despite the presence of "Big Brother" Brannum, Macauley took a beating almost every night. He would take it all, mainly because he would never quit on Auerbach or his teammates. "Red had a personality that would never help him win any elections. He was gruff, sometimes crude, and very difficult to get along with," Ed told me years later. "He bullied people. He used it as a tool to help his ball club. I always knew he did it because he was fighting for his players, not because he was showboating. I'm convinced he didn't want recognition, but he sure wanted to make certain we were recognized as a team that couldn't be intimidated."

It wasn't coincidence that Brannum would always end up in a fight with one of the opponent's top players. If Brannum got tossed by the ref, then it was almost a certainty that the guy he was fighting also got tossed. Syracuse forward Dolph Schayes, Knicks forward Harry "The Horse" Gallatin, Fort Wayne center Larry Foust and Mikan—all perennial All-Stars—were thrown out of games because of fights with Brannum. I asked Bob if Red ordered him to fight players in order to get them thrown out of games. "Let's just say Red was very pleased with my aggressiveness toward certain All-Stars. Before a game against Syracuse he might say to me, 'Don't be afraid to smack Schayes around if he's hurting us.' Truth is Schayes isn't a tough guy at all. So you figure out if Red's game plan is for me to find a way to instigate a fight and get a key player thrown out. I ain't talking."

Macauley, who became the youngest person (age 32) ever elected to the Hall of Fame back in 1960, never let an injury slow him down. At a banquet held in Red's honor in 1985, Macauley told me about the time he took an elbow square on the left side of his chest and Red sent him for X-rays.

The next day an envelope containing the results of the X-ray was delivered to Auerbach. When Macauley came in for practice, he asked Red if the doctors had found any broken bones. "Nah, it's just a bruise," replied Red. "Just wear a little pad on your left side when you're playing, and there won't be any pain."

Two years later, after Macauley had been traded to the Hawks as part of the deal for Bill Russell, Ed suffered a similar injury with the Hawks and again was sent for X-rays. The doctor looked at the X-rays and said, "You've got broken ribs again."

"*Again?* I've never had broken ribs in my life," replied Ed. Then Macauley suddenly recalled the injury he had sustained back in Boston when Auerbach told him to wear that pad. "Red knew all along my ribs were either broken or bruised badly, but he wasn't going to let me know. I think he honestly believed pain was all psychological. If you weren't on your death bed, you were OK to play," he said.

Ed's injury experiences were not limited to just one or two incidents. Against Syracuse, he had suffered a broken index finger. Because the Celtics were playing the Lakers in Minneapolis the next night, Auerbach ordered the trainer, Harvey Cohen, to tape the broken finger to the middle finger. Ed not only played against the Lakers, but he scored 46 points. Honest to God, at the next practice everyone was lining up at the trainer's table, asking to have their fingers taped together.

Once when the Celtics were in Philadelphia, Macauley called Red five hours before the game and told him he had a bad case of the flu. "Well, as long as you're already here, why don't you just show up at the arena?" Auerbach said. So Macauley followed orders. In the locker room, Macauley again told Red that he was sick as a dog. "Well, as long as you're at the arena, you might as well just warm up and see how you feel," said Auerbach. So Macauley went out on the floor and warmed up. As the game was about to start, Macauley, figuring he was finally going to get some rest, headed for a seat on the bench. "Look," said Red, "As long as you're warmed up, why not play a couple of minutes?"

As things turned out, it was a close game all the way and Macauley ended up playing 38 minutes and scoring 22 points. Afterwards Red sat down next to him, and said, "You feeling all right now? All you need is a good night's sleep."

"Red," Macauley said, "has a knack for embarrassing guys into playing when they are either hurt or sick. He acts like it's a sign of weakness if an injured player sits out a game or two. He makes sure everyone on the team knows a guy is injured and then he makes a speech in which he all but accuses the player of "milking a few bumps and bruises.""

I have to mention that Red wasn't always considered a coaching genius. Only twice in his first eight years had an Auerbach club so much as won a division title (with the '47 Washington Caps when Red was a rookie NBA coach and then with the '49 Caps). Both times his teams were eliminated in the playoffs.

In his first six years with Boston, Red's best finish was a tie for second in the regular season, and his teams never won a division title. In fact, during that time span the Celtics never had one year in which they had a winning record in the playoffs. However, no one could knock Red for developing and then perfecting Boston's fast-break offense, which accounted for the team leading the league in scoring in each of Red's first six years as Celtics coach.

Walter Brown liked the high-scoring style but had no patience for the losing. "I'm paying three guys—Cousy, Macauley and Sharman—more money than some owners are paying their entire squad," he complained to me on the air. "Maybe they're more concerned with their own press clippings than they are with our record. Something isn't right."

Or he might criticize Brannum or Barksdale in the newspaper. "They're not producing. All one of them [Brannum] likes to do is get into fights and the other [Barksdale] listens to music all day, stays up all night and hits every nightclub in town. They better start thinking of scoring baskets and playing good defense."

But Walter would calm down almost immediately. He'd come up to me and say, "I want you to interview me before the next game. I didn't mean those things I said about Brannum and Barksdale. I can be a little bit of a hothead at times, you know. I have to say some positive things about their play."

He'd do the same type of backtracking with the newspaper reporters. "Do me a favor," Walter would say to one of them. "Make sure you write something about how I think Brannum and Barksdale are underrated. I never should have said anything bad about either of them. We had just lost and I took my frustrations out on them."

The players understood how badly Walter wanted to win and always forgave him when he said something negative about them. "He always apologizes," Barksdale would tell me after I informed him one night that Walter was upset about his reputation as a nightclub regular. "It's nothing new. He'll get hot under the collar and make some critical comments. Moments later, he'll regret what he just said. Next thing I know, he's asking me what jazz groups are coming to town."

Brown's harshest comments were usually said in private to Red. If Auerbach only used seven guys in a game which the Celtics lost, Walter wouldn't hesitate to draw Red into a shouting match. "Why am I paying 10 guys if you only like using seven of them? Why are you wasting my money?" he'd scream.

Red would get angry and cut the conversation short: "Walter, why don't you cut the crap? We lost a God-damned game and you're looking for someone to blame. Don't bother me with your shit." For the next two or three days, the two wouldn't talk. But it was always Walter who made peace with Red, usually by offering to buy lunch or dinner.

Yet Walter, despite his complaints, would always call Red "the best coach in the league" when reporters questioned Auerbach's record. "All you newsmen want to crucify him every chance you get. Understand one thing: I'm Red's biggest fan because he can outthink every other coach in this league." Few people in the NBA agreed with Brown's assessment.

"Today," Macauley said to me at a Celtics reunion dinner held in '85, "everyone calls Red a coaching genius, which he is. However, when I was with the Celtics, he was viewed as a run-of-the-mill coach. Guys like Minneapolis' John Kundla and New York's Joe Lapchick were far more highly regarded than Auerbach. Red hadn't won a thing, and with his temper and brashness, many owners and players doubted that he would last more than a few years. But he was smart enough to realize that the only way to compete with the bigger teams was to outquick them defensively and outrace them on offense. That's why he ran us to death in practices."

Guard Bill Sharman, a 6'1" sharpshooter from USC who had been acquired along with Brannum by Red for the draft rights to 6'11" center Charlie Share in 1951, always understood why Brown had so much faith in Auerbach's abilities. "I knew from day one that Red was going to be a hell of a coach. I think every Celtics player believed in him," Bill told me. "It was just a fact that we just didn't have the size to win consistently. For the first five years Red was in Boston, the Celtics were a .500 team. It had nothing to do with coaching; it had to do with a lack of height and bulk. If we didn't have Auerbach, the team would have been close to last place because we had no true center.

"That's not a criticism of Macauley, because Ed was a tough, hard-working guy with a good offensive game. He just was too skinny to battle guys who outweighed him by 20, 30 or even 50 pounds. I'm not saying we were happy to be a .500 club, but we weren't ashamed of it, either. I think it's fair to say Red got more out of the talent we had than any other coach in the league could have. As players, we knew how intelligent he was. The rest of the league may not have recognized it, but they would learn soon enough."

From the start of his career, Sharman was a student of the game, a player Auerbach admired, and probably the foremost workaholic in Celtics history. His methods of training became standard procedure for today's NBA teams.

On the day of every game, Bill would go to a local high school gym and take 300 shots. When the Celts were at home, he would use the Needham High gym. When the team was on the road, he'd get in a taxi and go to the nearest high school gym and ask the athletic director if he could practice his shooting for an hour. When Red learned of Sharman's routine, he eventually decided it was such a good idea that he ordered the whole team to attend a short shooting session on game days. Soon other teams followed suit. Without a doubt, Sharman is the inventor of the modern-day shootaround.

Sharman was a deadly free throw shooter. He won the league's free throw percentage title seven times and still holds the NBA record for most consecutive free throws made in the playoffs (56). He never would leave a practice without first making 20 straight jump shots and then 50 straight free throws.

He was a very intense person who kept the same routine on every game day. Bill would never get less than eight hours of sleep, then he'd have a bowl of cereal and juice for breakfast. After resting for a half hour, Sharman would head to a gym for his private shootaround. At precisely 1 p.m. Bill would have what he called his "pregame meal," which consisted of steak, potatoes and a piece of fruit. Upon arriving for the game, he'd perform calisthenics for 15 minutes in front of his locker. He was the only player who stretched in those days. Because Sharman was so quick and agile, Red attributed Bill's exceptional speed to his calisthenics routine. It wasn't long before Red ordered the entire team to stretch before a game, with Sharman acting as the drill sergeant. Today, many of Sharman's exercises are part of every team's pregame warmups.

Bill was another great all-around athlete. Before he signed with the Celtics, he was a .300-plus hitter for the Dodgers' Triple A farm club in 1949 through August of '51. The next month, Brooklyn called him up to the majors. Even though he never actually got into a game, he was thrown out of one. It happened when an ump made an incorrect call on a close play at home plate. Immediately the Dodger dugout went wild. Sharman happened to be sitting next to my old broadcasting partner, Dick Williams, who had what you might call a real "garbage mouth." Dick was yelling a series of four-letter words in the direction of home plate when the ump ran toward the Dodger dugout and gave the heave-ho to Sharman instead of Williams.

"I was a rookie who wasn't about to cause any trouble," Bill told me afterward. "I didn't curse the ump. All I said was, 'Bad call, real bad call.' But the ump thought I was doing all the cursing and threw me out instead of Williams. Dick, of course, got a real kick out of me being tossed. I didn't share his sense of humor about the episode. I wanted to get into just one game that season, and here I was getting kicked out of a major league contest without ever playing so much as an inning."

The Dodgers liked Sharman's potential and wanted him to re-sign for the '52 season. The team insisted, however, that he had to give up his basketball career. Bill was willing to do that, but only if the Dodgers would give him a raise that would equal the money he would earn playing for the Celtics. The Dodgers refused, and Bill decided to choose basketball over baseball. It turned out to be a great decision for both Sharman and the Celtics.

When I became friends with Bill, I realized that he was destined to be a coach after his playing days. Whenever Sharman was on the Celtics bench, he would push players out of the way in order to sit next to Red and ask Auerbach questions about why he made certain moves.

"Aw, the guy can be a pain in the ass," Red said to me after the Celtics had just played a close game. "I'm trying to squeeze out a win, and there's Sharman, practically on my lap, asking me why I'm making this move and that move. He can't ever wait until the game ends to ask me why I made a particular substitution or called a certain play."

While Sharman and his teammates realized Red's coaching genius, Auerbach was certainly not viewed as a hero by the press and the fans in Boston—at least not for his first five years as Celtics coach. Members of the press, some of whom disliked Red's gruff, sometimes hostile, personality, never missed a chance to take potshots at him. There were even a few rumors in the newspapers that Red might be fired. Where these rumors came from was a mystery to me, because Walter Brown was totally loyal to Red. I suspect that because Red never catered to the media, writers made up negative rumors to sabotage him.

Walter, however, wasn't the type of person to be influenced by what he read in the newspapers. "Auerbach's gonna win championships for me," Walter told me when I confronted him about the reports that Red's job was in jeopardy. "As long as I'm here, Red will be here. I guarantee that."

4

CREAM OF THE CROP: AUERBACH AND RUSSELL

The creation of a championship team, one that would survive all challenges and dominate an entire sport for a record period of years, grew from an unlikely partnership—Walter Brown and Red Auerbach. They were as different as two men could be, yet in certain circumstances, they could be strangely alike.

The keys they both employed to unlock pro basketball success were words such as trust, loyalty, sacrifice, respect, affection, and heart. You don't hear those words used much in pro sports today. These words are almost anachronisms, having come from another era, a time before big money, contract incentives, holdouts, strike threats and agents.

When Walter and Red were establishing the team that would become a dynasty, they went about their task using what I call old-fashioned values. They didn't put a team together; they created a family. They did it without letting the words "prejudice" and "bigotry" enter their thoughts, which is why Chuck Cooper, upon retiring, wrote a four-page letter to Walter and Red thanking them for drafting him when other teams "dared not" draft a black man. Most amazingly, Red and Walter built their club with a budget that was among the league's smallest.

No owner in the history of sports ever had a better relationship with his players than Walter. Deep down, they respected the man because he always dealt with them fairly and was strictly above board. Frank Ramsey used to come into the Celtics' office and do something that was unique. He'd sign a blank contract, put it on Walter's secretary's desk, and say, "Please ask Mr. Brown to fill in the numbers. I know he'll be fair." Cousy once negotiated his contract while the two were eating a hot dog for lunch; Heinsohn negotiated one of his contracts with Walter in a men's room.

Today, the phrase "Celtics Family" may seem like a public relations gimmick to casual Boston fans, but I, like every person associated with the team during its early days, know it had deep meaning. If you had a financial or personal problem, you could go to any player, office staff member, or even Red and Walter. Whatever the dilemma was, it would be solved. The trust, the respect, the caring all started at the top, because Red and Walter treated each other like brothers.

Because of the team's limited funds, Red couldn't always pull off the deals he wanted. Yet knowing Walter's burning desire to produce a winner, Auerbach never complained about having his hands tied on occasion. When he thought he could swing a deal, he'd say to the other GM involved in the trade, "This is a good move for both teams. I want to make it happen, but it's Walter's money. If he gives me the green light, you've got yourself a deal."

Due to Red and Walter's teamwork, the Celtics managed to become "respectable" by the start of the '55-'56 season. Even with Ramsey in the army, Boston had Sharman, Cooz and Macauley, as well as the rights to Kentucky stars Cliff Hagan and Lou Tsioropoulos. They also had drafted a new enforcer, a 6'5", 230-pound forward named Jim Loscutoff from Oregon, to replace Brannum, who retired after the '54-'55 season.

Loscutoff wasn't quite the bare-knuckles brawler that Brannum was, but he possessed more pure basketball skills. Cousy, for one, believed Loscutoff was vastly underrated. "Loscy does the little things. He'll get rebounds and he'll never stop running," Cooz told me. "You know me. I'm not going to run my ass off up the court and then give the ball to some big lug of a forward who can't even convert a layup. Loscy's a guy who can hit the jumper consistently if I get him the ball when he's open. Because of our style, he helps our offense more than fans realize."

Like Brannum, Loscutoff never was one to shy away from a good fight. One night in Syracuse during his rookie year, Jim took on center Johnny Kerr and forward Earl "Big Cat" Lloyd at the same time. He didn't lose the battle, but he did get hit with a few solid punches. After the game ended, I went into the locker room and asked Loscy, who was resting on the floor, if he was injured. "Nah," he replied, thumping his chest with his fists, "You can't hurt steel." That's when I began dubbing him "Jungle Jim."

Red had also signed three-time All-Star forward Arnie Risen as a relief man for Macauley. The 6'9" Risen had been contemplating retirement from the Rochester Royals until Red convinced the 32-year-old that he still had a few good years left. "I couldn't reach an agreement with the Royals, and I had been injured quite a bit my last year with them," Arnie explained to me. "I didn't want to retire, but I thought I probably would have to. That's when Red called and asked me to give Boston a try for at least a year."

With Barksdale retired, I was looking for a new roommate, and Arnie needed a place to stay. So, along with reserve guard Ernie Barrett and sparingly used forward Red Morrison, we rented a house in Revere for the season. What poor Arnie didn't realize when we all moved in together was that Barrett, Morrison and I were all utter slobs. None of us had the slightest idea of how to cook so much as spaghetti or a hamburger. Arnie had no choice but to do all the housework and cooking. It was either that or face the prospect of starving to death, surrounded by mounds of empty beer cans.

In record time, Arnie was saddled with the nickname, "Mother Risen," which, of course, he detested. "I'm too old for your stupid jokes," he'd scold us. "I'm the old man. I'm the guy who should be sitting in a rocking chair while you guys make the meals and vacuum." A couple of minutes later, though, Arnie would announce, "I've got a roast in the oven, so you all better be here at six. Understand?" In unison, we'd reply, "Yes, Mother Risen, we understand."

Arnie had a million funny stories about his days in Rochester. One night he told me a classic story about Royals coach Les Harrison and referee Pat Kennedy, who was elected to the Hall of Fame in 1959. "Pat was the ultimate showman," Risen began. "He'd make a call on a simple hacking foul and proceed to do a four-minute reenactment of the play for the entertainment of the fans. I mean he'd sprint the length of the court, slapping his right arm with his left wrist repeatedly, blowing his whistle every three or four steps, and contorting his face as if he was in pain. Then he'd briskly march over to the scorer's table, get down on one knee and yell out, 'Foul is on Risen for extreme illegal contact on the arm.'

"Extreme illegal contact? I barely tapped the guy, but Pat exaggerated everything just in order to justify his calls. Well, one night he calls a foul on me and Harrison went wild. Kennedy walked toward him blowing his whistle, shaking his head from side to side, and screaming at the top of his lungs at Les. Just as he got within a few feet of Harrison, Pat actually swallowed his whistle. As it went straight down his throat, Kennedy fell to the floor. As Pat was choking and gasping for air, Harrison leaned over him and said, 'Hey, before you die, just say there was no foul.' Pat's face turned absolutely red. It took him a minute to recover after managing to spit out his whistle. Then, with a sheepish smile, he walked over to Harrison. 'Les, as I was saying, it's a foul on Risen. And you earned yourself a technical for being a wiseass.'"

Risen was an easy-going guy. I'd go out with Barrett or Morrison to Blinstrub's, a huge nightclub in South Boston where singers like

Eddie Fisher, Debbie Reynolds and even Frank Sinatra would perform. Then I'd invite a bunch of the customers, most of whom I didn't even know, to the house for a party at 1 a.m. Arnie, whose family remained in Rochester while he played for the Celtics, would never complain about the wild crowds who'd show up for my "open house" late-night parties. "Johnny, these are nice people you're bringing back with you, but the neighbors have been sort of complaining about the noise," Arnie would warn me.

"Don't worry," I'd reply. "I've taken care of that. I went around from house to house and told all of our neighbors that they were welcome, too. As long as they know they're always invited, they won't bitch about the parties."

There were a lot of great times for the four of us, but it wasn't a particularly satisfying season for the Celtics, who lost 2-1 to Syracuse in the Eastern Division semifinals.

Red knew he was not going to win anything until he could find a relentless rebounder who could also be physical at both ends of the court. "I need a guy who doesn't concentrate on scoring," he said to me. "I need someone who can defend, get us rebounds, and knows how to pass the ball quickly upcourt to Cousy."

The college senior who was the unanimous choice as the top player in the '56 draft was William Felton Russell, a 6'9" center from the University of San Francisco. Russell had led his team to two straight NCAA titles, and he finished his career by leading USF to 55 consecutive victories. He dominated the basket area by regularly grabbing 20-plus rebounds, and he redefined defensive strategy with his uncanny timing, anticipation, and above all, shot blocking.

It was UCLA's brilliant coach John Wooden, in describing Russ, who first used the now frequently mimicked sentence: "You can't stop him; you can only hope to contain him." Kansas coach Phog Allen witnessed Bill's 25-rebound, seven-block, 18-point performance against LaSalle in the '55 NCAA championship game and said, "After watching what Russell just did, I'm all for raising the height of the basket to 20 feet."

Despite Russ' nightly accomplishments, there were some NBA coaches who weren't convinced he'd be a force in the NBA. "This league places a premium on scoring," said Minneapolis Lakers coach John Kundla. "This kid from San Francisco can't score unless he's only a foot away from the basket. It's a big step up from college to the pros. Russell is an excellent rebounder, but very few NBA players are one-dimensional."

However, Auerbach had done his homework, even though he didn't scout Russell himself. He first learned of Russ' awesome potential in 1953 from Bill Reinhart, Red's coach when he played for George Washington University. "He's only a sophomore, but Russell can absolutely destroy an opponent's game plan. He runs faster than any big man I've ever seen, and he has an exceptional sense of how to outrebound even a player three inches taller than himself. Above all," Reinhart told Auerbach, "he's smart and he's clever."

As Russell's collegiate career continued, Red kept tabs on him, frequently calling USF coach Phil Woolpert, California coach Pete Newell and two of Auerbach's ex-players, Freddy Scolari, whom Red coached when he was with the Washington Caps, and my old roommate, Don Barksdale.

A lot of people may not realize this, but it was Don who convinced Red to trade "whatever it takes to get the draft rights for Russell." Barksdale, who was living in the Bay Area, was asked by Red to scout Russell for the final three months of the '55-'56 season. "Check out this kid for me," Red asked Don. "Let me know how he'd do against guys like [Ed] Macauley, [George] Mikan, [Philadelphia's 6'11 1/2" Neil] Johnston, and [Charlie] Share."

What Red didn't know at that moment was that Barksdale had already seen Russell 10 times that season. Don called Red back a couple weeks later after watching Russell play a couple more games. "He can't hit the broad side of a barn," Don told him, "but he can get you 18 rebounds a game, his passing ability for a big man is better than any college player I've ever seen, and he can block shots with such finesse that he can swat the ball directly to a teammate. Find a way to get this guy, because he can play against anybody in the NBA and come out the winner."

"This kid will be an All-Star in his rookie year and every year afterward," Don told me. "He's as fast as most guards, Johnny. He's as quick a big man as there has ever been. Most centers are awkward to some degree, but Bill Russell is totally agile. He moves with a certain gracefulness, yet he's aggressive. He'll be even more dominating than Mikan."

I believed Don when he said Russell would be a great pro, but I thought Barksdale might be exaggerating when he said Russell would be better than Mikan, because George had led the Lakers to five NBA titles in six years from '49 to '54.

Wanting Russell and actually getting him were two different things. The Celtics had the third draft pick, with the Rochester Royals drafting first and St. Louis Hawks second.

Walter Brown called Rochester coach Les Harrison and quickly learned the Royals weren't interested in taking Russell. They already had a good scorer and excellent rebounder in 23-year-old Maurice Stokes, who averaged 17 points and 16 rebounds as a rookie in '55-'56. Plus, Russell was demanding a $25,000 salary, far too much for Harrison's liking. Instead, Harrison told Walter, the Royals were going to take a highly touted 6'2" guard from Duquesne, Sihugo Green.

Now Red had to convince one of his archenemies, St. Louis owner Ben Kerner, that the Hawks needed veteran help, not a "raw rookie" like Russell. Kerner's teams had been at or near the bottom of the standings for six years. Attendance was so low that the Hawks were having trouble staying afloat financially. Red offered Ed Macauley for the draft pick, pointing out to Kerner that, as a former Saint Louis University star and a perennial NBA All-Star, Ed would bring people into the stands while also improving the team. However, Kerner didn't bite. "The only way I'll make the deal is if you throw in Cliff Hagan," he said.

"OK, OK, you've got a deal if Walter approves it," Red replied, pretending to hesitate about making the trade.

Walter Brown, however, liked Macauley as both a player and a person. So he called Ed and told him, "We have a chance to make a trade with the Hawks which could give us a true center. The Hawks, though, want you in return. If you don't want to leave Boston, tell me, and Red and I will find another way to make the deal work."

Ed, however, actually wanted to go to St. Louis, because his two-year-old son, Patrick, had been stricken with spinal meningitis. "Johnny, I love Boston, but I have to be with my family more now, and the doctors in St. Louis are all fine specialists," he explained. "Moving to St. Louis will allow me to be near Patrick and my family while still being able to earn a good living. If playing ball for the Hawks doesn't allow me enough time to devote to my family, then maybe I'll become a play-by-play broadcaster. You know, I'll be the Johnny Most of St. Louis."

To this day, Macauley is convinced that Walter Brown would not have traded him if Ed had wanted to remain a Celtic. "I'm not saying Red wouldn't have ended up with Bill Russell; I'm just saying that Walter would have insisted that Red work out a trade that didn't involve me," he said.

When Ed told Walter about his son's health problems, Walter offered to renegotiate Ed's contract for the express purpose of giving him a huge raise. "St. Louis will have to honor it," Walter told Macauley. "You'll need that extra money to pay the doctors' bills." Being a gentleman, Macauley thanked Walter for the offer but turned it down. "I just wouldn't feel right doing that," he said to Walter. "I'll play well, and then Kerner will have no choice but to give me a nice raise."

While Ed, a devout Catholic, admired Walter, he was never totally enamored with Red's personality. "All that swearing by Red really bothers me. He's so gruff and almost angry all the time. I don't even like saying hello to him because Red acts like you're bothering him. Deep down, I know Red is always willing to do you a favor. He'll even go out of his way to help you. But getting past Red's intimidating exterior can be very, very difficult."

The Russell-for-Macauley-and-Hagan trade was completed, but, believe it or not, it was hardly big news in Boston. Again, the newspapers all but ignored the Celtics, devoting maybe two or three paragraphs to covering what was to be eventually known as the biggest trade in NBA history.

"Now I've got a true center. It's going to make a big difference," Auerbach said to me when I interviewed him shortly before the '56-'57 season began. "All that's left is to sign the kid." The contract negotiations, however, would have to wait until after Russell played in the '56 Olympics, which were to take place in Australia in early December. When Russell returned after leading the U.S. team to a gold medal, the $25,000 figure that Russell had reportedly been demanding was quickly negotiated down to $19,500 during a half-hour meeting in Walter Brown's office.

Along with the acquisition of Russell, the Celtics also used their territorial draft choice to take Holy Cross scoring forward Tommy Heinsohn, who was to become my closest friend through all these years. Tommy was a perfect fit for the Celtics. He could rebound to help ease Russell's workload and could shoot from just about anywhere on the court. He had a sweeping hook shot in the lane and a nice jump shot, which he knocked down with regularity from the outside.

Besides drafting Russell and Heinsohn, Red made one more key move, picking up 34-year-old point guard Andy Phillip, who had led the league in assists twice, after the Fort Wayne Pistons decided to go with a younger player. "I need a guy who can relieve Cooz or Sharman for 10 to 12 minutes a game. Andy is a solid player who doesn't make mistakes," Red told me. "I've tried to get him for the past three years. He'll give us a nice lift."

Red would become a genius at acquiring players who were at the tail end of their careers but who still could provide the Celtics with quality play for short spurts at a time. Risen and Phillip were his first two "old pros."

"What Red knows for sure about Arnie and Andy was that these guys have a lot of pride," Cooz told me. "By no means are they trying to relive their glory days, but they still have enough gas in their tanks to give us quality play for at least 10 minutes a game. We need that, because with our running game, the starters can't be on the court for 40-plus minutes."

This may shock some people, but Russell was the first Celtic player I ever disliked—right from the first day I met him until I finally got to know a little bit about what made him tick four years into his career. He appeared arrogant, cocky, and at times hostile. Even when I would just say hello, he made it seem like a major effort to give me a one-second reply. Many times I tried to strike up a conversation with him, and he had always looked away or walked away. Finally, I decided that Bill just enjoyed being miserable.

On the air, I was objective about Russell's play. In fact, over the course of his first two years in the NBA, I totally fell in love with his game, but I always detested the shabby manner in which he treated everyone except his teammates, Walter, and Red. Off the court, I gave up on trying to engage Russell in conversation. If he was going to snub me, I'd do the same to him.

And I wasn't alone in my negative opinion of Russ. Even the ushers at the press gate resented Bill's "screw you" attitude. His refusal to sign autographs for youngsters angered the ushers so much that they demanded he show them some form of identification before they'd allow him to pass through the Garden turnstiles. They wanted to embarrass him because Russ never made an effort to even so much as say hello to them. "He's an SOB," the head usher said to me one day. "He thinks we're peons and that he owns the damned building."

The Boston fans had the same attitude toward Bill as I did. They'd come to the Garden on a regular basis to watch his amazing athleticism and applaud his unselfish play. However, he acted as if he was playing in an empty Boston Garden, rarely acknowledging the crowd's cheers.

In contrast to Russell, Heinsohn was a happy-go-lucky type of guy. He and I hit it off right away and soon began rooming together on the road on occasion. He was a genuinely down-to-earth person with a great sense of humor. In public, Tommy was friendly and outgoing, signing autographs all the time and always taking time to carry on conversations with any fan who approached him. As a basketball player, he was a competitor who took the game seriously and worked hard to excel.

On the road, the two of us would spend hours talking about World War II because Tommy was, and still is, a history buff. He knew everything about the major battles, the strategies of both sides, and the leaders. I guess what I was able to give him was some insight on what the war was like for the average guy in the military.

We also shared other common interests. He was an excellent artist who could draw detailed charcoal sketches of his teammates or paint magnificent landscapes. He'd show me his works and I'd show him some of what I considered my better poetry. Also, we were both fight fans. Whenever there was a fight card at the Garden, Boston Arena, or at Fenway Park, Tommy and I would be there if at all possible. Boxing promoter Sam Silverman owned a gym around the corner from the Garden, and we'd stop in regularly on our way to lunch at the local deli. That's how we became great friends with welterweight champion Tony DeMarco, whose brutal bouts with Carmen Basilio are considered classics. Through Tony and Sam, we also became friends with top middleweight contender Joe DeNucci, who would go on to enjoy a successful career in politics.

Despite the fact that Russell seemed determined to distance himself from the fans and the media by totally ignoring them, his teammates defended him. "Russ is one of the greatest guys I ever played with. He's not only unselfish and a winner on the court, but he can be a funny guy," Heinsohn would tell me. "With time, he'll grow on you." Well, I thought to myself, I've got better things to do with my time than wait for Bill Russell to treat me with a small degree of common courtesy.

I think it was Russell's fourth year in Boston when I learned from Tommy that Russell had been a victim of racial prejudice in suburban Reading, where he lived. He had wanted to buy a more luxurious home in the town where he already had owned a modest house. However, residents in the neighborhood where he hoped to purchase got together and managed to block the sale. Even though he remained in Reading and was finally able to buy a nicer home, Bill never was able to forgive and forget the way he was treated by a prejudiced group.

These same people wanted him to play for the Celtics, but they didn't want him in their social circle. They wanted to take, but they didn't want to give. They wanted to have him on their side, but they did not want to have him in their homes. Russ resented their attitudes tremendously, and I would have felt the same. For the first time, I adopted a new attitude concerning Russ. Because Bill wouldn't talk to me, I decided to approach him. "Bill, is there something bothering you about me?" I began. "No, there isn't," Russ replied. "It's nothing personal. My problems are about issues no white man would understand."

That response made me angry. "Hey, wait just a fucking minute," I said to him. "That's not true. You don't even know me as a person, and you have no right to judge me. I know you were screwed by some bigots in Reading. Well, I've been a victim of prejudice, too."

I then proceeded to tell Russ about an audition I attended years earlier for a play-by-play job to do some regional college football games.

"Bill, about eight years ago, a friend of mine, a Catholic by the name of Jack McGinnis, managed to help me get an audition with the sponsor of some football games, a national oil company. At the time, I already had completed one year of broadcasting the Dodgers. When I hadn't heard from anyone, Jack McGinnis called the sponsor and asked, 'Well, what did you think of Johnny Most?' The guy's reply startled Jack. 'Most was by far the best, but we can't hire him because he's a Jew.' Bill, prejudice prevented you from moving into a better home; in my case, prejudice actually took food off my table at a time when I didn't have money to buy enough food to eat three meals a day."

Russ got the message. Never again did he accuse me of not understanding the prejudice he faced. Since then, he has always been a total gentleman with me, an absolutely true friend. There were times when I'd interview him on the air and somebody would come up to me afterwards and say, "Do me a favor. Ask Russell what he thinks about the upcoming game. He likes you, but he won't cooperate with me." Well, I'd refuse because Russ is a sensitive person who has his reasons when he declines an interview. I won't question that sensitivity. I've always tried to respect Bill's individual opinions.

There was only one other time when Russell and I clashed. It took place after he retired, and he made a statement that offended me. Bill said that the media in Boston is full of prejudice. I immediately confronted him again. "Look, I'm deeply hurt by what you just said, because I, for one, am not full of prejudice and you know that."

"No, you're not prejudiced," he replied. "I do know that completely, Johnny."

"Then why didn't you just mention the ones you know for a fact are prejudiced instead of making it seem that all of us in the Boston media are racist? Or do you really believe every white person in Boston is prejudiced?" I told him, "If you're going to make a blanket statement like that, then anyone, white or black or green, who heard your little speech is going to conclude that you're really the one who is prejudiced. There are people in this town, white people, who genuinely like you as a person. I'm one of them. You can't generalize about sensitive subjects. Name names if you're going to accuse individuals of racism. I don't want to be lumped into a category. Like you, I want to be judged on an individual basis."

I was as angry as I have ever been at a Celtics player. Russ knew it and quickly apologized.

My point to Russell was that I understood his bitterness, and I didn't disagree with it. But I resented the fact that Bill took it for granted that I was incapable of understanding his being a victim of prejudice. It took patience to get to know such a complex man. He is intense, proud, humorous, ferocious, loyal and distrustful—all in one.

He has a big cackling laugh that can be heard from a hundred yards away. It isn't a phony laugh but a sound that shakes his entire body. His teammates enjoyed his company, which was very important to him. Although Russ cares deeply about what his friends think of him, he could care less about how the outside world views him.

Does Russ have an ego? You bet, and so do all players who want to survive in the league, because they are playing against a lot of other great athletes. You have to think you are a great player if you are going to compete and win. It's been my experience that the players with the biggest egos, the most pride, and the fiercest determination are the ones who succeed.

I know I have an ego. If I expect fans to listen to me for two and a half hours a night, then I better believe that I'm damn good at what I do. I have to assume that I'm among the best, or else I will end up being just another average radio voice.

Heinsohn also possessed an ego, at least when he was on the basketball court. He had that certain swagger of an All-Star even as a rookie. However, even before the draft, Auerbach had begun to criticize Tommy. On the air, Red told me, "Look, I've never said Heinsohn doesn't have talent. He's wasting some of it, though. I've seen him play in college. He's fat, lazy, lackadaisical, and he's not aggressive even though he's got the body to punish guys who get in his way for a rebound."

Still, Red drafted Tommy and had big plans for him. By then, however, Red's public criticisms had forced Heinsohn to give serious consideration to playing for an AAU team in Peoria, Illinois. There he could earn a decent basketball salary and a good side income by working for the team's sponsor, Caterpillar, a tractor manufacturer.

Discovering that Heinsohn was offended by his comments, Red dispatched Cousy to prevent a crisis. "If Cooz hadn't convinced me that Red was really a good person, I'd be on my way to Peoria," he later told me.

"Cousy said Red's remarks were all taken out of context," Tommy told me. "I knew damn well they weren't. However, based on what Cooz told me about Red's strange way of motivating players, I decided to at least meet with him. I found myself liking the guy and signing a contract." Heinsohn continued, "Once I signed, though, Red had to get in the final jab at me. 'I want you to report to camp at 217—and not one pound more. Got me?'

"Yup," Heinsohn said as he walked out of Red's office.

Then Tommy started laughing to himself, because he knew there was absolutely no way he could play at less than 225, which was ten pounds less than he weighed during his senior year at Holy Cross. "I wasn't about to starve myself or eat salads for breakfast, lunch and dinner. I'm a steak-and-potatoes man, baby," Tommy explained to me. "Red took one look at me and knew he wasn't going to transform me into 'The Thin Man.' He just wanted to let me know he was the boss. He wanted to scare me a little bit, while also making sure I knew he really wanted me on his team."

The public's perception of Red may be that of a dictator, but that wasn't reality. I remember interviewing 6'7" Jack Nichols, a reserve center-forward who earned his degree at Tufts Dental School while playing for the Celtics, and asking him how he managed to be both a full-time student and a full-time player.

"I have to correct you, Johnny," he replied. "Thanks to Red, going to dental school is my only full-time job. He knows I stay in shape and always play hard, so he lets me miss practices if they interfere with my studies, and he'll even allow me to miss some road games if I have tests which conflict with our schedule. All I do is tell him in advance about my class schedule, and he makes sure I get all the time off from the Celtics I need. And I never get a cent taken away from my paycheck, because Red and Mr. Brown know most of my salary goes toward paying for tuition. I don't think there's another coach or owner in the league who would be so understanding and generous."

Nichols' excused absences caused Red to constantly have to juggle his lineups for the four years Jack played in Boston, but I never heard Auerbach complain. When Jack finally earned his degree in 1958, Red attended the commencement and gave Jack a standing ovation when his name was announced. (Today Jack has a thriving practice in Seattle.)

With Russell unavailable until after the '56 Olympics concluded in mid-December, Red had to improvise as the Celtics began the regular season. His guards were Cousy and Sharman, with Phillip coming off the bench. Heinsohn and Loscutoff were the starting forwards. At center, Red went with Risen, with 6'7" Nichols backing him up.

Heinsohn, with Cooz setting him up offensively, got the Celtics off to an excellent start in '56-'57. By the time Russell arrived, Tommy had averaged 20 points and about 11 rebounds a game as Boston jumped out to an incredible six-game lead in the Eastern Division.

During Tommy's first month as a pro, he made the mistake of hitting Sweetwater Clifton with an elbow and then a jab to the stomach. "Sweets" could easily have pounded Heinsohn, but instead just scolded him by saying, "Son, if you want to have a long career in the NBA, you'd better cut that crap out."

All Tommy could manage to say when he realized his blows had no effect on Clifton was to politely respond, "Yes, sir, Mr. Sweetwater."

When Russ made his pro debut on December 22, 1956, against the Hawks, 11,052 fans showed up at the Garden to find out if Russell was indeed as good as Auerbach claimed he was. Red kept Russ on the bench for more than half the game, but in his limited time on the court, Russ made believers of the fans, as well as his teammates, by grabbing 16 rebounds and scoring a half-dozen points. Although the Celtics trailed by 16 midway through the final quarter, Russell demonstrated his amazing leadership potential by blocking three of Bob Pettit's shots down the stretch, enabling the Celtics to rally for a win on a last-second jumper by Sharman.

Up in my broadcasting booth, I was hoarse by the time the game ended. "You'll have to forgive me for losing my voice," I barely managed to whisper, "but I think we just witnessed the birth of a star and the start of a bright new era in Celtics history...I just saw Bob Pettit shaking his head in total disgust—and is that a great sight for every Celtics fan."

In his third game as a Celtic, Russ recorded 34 rebounds and what I counted as at least nine blocked shots in leading Boston to a 23-point win over the Warriors. He followed that performance by holding Philadelphia's six-time All-Star center Neil Johnston, with his 22-point average, scoreless for 42 minutes in another Boston win. After the game, Cousy was ecstatic.

"This kid is like no rookie I've ever seen. He's just so poised and confident out there. I know his play has given us an entirely new game plan," Bob said. "Now I know I can gamble more with my passes, because Russell is there to stop teams from scoring off a mistake I might make. On defense, all of us can take more chances, because we're now the team which is controlling the rebounds. Usually it's Russ, but we've got Heinsohn, Loscutoff and Risen getting their share, too."

A few days later, the offense got a boost when Frank Ramsey returned from the service after a year in the military. Auerbach immediately used him as the first man off the bench because he could play as a guard or a forward. "The thing about Frank," Auerbach explained to me, "is that he's a scorer. He may only be 6'3", but I can use him at forward, because no matter who guards him, Ramsey will be too quick for them." And so Red's sixth-man strategy, which has been copied by every team, was born.

As the Celtics continued their winning ways throughout the regular season, the atmosphere around practices became comical at times. For instance, the guards always wanted to scrimmage against the big guys. There was one condition that the smaller players insisted upon. Russell had to be the referee instead of playing. Cousy, Ramsey and Sharman knew they could win the shooting battle, and they also thought their quickness could help them get enough rebounds to teach Risen, Heinsohn and Loscutoff that the "munchkins," as Loscy called the Celtic guards, weren't about to be bullied. They'd shove, throw elbows, and grab to get an edge and win the practice games, which provoked only laughter from guys like Heinsohn. "It's like flicking off flies from your arms," he'd tell me. "Cousy especially loves to try and time his jumps for a rebound. Unfortunately for him, his best leap only brings him up to my elbow. And that's without me even jumping. Sharman tries to literally tackle Loscy and always ends up on his ass as Jim stands over him with a fake scowl on his face."

The bigger Celtics claimed they won 90 percent of those scrimmages; the little guys bragged that they were unbeatable. "It's brains over brawn every time," Cooz would crow.

On rare occasions, Red would become a victim of the players' pranks. I'm not quite sure if it was Heinsohn, Loscutoff or Ramsey who did this, but one of them sneaked into Red's office before practice and switched his green shorts from a size 36 to a size 34. Then three or four players peeked in to watch Red as he squeezed into his "altered" pair of shorts. A week later, the shorts would be switched again, this time from size 36 to size 38. Red would put them on and stare down as the shorts starting slipping down on him. "Knock it off," he'd finally yell out as players in the locker room at the Cambridge "Y," where the team practiced, roared with laughter.

When the Celtics finished the regular season at 44-28, the best record in the NBA, all the day-to-day humor suddenly stopped. "Everything seems so different," Red said to me a day before the playoffs began. "Heinsohn is trying to give up smoking. Nobody is breaking curfew. Ramsey hasn't pulled a practical joke in weeks. Even Walter Brown hasn't second-guessed me once in the last couple of months. That's definitely a record."

Like everyone else, I was getting excited. People would approach me on the street and kid me about how differently I sounded on the air than I had in the past. "You start screaming and yelling at the refs as soon as tipoff begins," my old friend from the Giants, Ken McAfee, said to me one day as we headed into the Garden together. "You seem to get angry at every call that goes against the Celtics, even if the they're winning by 30."

"Is that right? Does it sound bad?" I asked him, in all seriousness.

"Hell, no," he replied. "Everyone in Boston is greedy. We want to see the Celtics win by 50. After so many years of seeing the other teams beat us, we want revenge. When I listen to you call a game against Syracuse, I can tell you're rooting for Boston to bury the other team. I remember when Syracuse would love to hit the last shot of the game even when they had a huge lead. Well, now it's time to even things up a little."

The Celtics had no problem winning the Eastern Division playoffs, wiping out none other than Syracuse in three straight games. However, beating the Hawks in the NBA finals would be an entirely different story. Even though St. Louis had only won 34 games in the regular season, they featured two of the top eight scorers in the league in Macauley and Pettit, along with a quick, reliable playmaker named

Slater Martin, who had his best games whenever he played against Cousy.

When the Hawks won the series opener in Boston 125-123 in overtime, I started worrying. Pettit had scored 34 points in that game and looked unstoppable. But Red didn't seem all that upset. "We had a bad game, that's all," he said to me in my pregame interview before Game 2. "We're going to let Russell roam more this time around. He'll slow Pettit down inside. I want him to take jumpers, not layups." Which is exactly what occurred as the Celtics evened the series with a 20-point win at home.

Before the start of Game 3 in St. Louis, I witnessed one of the classic confrontations of my career. Sharman had complained that the basket Boston would be shooting at to open the game was higher than 10 feet. Red immediately asked referees Sid Borgia and Norm Drucker to measure the distance from the floor to the rim. It was 10 feet high exactly, which gave Hawks owner Ben Kerner a chance to get in his two cents. "Auerbach, you're bush," he yelled from 10 feet away. Without hesitating a second, Red broke into a full sprint and landed a wild right-hand hook to Kerner's mouth. Kerner responded with a slap, which barely touched Red's face. As Kerner's lip began to swell, the St. Louis owner baited Red once again. "Not only are you bush, but you can't throw a punch, either." Auerbach, walking away with his back now facing Kerner, just waved him off and said, "Ben, why don't you go find some ice to put on that fat lip I just gave you?" Norm Drucker couldn't resist the opportunity to rib Auerbach. "Hey, Red, how can a heavyweight like you manage to allow a middleweight like Ben to land a punch? You're as bad a boxer as you are a coach."

"Well, I'm not the guy who has to get first aid," Red answered immediately. "I could have knocked him out except the son of a bitch would have sued me." Although the Celtics lost the game that followed the Auerbach-Kerner clash, Boston managed to win two of the next three games to force a Game 7 at Boston Garden.

For me, it represented the first opportunity to broadcast a game in any sport that would decide a championship. I remember pacing in the hallway three full hours before tipoff just in case Auerbach and Kerner decided to renew their warfare. I also recall checking my supply of English Ovals—a pack of cigarettes for each of my pants pockets, another pack for my sport coat, and a pack in my briefcase. Little did I envision that I'd have to "bum" cigarettes before the game concluded.

It just so happened that Cousy and Sharman both played their worst games of the year that night. They combined to hit just five of 40 shots in what turned out to be a double-overtime game. It was Heinsohn (37 points and 23 rebounds overall) who led the Celtics offensively in the second overtime by hitting three crucial shots that helped Boston edge the Hawks 125-123, with Pettit missing a desperation rushed jumper from just inside the foul line as the final buzzer sounded.

I was both elated and mentally drained at the same time. There were so many lead changes, so many plays that could have changed the outcome of the game. I second-guessed a few of my play-by-play calls as I headed into the locker room. The first person I saw, Walter Brown, made me forget about individual plays and think only about what this team had just achieved. "This is incredible. I'm just so proud of everyone connected with this team, including you," he said to me. "I know you're this team's biggest fan and everyone loves you for that." Typical Walter.

You might notice that most pictures of the celebration in the Celtics locker room did not include Walter. He wanted it that way. After posing with Red and some of the players, he would step to the back of the locker room and just stand there with a wide grin as the players and Red jumped all over each other. I was soaked in beer and champagne that day as I interviewed Red and the players.

The Red Auerbach I interviewed was practically a new person. I'd ask him a question and he'd shake his head for a moment, grinning and with tears in his eyes. Then he'd try to compose himself. "I waited a long time for this moment. With this bunch of guys, though," he said, pointing his finger randomly at players in the room, "I was as confident about pulling out a close game as I've ever been. These players are something special, each one of them."

I was particularly happy for Heinsohn, who was the NBA's Rookie of the Year and had also perhaps played the finest game of his career in this championship battle. He and Russell, who had 19 points while totally dominating the boards with 32 rebounds, were the obvious heroes of the day.

I was just as pleased for both Cousy and Sharman. Had the Celtics lost, the two of them would have accepted the blame for the deciding game's outcome because their shooting was off target all night. Neither would have made up excuses. Truth is they were the veteran leaders of the team throughout the entire season, two competitors who never got rattled. They set the standard for the younger players, like Tommy, Loscutoff and Russ, who matured so quickly, not only because of Red's coaching, but also because of Cousy's and Sharman's hustle and desire.

There were two other guys who rarely are mentioned when fans look back on Boston's first title. As the years go by, people forget that Risen and Phillip were instrumental in getting Boston's season off to a great start despite the absences of Russell and Ramsey. Those two veterans gave Boston the confidence to erase any self-doubts about their abilities. "Way before Russell had joined us and Ramsey had returned from the military," Cousy told me after the championship game, "I honestly believed we had what it takes to go all the way."

Risen played 40 minutes a game at center until Russ arrived. That's a lot to ask of a guy who doesn't weigh more than 195 pounds, especially when he's going up nightly against guys like Philadelphia's Johnston, Syracuse's Johnny Kerr, and New York's center combination of Sweetwater Clifton and Ray Felix. Each game, Arnie would give up an inch or two in height and usually 20 or 30 pounds.

In Ramsey's absence, Phillip played almost 30 minutes a game as Cousy and Sharman's relief man and averaged seven points and four assists. "I don't give a shit about his numbers. They don't tell you anything about how many wins he got for us," said Red. "He knew he was in there to slow the pace of the game down and give us mistake-free minutes. I didn't want him to try and duplicate Cousy's fast-break skills or Sharman's scoring. I wanted him to just be himself out there, which meant he'd run only when we had an advantage and he'd shoot only when he saw an opening. I didn't have to coach him, because he automatically did what I expected from him."

The first Celtics championship was indicative of how Boston would go on to pile up titles, using a complete team effort to gain its objective. There wasn't one player in Red's locker room, after beating St. Louis, who didn't believe he played a substantial role in securing the championship. "It was the greatest experience," Risen told me years later. "Red rescued me from the scrap heap, because I had made up my mind to retire when Rochester wouldn't offer to pay me anything close to what I thought I was worth. Then came Red's call, and I became a Celtic, played for three more years, and got a championship ring."

Risen and Phillip truly treasure their rings. Arnie had helped Rochester win an NBA title in 1951. However, neither teams nor the league were handing out championship rings back then. "You basically got your playoff share and a pat on the back when you won championships," Risen explained to me. "It wasn't until [Warriors owner] Ed Gottlieb gave them to members of his '56 championship club that players received rings. Getting mine from Walter Brown was the greatest honor of my career."

For Phillip, 1957 was the third time he had made it into the NBA finals (twice previously with the Fort Wayne Pistons) but the only time he had been on the winning team. "I've been playing pro ball for 10 years, and I had almost given up on winning a championship. Like Arnie, I was ready to retire when Red convinced me to come to Boston," Andy said to me. "I knew the team's personnel, and I had heard all about Bill Russell's rebounding and shot-blocking abilities. I felt like I could still play effectively, especially in the role Red envisioned for me. I had to take one more legitimate shot at going after a title. Now I look at that championship ring and really feel my career is complete in every way."

(In 1961, "Handy Andy," as I call him, was elected into the Hall of Fame. Although he had certainly been one of the top playmakers in the game, I'm 100 percent sure he would not have been a Hall of Famer so soon after retiring had it not been for his role in helping Red gain that first Celtics championship.)

5

BUILDING A DYNASTY

With the rise in the Celtics' popularity following that first championship, I began to receive some offers to make off-season appearances at some unique events. For instance, I was actually the ring announcer at a "championship" wrestling match at Boston Garden, featuring a main event of Walter "Killer" Kowalski versus the always "fashionably dressed" Gorgeous George. When the match ended, I marched past Gorgeous George, who was on his belly kicking his feet and crying at the same time, and announced, "Winner by submission, the King of the Claw Hold, Killer Kowalski," as Walter shook my hand and waved a Celtics jersey. Among my other "oddball" jobs were judging a beauty contest for dogs held at Lincoln Park and serving as the master of ceremonies for an Elvis Presley impersonator contest at Boston University during its orientation week.

The chances of a second straight title for the Celtics looked very bright when Auerbach brought his team to training camp. As I have mentioned, Red didn't have time to do any scouting, but he did have a network of unpaid former Celtics players who would call him if they saw a player worth drafting.

In March of '57, "Bones" McKinney, who had played for Red in Washington and Boston, phoned Auerbach to tell him about a tremendous shooter from an all-black NAIA college, North Carolina Central. The kid's name was Sam Jones.

"Red, this kid has ice water running through his veins. I saw him play twice, and he just is totally confident in any situation. He'll shoot the ball, turn, and trot back before the ball is halfway to the basket. He's another Ramsey, except Sam has better range and a deadly two-handed push shot, and he's a lot quicker," McKinney said to Red.

Based largely on that one phone conversation, Auerbach used his first-round pick to select Sam, who, incidentally, had been drafted three years earlier by Minneapolis as a junior eligible. However, because the NBA draft rules had since changed (due entirely to Red's crafty drafting of Ramsey, Tsioropoulos and Hagan as juniors from Kentucky in '53), the Lakers had lost their rights to Sam while he served a two-year hitch in the military and then completed college.

When Sam first arrived, Red must have wondered what had possessed McKinney to rave so much about this 24-year-old 6'4" guard. Watching Sam play as a rookie in training camp and then through the first month of the season, it was clear to me, the players, and to Auerbach that Sam was almost "gun-shy" rather than being a fearless shooter. As soon as Sam would receive a pass, he'd immediately look to get rid of the ball, as if it were a hot potato.

Russell began calling Sam by the nickname "Right Back," because if he or Cousy passed the ball to Sam, it always came right back to them. When I asked Sam why he passed the ball so much instead of looking to dribble and shoot, he told me, "I've always played the point guard spot from high school through college. I like being the shooting guard, but I don't really want the ball until I'm ready to shoot. I can read the defense and know how I'm going to get a good shot much easier when I'm moving without the ball than when I have to dribble it. I'd rather have Cousy, the best assist man in the game, setting me up than trying to set myself up."

Another slight problem Auerbach faced was teaching Sam the Celtics' offensive system. Sam, like most rookies, had a difficult time remembering all the plays and their numbers. Andy Phillip would call the "two play," designed to get Sam an open shot, and Sam would immediately go and set a pick for Heinsohn or Cousy or Sharman instead of looking to free himself for a shot. Phillip, realizing that Sam hadn't mastered the plays, would occasionally have a little fun by calling out the "seven play." Sam would run to a spot and wait to see what developed, pretending to know what he was supposed to do. There was one problem: the Celtics didn't even have a "seven play." All the other Celtics were veterans who knew Phillip was just having a little laugh at the rookie's expense, so they would sort of jog in circles, chuckling to themselves, and sneaking peeks at Sam as he tried to do all the right things to make the bogus "seven play" work effectively.

Ten games into the regular season, Red knew he had drafted a gem of a player. "This kid is a great shooter and probably our quickest defender," he told me after a practice in which Sam was matched up against Sharman. "At 6'4", he can guard just about anyone except the other team's center. He's very shy, a nice kid. I think Russ will make him feel comfortable here in no time flat."

Russ did just that. First, he invited Sam to live with his family in Reading while he looked for a place of his own. During games and practices, Russ would take Sam aside and remind him that his job on offense was simple. "When you're open, shoot. I mean every damned time." In a game against Syracuse, Sam passed up a wide-open short jumper after he had missed six shots in a row. Russ calmly walked over to him during the next timeout, put his arm around Sam's shoulders, and said, "Sam, you've got to take that shot. Your role on this team is to score."

Sam looked puzzled. "I know, I know, but I haven't hit a single shot yet. I'm way off the mark and I'm killing the team."

"Look, I'm speaking for every single guy on this team," Russell said. "We don't care if you miss 20 in a row. We still want you to take that 21st shot the very next chance you get. We all have confidence in you. I promise you that nobody, not even Red, will ever criticize you for shooting the ball too much. That's your job, and you're the best shooter we've got." From that moment on, Sam was transformed into a deadly weapon and a much more self-confident basketball player.

What Auerbach liked especially about Sam was his competitive nature, both on and off the court. No one on the team could beat him in tennis, because he had lettered twice in that sport while in college; no one could come close to upsetting him in pool or ping-pong. In track, the only player who could go stride for stride with Sam in a sprint was Lou Tsioropoulos, another incredible athlete.

During one practice, Loscutoff was boxing out Lou under the backboard when Tsioropoulos suddenly put one hand on Jim's shoulder and actually leapfrogged over him to get a rebound. Lou also loved to run on outdoor tracks as a way of maintaining his speed, and one day he challenged the state high school 220-yard champion, a kid from Lynn, to a race in front of the whole Celtics team. Well, Lou beat the kid by a couple of steps, pulling away at the finish line.

When Sam heard about Lou's running abilities, he challenged Tsioropoulos to a race. Lou managed to win, but only by a fraction of a second, which brought out the competitor in Sam. "Let's go again," Sam begged Lou. "One more time when you're ready." Lou wisely declined. "I've lost to you in everything—cards, pool, foul shooting, even fricking dominoes. As of today, I'm retiring from the 220 while I'm still undefeated. I know you, Sam. You won't quit challenging me until you beat me. Then you'll never give me a rematch."

One quick Tsioropoulos story:

Lou was a good friend of mine. He didn't get much playing time with the Celtics, but he was the perfect teammate, a guy who practiced hard just in case Red called out his number. Whenever he got into a game, I'd really root hard for him to do well during my broadcasts. During the '56-'57 season, Loscutoff injured his leg and was forced to miss a game against Rochester. Red decided to start Lou and give him the assignment of guarding the Royals' top scorer, Jack Twyman. As usual, Lou got on the court and was full of energy. He shadowed Twyman on every play and, in my mind, was doing a great job of limiting Twyman's production.

By the midway point of the fourth quarter, the Celtics had a huge lead. I got carried away and began to salute the effort of my buddy, Lou, on the air. I admit, however, I hadn't paid much attention to the game stats when I started dishing out my praise. "Lou's been a thorn in Twyman's side all game," I told the audience. "He's been in his shirt all night. Twyman is being pestered nonstop and he's showing his frustration. You can see Twyman's been totally thrown off his game by Tsioropoulos. He's all but stopped trying to get off his shot against Lou." Then I passed a piece of paper to my statistician that read, "TWYMAN—HOW MANY POINTS?" "Well, it's clear that Tsioropoulos has been the clear winner of his muscle tussle with Twyman," I remarked.

Just then the statistician handed me Twyman's point total. I continued to praise Lou until I happened to glance at the statistician's note. "Twyman's played every minute and, thanks to Lou's work, he only has...*42 points*?" I couldn't believe it. I guess I had been rooting so hard for Lou, I just somehow overlooked that Twyman was piling up the points. So I quickly thought of something positive to add: "That's a lot of points, but Twyman's probably taken half of Rochester's shots and each one has been under extreme duress—thanks to the nonstop tenacious defense of Tsioropoulos."

But back to the '57 season.

With "Slippery Sam," as I nicknamed him, coming in off the bench to relieve Sharman while Phillip was relieving Cousy as the playmaker, the Celtics won their first 14 games en route to a 49-23 record in the regular season. So balanced was the Boston scoring that Russ, Cousy, Sharman, Heinsohn and Ramsey each averaged better than 16 points. Russell led the league in rebounding, and Cousy was the NBA's best in assists.

Russell, who also earned the MVP award, was so dominant that some opponents resorted to cheap, vicious elbows and punches in blatant attempts and get him thrown out of games. What many of the league's "tough guys" didn't grasp was that while Russ may have looked skinny and fragile, he was actually deceptively strong, especially when someone made the mistake of provoking him. Lakers power forward Jim Krebs was one enforcer who found out the hard way that Russ's game was more than simply finesse and timing.

In a game in Providence, Krebs became frustrated after Bill had blocked three of his shots in a row. He waited until Russell was looking away and then threw an elbow that connected squarely on Russell's chin. Bill staggered back a few steps and then went after a quickly backpedaling Krebs. One right-handed punch was all Russ needed to knock out Krebs for 20 minutes and send him to the hospital. It didn't take long for the entire league to conclude that you just didn't mess with Boston's center. The reality was that the only reason Bill preferred to avoid contact was solely because he wanted extra space to create jumping room, not because he feared anyone.

As the playoffs began, it looked like a second straight Boston championship was on the horizon. The Celtics crushed Philly in the Eastern Division finals and seemed ready to handle the Hawks for the second straight year in the NBA finals. In Game 3, however, Russell severely sprained his left ankle while attempting to block a Pettit layup. That proved to be the end of Boston's chances as Bill would miss the next two games and see only limited action in Game 6 when St. Louis, behind 50 points from Pettit, wrapped up the title, 110-109. Ed Macauley knew the Hawks had caught the luckiest of breaks. "If Russell hadn't sprained his ankle," he said, "I don't believe we'd have won. It's that simple," he said. Shortly after the playoffs ended, the Celtics' three "old pros"—Risen, Phillip and Nichols—announced their retirements.

Red had known well in advance that he was going to need a backup for Russell, as well as a fourth guard, for the '58-'59 season. There were rumors circulating that 6'8" Gene Conley, a Red Sox pitcher who played briefly for the Celtics back in the '52-'53 season, wanted to attempt to play both sports again. Conley and Red agreed on a contract, but Red wasn't sure Conley, who hadn't touched a basketball in six years, was the best choice to spell Russell. Out of loyalty, he brought him to camp anyway. "To be honest, I'm looking for a guy who was in the league last year, a guy I know for sure can give me 10 steady minutes a game. I don't know if Gene can do that," Red told me. By the end of training camp, Red realized Conley was better than any other player he could find. "Damn, he just may be better than he was as a rookie," Red told me. "He's managing to hold his own against Russ in practice. He's not intimidated one bit. If he can play that way against Russ, he can be effective against anyone."

Conley knew his limitations. He couldn't put the ball to the floor, he wasn't a consistent shooter, and he was only an adequate passer. Yet Gene knew how to box out, outjump his opponent for rebounds and run the court. And with Heinsohn tutoring him on a daily basis, Gene eventually developed a reliable 10-foot jump shot. Although Gene's position was power forward, Auerbach always referred to Conley as "Russell's backup."

"That was sort of embarrassing," Gene said to me. "Hell, Russ plays 45 minutes a game. Sure, I play maybe three or four minutes a game at center, but I'm really Heinsohn's backup, because I get 10 minutes at the forward spot every game," he said. "Red made it sound like Russ and I shared the center spot. It felt awkward when Red would mention me in the same sentence with Russell. Truth is, if Russ and I played a one-on-one game, not only would I get shut out, but Bill would have blocked every shot I attempted."

Fact is, however, that Red did use Gene to ease Russell's work load. When the two were on the court at the same time, Red used Russell to cover the scoring forwards on the defensive end, while Gene got the unenviable task of guarding the big centers like Charlie Share, Johnny "Red" Kerr, and seven-foot Detroit center Walter Dukes, whom I referred to as "Walter the Wailer" because he was always complaining to the officials about being manhandled. Manhandled? The guy weighed 230 and loved to use his closed fists to jab his defender right between the shoulder blades.

"Basically, my responsibility is to get the crap kicked out of me by blocking out the big men, who all outweighed me by at least 20 pounds, once an opposing guard or forward shot the ball. The one thing I do very well is to take up space, use my elbows to carve out room, and get position between my man and the basket, which leaves Russell to grab the defensive rebounds," Gene explained to me.

Conley was such a good leaper, I nicknamed him "Jumping Gino," which the Garden fans loved. "Johnny," Gene said to me, "you've managed to turn me from an Irishman into an Italian with that nickname. The people in the North End buy me free meals because they actually think I'm half Italian."

Because of Gene's major league pitching career and my experiences broadcasting the Dodgers, he and I would sit next to each other and talk baseball for hours at a time on almost every road trip. This would drive Red bonkers. "For Christ sakes, why don't you concentrate on basketball and think about what you have to improve on, Conley?" he would complain. "And you, Johnny, talking baseball isn't going to make you a better basketball broadcaster." So Conley and I would always sit as far away from Red as possible just so we could trade stories about our baseball experiences.

Gene didn't mind getting an occasional lecture from Red because he knew Auerbach was satisfied that he had found a reliable role player to help out Russell and the Celtic big forwards. I also believe Red didn't want to yell at Conley too often, because Gene did have a reputation of being just a little "unpredictable." Gene always cautioned me not to refer to him as "flaky." "Flaky is what lefties are," he'd say. "I'm a righty, so call me unpredictable."

Of course, most Boston sports fans are familiar with the story of Gene and infielder Pumpsie Green's infamous "vacation" from the Red Sox. It seemed they both had one too many cocktails, and because Conley had begun to read the Bible on a daily basis, he convinced Pumpsie to take a trip to Israel to visit some of the religious landmarks. Fortunately, they were turned away at airport customs because they didn't have their passports with them. They missed a game and were AWOL for several days as their drinking binge continued. Naturally, their "non-adventure" became legendary. Years afterward, Gene's wife even wrote a little book about Gene's sports adventures that she titled *Goodnight Pumpsie Green, Wherever You Are.*

Besides adding Conley to the Boston roster, Auerbach also received an unexpected call from KC Jones, Russell's roommate at the University of San Francisco, a second-round draft choice of the Celtics in '56 and a member of the U.S. Olympic gold medal team later that same year. Following the Olympics, though, Jones didn't follow Russell's path to the Celtics.

"I was originally drafted as a junior eligible in 1955 by the Minneapolis Lakers," KC told me when he first arrived in Boston. "The Lakers had a year to sign me or lose my rights. Every one of the so-called experts told me the same thing back then. They were pretty blunt about my chances. 'You can't get away with being a guard who can't shoot in the NBA and you're too small to be an effective defender,' they all said. I decided the experts just might be right. At that stage in my life, I confess I was afraid of failing. Instead of heading to the Lakers' training camp, I joined the army."

While in the army, KC played football and was so good that one of his teammates, a guy named John Morrow who had been a lineman for the Los Angeles Rams, called the team's general manager, Pete Rozelle, who would eventually become the NFL's commissioner.

Rozelle didn't have to be convinced of KC's potential, because he had once tried to convince Jones to play pro football. Upon being discharged from the military, KC headed to the Rams' training camp, where he looked like a cinch to start as a rookie at defensive back. He started the first three exhibition games, and not a single pass was completed against him.

However, when KC tore a muscle in his leg and suffered a rock-hard contusion as the regular season approached, the Rams' trainer told him the injury was minor and that he would be able "to play through the pain." KC knew better and chose not to wear his pads to practice the day after suffering the injury. L.A.'s coach Sid Gillman asked KC why he wasn't taking part in the contact scrimmage, and KC explained the injury. The trainer disputed KC's statement. Upset that his honesty was being questioned, KC told Gillman he felt the injury was career-ending and left the Rams' camp.

Gillman tried to call KC in an attempt to convince him to return. KC, however, had already called Red and agreed to a contract with the Celtics. When I interviewed Gillman four years later while he was head coach of the AFL's Los Angeles Chargers, Sid was still absolutely seething that KC had left the Rams. "Not only would he have made the team, but he would have started," he told me. "Looking back, I should have fired that dumb son of a bitch of a trainer, because he cost me the services of a guy who just might have ended up being an All-Pro. That's how impressed I was with KC. My loss was Red Auerbach's gain."

After his football experience, KC decided that just maybe his basketball critics were wrong. "I phoned Red and told him that I'd like to try my hand at pro basketball," he said to me. "Red knew all about my tryout with the Rams, and he also knew I was not a shooter. I still remember him telling me that he didn't care if I ever made a shot. 'I've got plenty of scorers. What I need is someone who can stop the opponents from scoring, someone with quickness, strength and anticipation. That's you. That's why I drafted you. You don't have to please all the critics; you only have to please one guy—and that's me. If you do that, you'll be a Celtic for as long as you want.'"

KC was Russell's biggest fan, even as a rookie. "I never played with a more unselfish guy in college, and I know I will never have a better teammate in the pros," KC told me. "What the fans will see is that he is just as smart as he is talented. He's all about team success, not individual glory. As long as Bill is in Boston, I have no doubt the Celtics will be winners."

People ask me all the time about whether Russell was the greatest leaper of all time. My answer shocks people, because Bill wasn't a guy who could hang in the air and soar way above the basket. In fact, there were a number of players who could outjump Russell. Just with the Celtics alone during Bill's career there were three teammates— Tsioropoulos, then Gene Conley, then Willie Naulls, who could jump much higher. None of them, however, possessed anything close to Bill's ability to time his jumps to perfection and to jump as quickly as he did. Russell, with his superhuman reflexes, was a basketball genius. He knew how to use his skills to maximum effectiveness and he had a sixth sense when it came to judging the exact second to go for a block or a rebound.

When it comes to shot blocking, I doubt there will ever be a player who matches Russell. He didn't "swat" shots away; he "directed" and "deflected" shots to either send the ball to teammates or to himself. His most often used method of blocking a shot to himself was to gracefully and quickly use his hand to slip underneath the basketball just before an opponent could release his shot. The ball would simply float up, and Russ would have to move no more than a step or two to pluck it out of midair.

I have never believed that statistics tell the true story of a player's contributions to a team, but some stats can't be ignored. I'm guessing—but it is an educated guess, believe me—that Russ blocked 400 shots in his second season, which was probably 250 more than the next best shot blocker accumulated. As far as his rebounding that year, he averaged better than 22 a game, which was five more per game than Bob Pettit, the second-place finisher, grabbed.

Boston's fast-break machine was fueled by two constants: Russell's anticipation of rebounds or blocks and Cousy's anticipation of Russell's short, accurate outlet passes. Cooz would see Russ go into action, and he'd immediately get a head start on the break. As a result, the opposition would be totally off balance before the ball crossed the midcourt line.

Cooz was and still is the greatest passer the game has ever had. He invented so many different ways of getting the ball from Point A to Point B, like his fullcourt discus throw, his backwards between-the-legs drop pass to a trailer, his look-away behind-the-back flip on the fast break. What further set him apart from all the other good point guards was that he only called a play for himself as the fifth option. If options one and two weren't available, he'd try options three and four. Only when all his teammates were covered did Bob even think about taking a shot himself.

And when he did shoot, Cousy usually did so with a definite purpose in mind. For instance, an opponent would score a go-ahead basket late in a game, and Bob would grab the inbounds pass, race up court, and take a running 25-foot one-hander off the wrong foot, with only five or six seconds having ticked off the clock. And he'd make it, effectively taking the wind out of the other team's sails and swinging the momentum completely over to the Celtics. Or he might go straight to the basket and flip in a short hook shot over the opposition's center, just to make a point that no one was capable of intimidating him or any member of the Celtics.

After the disappointment of the '57-'58 season, Red desperately wanted to prove that Boston's first NBA title was no fluke. He held what can only be described as a boot camp-style training camp, which consisted of two two-hour conditioning sessions a day.

When training camp broke up, Red eased up on the players—all except for Heinsohn. "Heinsohn, you're fat...Heinsohn, you're late...Heinsohn, you're loafing...Heinsohn, you're smoking too much...Heinsohn, you eat too much candy...Heinsohn, you drink too many beers...Heinsohn, you miss too many easy shots." And so forth.

Red picked on Heinsohn because he knew Tommy could shrug it off. He also knew that no one else on the team wanted to be picked on the way Tommy was scolded. By yelling at one guy, Red succeeded in getting every member of the team to do his job with a minimum of errors. Using Tommy as a scapegoat was perfect motivation—even if Tommy didn't quite grasp the reason that he was always Red's target.

Tommy usually took his frustration out on Frank Ramsey, who was the team's "little old lady," sort of a tattletale. For example, Tommy nearly always hitched a ride to practice with Cousy, because they both lived in Worcester. Cousy was the type of guy who arrived barely five or 10 minutes before practice. Because Bob didn't tape his ankles, he'd be ready to go when Red blew his whistle. Heinsohn, however, always had his ankle taped, usually causing him to be a few minutes late for the start of practice. Whenever this happened, Ramsey would immediately run to Red and demand that Tommy be fined for his tardiness. "He's three minutes late," Ramsey would whine to Red. "That's 50 cents a minute. He owes $1.50. Make him pay, Red. Rules are rules."

None of the other players cared about the fines, but Ramsey would whine and pout until Red agreed to enforce the $1.50 penalties. Tommy paid the fine, but he always found a way to get even with Frank. He'd patiently wait for a chance at revenge. Sometimes Tommy would let a week or two go by before getting even.

I remember one night when we were taking a train back to Boston from New York after a double-overtime loss to the Knicks. Tommy, obviously dead tired, was sitting next to me. I could tell he wanted to fall asleep, but he kept staring at Ramsey, who was sitting two rows in front of us. Ramsey loved mystery books and usually would read from the time we boarded the train until the time we arrived at our destination. On this occasion, however, Ramsey put his book aside and fell asleep.

Tommy got up from his seat and tiptoed up to Ramsey. Then Heinsohn carefully snatched Frank's mystery book and returned to his seat. "What are you doing?" I asked. "I'm paying Frank back for getting me in trouble, Johnny. Just watch this," Tommy replied. As Heinsohn held up the book for everyone on the team to see, he proceeded to tear out the final chapter from Frank's book. Then he sneaked back to where Ramsey was sleeping and put the book back exactly where he had found it. It wasn't until the next day that Frank realized he had been the victim of a practical joke.

"I want the pages returned," Ramsey demanded. "I know who's responsible, and I think the guy who did it is very childish." With that, a straight-faced Heinsohn chimed in, "Hey, Frank's right. Whichever one of you guys ruined Frank's book should be ashamed. I know who ripped those pages out, and I'm going to tell Frank who did it unless those pages are returned." Needless to say, Tommy didn't quite sound convincing and, needless to say, Ramsey never did recover the missing pages.

Tommy also devised other ways to get back at Frank for costing him fines. Ramsey had a routine where he'd stay 15 or 20 minutes after practice to work on his free throw shooting. While Frank was tuning up his game, Heinsohn would walk into the locker room and grab a pair of small scissors. Then he'd go over to Ramsey's locker and snip off all but one or two threads from Frank's shirt buttons. He also cut through all but a sixteenth of an inch of Ramsey's shoelaces. When Ramsey would enter the locker room, Tommy would casually head to the showers. Ramsey would shower a minute later and then start to get dressed. Shortly afterward, with Tommy sneaking a peek, Ramsey would be muttering to himself.

As Frank put on his shirt, one button after another would snap off. Then he would attempt to tie his shoes, only to get angry as the laces ripped apart as he was tying the knots. "Anyone have a shirt I can borrow?" he'd ask. Of course, none of the players were about lend Frank a decent shirt and spoil the joke. So Frank would walk out of practice with a wide-open shirt that was missing three or four buttons and with a pair of brown shoes that were tied with white sneaker laces. What was even more comical was that Frank didn't put two and two together and figure out that Heinsohn had tampered with his wardrobe. Instead of blaming Tommy, Frank blamed his own wife for not spotting the "frayed" threads and the worn out shoelaces.

The joking and carefree atmosphere continued throughout the '58-'59 season. Every so often, Auerbach would remind his players how one injury, such as Russell's ankle sprain the year before, can have a devastating effect on a chance to win a championship. Still, the Celtics were so deep and so talented that they were toying with teams on a nightly basis. And I was having a blast. I'd even have a little fun at the expense of the referees. Like the night Boston was beating up on the Knicks in New York by 30 points.

I was sitting at courtside and Mendy Rudolph, an excellent official, was standing in front of me. "Well, fans," I told the audience, "I think Rudolph has blown about five calls tonight, and I'm not even upset."

Mendy, of course, overheard me and turned around. "Johnny, according to you, I've never made a correct call against the Celtics. So if you say I only missed five calls, then I'm probably officiating the best game of my career. Thanks for the compliment."

While my exchanges with Rudolph were usually all in good fun, I did have some not-so-humorous debates with Syracuse Nats guard Al Bianchi, a 6'3" guard, whom I swear must have practiced every little dirty trick in the book. His favorite move was running beside Sam Jones or Frank Ramsey at full speed and then sliding his leg in front of them to make them sprawl head-first to the floor as he also "collapsed" on the court. Then he had the nerve to get up and claim he was being "tripped" on purpose by Sam or Frank. After this potentially dangerous play had occurred three or four times, I waited until Bianchi got close enough to hear me.

"Bianchi is a poor excuse for a human being. He gets humiliated out there because he couldn't defend a one-armed midget. And he knows it. He thinks he's a hard-nosed player, but he's nothing more than a coward." Bianchi stared me down, and I began to laugh at him. "What's the matter, Al? The truth hurts."

"I'll never do an interview with you again, you jerk," Bianchi finally yelled at me.

"Who cares about you?" I replied. "You're nothing but a scrub, anyhow. Al, do me one favor, will you? Retire before someone exposes you for what you are, a no-talent fraud."

This little exchange went over the air—and Al and I still laugh about it, because we eventually became good friends who respected each other for the passion we shared for the game.

Late in the regular season, I was lighting up my own victory cigar, because on February 21, 1959, I became a father for the first time when Sandra gave birth to a son, James Andrew. I chose his middle name in honor of Celtic Andy Phillip, my close friend and a person whose character and work ethic I had always admired.

Boston ended the regular season with a 52-20 record, best in league history. Their most impressive win of the year came at the expense of the Lakers, who had lost Mikan to retirement two years earlier. In that game, Boston scored a league-record 173 points, with Cousy handing out 28 assists. In the Eastern Division finals, the Celtics edged Syracuse 4-3. During that series, one of the classic moments in my broadcasting career occurred.

Boston had an 18-point lead early in the third quarter of Game 5 at the Garden. When Russell made an unbelievable block, I began to shout, "Russell came from out of nowhere..." Just then, my false teeth popped out of my mouth and headed over the balcony railing. In desperation, I reached out with my right hand and snatched my choppers just before they started heading downward toward the people in the loge seats. I quickly put them back in. After sheepishly explaining to my audience what had just occurred, I turned to my color commentator, longtime and highly respected St. Anselm coach Al Grenert, and proudly asked, "How's that for quick hands?"

The championship series was almost anticlimactic after Boston had scratched and clawed its way past the Nats. Minneapolis, with only a 33-39 regular-season record, was swept 4-0 by the Celtics, who gained their second title in three years. It was the first time in NBA history that a team had swept a title series.

As I interviewed Elgin Baylor after the series ended, I almost felt sorry for him. "We tried everything we could think of. We had no one to match up with Russell and no one to stop Cousy on the break. I must have shot the ball 50 times a game, but Boston's whole team seemed to surround me each time I got within 15 feet of the basket," he said. "What I hated the most was watching Auerbach's smug grin each time I went past him. It was as if he was saying to me, 'I don't care if you score 100 against us. We still can't lose.' And maybe he was right. I give them credit, but I hated Auerbach's cockiness."

This was the first Celtics team whose trademark was depth at every position. It was Sam Jones who had emerged as Boston's most reliable outside shooter. And by now, Sam had no conscience and absolutely no lack of confidence. He knew exactly how much room he needed between himself and his defender in order to get a smooth, unhurried look at the basket. Opponents like Pistons guard Gene Shue or Knicks scorer Richie Guerin were constantly frustrated by Sam's uncanny sense of timing. "I hated guarding Sam," Shue told me when he became the Bullets' coach following his playing days. "I was always just a half-step slow when it came to getting perfect defensive position against Sam. And unfortunately, you needed to be absolutely perfect if you were going to stop him from scoring."

Following the '59 title, I spent a great deal of time in the off season with KC Jones at various nightclubs in the Boston area, particularly at the Meadows, a club on Route 9 in Framingham. Like Don Barksdale, KC was a big fan of jazz and pop music. As we sat listening to the Noteables, a jazz trio from Worcester, KC would softly sing along. I was so impressed with the quality of his voice that I asked the horn player, Emil Haddad, to invite KC up to the stage to sing a number or two.

KC was very shy and didn't really want to sing in front of hundreds of people. "Please, give it a shot. You've got as good a voice as a lot of professionals I've heard," I encouraged him.

Finally KC went up and performed a couple of ballads. At the end of each song, he received a standing ovation and even did an encore at the insistence of Haddad and the entire audience. From that night on, KC became a welcomed, regular, non-paid performer at the Meadows.

It wasn't long before KC was hooked on singing at clubs, even getting paid to do an act down on the Cape. Today, if there's a piano player in any bar KC might walk into, you can count on him stepping up to the mic and belting out a few tunes. In fact, he performs quite often with the Bo Winiker Band at the Parker House in Boston and other locations. I swear if he wasn't an athlete, he sure as hell could have made a good living as an entertainer.

KC also had another talent. He could imitate anyone connected with the Celtics, from Heinsohn to Sam Jones to Russell to Auerbach. He would zero in on a distinctive characteristic such as a player's walk, shooting motion or even facial expressions. His favorite target was Ramsey, because Frank would stick his butt way out whenever he shot a free throw. He also did a great imitation of Red getting in an argument with a ref because he knew exactly what curse words Red would use, what hand gestures he'd make and how Auerbach would stomp his foot and then spin around on his heels and march back to the bench in disgust. Cousy was another player KC loved to imitate. He'd grab a basketball and pretend that he was Cousy running a fast break, and then he'd make a behind-the-back flip which he would heave 10 rows into the stands.

As soon as the ball went out of bounds, KC, imitating Cooz, would start yelling at Heinsohn. "God damn it, Tommy, if you weren't loafing, you could have caught that pass. It's all your fault. You made me throw a bad pass. And you know I never throw a bad pass." Even Red howled with laughter at the way KC mocked Cousy's occasionally off-target passes.

When Red opened training camp for the '59-'60 season, he didn't have say a word to motivate the players, because the media wasn't giving Boston even an outside chance to repeat as champions. The reason: Philadelphia had drafted Wilton Norman Chamberlain, who was being touted by many "experts" as the greatest offensive scorer and all-around defender the NBA would ever see. Warriors owner Eddie Gottlieb signed the rookie to a record contract that called for a $30,000 base salary and another $20,000 if certain incentives were achieved. Needless to say, Russell took notice of Wilt becoming the highest-paid player in the league before he ever played a game.

Wilt's size, strength and stats all seemed to indicate that Russell, at 6'9", 220 pounds, would be no match for the 7'1", 280-pound Philly center. After all, the "experts" pointed out, Wilt was a scoring machine with his dunks and his short jumpers, a prolific rebounder, and an intimidating shot blocker. Every coach in the league, with the notable exception of Red, seemed to be in awe of his abilities and his potential. Halfway through Wilt's initial exhibition season, he was being proclaimed as "a stronger, meaner, and far more agile George Mikan." The Celtics, as reigning NBA champs, were in awe of neither Chamberlain nor the Warriors.

Why? Because the Celtics had Russell, who was the smartest player in the league, the most unselfish big man, and a player who understood what winning was all about. Above all, he had the heart of a champion, which gave each and every one of his teammates supreme confidence in their abilities as a team. Still, the consensus was that Philly had a virtual lock on the title. Not only did the Warriors have Chamberlain to "dominate" Russ, but they had a supporting cast that included All-Star-caliber players such as forwards Tom Gola and Woody Sauldsberry, outside shooter Paul Arizin and playmaker Guy Rodgers.

Personally, I thought the beginning of the "Wilt the Stilt Era" was half hype and half horse shit. I knew all about Russell's team-oriented mentality and his unmatched caring about winning. I was also very familiar with Chamberlain's concern with individual statistics and being the star attraction. Boston, in my opinion, had a huge advantage over Philadelphia in every other aspect of the game. Warriors coach Paul Seymour was no mental match for Red, Gola was too slow to guard Heinsohn, and Arizin was too old and too slow to keep up with Sam Jones or Ramsey. Further, Philly's point guard, Guy Rodgers, whom I referred to as "a dribbling fool" because he would often use almost the entire 24-second clock to demonstrate his "clever" ball-handling skills, was an absolute amateur compared to Cousy.

Rodgers' "Globetrotter-style" showboating was caused in large part because Chamberlain would literally walk up the court rather than "waste his energy" running or even jogging. I guess he figured that since he was the league's top scorer, his teammates would just have to wait for him to take his position before Philly began its offense. The sight of Wilt taking his strolls while Rodgers did his dribbling routines was pitiful but priceless. KC was so amused that he actually would imitate Rodgers at Celtic practices.

The Chamberlain-Rodgers act had to drive guys like Arizin, Gola and Sauldsberry absolutely crazy, because they were very capable shooters and passers who simply weren't allowed to get their hands on the ball because Philly's offense revolved around Rodgers' hot-dogging and Wilt's power game inside. Only on occasion would Arizin get a chance to shoot his accurate 20-foot shots. Gola, a tough player with a decent shooting touch, basically shot the ball only when Wilt got the rare urge to pass the ball out of a double-team. Sauldsberry had to settle for the leftovers.

For all of the above reasons, I thought the idea of Chamberlain being viewed as superhuman was pure, unadulterated bull. In fact, I was amazed that so many GMs and coaches bought into the ridiculous notion that Wilt could win championships even if he had four midgets playing with him. When Chamberlain arrived on the scene, everyone around the NBA seemed to totally ignore the cardinal principle that basketball is a team game.

As Red's teams had already proved twice, you need five players on the court who all are willing to sacrifice individual glory in order to achieve success as a group. Philly, especially with Wilt and Rodgers playing together, would never function smoothly as a unit.

While the Celtics were battling the Warriors on the court, I began to take on members of Philadelphia's front office staff. My first target was Dave Zinkoff, the team's public address announcer, whom I referred to as "Hysterical Harry," because he thought he had to shout and be dramatic in order to excite the crowds. Zinkoff's antics forced me to talk twice as loud as normal just to be heard on the air while he was playing to the crowd.

"Hey, Dave, do you think everyone in Philadelphia is fucking deaf?" I asked him. "You're screaming so loud that even your own players wear ear plugs. Give us all a break and stop trying to impress people with the sound of your own voice. By now, everyone knows you've got a big mouth."

"Don't lecture me," he replied. "I'm not here to please you, Auerbach, or the dummies who listen to your long-winded, boring broadcasts."

Although Zinkoff and I frequently traded barbs, I should point out that he was a true original. Today the NBA public address announcers are nothing more than second-rate imitators of Zink. And none of them possess an ounce of originality or talent. They're nothing more than cheerleaders whose only job is to shriek the starting lineups to the crowd in order to create an atmosphere of artificial enthusiasm.

Zinkoff, despite his shout-and-scream PA work, invented some clever expressions to describe a basket. His most famous was his call of a Chamberlain slam as a "Dipper Dunk." In addition, he would also use alliteration to come up with such phrases as "Gola Goal" and, a few years later, "Two for Shue." His pregame introduction of the "Doctor" as "Julius E-r-r-r-r-v-ing" "inspired" other PA announcers to stretch out the names of their team's top player.

On February 26, 1960, Sandra gave birth to our second child, a daughter whom we named Margery Ann. I was on cloud nine. Until we had children, Sandra and I had never viewed my job as having too many drawbacks. Now, however, the constant traveling was more than a minor irritation, because it meant being away for extended periods from my growing family. Still, Sandra was very understanding and did a great job keeping Jamie and Margery healthy, happy and active while I was on the road.

By the end of the regular season, the "Whose Better? Wilt or Russ?" debate was the chief topic in every NBA city. The individual stats "favored" Chamberlain, who led the league in scoring (37.6 a game) and rebounding (27 a game). For his individual efforts, Wilt was named Rookie of the Year, MVP of the All-Star Game, and the league's MVP. Yet his team finished 10 games behind Boston in the regular season.

Although Wilt continued to put up big numbers in the playoffs, his team was no match for the Celtics in the Eastern Division finals. After we had jumped out to a 3-1 series lead, Wilt became totally frustrated. In Game 5, he got into a scuffle with Heinsohn and threw a vicious punch that missed Tommy's head and landed squarely on the jaw of Philly forward Tom Gola, who was simply trying to break up the fight.

"Believe it or not, the Stilt's punches are even less accurate than his free throw shooting," I said on the air. "He just decked his own teammate!" Still, the Warriors managed to win 128-107 as Chamberlain scored a Boston Garden-record 50 points.

Two days later the Celtics eliminated the Warriors, 119-117, at Philly's Convention Hall, as Heinsohn sneaked in between Wilt and Gola to tip in the deciding basket at the buzzer. After the game, Wilt threatened to quit because he claimed he was tired of being beat up. "Poor Wilt," I commented. "At 7'2" and 280 pounds, he's complaining about all his little bumps and bruises. Please, someone go get him some Gerber's baby food and a pacifier."

Following their win over the Warriors, the Celtics proceeded to secure their second straight championship by knocking off the Hawks 4-3 in the title series. Russ, the proud owner of another championship ring, was quick to praise the choice of Wilt as the league's MVP. "I'm happy, and Wilt has to be happy," Bill said to me during an interview following Boston's championship game victory. "I'm sure Wilt would have liked to have won a championship, but he accomplished just about everything else as a rookie. He should be congratulated." That statement was made for a reason. It was Russell's subtle method of employing psychological warfare to make sure Wilt's focus remained on individual statistics rather than on wins and losses. And it worked to near perfection year after year.

Personally, I've never put a great deal of emphasis on statistics. During a broadcast, you will seldom hear me use more than a dozen stats a game. Why? Because I have never believed they give an accurate picture of how a player is performing. Statistics don't tell about effort, hustle, desire, leadership or toughness. In my opinion, too many broadcasters rely on statistics to tell the story of a game rather than painting a description with their own words and emotions.

For instance, I know one well-known national TV broadcaster who faces his stat man while turning his back on his own color commentator throughout the course of a game. To me, that's ludicrous. Yes, it's important to announce that a star player has five fouls. Yes, it's essential to state that a guy has nailed seven straight shots. However, why is it so damn important to note that so-and-so is five for 12 in field goals or that Joe Blow has picked up his second foul? Air time is precious, and your audience wants to hear opinions and insight rather than listening to a bunch of meaningless numbers. In many cases, broadcasters use a thousand stats for only one reason: to cover up their own lack of knowledge about the game. They're phonies, and they're too ignorant to realize their listeners are knowledgeable enough to conclude they are fakers.

Oddly enough, the two most important stats—the score of the game and the time remaining in a quarter or in a game—are the ones that usually are not mentioned enough by those broadcasters who love to rattle off trivial numbers. Personally, I like to mention the score at least every couple of minutes. Why? Because there are people driving their cars who have just turned on their radios or people tuning in the game after just finishing a late dinner. They want to find out quickly how their team is faring. If I make them wait 10 minutes to hear something so basic as who's winning and by how many points, then I'm doing a poor job.

Just to give you an idea of Wilt's obsession with personal stats, I recall what happened after one game during Chamberlain's third year in the league. The Celtics had beaten Philly by 18 points at Boston Garden. When the Warriors returned to Philadelphia, Wilt, stat sheet in his hand, stormed up to Warriors public relations director Harvey Pollack. "I had at least 30 rebounds and they [the Celtics stat crew] only gave me credit for 22," he whined. "They gave Russell 32 and he didn't have more than 20."

Pollack, who kept every imaginable statistic you could think of at the Warriors home games, promptly told Wilt he would investigate. So when Philly visited Boston the next time, Harvey accompanied the team and kept his own stats on Wilt's and Russell's rebounding. After the game, which the Celtics won easily, Pollack approached the scorer's table and challenged the Boston stat crew. "You guys gave Russell six more rebounds than he really got, and you gave Chamberlain eight less rebounds than he actually pulled down. You're screwing Wilt every time he plays here, and I'm going to let the league know about it."

A *Sports Illustrated* reporter overheard the remarks and interviewed Harvey about his comments. The next week the magazine ran an article with a headline that read, "IS BOSTON CHEATING WILT?" Needless to say, Red was irate. He contemplated banning Pollack from the Garden, and he even debated assigning the worst seat in the Garden to anyone from *Sports Illustrated* who covered a Celtics home game. For 10 years he refused to talk with Pollack. "I could care less about individual stats. Russ could care less about them. But we don't cheat anybody. Let him run the stat crew in Philadelphia, but he's not going to criticize our guys," Auerbach said. "Who appointed him supervisor of our stat crew, anyhow?"

The Celtics made winning look even easier during the '60-'61 season when they captured their third straight title. They won the Eastern Division by 13 games over Philadelphia with a 57-22 record. Then they beat Syracuse 4-1 for the division title and ripped through St. Louis 4-1 for the championship, with Russell scoring 30 points and grabbing 38 rebounds in the series finale. (Wilt's Warriors, by the way, couldn't even manage a single win in being eliminated, 3-0, by the Nats in the Division Semifinals.)

During Wilt's first year, referee Mendy Rudolph told me one of the funniest exchanges he had ever heard between players. The mini-confrontation involved Philadelphia rookie point guard Vern Hatton and Detroit Pistons veteran Dick McGuire, whom I knew very well from my days working the Knicks games with Marty Glickman.

Dick had learned beforehand that Hatton was a devout Mormon who didn't curse and didn't appreciate it when others used foul language. At every opportunity, McGuire, who was known to use some salty language during the heat of battle, tried to throw Hatton off his game by guarding him closely and using every curse word he could think of to make Hatton nervous. For 48 minutes, Hatton listened to McGuire's non-stop off-color vocabulary. The poor kid became so flustered and made so many mistakes that he finally blurted out, "Come on, please just play and stop cursing me out. I haven't done a thing to you." To which McGuire, ever the antagonist, replied, "Aw, stop your goddamned bitching. You go ahead and play your game and I'll play mine. Screw you, asshole."

"I had a hard time keeping a straight face," Rudolph told me. "I mean Hatton was practically in tears, and McGuire was enjoying every minute of it. I felt sorry for the kid, but technically, McGuire wasn't doing anything wrong. Dick wasn't yelling at Hatton. In fact, he hardly raised his voice as he kept up his verbal assault. The only people who knew what was going on were McGuire, a few of his teammates, Hatton and myself."

A big factor in Boston's improvement during Wilt's rookie season was the addition of Tom "Satch" Sanders, the Celtics' first-round draft pick.

My first impression of Satch, who had to be convinced by Auerbach to sign with the Celtics instead of accepting a job in the business world, was that he was too skinny (200 pounds) and too small (6'6") to play a lot of minutes at the forward spot in the NBA even though he had averaged 22 points a game for NYU. "Listen," Red said to me, "I didn't draft this kid to be a scorer for us. We've got plenty of guys who can put the ball in the basket. What I want Sanders to do is be a defensive stopper. He's quick, he can jump, and he's a very smart player."

Then I relayed Red's assessment to Satch, who was and still is one of the most well-spoken, polite and candid people I ever met. "I'm not sure how well I'll do," he responded. "I have my own doubts about my physical abilities. However, when somebody like Red

Auerbach says I can help a team like the Celtics, well, I just have to find out for myself if I can do what's expected of me."

Satch was, without a doubt, the one Celtics player who shocked the hell out of me with his game. Throughout his career, he would be used on defense to cover the opponents' top-scoring forward. He'd cover Bob Pettit, Philly's Chet Walker, the Lakers' Elgin Baylor, Cincinnati's Jack Twyman, Philly's Billy Cunningham and even Knicks center Willis Reed whenever he played the high post.

"It's never any fun playing against Sanders," Baylor told me. "You know you're in for a long night every time he's guarding you. He can match up with anybody, he has a knack of anticipating your moves and he loves to give you a little bump now and then. Most of all, Sanders is very deceptive, because he has such long arms and quick reactions that he always plays two steps off you. You think you have a wide-open shot and then he explodes toward you and alters your shot."

And that was just Satch's value to the Celtics on the defensive end. Offensively, his long strides and excellent hands made him a perfect fit for the fast breaks generated by Russell's rebounding and Cousy's passing, however, Red could have cared less about Satch's offense. "We've got plenty of scorers, but no one defends forwards like Sanders," Auerbach said.

Of course, Satch wanted to show Red that he was capable of being an offensive weapon. During his second year, Satch had a string of double-figure games, including a 28-point game against Syracuse. Unfortunately, Boston lost to the Nats that night. "It taught me a lesson I've never forgotten," Satch told me. "Every player has a very defined role. If just one player forgets his role, if just one player crosses over the line and forgets what his role is, the whole team's chemistry is thrown out of kilter. After we had lost the game, Red didn't say a word to me. He knew I had learned my lesson."

Satch was a true gentleman. He'd greet me with a very formal, "And how are you tonight, Mr. Most?" even after we became good friends. As a rookie, though, Satch had a few quirks.

He'd wear a pair of ugly, torn and dirty white knee pads. Loscy hated those things. "They look like crap," he scolded Satch. "You make us all look bad when you wear those raggedy pads." Red also didn't like them because he believed the opposing teams would start thinking Satch had bad knees and might start taking aim at his knee caps whenever he went up for a rebound. "Besides," Red told me, "I want my guys to look tough. I didn't want guys wearing elbow pads, knee pads or even bandaids."

So Loscutoff, supposedly under orders from Auerbach, hid the knee pads. "I knew where he put them," Satch told me. "I also knew that Red didn't want me to wear them. Using my common sense, I let them remain permanently 'lost.'"

Because Satch had suffered a series of sprained ankles when he was at NYU, he wore three times the amount of tape that every other Celtics player wore throughout his rookie year. "I don't know how you can walk, let alone run, with two inches of tape around each ankle," Heinsohn would tell Sanders. "You're wrapped up more than a goddamned mummy."

"I gave up my knee pads. I won't stop wearing my layers of ankle tape," Satch announced firmly. "I get here an hour early to get taped. I don't cause any delays. I'm not going to suffer a sprained ankle because certain people think so much tape looks funny. Laugh all you want, but I'm sticking to my guns."

My favorite story about Satch is when he was learning to drive. Because he grew up in New York and then attended NYU, he simply never had a need for a car. He'd either take the subway or walk to wherever he was going.

Once Satch moved to Boston, a car was essential for getting to and from practices and games. In a two-day "crash" course, KC Jones taught Satch the basics of driving. On the day Satch took his driver's test, KC went with him and sat in the back seat as the driving instructor tested Satch.

The next day KC came into practice and proceeded to give a play-by-play on how Satch fared during his test. Now, KC isn't the excitable type. But on this particular day KC was as animated as I have ever seen him. "You're not going to believe this," he told his teammates. "Satch turned a mild-mannered instructor into a nervous wreck in a matter of 15 minutes. I thought the guy was going to jump out of the car."

Then KC mimicked Satch's actions behind the wheel as he recounted the driver's test adventure. "First of all, it took Satch five minutes just to get comfortable. He adjusted the car seat three times. Then he spent another couple of minutes fixing the rear-view mirror. Finally he took another five minutes making certain there was no traffic," KC related. "The instructor practically had to beg him to start driving. As Satch drove down the street, he never went faster than 10 miles an hour. I could see the instructor was getting impatient as he asked Satch to make a left turn. Satch, however, was so nervous, he missed it. At the time we were on a four-lane street, with heavy traffic moving in both directions.

"Having missed the turn, Satch decided he'd make a U-turn to go back to where he was supposed to have turned originally. The instructor looked like he was having a heart attack as Satch made his U-turn with oncoming traffic bearing down on us. As Satch slowly maneuvered the car forward and backward, traffic on both sides of the road had to come to an abrupt stop. The instructor, who now was a nervous wreck yelled out, 'Hurry up, hurry up...you're going to get us into a damned accident.'

"Satch finally made the U-turn, though. I can't tell you guys how he managed to do it, because by then I had my eyes closed. The next thing Satch was asked to do was to parallel park. That maneuver must have taken 20 minutes as he inched the car back and forth, back and forth. Just when I thought he was going to successfully complete the parking job, Satch tapped the car in back of us with enough force that the instructor dropped his clipboard.

"When Satch completed the test, I expected the instructor to give him the bad news that he had flunked the test. Instead, the guy told Satch he had passed."

With everyone on the team, including Red, doubled up with laughter, Satch bowed and spread his arms. "Gentlemen, if any of you ever need a ride, just let me know."

KC must have been a glutton for punishment, because the next day he drove Satch to buy a car from a dealer in Cambridge. After completing the deal, KC followed Satch as he drove his car home.

"Johnny, he was going five miles an hour as he approached the Massachusetts Avenue bridge. As we got to the bridge, the traffic was really heavy and there was a cop directing traffic. He was signaling the oncoming cars to stop, but Satch got confused and distracted by a heavy truck right behind us," KC told me. "He didn't see the cop's signal and kept going at his five-mile-an-hour-pace. Next thing I knew, Satch's car nudged the cop, who ended up spread-eagled on the hood of Satch's car. 'What the hell are you doing?' he asked Satch. 'Didn't you see me telling you to stop?'

"'No sir,' said Satch. 'I apologize.'"

The cop, checking Satch's license, realized it was his first day behind the wheel and, no doubt recognizing the Celtics duo, waved them off with a frown and a grin. "Just get over to Boston and don't ever come to Cambridge," the officer joked.

After KC's teammates heard the stories about Satch's driving abilities, no Celtic was brave enough to accept a ride from him for years. As Heinsohn said, "If I was an hour late for practice, I think I'd rather ride the 'T' or walk than take my chances riding with Satch."

Shortly after Boston won the title, Sharman, now 35, announced his retirement in order to become head coach of the Los Angeles Jets of the newly formed American Basketball League. The ABL had signed some excellent coaches, including Andy Phillip and former

Philadelphia star Neil Johnston, but it couldn't attract star players. Not surprisingly, the league folded after a year and a half. When the Jets folded three months into the league's inaugural season due to poor attendance, Sharman became coach of the Cleveland Pipers (owned by a newcomer to the sports world, the one and only George Steinbrenner) and was able to lead that team to the ABL title in his first year on the bench by compiling a combined .615 winning percentage with his two teams.

"I knew I could have stayed and played for Red another year or two. And I also realized the ABL was probably doomed from the start," Bill told me. "I chose to coach in that league because it was the quickest way to let NBA executives see that I had what it took to be a head coach. Yes, I missed out on winning more titles with the Celtics, but I also think I proved to people that I could be a winner as a coach. I never regretted my decision."

Sharman went on to enjoy a spectacular bench career, becoming the only coach to win championships in three different pro leagues (the ABL, the ABA with the Utah Stars in '71, and the NBA with the Lakers in '72).

During his seven-year NBA coaching career, he managed to win four division titles, one with the Warriors and three with the Lakers. Following his final division title, he left the bench to become L.A.'s general manager.

And Bill credited Red with all his success. "I patterned my coaching after Red. I believed in his philosophy that good chemistry is every bit as important as good talent," he said. "I studied Auerbach's methods from my first day as a rookie until my last day in a Celtics uniform. Sure, I learned a lot about the game from Red, but he taught me even more about how to motivate players. I didn't try to copy Red's personality. I just tried to copy his knowledge of the game and his understanding of getting the most from his players."

Despite the loss of Sharman, the Celtics continued to dominate the NBA during the '61-'62 regular season. Chamberlain averaged

50 points and 25 rebounds a game for the Warriors, Cincy's Oscar
Robertson averaged a triple-double for the season, and the Lakers
scoring duo of Jerry West and Baylor combined for 69 points a game.
But it was Boston that outdistanced everyone with a 60-20 record.

By now, the Celtics had perfected their winning formula.
Everyone knew their roles: Heinsohn, Ramsey, and Sam were the
scorers; Russell ignited the fast break with his defensive rebounding
and shot blocking; Cousy created the easy baskets for the entire team;
Satch and KC created havoc on defense.

If there was one new wrinkle to Boston's game, it was the
constant fullcourt pressing by Sam and KC Jones. Both were quick;
both were relentless. They knew how to work in tandem to force
turnovers or completely disrupt a team's set offense.

When I interviewed Detroit's Gene Shue, an excellent
playmaker, he summed up the feeling of frustration that opposition
guards experienced against Sam and KC. "Boston has so much depth
at guard. Your first reaction when you see Cousy on the bench is that
at least that's one less All-Star to worry about," he said. "But then,
while Cousy is sitting back in his chair resting, you find yourself
constantly being hounded by Sam and KC. It takes all your energy
just to get the ball into the frontcourt. When you finally get across
midcourt, you really don't have time to set up a play. You just pass
the ball to anyone who is open enough to get off a quick shot. I've
seen guys who are just relieved to get rid of the ball because of all the
pressure applied by Sam and KC. They're not looking to set up a
play; they're just glad they didn't get the ball stolen."

As the Celtics kept winning, opponents looked for excuses. This
was the year when teams started accusing Red of using "dirty tricks"
at the Garden to help Boston's cause. Lakers coach Fred Schaus claimed
Auerbach opened L.A.'s locker room windows during the first half of
games in order to make the players feel like they were in a "refrigerator"
during halftime. Philadelphia coach Alex Hannum complained that
Red instructed the ballboys to give his team half-inflated balls to use

in warmups. Players threw tantrums because the showers either were ice cold or scorching hot. And, for some strange reason, the opposition teams never had a sufficient number of towels.

I'm going to let you in on a little secret. Most of the complaints were legitimate. However, Red was not the principle culprit. For the most part, the Celtics' chief mischief maker was, in fact, the late Walter Randall, the team's longtime equipment manager. Walter was quite a character. Almost always, he called the players by their numbers rather than by their names. Like Red, he had a tough exterior but a heart of gold. Whenever he was up to no good, you could see a little grin on his face as he moved about the Boston locker room.

If the Celtics got off to a slow start in a game during the winter months, Walter would walk down to the opponents' locker room and use his master key to go inside and open the windows as wide as possible. By halftime, the locker room would be so cold that a few coaches gave their halftime talk in the Garden hallway. During the playoffs, when the building was steamy, Walter would sneak down to the visitors' locker room and shut and lock the windows.

When the Celtics were on the verge of losing a game late in the fourth quarter, Walter would become angry and instruct a ballboy to run down to the opponents' locker room and grab a handful of towels. The result—much to Walter's delight—was that visiting players would have to share towels. "Johnny, I got those bastards good tonight," he'd tell me. "Not one of them could dry themselves off completely."

As for the hot and cold showers, Walter knew where the shutoff valves were located. If he was in a bad mood, he simply turned one of the valves off and then enjoyed himself as the opposing players, coaches and trainers ranted and raved.

"I have a million little jokes I play on teams," he told me. "I guess my favorite is giving a team plenty of good towels before a game and then replacing them while the game is going on with towels that are so damp they won't sop up any water. I love standing out in

the hallway and watching these guys walking out with their shirts
and pants soaking wet."

Was Red aware of Walter's "dirty tricks?" I have no idea.
However, if Red did know about them, I'm sure he probably smiled
when he heard about Walter's methods of trying to give Boston a few
little advantages here and there.

When the '62 draft rolled around, Red passed on some "big-
name" offensive players, such as Purdue's high-scoring forward Terry
Dischinger, Bradley's power forward Chet Walker and St. John's guard
Kevin Loughery. Instead, he chose Ohio State swingman John
Havlicek. Even after winning four straight titles, Red was second-
guessed. Despite the fact that his Ohio State teams had won an NCAA
title and twice finished second, Havlicek, the critics claimed, was not
even the third or fourth best player on those teams.

As soon as Auerbach made his choice, I found myself in a verbal
battle with *Herald Traveler* columnist Clif Keane, who always seemed
to find some fault with Red.

"Why Auerbach didn't take Dischinger or Walker is beyond
me," Keane said. "This team needs another scorer up front. Heinsohn's
the only consistent shooter, and he's getting up there [in age]. Both
the guys I liked could help on the boards, too. Have you ever seen
Havlicek? A strong breeze could knock him to the ground."

"Clif, no matter who Red took, you wouldn't like his pick. You
make your living by being a negative son of a bitch," I told him. "I
don't think you've even seen much of Havlicek, or you'd know this
kid can really play."

(Truth is I had only seen John play once or twice on TV. He
really didn't stick out in my mind as one of the top players available.
I wasn't, however, going to let Keane second-guess Red, because I was
sure Keane probably had seen Havlicek play even less than I had.)

I immediately asked Red about his draft choice, a player who
also had been drafted by the Cleveland Browns as a wide receiver in
the seventh round and then cut late in the preseason.

"I've seen enough of Havlicek to know he's my type of player. He's got great hands, he's quick, he was Ohio State's best defensive player, he's smart and he never stops hustling," Red said. "Everyone wants me to explain why he only averaged 14 or 15 points a game if he's so damned good. Well, they didn't need him to score. They had a lot of talented scorers. Shit, the guy only took 10 shots a game and would hit more than half of them. He's a very unselfish player. If they had asked him to score more, he could have. Screw the critics. If they knew anything about basketball, they'd know John Havlicek is going to be a hell of a pro."

Meeting Havlicek for the first time, I immediately loved his attitude as he talked about his experience with the Browns. "I hadn't played football since high school. When Cleveland drafted me, I was sort of shocked. Why me? Then I thought about it some more and said to myself, 'Hey, if the Browns think I can play for them, then maybe I can. It can't hurt to give it a shot,'" he said. "They had a great veteran receiver in Ray Renfro and they also had selected Maryland's All-American, Gary Collins, in the first round. I knew the odds were against me, but I also believed that if I didn't try to make the team, I would always wonder whether I had made a mistake by passing up the opportunity.

"Besides, I was very confident about my basketball ability. I know I can play in the pros, especially here, because they do what I do best—and that's run."

In addition to drafting Havlicek, Red signed nine-year veteran center Clyde Lovellette as a backup for Russell. Conley had left following the '60-'61 season, and even though Boston had secured another title in '62, Auerbach realized that Russell had been overworked.

"Russ never complained about it, but he played 45 minutes a game," Red said to me. "I tried to get some help for him, I tried back then to get Clyde, but I just couldn't pull it off. When Lovellette became available this summer, I grabbed him. He may be 33 years old, but he's very physical, with a mean streak. If I can get 10 minutes a game from Clyde, it'll mean less minutes and more production from Russ."

Typical Auerbach. His coaching philosophy revolved around solid depth. Less minutes, better production. Such thinking was by now part of the Celtic tradition.

The '62-'63 season was to be Cousy's finale. Originally Cooz planned on retiring a year earlier to become the head coach at Boston College, but Red persuaded Bob to stay on for one more season. "BC agreed to hold the job for me," Cooz said. "So I'm going to play just one last season."

Cousy's skills hadn't diminished, but at age 34, Cooz wanted to leave while his game was still at the All-Star level. "Being surrounded by five or six All-Stars, I know I could play at least three more years and be effective," he said to me. "But the travel, the practices, being away from my family all are becoming too much. The only part of the basketball business I enjoy are the games themselves. Now it's time to move on."

In his final year, Cooz indeed performed at his usual high level of efficiency. Every road game was a tribute to Cousy, as opposition fans gave him standing ovations as the Boston lineup was introduced. In fact, his slightly reduced playing time allowed him to have one of his best seasons, leading the Celtics to a league-best 58-22 record. On the final day of the season, Bob Cousy Day was held at the Garden.

As master of ceremonies, I was a little concerned about how Cooz would handle all the emotions he would experience. "Johnny, I have my whole speech written down, because I don't want to stumble through my remarks if I start to cry." Cooz began by apologizing for having to read his speech—but it didn't matter one bit to the fans.

As Bob read the speech, a lone voice from the balcony cried out, "We love ya, Cooz." The Garden erupted in applause, and Cooz struggled to keep his composure. "It was a wonderful day," Bob said to me afterward. "But I'll tell you one thing: I felt more pressure that day than I ever did playing for a championship."

The media dubbed Cooz's Day as the "Boston Tear Party"—and you wouldn't get an argument from Red, any of the Celtics players, or me.

Of course, all of the Celtics wanted desperately to see Cooz retire as a champion, which proved to be no easy task. The Royals, led by Oscar Robertson, Jack Twyman and their no-holds-barred enforcer, Wayne Embry, pushed Boston to a seventh game in the Eastern Finals. Fittingly, Cousy led the Celtics into the title series with a 21-point, 11-assist performance as the Celtics ran off to a 142-131 victory.

Earl Strom, who officiated the game, told me afterward that Robertson came up to him in the closing minutes of the game and said, "You know that I hate losing. This time at least there's a silver lining. I won't ever again have to worry about trying to keep up with Cousy. I won't ever have to guess again what the hell that little guy is going to do with the ball when he's darting upcourt, plotting how to get the easiest basket for his team. I've always thought I was pretty good at guessing what my man was planning to do against me. Cousy was the exception. Too many times I guessed wrong. You realize everyone in the arena knows you've just been suckered."

In the finals against the Lakers, Cooz again was among the heroes as Boston won the title in six games with a 112-109 victory at the L.A. Sports Arena. In closing out his career, Cousy scored 18 points and seven assists. He dribbled the ball for the final six seconds of the game and then hurled the ball toward the ceiling in celebration as the buzzer sounded. Of course, the Boston media critics were already demanding to know how Auerbach could possibly replace the heart and soul of its fast break.

Sure, KC Jones was a smart, exceptionally dogged defender who, on the offensive end, seldom made mistakes as a ball handler and playmaker, the writers admitted. But, they repeatedly pointed out, he didn't possess the on-the-run passing ability or imagination of Cousy.

What the scribes failed to note was just how much KC could disrupt an opponent's offensive style. As Lakers All-Star guard Jerry West told me on the air about KC, "He forces me to change my game. He always saddles up and rides me, so he takes away my jumper, which is my best shot. Because of his defense, I'm learning to drive to the basket more. Because of his non-stop defensive pressure, I think I'm becoming a better all-around player."

The media's guessing game had begun. Would Red draft a playmaker? Did he plan on making a trade? Or would he sign a free agent who could come close to filling Cousy's offensive role as "master of the fast break?"

The answer was none of above. What Auerbach decided was to revamp his offense to fit his personnel. "You just don't go out and find 'another Cousy.' He's one of a kind," Red told me. "We obviously won't use the fast break half as much as before, but we still have guys like Heinie and Sam who can score, we still have Russell to rebound and block shots, and we have KC, who was Cousy's protege for five years and can easily step into a starter's role as a playmaker, who also happens to be the best defensive backcourt man in the league."

That's the type of thinking that made Red a coaching genius.

Too many coaches believe they have the "perfect system." Any players these coaches draft, acquire in trades or sign as free agents must adapt to that system. If the team fails, then the coach blames the players, not the system. Red, on the other hand, was smart enough to realize that you have to mold a system to fit your personnel.

"I've got the best defensive guards in the league," he said. "I've got the greatest center in the history of the game. I've got toughness in Heinsohn, Satch, Loscy and Lovellette. Plus, I've got Ramsey and Havlicek coming in off the bench. Teams aren't going to score easily against us. If we execute offensively, we'll still be the team to beat. That's what I'm going to tell my guys. And it'll be the truth, too."

Only once during my entire Celtics broadcasting career did I ever give serious consideration to another job offer. That came shortly after we had won the '63 championship when the executive board of Carling Brewery, which owned the Bullets, asked me to come down to Baltimore and be the radio voice of the team. I met with the several members of the board at their offices in Natick, Massachusetts, and they presented me with a proposal that would have nearly doubled my salary.

While I was flattered and tempted by the offer, I told them that the only way I'd take the job was if I was also appointed to the Bullets' vacant general manager's post. In those days, the GM's job wasn't as complicated as it is today. You didn't have to be a legal genius. Your basketball knowledge was the all-important factor, and I figured I had more knowledge of the game than any number of people in the various teams' front offices. After all, I had been a student of the game for a decade—with Red Auerbach as my teacher. I knew what Red looked for when he drafted players, I knew his coaching strategy, I knew how he went about improving his roster with free-agent acquisitions and trades.

Although my proposal was given serious consideration, the Carling board rejected it. They countered with an offer that included the pay raise and as the position of assistant general manager. The Bullets owners were brutally honest with me. They said they were afraid that if they offered me the general manager's position and the team didn't do well, their fans and other teams would ridicule them for choosing a "novice" with no coaching or front office experience to run the club.

I thought they were merely offering a title without any real power, so I turned the job down and recommended my partner, St. Anselm's coach Al Grenert, for the job. But Al, who went on to coach St. A's for 22 years, loved coaching too much to become a full-time broadcaster, even though he was close friends and a former teammate of Baltimore coach Buddy Jeannette. I then recommended a young, talented broadcaster named Jim Karvellas for the position. Jimmy got the job, was very talented, and went on to be the longtime TV play-by-play man for the Knicks' cable operation.

(One more little-known fact about Al Grenert. He was the first college or pro head coach to advocate the three-point shot, because he felt it would help equalize the roles of the smaller and bigger players. His idea was rejected as "ridiculous" in the press. Yet today the three-point shot is a major offensive weapon in high school, college and the pros.)

During the summer of '63, I began a three-year stint as the track announcer at Norwood Arena, a quarter-mile high-banked asphalt track where modified stock cars raced. The outdoor arena, which operated from May to September each year, was located on Route 1 and attracted some of New England's top drivers.

Because the track was so small and steep, there were bumps, spinouts and crashes every night. Whenever there was a crash or a car out of control, I would scream, "STOP THE ACTION! STOP THE ACTION!" By using those words, I was trying to alert the drivers that there was danger ahead. However, one night a leading racer, Bill Slater, who was sidelined by an injury, was sitting with me in the announcer's booth. As I yelled at the top of my lungs, "STOP THE ACTION!" he began to chuckle.

"What's so fucking funny?" I angrily said to him. "Don't you want me to make sure your fellow drivers know there's a pileup ahead of them? I can see the whole track. They can't. Even if you don't appreciate my warning call, I bet they do."

"I didn't mean any offense, Johnny," Slater replied, "but none of the drivers on the track can hear a single word you're hollering. They're driving unmuffled cars at high speeds. With their helmets on, all they're capable of hearing is the sound of their engines roaring. I know you're trying to warn them of potential danger, but, trust me, the drivers can only rely on their eyes, not their ears, to spot trouble ahead. Don't stop yelling, though. The crowd loves it."

A week before the Celtics opened the '63-'64 campaign, Auerbach added Havlicek's former Buckeye teammate Larry Siegfried to Boston's roster. Just how Siggy, who would go on to earn seven championship rings, ended up in Boston involved many bizarre twists and turns.

As a 39-points-per-game scorer in high school, Siggy, as everyone called him, was recruited by more than 40 major colleges. He chose Ohio State and was the Buckeyes' leading scorer as a sophomore in 1959. However, when Jerry Lucas and then John Havlicek joined the OSU varsity, Siggy suddenly was only the team's third offensive option. "I always viewed myself as a guy who could have been far more productive in my final two years at Ohio State if [coach] Fred Taylor had allowed me to post up. I was 6'4" and usually had midgets guarding me," he told me. "Instead I had to set up outside and take jumpers. Lucas could shoot well from 16 feet and Havlicek could always nail his shots. So I just accepted a lesser role. Since we were beating everyone, I couldn't complain."

Despite the fact that Siegfried's stats dipped his final two years in college, his all-around skills didn't go unnoticed. In fact, when the NBA held its '61 draft, Larry was selected as the third overall selection by the Cincinnati Royals. Because of the Buckeyes' intense rivalry with the University of Cincinnati, Siggy was so convinced the Royals' fans would never accept him that he chose to sign with the Cleveland Pipers of the newly created ABL.

Much to Siggy's disappointment, the ABL folded after his rookie season with the Pipers, which had won the ABL title under Bill Sharman. Although the Royals, who still had his NBA rights, made another pitch to him, Larry stubbornly turned them down and signed on with a Midwest semipro league team. "The Royals offered me about 20 times what I made kicking around as a semipro, but I just couldn't bring myself to play in Cincinnati," he told me when I first interviewed him. "Ohio State players hated Cincinnati and Cincinnati fans hated us. I would have felt like a total traitor if I played for the Royals."

Once the semipro season ended in February, Siggy became a high school substitute teacher for four months just to survive financially. "Then Havlicek put in a good word for me with Red and the Celtics tried to make a deal with Cincinnati, but the Royals decided to trade my rights to St. Louis," he said. "Basically, I went to Hawks camp hoping they'd cut me. They had two quality veteran guards in Richie Guerin and Lenny Wilkens. Plus, their first-round draft pick that year was a 6'4" guard named Gerry Ward, whom they obviously liked a lot. Going into training camp, I knew I wouldn't play a minute, even if I made their team."

Two weeks into the '63 training camp, St. Louis released Siegfried and Red promptly signed him. However, with Sam and KC Jones starting in the backcourt and Ramsey coming off the bench, Larry spent almost all of his first season with the Celtics on the taxi squad. He was clearly frustrated, but he didn't give up. As he told me, "It seems like I've been knocked down a hundred times over the past three years. Each time I manage to get back up and keep plugging away. I don't regret my decisions, and I haven't lost confidence in my abilities. I can help this team, and I'll eventually prove it."

Boston, which added a scorer up front by signing seven-year veteran and five-time All-Star forward Willie Naulls, met little resistance in its first Cousy-less season. With KC orchestrating the offense, the Celtics cruised to a 59-21 record, best in the NBA. This team's extraordinary depth and balance was reflected in the fact that Havlicek—despite not starting a single game—was the Celtics' leading scorer, averaging 19.9 points.

It was an eventful season for me personally, with Sandra giving birth to our third child, Robert Douglas, on February 6, 1964.

In the playoffs, the Celtics lost only two games, as they hammered Wilt's San Francisco Warriors, 4-1, in the final series. "Unbelievable. This dynasty is now officially the greatest in sports history," I emphatically told my audience after Boston's 105-99 victory in Game 5 at the Garden. "The ['49-'53] New York Yankees and the ['56-'60] Montreal Canadiens managed to each win five championships in a row. The Celtics have just captured their sixth straight....and [pause] we're [pause] still [pause] counting."

The '64-'65 season was a difficult time for Red, the Celtics players, and myself. On September 7, Walter Brown died of a heart attack at age 59. As Bill Russell said upon hearing the sad news, "The huge heart has stopped beating."

Personally, I was devastated. This was the man who gave me my biggest break, who encouraged and praised me from day one, who wisely counseled me on personal matters, who let me know he was "only a phone call away" if I needed anything, who told me, "I'm not your boss; I'm your friend."

Tears came streaming down the faces of the players and me while the Garden fans stood in silent tribute when the Celtics raised "No. 1" to the rafters in honor of Walter on October 17, 1964. "Anything but winning the championship will make us feel we have somehow forgotten what Mr. Brown did for this team and everyone who ever played for him," said Sam Jones.

To a man, the Celtics dedicated the '64-'65 season to Walter. And it showed in their performance, as Boston ran away with the league's best record at 62-18. But as the Eastern Division finals against the Philadelphia 76ers, who formerly were the Syracuse Nats, would prove that another Boston championship was not a foregone conclusion.

The 76ers were a sub-.500 club when they acquired Chamberlain from the San Francisco Warriors during the All-Star break for what I angrily referred to as "a small bag of peanuts and a suitcase full of thousand dollar bills." All the Sixers gave up were guard Paul Neumann, power forward Connie Dierking, 6'7" forward Lee Shaffer and cash. Now they had a very solid, very tough, eight-man veteran rotation, led by Wilt, forwards Chet Walker and Luke

Jackson, and guards Hal Greer, Larry Costello and Dave Gambee. The trade instantly made Philly a threat to dethrone Boston. "This team dedicated its season to Walter Brown," I commented before the Celtics' first game after the All-Star break. "Even with Wilt, I am telling you Boston will not fail in its quest for a seventh straight championship. Philadelphia might now match the Celtics' talent, but they can never match Boston's desire to win for Walter A. Brown."

6

"HAVLICEK STOLE THE BALL"

The 76ers-Celtics '65 divisional championship series was, as expected, a war. The first six games were each won by the home club, setting up a deciding game at the Garden on April 15, 1965. I had no inkling that this day was to be the most memorable of my entire career. Having seen this Celtics team methodically rip apart the league throughout the regular season, I envisioned a Celtics blowout, especially since Red had told his players and officially complained to the league that the officiating already cost Boston two victories. "We can't let the refs [Richie Powers and Earl Strom] decide the next game on a last-minute call," Auerbach emphasized to his team after Philly had evened the series, 3-3, at the Spectrum. "The refs aren't going to give us any calls, so we have to be in complete charge in the fourth quarter...give them [the Sixers] no hope."

Two hours before Game 7, I sat in the press room with my color commentator, Jimmy Pansullo, and our third man in the booth, Al Grenert, whom I had been friends with since we played against each other in college when I played for Brooklyn College and Al starred at NYU. Both Al and I predicted a Celtics blowout. Jimmy conservatively picked Boston by a basket. All three of us agreed the series winner would undoubtedly take the NBA title since the Western

Division-champion Lakers would be without the services of 27-points-per-game scorer Elgin Baylor, who had suffered torn knee ligaments during L.A.'s division title game.

When the Celtics took an 18-point lead just eight minutes into the game, I became too cocky. "Boston is just shredding up the Sixers at both ends of the court. Wilt the Stilt Chamberlain is pouting, because all his teammates are doing against the Celtics' defense is shooting off-target jumpers 25 feet away from the basket. They're in a state of sheer panic."

But I jumped the gun. The 76ers regrouped and by halftime had come back to lead by a point. When Philly took a 66-61 lead early in the third quarter, Red angrily signaled for a timeout. "I cursed them out. That's what I did," he said to me during my postgame show. "I reminded them we had to take charge right then, or Philly was going to embarrass us."

The Celtics proceeded to use Russell's picks to free Sam Jones and Havlicek, whom I had nicknamed "Jarrin' John, the Bouncing Buckeye," for easy jumpers. On the defensive end, KC Jones and Sam began to turn up the heat with their "in their shirts" defensive fullcourt pressure. Entering the final quarter, Boston held a 90-82 advantage. With a little more than a minute remaining, Boston was up, 110-103, as Red began to light his victory cigar. Al Grenert then commented that the Celtics "might want to foul Wilt, a 46 percent free throw shooter, every time he touched the ball." Instead, the Celtics, who had four players with five fouls, decided to loosely guard Chamberlain rather than risk giving up any possible three-point plays. Six straight points by Wilt, ending with an emphatic dunk, cut Boston's lead to a single point. Still, there were only five seconds on the clock.

With Russell inbounding the ball, Philly double-teamed him while the three other 76ers scrambled frantically to force an errant pass. Russ took a step backwards and jumped as he fired the ball. It traveled only a few feet before hitting the guy wire that supported the basket. "Russell lost the ball off the support," I bellowed into the microphone. "And the Celtics are claiming Chamberlain hit him on the arm...The ball goes over to Philadelphia. Time is out. And time is in for Jim Pansullo."

"Just five seconds left," Jimmy calmly reminded the audience. "But Philadelphia has the ball under the basket [in the offensive end]. Now this change of events, Al, has hit us right smack in the nose."

Grenert then offered his opinion of what Philadelphia, coached by my old friend Dolph Schayes, might attempt to do. "I think you'll see them try to get the ball into Chamberlain, or else you'll see [Hal] Greer fool around for three or four seconds and then throw that thing at the basket. If they foul him [Chamberlain], they get three [attempts] for two. It's a real bad situation."

As soon as Philadelphia was awarded the ball, Russell went down to one knee, pounding his fists on the court and muttering, "Oh, my God! Oh, my God!" Then, head down, he arose and almost reluctantly walked over to the Celtics huddle. "Somebody bail me out," he pleaded. "I just blew it."

Fortunately for Boston, the Philly huddle was absolute chaos. "Everybody was trying to make up a play," Schayes said afterward. "Everybody was yakking, screaming and talking at the same time. Finally I screeched, 'Hold it. Let me talk.'"

Philly had a few options. The most obvious was to get the ball into Chamberlain, with his five-inch height advantage over Russell. The second was to get the ball on the outside to Chet Walker, who would then look for either Chamberlain or Greer, whichever one was more open. Walker also might shoot, hoping that even if he missed, Chamberlain would have time to tip in the rebound.

The huddles broke, and I began my play-by-play:

"Greer is putting the ball into play. He gets it out deep...And Havlicek steals it...over to Sam Jones...Havlicek stole the ball...it's all over! It's all over!

"Johnny Havlicek is being mobbed by the fans. It's all over! Johnny Havlicek stole the ball! Oh, boy, what a play by Havlicek. A spectacular series comes to an end in spectacular fashion. Johnny Havlicek is being hoisted aloft. He yells and raises his hands...Bill Russell wants to grab him. He hugs him. He squeezes Havlicek.

"Havlicek saved this ballgame! Believe that! Johnny Havlicek saved this ballgame. The Celtics win it, 110-109."

In the locker room afterward, Heinsohn explained to me Boston's strategy. "First off, we were glad to see Greer inbounding, because that meant we had him covered," Tommy began. "We figured that the ball would probably be lobbed into Chamberlain, so Russ was just going to keep him as far away from the basket as possible. If Greer tossed it in to Wilt, we were going to hack the shit out of him as soon as he touched it. He was only five for 13 from the line in the series and the pressure would be on him. We knew we would have to foul him before he attempted a shot. Even Wilt can make one or two [free throws] out of three. I guess Red figured if we only had two shots, the odds were he might miss them both or, at most, make one."

Havlicek, though, roaming on the outside like a safety in football, was fully prepared for an inbounds pass to the outside. "I knew he had five seconds to get the ball in, so I started counting, 'One one-thousand, two one-thousand, three one-thousand.' That's when I turned my head toward Greer and spotted the ball coming toward Walker. I was already running towards him. It was sort of a high-arching pass. All I did was jump, reach up and get a hand on the ball."

Years later, Schayes would tell me, "Every time I happen to see Havlicek even now, I want to punch him right in the nose."

After the game, I thought my play-by-play call had been a good one. With so little time, the only fact I left out was that Greer's target was Walker. Little did I imagine that my frantic, high-pitched call would become famous. I began to realize that Boston fans enjoyed it when I heard it on TV and the radio almost every 15 minutes the next day. Fans would stop me on the street and ask me to do "that 'Havlicek stole the ball' thing for me."

And Havlicek was also very aware of the instant popularity of my call. "Everywhere I go, people are doing their Johnny Most imitations," he told me when I saw him the day after the game. I've heard it at least a hundred times already. Either I'm making you awfully famous or you're making me awfully famous. Which is it?"

Grinning, all I could manage to say was, "I think you deserve 99 percent of the glory. I'm satisfied with my little piece of the action."

As expected, the championship series with the Lakers was anticlimactic. Boston crushed L.A. in five games, winning by an average margin of 24 points per game. The title streak was now at seven, and the Celtics had kept their promise of giving Walter Brown a fitting tribute.

To my surprise, the notoriety of the call kept growing throughout the summer and throughout the years. I recall one night around 1 a.m. when I bumped into boxer Joe DeNucci, a friend of mine, outside Jack and Marion's restaurant in Brookline. "C'mon, Johnny," he said. "Do that call for me one more time. So there I was on Harvard Avenue shouting at the top of my lungs, "HAVLICEK STOLE THE BALL! IT'S ALL OVER! IT'S ALL OVER!" Next thing I know Joe is laughing, and my little bit of showmanship had drawn a crowd of about 50 people. "You gotta do it again," Joe yelled. "We want to hear it again, don't we?" Now the people are giving me an ovation, and I'm worried about some resident in the area calling the cops. "OK, but this is the last time." I repeated the call, received another ovation, and ran to my car before Joe could get the crowd riled up once more.

Much to my surprise, the publicity I received from that one call led to an interesting business opportunity. A month after Boston won the title, an investors group contacted me about becoming general manager of the New Bedford Sweepers of the Atlantic Coast Football

League. In return for my services, which included handling PR and being the team's public address announcer, I would receive a five percent stake in the team.

Because their season overlapped with the Celtics schedule, my duties principally would be to recruit players and negotiate their contracts. I did my research, conducted tryouts, and managed to sign five ex-NFL players, including two former Raiders, Riley Morris, a linebacker/defensive back, and James "Jetstream" Smith, a halfback. I also signed quarterback Charlie Green, a Patriots draftee.

On the field, the team enjoyed success, winning the ACFL title, with "Jetstream" leading the league in both yards gained and TDs. While attendance at the Sweepers' home games averaged an impressive 5,500 fans, the investors group claimed it was losing money. All I knew is that, on paper, the '65 Sweepers should have turned a decent profit. When the investors group folded the team after one season, a championship season, I was irate because the team's financial statement was pure fiction and showed that funds had "disappeared." I ended up not making a penny. In fact, I wasn't even reimbursed for my expenses. I loved the effort my players gave the team, I loved being the GM, but I came away from the experience with bitter feelings about some of the key people (I won't name specific individuals) involved in the Sweepers investors group.

Just before the Celtics began the '65-'66 season, I received a call from the radio station that broadcast the Bruins games. It seemed Fred Cusick, the Bruins' play-by-play man, had caught a severe cold and wouldn't be able to call the Bruins-Maple Leafs game in Toronto.

The sports director asked me if I had ever broadcast hockey.

"Oh, sure, I did a couple of Ranger games about 10 years back." Of course, I was lying through my teeth. In fact, I had never once called a hockey game and probably only attended a handful of Rangers and Bruins games in my entire life. "Could you catch a plane to Toronto in an hour? You'll handle the color commentator's job, with

Bob Wilson doing the play-by-play. We'll pay you $1,000 plus expenses, and you'd be doing us a huge favor."

I accepted the challenge and arrived at Maple Leaf Gardens an hour before game time. I thought I did a decent job—even though I wasn't entirely familiar with all the hockey terms. I decided to use some of my basketball phrases to describe the play. For instance, I had Boston defenseman Gary Doak "shooting from downtown." I also mentioned to my audience that Johnny Bucyk was "tricky dribbling" the puck in front of the goal. And when Bruins forward Bill Goldsworthy scored, I came up with this description: "He stops, he pops, goal. Boston takes the lead."

When I returned to Boston, I discovered that Weston Adams Sr., who was a Celtics hater because he felt Walter Brown abandoned the Bruins and because the Celtics were more successful than the Bruins, was irate that I had handled the color commentary. "Most made a joke of the broadcast," he told a few newspapermen. "He insulted the whole organization."

Adams even went so far as to call the Bruins' radio station and threaten to immediately cancel the Bruins' contract with the station. Personally, I thought I did a good job. Weston Adams was making a mountain out of a molehill because of his jealousy of the Celtics and their championships. To put it mildly, old "Westy," as his cronies called him, was a bag of wind and a bit of a jerk, which was proved by this incident.

There's a little more to the story of my one-game stint as the Bruins' broadcaster. It seems some members of the media recall my description of one play a lot differently than I do. Boston was on a power play, and one of the Bruins' defensemen took a shot from the point. As I recall the broadcast, I told my audience, "He hit the far right post." However, some insist my call was: "He hit the fucking post." Personally, I'm 99.9 percent sure I didn't used the four-letter word on the air. If I had used that particular adjective, old "Westy" would have sued me, and the FCC would have been knocking on my door.

Throughout the years, more than a few Bruins fans have told me they had heard the story about me using the "F-word" during the Boston-Toronto game. All of them ask me if the incident actually occurred. I just tell them, "Nope, I didn't." Then I pause for a second and add, "But if I did, screw it. There's nothing anybody can do about it now."

7

A CHANGE IN
COACHING LEADERSHIP

Prior to the '65-'66 season, Red announced that he would be retiring as coach at the end of the year. No "ifs, ands or buts." It was a typical bold Auerbach move. He was telling every team in the league: "If you want to beat me, this is your last chance." He believed in his team and his own abilities that much. In effect, he lit his championship victory cigar six months before the playoffs even began.

To replace the retired Heinsohn, Red signed fourth-year forward Don Nelson, who cleared waivers after being cut by the Lakers. "Why L.A. would let this guy go is a mystery. He played well for them. Then I thought for sure some team would claim him. Regardless, I'm just glad we were lucky enough to end up with him," Red told me. "Nelson knows how to play the game, he shoots the ball well, and he's an excellent passing forward. He's not the quickest guy, but he knows how to move without the ball and use screens. He's a good team guy, a good fit for what we need."

Besides his skills on the court, Nellie also proved to be the type of person who kept things loose in the locker room and on the road. For instance, there was a night in New York when Nellie, following a Celtics victory over the Knicks, went to the hotel bar for a couple of drinks. A Knicks fan who had played some college ball challenged

Nellie to a game of one-on-one for some money. At first, Don declined. But when the guy persisted, Nellie, now having downed a half-dozen drinks, accepted the bet. The two "competitors" got into a cab and drove to a lighted basketball court somewhere in downtown New York City. Of course, Nellie destroyed the guy and won the bet. Somehow Red managed to find out the next morning about Nellie's late-night victory.

As the team prepared to leave the hotel, Red approached Don. "Nice game last night," Auerbach said.

"Thanks, Red, I appreciate that," Nellie replied.

"Hey, I'm not talking about our win over the Knicks. You didn't play so great in *that* game. I'm talking about your goddamned 1 a.m. game against the guy you met in the bar. Next time save your energy for games that count."

The Celtics finished second to Philly in the East during Red's final year as coach. Cincinnati gave Boston a scare in the opening round by taking a 2-1 advantage in a best-of-five series. However, led by Sam Jones' shooting, we went on to win the next two easily. After Boston breezed past Philly, 4-1, the team faced L.A. for the championship. Before the series, Red had named Russ as his successor on the bench in order to end speculation and allow his team to concentrate on winning its eighth straight title.

The Lakers forced a seventh game at the Garden but seemed doomed when the Celtics took a 53-38 halftime lead. Although L.A. kept battling back, a Russell slam put the Celtics ahead 95-85 with only 30 seconds remaining in the game.

"Thirty seconds left and the Celtics are on the verge!" I yelled. "This crowd is going completely berserk!"

Despite Jerry West hitting two straight jumpers, Red invited Massachusetts governor John Volpe to light his victory cigar with 16 seconds remaining. That act not only ignited the stogie, it ignited the crowd, which began to swarm the court. "Now Havlicek has to call time, because he can't get the ball in play. The crowd has surged down the end line," I screamed. "They can't finish the game. The crowd in its delirium and joy has thrown things onto the court...Red Auerbach is being mobbed...officials are asking the crowd to please pull back. The crowd wants to get at these guys and hug 'em."

Remembering how Russell had hit the guy wire a year before in the final seconds, I still wasn't 100 percent confident of the outcome. "The fans are on the supports of the baskets," I reported. "I have never seen anything like this."

After the Celtics players were finally able to push back the fans, play resumed, as Red, still mobbed by well-wishers, was forced to jump up and down to get a glimpse of what was taking place on the court. What he saw was almost the worst disaster in Celtics' history. Four times in a row, Boston quickly committed turnovers.

With six seconds left, the Lakers' Leroy Ellis attempted a 14-foot jumper. "It's [pause] good," I announced, with panic in my voice.

"Four seconds left and the lead is down to *two points*!" I breathlessly screeched.

At that instant the Garden was almost silent. Red appeared angry and was shoving fans so he could see his players and they could see him.

"KC with the ball...gets surrounded...one second. THAT'S IT! ...it's all over. Havlicek got the pass and gets mobbed. It's all over," I exclaimed in a croaking voice. "What a finish...unbelievable... unbelievable."

In the locker room afterward, Red said to me, "I almost didn't see the end of my own coaching career. That's too crazy. Even when Russell hit the guy wire last year, I felt much more confident, because I had a timeout to set our defense. This time, though, things were out of control. My final game and I've never experienced a feeling like that. I couldn't help thinking, 'What a fucking nightmare. Just let me hear the damned buzzer.'"

I can only describe the '66-'67 season with a four-letter word— WILT.

Despite the fact that the Celtics had a deep, talented team and had added two veteran, hard-nosed competitors, center Wayne Embry and 6'8" rebounding forward Bailey Howell, to their roster, Philadelphia was the most dominating and most feared team in the league. Russell, the first black head coach in NBA history, did a hell of a job in directing Boston to a 60-win regular season, yet the 76ers won the division by eight games.

The reason: Wilt Chamberlain, for the first time in his career, was a complete, unselfish team player. He finally understood why Russ had enjoyed so much team success while Wilt had to be content with personal accolades. In leading the 76ers to an eventual championship, Chamberlain shot less but still took high-percentage attempts and rebounded as well as ever. More importantly, he blocked shots to his teammates and was constantly looking to pass to open players, including such talented outside shooters as Wali Jones, Hal Greer and Billy Cunningham.

Before Philly eliminated Boston 4-1 in the division finals, Russell confided in me, "I've never gone into a series without believing we would positively win. This is the first time I 'hope' we can win, but I can't honestly say I'm confident."

When the series ended, KC Jones retired, and Russ, after congratulating Wilt, told me on the air, "When you lose, you shut up. No excuses. It happened. You don't like it, but you have to accept it."

Havlicek was similarly candid with me. "Sooner or later, this was going to happen. It isn't the end of an era. It's the end of a string of titles. We start fresh in a few months. No one is lowering expectations because of this defeat. We know we can be champions again. It's the waiting which will be a killer."

Again, in '67-'68, the Celtics finished eight games behind Philadelphia. Fans questioned whether Russ, as player/coach, was too old or, even worse, whether he was losing his desire. The most frequent question I was asked was: "Is Russell 'loafing' his way through the regular season?" To be honest, he was conserving his energy for the playoffs. His goal was to play hard enough to ensure Boston would not face Philly until the division finals.

So, yes, there were games when Bill would go through the motions, take a seat on the bench, and let Wayne "The Wall" Embry do battle with some of the NBA heavyweights for most of the night. Russ, at 34, was more than four years older than Wilt, and from his point of view, he had to be rested and healthy if he was going to outplay Wilt.

His strategy worked, but Philly still managed to take a 3-1 series lead against the Celtics. No team had ever come back from that deficit to win a series. Adding to Boston's problems, two of the three remaining games were in Philadelphia.

Before Game 5, Embry and Havlicek came into the locker room together and wrote one word on the chalkboard—PRIDE. Considering the dire circumstances, I wasn't totally convinced any one-word motivational message was going to bail out the Celtics. But I hadn't lost faith in this team's desire and willpower, by any means.

A convincing Celtics win at the Spectrum raised my optimism for a series comeback. "This *is*, without a doubt, a proud team," I said on the air during the closing minutes of Boston's 122-104 victory. "Anything is possible now. If there's a team which now may be doubting itself, it's not the Celtics."

Using the pick-and-roll play repeatedly in the final two games, the Celtics had Wilt off balance. When Russell set a pick, Chamberlain was "in a pickle." He didn't want Russell to slide to the basket for a layup, and yet Russell's picks were creating open jumpers for both Havlicek and Sam Jones.

"Wilt would hesitate for just a fraction of a second," said Satch Sanders. "That's all we needed to make the play work time and time again."

The result: The Celtics took a 114-108 decision at the Garden and then put the 76ers away, 100-96, in Game 7 at the Spectrum. The phrase "Celtics Pride" was now forever the team's rallying cry. "At the time when Wayne and John wrote the word PRIDE on that chalkboard, if fans had seen it, they might have found it laughable," Satch said following the series win. "But what others laugh at, we believe in."

In that series finale, Wilt took only one shot during the entire second half. When I asked Russell if he thought Chamberlain had given up on his team by not shooting, Russ replied, "Why should I think that? Just look who was guarding him."

"Wayne the Wall" happened to overhear Russell's comment and half-jokingly interrupted, "Thanks for the compliment, Bill. You do remember that I was guarding Wilt for most of that second half." Russ laughed and then backtracked, "Well, yes that's true. But remember that I was the coach who was smart enough to put you in there to guard Wilt."

In the finals against L.A. the Celtics won the title, 4-2, at the newly built Forum, with Havlicek scoring 40, "Buckshot" Bailey Howell 30 and scrappy Siggy adding 22, along with twice diving head-first to the floor to recover loose balls to lead Boston's defensive effort.

On September 19, 1968, I became the proud parent of our fourth child, Andrea Leigh. Now my family was complete, and our home was a wonderful madhouse, with kids laughing, playing and crying from dawn to dusk. I loved every minute of it.

Late in the off season, Siggy found out that a trade had been worked out that would send him to the Hawks for guard Lenny Wilkens. Even though he would get a raise if the trade went through, he decided to hold out. It was a strange move for a player who wasn't seeking a raise and knew he wasn't going to get any guaranteed money. "Red can't trade me if I'm not signed," he told me. "I'm not going to sign until the Hawks trade Wilkens to someone else. I want to stay here. I'm a holdout until Red tells me he won't trade me." Now, that's the classic example how much being a Celtic meant to players.

Siggy, whom I occasionally called "Leapin' Larry," got his wish, and after Wilkens was traded to the Seattle Sonics, Red re-signed him. "It isn't that I wanted to get rid of Siegfried. I love his all-out hustle and enthusiasm. I just thought I couldn't pass on a chance to obtain a veteran point guard like Wilkens at that particular time," Red explained to me. "We have Sam Jones and [first-round draft pick] Don Chaney at shooting guard, but our only true veteran playmaker is Emmette Bryant. Russ loves Siggy's game, so we'll just have to see if we can get away with only one true playmaker."

This was the season I began using one of my trademark phases, "pulling a Stanislofsky flop." Stanislofsky was a Russian actor whose acting methods were overdramatic and exaggerated. So when guard Jerry Sloan of the Bulls blatantly began faking that he had been knocked down by the slightest bit of contact, I disgustingly referred to Sloan's ridiculous histrionics as a "pulling a Stanislofsky." By the way, I "borrowed" that phrase from Tommy Heinsohn, who was handling the Celtics' TV play-by-play at the time.

Russ was now pacing himself more than ever. He still could dominate a game with his rebounding and shot blocking, but Russ the coach was content to let Bryant lead Havlicek, Sam, Nellie and Siggy on the fast break while Russ the player trailed the play. As a result, the Celtics finished fourth in the East, the first time that had happened in 20 years. Yet no one seemed particularly worried. "Just wait," Sam, who had announced he was retiring after the playoffs, told me. "You're going to see Russ play like he's 25 instead of 35 once the money games start. That's been his game plan from the start. He wants our opponents to think of him as a tired old man."

Boston breezed through the East as Russ played 47 minutes a game in defeating New York, 4-2, in the division finals.

Then came the championship series against the mighty Lakers, who had acquired Chamberlain from the 76ers in the off season for three mediocre (and that's being charitable) players—center Darrall Imhoff, 6'2" shooter Archie Clark and 6'5" reserve swingman Jerry Chambers.

The Lakers had three 20-plus point scorers in Wilt, West and Baylor. They also had capable point guard Johnny Egan and outside shooter Keith Erickson in the starting lineup. Their sixth man was Russell's former backup, Mel Counts. Despite the fact that L.A. had no depth, Boston was given little chance of "upsetting" L.A.'s cocky, obnoxious and loud owner Jack Kent Cooke's self-proclaimed "greatest team ever assembled." I was quick to point out to my audience that "Cooke must have been locked away in an isolation ward at some mental institution while the Celtics had won 10 of the last 12 NBA titles."

The series came down to a seventh game at the Forum. Cooke went to great lengths to prepare for the Lakers' postgame celebration. Nets holding thousands of balloons were tied to the ceiling, the USC Trojan Marching Band was rehearsing "Happy Days Are Here Again" as the Celtics arrived for the game, and cases of champagne were stacked high outside L.A.'s locker room. The media were even handed press releases before the game which began: "When [not if] the Lakers win the championship..."

"What's this all about?" I said to my Laker counterpart, Chick Hearn.

"It's dumb, that's what it is," Chick candidly replied. "I can imagine what Russell is going to say to his team about this nonsense."

Russell, unbeknownst to me or anyone else on the team, with the possible exception of Sam Jones, had already decided he was retiring after the '69 finals. "I think Bill viewed Sam as the last of the old gang," reserve guard Mal Graham told me. "Even though he had another year remaining on a very lucrative contract, he just thought that the fun wouldn't be there any longer. We weren't a young team by any means, but I think Russ, without Sam being around, just would feel out of place." The Celtics, who led by as many as 17 in the closing seconds of the third quarter, saw their lead cut to nine with five and a half minutes remaining in regulation as Jerry West, who finished with 42 points, 12 rebounds and 12 assists led L.A.'s charge. Just when the Lakers seemed to have all the momentum, Wilt bumped his knee and took himself out of the game. Russell later told me, "I couldn't believe my eyes. My leg would have to be broken for me to leave the court just when you have a visiting team a bit shaken and nervous. You get a team worried, and that's when mistakes come one after another."

With Counts replacing Wilt, the Lakers closed to within a point with 3:07 on the clock. Now Wilt got up to return, but L.A. coach Butch van Breda Kolff told Chamberlain to sit back down on the bench. It was a classic moment: Here the final minutes of the championship game were being played and the coach and Wilt are cursing at each other. I give van Breda Kolff credit for having the grapes to basically accuse Wilt of quitting on the team, but I think common sense would have dictated pampering Chamberlain at that critical stage of the game and sending him in for Counts.

With 80 seconds remaining and the 24-second clock about to expire on the Celtics, Don Nelson grabbed a loose ball and heaved it towards the basket. "It's short," I said. "Hits the front of the rim and bounces straight up...and in. The ball went in after bouncing a full three feet above the basket...and now Boston leads by three." Nellie's shot settled down the Celtics, who proceeded to push the lead to six. A pair of free throws and a meaningless basket at the buzzer made the Celtics' 108-106 victory sound closer than it actually was.

"We busted their balloons," I screamed. "The USC Band is packing their instruments and all the champagne has suddenly gone flat. And then there's poor Wilt, who probably is icing his boo-boo right now while picking up a crying towel."

In the Celtics' locker room, Nellie admitted that his shot "didn't feel right. I just was hoping it would hit the rim so we might have a chance to get the rebound. It was a shit-assed lucky perfect bounce, but it still put two points on the scoreboard."

Boston's eleventh championship in 13 years was the first time in league history that a team won a title without ever having the homecourt advantage in the playoffs. As Russell said proudly, "We've had far more talented clubs than this one, but no Celtics team ever had more guts."

Speaking of guts, van Breda Kolff told me after that game that he knew he would be fired for not putting Wilt back into the game. "I thought Counts was playing hard and *wanted* to be out there. I know I'll be criticized in the media, and I know I'm a goner. But I think I made the correct decision."

Shortly after the Celtics' victory, the Lakers announced that van Breda Kolff was officially unemployed.

Russell announced his retirement by writing an article in the August issue of *Sports Illustrated* in which he explained that he had "lost his competitive edge." He reportedly was paid $10,000 for the exclusive. Not unexpectedly, he was roasted for doing so by the Boston media. I didn't see anything wrong with Russ' decision. If *Sports Illustrated* was willing to pay Russ, why shouldn't he have the right to announce his retirement any way he wanted to? I could understand why *Sports Illustrated* was criticized for "checkbook journalism," but I didn't blame Russ for selling the rights to the magazine.

8

HEINSOHN TAKES CENTER STAGE

Speculation ran wild in the media as to who would be the next Celtics head coach. Would Auerbach himself return to the bench? Would Red be able to coax Bill Russell into returning as player/coach for one more season? Or would Auerbach turn to another of his former players—Heinsohn and Sharman were the two candidates most often mentioned—to guide the '69-'70 club?

Red made every effort to convince Russell to change his mind; he didn't succeed. "I couldn't bring myself to beg the guy. Like myself, Russ wanted to go out a winner. I couldn't blame him for leaving on his own terms, even though I now had to find a way to rebuild this team at least a year earlier than I expected," Red said to me. "Still, it was tough to lose someone whom I still considered to be the best player in the NBA, even at age 35."

As the speculation increased, *Boston Record* sports editor Sammy Cohen, my mentor, asked me to write a column on whom Red should choose as Russell's successor. "To me, Tommy Heinsohn represents the closest total of Auerbach's coaching attributes of all the the ballplayers who have played for Red," I stated in the article. "Tommy will be an advocate of wide-open, firehouse basketball, with an occasional explosion of violence. Under Heinsohn, the Celtics will be a 'go to hell' ball club."

Eight hours after my column appeared in print, Red officially named Heinsohn coach. My friendship with Tommy aside, I was certain he understood the game and could communicate with the players. The only question was whether or not he would have the patience to rebuild a team that lacked a legitimate 30- to 35-minutes-per-game starting center.

Heinsohn decided to rely principally on seven-foot Hank Finkel, a three-year veteran whom Red had signed as a free agent. While "High Henry," as I nicknamed him, was neither extremely talented nor athletic, he was a favorite of mine, because Finkel was always the optimist. For instance, if he was matched against the Knicks' wide-body center Willis Reed, for instance, Hank would say to me beforehand, "I may get my ass kicked tonight, but I won't get outworked or outhustled."

During the first two weeks of the season, Tommy decided to experiment by starting rookie Steve "Stosh" Kuberski at power forward against the Baltimore Bullets. "This has been a day I'd like to forget," Steve told me afterward. "On my way to the game, I went to cash my first paycheck. It bounced, leaving me completely tapped out. Then, on the opening tipoff, Gus Johnson whacked me with an elbow to the side of my head. Boom, I had suffered a concussion. The rest of the game is a blank, even though I played about 20 minutes."

By the time rookie JoJo White returned from a stint in the marines and joined the Celtics in January, Boston had no chance of making the playoffs. Tommy had made the decision he was going to use the remainder of the season to develop Boston's young players—White, Kuberski, and second-year guard Don Chaney. Larry Siegfried went from starter to sixth man.

"I didn't like it at all," Siggy told me years later. "I sort of began going off the deep end. If Tommy had explained why he was making the change, I could have accepted it. Instead, he never said a word to me. I thought it was a demotion, plain and simple. In hindsight, which is always 20-20, I wish Tommy just would have told me he was making me the sixth man in order to give our younger players more experience. If he had just talked to me one on one, I would have had no gripes. Being sixth man for Boston might have extended my career by two or three years."

Instead, Siggy and the Celtics would part company at the end of the '69-'70 season.

The Boston fans became hostile as the '70 Celtics struggled to a 34-48 record. More often than not, they'd vent their frustration on "High Henry," who'd hear boos whenever the Celtics were losing badly at the Garden. For one of the few times in my career, I "lectured" my audience. "Booing 'High Henry' is totally uncalled for and absolutely unfair. Finkel isn't the Celtics' problem," I said. "The guy doesn't deserve this type of treatment. He's giving a hundred percent effort every night. His teammates appreciate his effort. Why can't you Celtics fans do the same? Johnny Havlicek, for instance, has told me he loves playing with Finkel because 'High Henry,' with those wide shoulders of his, sets the best picks John has ever seen. You won't hear a single Celtic ever criticize Hank's effort. It's ignorant to blame Finkel for this team's problems. He didn't ask to be Russell's successor. You're too knowledgeable to act like this."

Speaking of "High Henry," I should mention the time his five-year-old son, Dennis, singlehandedly caused the start of a game to be delayed.

It seemed Dennis decided to climb to the top of the backboard just before the Celtics walked onto the floor for warmups. For five minutes, Henry attempted to coax his son down, without any luck. Then Don "Duck" Chaney climbed up, but young Dennis, obviously enjoying his version of "Catch Me If You Can," managed to crawl across the backboard top and avoid capture. Finally, referee Earl Strom begged Heinsohn, "Please, Tommy, find a way to get 'Tarzan' down from there. This is embarrassing. We're going start 10 minutes late because of this little boy."

I then spotted an ice cream vendor and offered a vanilla cone as a bribe that eventually enticed Dennis to "take the bait." As Dennis reached for the cone, "Duck" grabbed him around the midsection and carried him down to safety and into the arms of his now-sweating dad.

During the third month of the college season, Red sent scout Mal Graham, who had been forced to retire as a player due to a physical ailment following the '69 championship, to evaluate Florida State center Dave Cowens.

"FSU was playing at Kent State, a small program. Cowens' team was on probation and couldn't play any games on national TV. They were also banned from all postseason play. I didn't think there'd be any scouts there except me," Mal said. "Well, there must have 20 scouts, coaches, and GMs there, all with their eyes on David."

When Graham reported back to Auerbach, he told Red, "I loved the kid. He's the best-jumping white man I've ever seen. He's tough, aggressive, strong, and quick."

I know the story of how Red scouted Cowens and, pretending to be disgusted at Cowens' play, stormed out after watching David play for only 10 minutes. It's true—but Auerbach wasn't the first coach or GM to pull that trick.

When Graham scouted Cowens, he sat next to Bob Cousy, who was then the head coach of the Cincinnati Royals. As Mal reported to Red, "I loved the kid. I've got to tell you, though, that Cousy was there, too. He walked out after watching Cowens for about five minutes. I asked him if he liked Cowens, and Bob just said, 'Nope, not one bit.'"

Red began laughing. "Look, Mal," Red said. "Cousy just was playing a mind game with you. He just wanted to throw you off track."

Two weeks after Graham's scouting trip, Red went to evaluate Cowens. He watched the game for two or three minutes, got up from his seat, and walked out, shaking his head as if to say, "I wasted my time. The guy is nothing special."

Pure bull, because watching David for just those few minutes convinced Red that Cowens was the one player in the draft who could be the foundation of Boston's rebuilding process.

The Celtics chose fourth in the '70 draft. Ahead of Boston were Detroit, San Diego and Atlanta. The Pistons made it clear they would draft 6'11" center Bob Lanier. San Diego, which could not afford the salary demands of All-America guard Pistol Pete Maravich, was not tipping its hand. Atlanta, though, definitely would take Maravich.

Prior to the draft, Mal clued me in. "Cowens is the guy we want, the guy we really need. We need a little luck because we don't know what the [San Diego] Rockets will do," he said. "Red couldn't even talk to them about a trade because then they might have started taking a closer look at whom we might want."

Moments later, San Diego announced it was taking Michigan's high-scoring forward, Rudy Tomjanovich. "Red Auerbach just jumped six inches off his chair," I reported. "He's actually smiling."

When Atlanta chose Maravich, Auerbach paused for a minute, leaned towards the microphone and announced, "Boston selects David Cowens from Florida State."

9

REGAINING THAT CHAMPIONSHIP FEELING

From day one, I loved watching Dave Cowens play the game. I'm not going to make any comparisons between his game and Bill Russell's, because they were two entirely different types of players. I'll say this, though: Cowens, with his high-energy, physical style of play and his soft, accurate 16-foot jumper, would have been the perfect power forward to play next to Russ.

After starting Cowens at power forward for the first few games, Tommy decided to see whether David, at 6'8 1/2" and 225 pounds, could handle the center position. "He loves the contact. He's totally unafraid, no matter whom he's guarding," Tommy said. "I just don't know if his body can take the nightly poundings he'll get battling guys like [Milwaukee's Kareem] Abdul-Jabbar, New York's (Willis) Reed, [Atlanta's Walt] Bellamy, and [L.A.'s Wilt] Chamberlain. David wants to be in the middle, so we'll find out soon enough."

Throughout his rookie year, Cowens played his best games against the centers who were three, four or five inches taller and usually 20 or 30 pounds heavier than he was. He utilized his quickness to outrebound them and his speed to score easy fast-break baskets, wearing down opponents in the process.

Although the Celtics failed to make the playoffs in David's rookie year, they did improve their record to a very respectable 44-

38. Cowens was his own toughest critic, which impressed me. "I fouled out of 15 games because I made some dumb mistakes. I passed up some easy shots and forced up some bad ones," he told me. "I won't make the same mistakes next season."

Despite Cowens' far too harsh self-evaluation, I thought he would be the runaway winner for Rookie of the Year. After all, he had averaged 17 points and 15 rebounds. So when it was announced that Portland guard Geoff Petrie and David had been named co-Rookies of the Year, I went ballistic. "It's an absolute joke," I told *Record American* reporter Ed Gillooly. "Sure, Petrie averaged almost 25 points a game. Big deal, it took him 22 shots a game to do it. He doesn't look to pass, and he's not even a mediocre defensive player. He's one-dimensional. How does that compare to David's many contributions at both ends of the court?"

When David heard about my remarks, he phoned me. "Hey, Johnny, don't worry about that best rookie award stuff," he said. "My only concern is helping this team win...thanks for speaking up, though. At least now I'm certain I got your vote."

Throughout his career, I admired David as both a player and a person. Some labeled him a bit "flaky." I viewed Cowens as someone who was determined to always be his own man. No doubt about it, David definitely had no use for his "celebrity status."

There are plenty of stories about Cowens' lifestyle. As a rookie, he lived in a one-room cabana/cottage on a Weston estate. In his spare time, David took a course in auto mechanics and loved tearing apart and then rebuilding engines as a hobby. One year he decided to learn the basics of sign language at the Framingham School for the Deaf in order to teach basketball to the students there. One night, wearing a cap pulled down to his eyebrows, he drove a cab in Boston, because he thought it would be a fun way of talking with average people about subjects other than basketball. When he relaxed, he preferred to go to working-class suburban taverns such as "The Happy

Swallow" in Framingham for a beer or two rather than get involved in the Boston social scene.

Call me "flaky," too, but I found David to be both down to earth and refreshing.

Only one month into the '71-'72 season, I realized the Celtics had an outside chance of challenging for a title. The old vets—John Havlicek, sixth man Don Nelson, and Satch Sanders—were comfortable in their leadership roles. Cowens was maturing rapidly, committing fewer fouls and using his speed and quickness to destroy one opponent after another. The starting backcourt duo of JoJo White, now a 23-points-per-game scorer, and Don Chaney, the defensive stopper, gave Boston perfect balance. With Hank Finkel, Steve Kuberski and "Hambone" Williams on the bench, Boston was well equipped to carry out Heinsohn's "Attack, Attack, Attack" game plan.

In my opinion, the Celtics lacked one key piece of the puzzle. "Tommy, Red needs to find you a guy who can give David some help on the boards," I mentioned to Heinsohn. "Hey, tell me something I *don't* know," he replied. "We've tried to get one, but it's not easy. Red's not going to give up a first-round pick, and we just don't have a top-notch scorer we're willing to trade for a quality rebounder. You know the old saying, 'Play to your strengths, and you'll hide your weaknesses.' Well, we're going to run every chance we get and hope David can keep dominating inside."

In March of '72, the Celtics traded the rights to guard Charlie Scott, whom Auerbach had selected in the seventh round of the '70 draft, even though Scott had already signed with the ABA's Virginia Squires, to the Phoenix Suns for "future considerations." No one could foresee that this "minor deal" would lead to another Auerbach coup a few months later.

Heinsohn's game plan resulted in a 56-26 regular-season record. In the playoffs, however, a veteran Knicks club had too many weapons, beating Boston, 4-1, in the Eastern Conference finals.

In the off season, the Suns sent their top rebounder, Paul Silas, to Boston to complete the Scott trade. "Red did it again," said JoJo at the start of training camp. "Here's a guy [Silas] who's an absolute animal under the boards. He's averaged 14 rebounds a game for Phoenix over the last two years, and he's shed 30 pounds this past off season. He's leaner and meaner than ever...and we're getting him for a player who has never played a single game for us. Red's not lucky, he's just smarter than everyone else."

In addition, Auerbach drafted USC's scoring guard, Paul Westphal, to add to the Celtics' backcourt firepower.

I couldn't believe Auerbach's uncanny maneuvers either. "With Silas here, David can force his man away from the boards by shooting that foul-line jumper of his. That will leave 'Tall Paul' [my new nickname for Silas] to just concentrate on grabbing the offensive rebounds," I said during the preseason opener. "And our rookie, 'Small Paul' [Westphal] can run and gun on the break when Chaney is resting on the bench. We're back in business, babe. We're going after championship number 12."

This was the season in which Cowens had a heated disagreement with the officials concerning the definition of a foul. Playing against the Houston Rockets, David was called for two charges against guard Calvin Murphy, who had pulled a pair of "Stanislavsky" flops. "C'mon, it's not like I'm beating up the guy," David yelled at official Jake O'Donnell. "I barely touched the guy. Murphy's acting like he got mugged, and you guys are buying it."

When the ball was put into play seconds later, David sprinted towards Houston guard Mike Newlin and whacked him on the shoulder with an elbow. Turning to the nearest official, he yelled, "NOW THAT'S A FOUL." From my broadcasting position high above courtside, I could hear every word as David made his point to the referees and the 13,909 fans at the Garden.

(Several years later, David had another dispute with officials concerning what was and what wasn't a foul. He was guarding

Chicago's 7'2" center, Artis Gilmore, and got called for two quick fouls in the first minute of the game. "If I can't put a body on Gilmore, he'll score 50 points," David told referee Don Murphy. Then David went over to Gilmore and told him, "Next time you get the ball down low, I'm not going to guard you. Just slam the ball in. I won't get in your way." At first, Gilmore didn't quite believe David. When he got the ball, he slowly backed in toward the basket and proceeded to dunk the ball uncontested. David, standing at the foul line with his arms folded, yelled at Murphy, "Is that how you want me to defend the guy?" For the rest of the game, David, in his own words, "clobbered" Gilmore every time he touched the ball and never was called for another foul.)

The Celtics, outscoring their opponents by an average of 8.2 points a game, finished the regular season with a club-record 68 wins, with Silas and Cowens combining for 29.2 rebounds a game. "Every one of us goes into a game just knowing those two guys are going to dominate the boards," Havlicek told me on the air. "As soon as the opposition shoots, we've got three guys running upcourt, because, in our minds, it's a certainty Dave or Paul will come down with the rebound. There's no way the opposition can catch up to us."

From the day he took over as coach, Heinsohn had patiently molded his team, piece by piece, into what was now an unrelenting fast-break machine.

Tommy's pet project during his first three years was transforming JoJo into a high-scoring, fast-break-leading playmaker. At Kansas, White was a pure playmaker who methodically walked the ball upcourt to set up the Jayhawks' halfcourt set offense. Seldom did he look to take charge of a game with his shooting. Now Tommy would change all that. "I want JoJo to push the ball upcourt every time he touches the ball. I want him to drive to the basket and shoot the jumper whenever he's open. He doesn't realize it, but he's a better scorer than a passer. And, let me tell you, he's a damn good passer."

Another Celtics championship seemed a foregone conclusion until disaster struck when Havlicek suffered a severely strained right shoulder in Boston's Game 3 loss to the Knicks in the Eastern Conference finals. John sat out Game 4, which the Celtics lost. Despite the injury, he returned, and, playing with a shooting arm he couldn't raise above shoulder level, scored 18 points as Boston took Game 5. Although the Celtics went on to force a seventh game at the Garden, New York attacked the "one-armed" Havlicek and cruised to an easy 94-78 victory. Afterward, Satch announced his retirement.

Despite the playoff disappointment, the league recognized the Celtics' achievements. Cowens was named MVP, and Heinsohn was voted Coach of the Year.

There was no need for major personnel changes as the Celtics prepared for another run for a title in '73-'74. "We've got one more year of experience under our belts, and we are still stinging from what happened to us against the Knicks," Heinsohn said. "This time I know any one injury isn't going to destroy our chances. My guys are that determined."

Boston's confident attitude resulted in a 56-26 record, best in the Eastern Conference. Late in the regular season, there was a minor confrontation between Tommy and "Hambone" Williams.

It seemed Williams had one too many beers on a plane ride and became loud and somewhat obnoxious. Heinsohn decided to talk to "Hambone" in an effort to get him to relax. However, "Hambone" refused to heed Tommy's advice. "Leave me alone," Williams said. "You act like you're the guy responsible for us winning. Hell, Ray Charles could coach this team and we'd still win the same amount of games."

Tommy gave Williams "The Heinsohn Stare," and went back to his seat without saying a word.

"Hambone's a little tipsy," I told Tommy. "Don't pay any attention to him."

"I'm ignoring him, but he'd better apologize tomorrow," Tommy replied. "He's not irreplaceable. He'll find that out if he thinks I'm going to let him get away with that kind of crap." (Three months later, "Hambone" was told his services were no longer wanted.)

In the playoffs, Boston cruised into the NBA finals, where they faced Abdul-Jabbar's Bucks. When I asked Heinsohn what his strategy would be, he responded, "I want Chaney to dog [Milwaukee point guard] Oscar Robertson from end line to end line. 'Duck' is six years younger than Oscar. He'll wear down Robertson. Our fullcourt pressure also will give Kareem less time to set up down low. David can handle Kareem one on one, but even Cowens can't stop Abdul-Jabbar's skyhook if Kareem gets 10 seconds to back in towards the basket and get comfortable."

Still, the experienced Bucks threatened to ruin Boston's title dreams when they won an emotional Game 6, 102-101, on a 17-foot Abdul-Jabbar hook from the right side in the closing seconds of double overtime at the Garden, forcing a showdown for the championship in Milwaukee.

Before that game, Cowens was in one of his "don't mess with me" moods. He started the game by hitting eight of his first 13 shots. On the defensive end, he held Kareem scoreless for the last seven minutes of the first half until there were only three minutes remaining in the third quarter. With Westphal, White and Chaney all contributing at both ends of the court, the Celtics pulled away to a 12-point lead early in the final quarter and never were challenged again.

"And the critics said we were underdogs," Heinsohn said to me in my postgame interview. "All I can say is I hope they call us underdogs again next year."

The Celtics seemed headed toward a second straight title after winning 60 games in the '74-'75 regular season

Entering the final day of the play, Cowens was leading the league in rebounding. However, the Bullets' Wes Unseld was only five rebounds behind him. The Celtics played an early afternoon game, and David grabbed 14 rebounds; the Bullets played later in the day. When Unseld's teammates learned how many rebounds Unseld would need to win the rebounding title, they purposely missed shots in order to allow their center to grab 21 caroms, enough to edge out David as the league's top rebounder. My old "enemy," Philadelphia statistician Harvey Pollack, surprised me by criticizing the Bullets for "artificially inflating" Unseld's rebound totals.

"It's a farce," Harvey told the media. "If I were Unseld, I'd be embarrassed." Auerbach, who hadn't spoken a word to Pollack since 1964 when Harvey claimed Boston's stats crew had "cheated" Wilt Chamberlain out of his true number of rebounds, immediately called Pollack and thanked him for his comments concerning the Bullets' unjust tactics.

Unfortunately, the Celtics were upset by the Bullets in the '75 Eastern Conference finals as Unseld and Elvin Hayes neutralized the inside game of David and "Tall Paul."

Following that disappointing result, Chaney, unable to reach an agreement with Red on a new contact, signed on with St. Louis of the ABA. Auerbach also dealt Westphal, who was demanding a salary exceeding White's, to Phoenix for Charlie Scott, whose move from the ABA to the NBA in '72 brought Silas to Boston.

The media questioned whether Charlie and JoJo, both big-time scorers, could co-exist in the same backcourt. "Two shooters, but only one basketball," said the *Record American's* Larry Claflin. "White and Scott will be fighting every game over who gets the most shots."

I wasn't worried, because JoJo had always been willing to do what's best for the team. "JoJo isn't liked by a certain few members of the media," Heinsohn told me on the air. "He can be cocky at times, but he produces. Whatever I ask of him, he does willingly. I will never understand why fans don't appreciate him more. Honestly, I think people pay too much attention to the so-called media experts rather than making their own judgments. If I need him to score, he comes through. If I need him to run the offense, he takes charge. If I would tell him to play center, he'd battle the big guys without ever backing down."

Scott, too, was willing to modify his game. He would shoot only when he had high-percentage opportunities. "In Phoenix, I was told to shoot whenever I got the chance. We didn't have a lot of other weapons. Here, though, we've got Cowens inside, Havlicek coming off screens for easy baskets, and Nellie driving the lane for his push shots. Outside there's JoJo and myself. There's great balance, and I'm not going to mess with that. I'll shoot only when I'm open, just like everyone else does."

Charlie wanted that championship ring—and proved it with his unselfish play.

Boston made it to the NBA finals and caught a break when Phoenix, a team that had only won 42 games in the regular season, upset Golden State, the league's defending champions, in the Western Conference finals, 4-3.

The series was tied 2-2 heading into what I rank as the most exciting, nerve-wracking game in history. The contest started off calmly enough as the Celtics built a 15-point halftime lead. But the Suns wouldn't quit. They battled back to force an overtime, which ended in a 101-101 tie.

The Celtics almost lost the game in the first OT when Silas signaled for a timeout, even though Boston had already run out of them. Official Richie Powers saw Silas' timeout request, but waved it off. "I wasn't about to have a game decided because of an error of that type," he told me after the game.

In the second OT, Phoenix forward Curtis Perry's 19-foot jumper gave the Suns a one-point lead with four seconds remaining—just enough time for Havlicek to bank in a leaner. As the Garden fans poured onto the court, I yelled, "That's it! Boston's pulled it out, 111-110, on John Havlicek's leaner!"

But the officials ruled there was still one second remaining. While Heinsohn pleaded his case with the refs and security personnel chased fans from the court, Westphal told Suns coach John MacLeod to call timeout, even though the Suns had none left. "I told him the timeout would only cost us a 'T' and we'd get the ball at halfcourt instead of having to go the length of the court. Even if Boston made the technical, we had a chance to tie with a final shot."

MacLeod agreed with the strategy. Admittedly, I was initially confused at what the Suns were trying to accomplish. "This is bizarre," I said. "Phoenix actually wants to be called for a technical." When I realized the Suns would inbound the ball at halfcourt, I became angry. "What a ridiculous rule. Why should a team be rewarded for calling an extra timeout and getting a technical? What sense does that make? It's ludicrous."

When White converted the free throw, Boston was up by two. Then the Suns set up for a desperation shot with their inbounds pass at midcourt. The ball came in to Gar Heard, some 25 feet from the basket. He spun and heaved an attempt that went through the net, beating the buzzer and forcing OT number three.

Boston, with four of its players already fouled out, then found an unlikely hero in reserve swingman Glenn McDonald, who had been in Heinsohn's doghouse for most of the regular season. His six points carried an exhausted Celtics team to a 128-126 win and a 3-2 series advantage.

"Everyone's a hero today," I said as the game ended. "I thought Boston had lost the game at least five times; I thought Boston had won at least 10 times. I've never seen anything like this. And I never will again."

In the game that clinched Boston's 13th title, it was Charlie Scott who fittingly led the Celtics to an 87-80 victory by scoring 25 points and 11 rebounds.

"I hope the fans appreciate Charlie and JoJo now," Heinsohn said. "All they did was give us 40 points and ten assists a game. That's a pretty effective backcourt in my book."

10

TWO YEARS I WOULD RATHER FORGET

Entering the '77-'78 season, I was cautiously optimistic about the Celtics' chances to capture their 14th championship. There were few off-season moves of note, with the exception of signing free agent guard Dave Bing. On paper, at least, Boston had talent and experience, with seven players having played in at least one All-Star Game.

After a 1-8 start, though, it was very evident Tommy Heinsohn was facing huge problems, because with few exceptions, the players weren't as distraught as I was. John Havlicek, at age 37, was working his tail off, running perpetually in zig-zag patterns to make use of his teammates' picks to find open shots. David Cowens was butting heads with the opposition night after night and winning his individual battles against taller centers. Cedric Maxwell showed no signs of having the rookie jitters. Off the bench, Kevin Stacom supplied energy, hustle and some unselfish offense. Unfortunately, the rest of team was the most inconsistent Celtics team I can recall.

"I'm embarrassed and confused," Havlicek said privately to me. "We're making three or four passes and still ending up with God-awful shots. There's no flow to our offense. I thought I knew this game. Now I'm not so sure. I thought we had other people on this team who knew how to play. One guy shoots, then it's someone else's turn, then someone else's. Guys just stand around waiting for the ball to come to them. If they're open, they shoot. All we end up taking is 18-foot jumpers. Nobody is looking for ways to get layups or easy 10-footers. It's pathetic. There's no movement at all. What's worse is that we're doing it game in and game out, which makes me think we don't even realize anything's wrong. Tommy tells us what were doing wrong, and either nobody is listening or nobody cares. It's one, or the other, or both.

"I don't think of myself as a great shooter or a great rebounder or a great passer. I've always been an opportunist. But with the way this team is playing, there are no opportunities, because we're not looking to work together to get the best possible shots. We settle for shots that the defense wants us to take."

By mid-December the Celtics had lost 18 games, and rumors began circulating that Tommy was about to be fired. "Hey, I'm a realist. I could be gone. I've tried everything to motivate these guys. I've tried kicking their ass at practice. I've met with each player one on one. I've let the players hold team meetings. I even stayed out of the locker room for an entire halftime when we were down by 20 points to New York," Heinsohn told me. "Nothing is getting through. I keep hoping no one is quitting on me or themselves, but the bottom line is that we seem to accept losing. It's killing me inside, because if we play as a team, we have the talent to win. What I'm seeing is a bunch of individuals all going in different directions."

Cowens was equally disgusted. "This is a new experience for me. It stinks. We have talented players who just aren't making use of their skills. I don't blame Tommy. You can't motivate guys who aren't bothered by losing because they're telling themselves, 'It's not my fault.' I'm not going to criticize this guy or that guy. It's a team problem," David said to me. "I've thought about our situation day and night, and all I can say for certain is that there isn't a sense of desperation to turn things around. Just once I'd like to see us play a physical, intimidating style instead of getting our asses kicked night after night. Just once I like to see us get mean on defense. Guys are scoring on us with layups, and we don't even lay a hand on them. That's inexcusable because we're supposed to be experienced professionals. *Professionals*—that's the key word. Teams don't show any respect for us. We're being viewed as patsies. And that hurts."

Auerbach tried to back Tommy by addressing the team. "I never thought I'd be saying this to a Celtic team," Red said, "but most of you guys are quitters who like to use half-assed excuses after every goddamned game." Then, according to Tommy, Auerbach really let off some steam. "There's a few basic reasons why you're losing. There's no fucking effort, no fucking hustle and no fucking teamwork. Too many of you are playing like you don't give two shits. You know who you are, and so do I. That's why you'll be someone else's headache pretty soon."

I reluctantly admit I knew there were players who were going through the motions, using false hustle to act like they were playing hard and then bitching about the coaching or their teammates. As Bing told me, "I went through a lot of losing seasons in Detroit. Once you start losing regularly, the blame game starts. No one takes responsibility. It's always somebody else's fault. Soon you have 12 guys who don't trust each other."

When I got a chance to talk with Red, he told me he wanted to dump at least three players. "When I come into the locker room after a game, I see guys checking out their own stats," he said. "If their individual stats look good, they're smiling and laughing—even though we might have lost by 20 points. It's enough to make me puke."

Red wanted to make roster changes immediately. He attempted to acquire players known for their hustle and toughness. Tops on his list was Houston's 6'4" guard Mike Newlin, whom I had always admired.

I had been friends with Newlin since 1970, his rookie year. Mike had been a Rhodes Scholar finalist who played the game with smarts and toughness. Somehow he had found out I wrote poetry, and he would usually seek me out an hour before game time and ask me to recite one or two of my works. I enjoyed interviewing him because he was such a student of the game, as well as being a student of history, which was one of my interests. Newlin was a blood-and-guts type of player, a true warrior. As I would tell reporters after Mike retired, "He was the greatest Celtic that never was."

I believed Mike's always competitive nature would have made him a perfect fit in Boston. As he told me, "I won't back down from anyone. I love to move without the ball, use picks, and take only high-percentage shots. I pride myself on never losing the mental game that is involved with basketball."

Fact is, Newlin came very close to actually wearing the green and white uniform. Houston GM Ray Patterson told me that on December 8 of '77, he and Red Auerbach had basically agreed on a deal that would have brought Mike to Boston. Unfortunately, the trade never took place, because on the very next day, Lakers forward Kermit Washington threw his infamous punch that crushed the face of Houston's star forward, Rudy Tomjanovich, creating a league-wide uproar and causing Patterson to put all personnel moves on hold.

When Boston went on a five-game West Coast trip in late December and lost every game, it was inevitable that Tommy was going to be fired. I didn't think it was fair, because even Red himself couldn't have gotten positive results from this particular group of players. Yet I knew it was necessary. "Yeah, Johnny, I'm gonna be history," Tommy told me. "You can't coach players who have no self-pride. All I'm asking is for effort, hustle and teamwork. I'm getting none of that from about three or four players. They're all in their own little isolated world. I know Red doesn't want to fire me, but [Boston owner Irv] Levin needs someone to blame." On January 2, 1978, Red met privately with Tommy and told him that his assistant, Satch Sanders, would be taking over as head coach.

Early in January, Red traded Charlie Scott to the Lakers for former Celtic Don Chaney, Kermit Washington (who was serving a

60-day suspension for punching Tomjanovich in the face), and a first-round draft choice. It was a good move, but the trade wasn't going to turn things around. Believe me, Scott was not the principal cause of the Celtics' numerous problems. He just happened to be one of the few players who actually had some legitimate trade value.

Soon a disgusted Havlicek announced that he would be retiring at the end of the season, and JoJo White's iron-man streak of 488 games came to an end when he no longer could tolerate constant pain in his heels.

In an interview with me, Cedric Maxwell talked about a lack of team chemistry. "The fans focus a lot of their hostility on [Sidney] Wicks and [Curtis] Rowe. I think that's a bit unfair," he said. "They came here from bad teams where they were basically the top scorers. All their teammates would look for them. They'd get to their spots, wait for the ball, and shoot, period. Here it's a more team-oriented offense. There's a lot more motion. It's a major adjustment for them and they're struggling to adapt.

"They're not bad guys. Curtis, in fact, gave me some good advice. He saw that I was trying to do too much too fast. 'If you get a couple of baskets and a couple of rebounds each quarter, there are plenty of nights you'll end up with a double-double. Just don't force things.' His words helped me. Contribute when the opportunities are there. That's how I've been approaching each game."

Not only was I finding it difficult to broadcast so many embarrassing blowout losses, I was again having major problems with my voice. I thought my career might be coming to an end, because I couldn't speak above a raspy, shaky, cracking whisper. The radio station decided to bring in Bob Lobel, a knowledgeable newcomer, as my partner so that he could take over the play-by-play whenever my voice gave out.

Bob did an excellent job, considering the fact that I was absolutely a miserable SOB as I sat in the booth listening to him handle *my* job. I'd try to make a comment every now and then, but my words were so inaudible that Bob would have to serve as my translator. He'd repeat my thoughts loud and clear, and I have to admit I thought he might be trying to show me up. Of course, that wasn't the case at all. But by this time, I was actually a bit paranoid and downright scared about my future as the Celtics' broadcaster. I must have seen no less than 10 throat specialists and they all came to the same conclusion: complete rest was the only cure. Being stubborn, I wasn't about to sit home and go stir crazy. Instead I temporarily cut down my cigarette habit from four packs to one and a half and went through three boxes of Luden's cough drops and a bottle of Robitussin cough syrup a day.

Somehow my home remedies got me through the season as I usually alternated quarters with Lobel. "Bob, I don't know which is tougher for me to handle, losing my voice or watching the Celtics look like a rag-tag semipro club."

"Johnny, don't worry so much about your voice, because this team is so bad that I doubt anyone in Boston is listening to us describing one disaster after another," Bob replied. And he was correct. I couldn't honestly blame the refs or the opponents' tactics for Celtic losses that resulted from too many players displaying what I knew to be blatantly false hustle.

As I've mentioned, individual stats are not usually an indication of how the Celtics fare as a team. However, during this disastrous season, they were difficult to ignore. Cowens grabbed one-fourth of all the Boston rebounds and led the team in scoring, assists and steals. Havlicek was third in scoring and second in both assists and steals.

When your center is by far the team's most effective passer and quickest defender, and your 37-year-old guard is the only other consistent effort player, it means too many players have a "me-first" attitude, something that went completely against Red's philosophy.

To make a long story short, the season's only bright spot came on April 9 when the Celtics held "John Havlicek Day." John walked into the locker room wearing a tux and told his teammates that he was wearing the tux because he wanted to go out with class. Then he told Satch that he wanted to play the entire 48 minutes. As I interviewed him, he put his arm around me and began, "I never pictured retiring from a Celtics team that lost 50 games, but there's nothing I can do about that now. I can say that I still have pride in how I played every game. I came into this league running, and that's how I am going to finish up."

Although John didn't quite play the entire game, he provided New England fans with memories they would never forget. During the pregame ceremony he received an eight-minute standing ovation. Then he proceeded to lead the Celtics to a 131-114 win over the Buffalo Braves as he scored 29 points and handed out eight assists. With 15 seconds remaining, Satch took him out of the game as John wiped away tears and waved to the Garden fans. As he walked to the bench, I commented, "There goes a man who demanded perfection from himself. And many nights he was indeed perfection personified. It's difficult to say goodbye to Johnny Havlicek, a man who gave his heart and soul to this team every time he stepped onto the court."

During the off season, I decided I needed a break from basketball. And when I got a call from the owner of the Plainfield, Connecticut, Greyhound Race Track asking me if I wanted to be the track announcer, I jumped at the opportunity, even though it meant a round-trip commute of three hours. After suffering through the Celtics' season of internal crises, I needed a challenge, something new and different. I had no experience with calling races. Still, considering my sports background, I figured the Plainfield job would be a piece of cake. Man, was I dead wrong.

As greyhound race spectators know, the finishes are usually so close that it's difficult to judge which dog wins with the naked eye. A fraction of a second can separate the winner from the dog who finishes third or even fourth. During my first couple of days on the job, I managed to make hundreds of enemies because my calls weren't exactly correct. Because I was never a gambler, I didn't realize the importance of calling the finish in precisely the exact order. As a result, when the dogs would cross the finish line, I'd excitedly announce: "It's two-four-seven in a wing-dinger." I didn't mean to imply that the two dog was first, the four dog was second and the seven dog was third. All I was trying to tell the fans was that those three dogs all crossed the finish line almost simultaneously.

However, some fans, believing I had called the exact order of finish, either tore up their tickets or threw them away. Then, when the official photo showed that the exact finish was really four-seven-two instead of two-four-seven, fans who had discarded winning tickets were ready to crucify me. In addition, fans who had placed wagers on the two dog, which I had announced as coming in first place, presumed they had won their bets when, in reality, their dog hadn't won the race. They would be standing in line waiting to cash their tickets when all of a sudden the tote board would light up, and they would discover their tickets were completely worthless.

Needless to say, track officials spent many hours listening to hundreds of bettors complain about my authoritative but totally erroneous calls. Before I even began my third day on the job, one of the track officials angrily lectured me. "I've been cursed at, spit at, kicked in the shins by an old lady, and called a crook," he said. "The next time you call one of your goddamned so-called 'wing-dingers' wrong, I'm going to personally introduce you to the mob of irate fans who want to use you as a human punching bag."

To my amazement, management decided not to fire me. They just pleaded with me to slow down my play-by-play and use the term "wing-dinger of a photo finish" to describe a close race. Gradually I got the hang of being the track announcer and even became a member of the track's public relations staff.

One of my PR brainstorms was to have a kennel owner name one of his greyhounds "Tommy Heinsohn." Having heard of my early problems at Plainfield, Heinie told me he'd be glad to go with me to the track and sign autographs and pose for pictures with "Little Tommy Heinsohn, the greyhound" if it would help me stay in the good graces of the track's owner.

Unfortunately, the dog named after Tommy ran more like a bassett hound than a greyhound and was soon disqualified from further competition. When I found out from the racing secretary that the dog's career was officially over, I called Tommy at his home in Natick. "Hey, I'm down at Plainfield. The kennel owner is giving you a present. You're getting 'Little Tommy Heinsohn' as a pet."

"I don't want a damned dog," Tommy told me. "Pets are just too much trouble to feed and walk."

"But they'll have to destroy the animal if you don't take him," I told Tommy, knowing he would never allow his namesake to be put to sleep.

There was a few seconds of silence on the phone. Then Tommy said, "Well, I'll take him in that case. He really is such a nice-looking dog."

"Good. I'll bring him to you tonight. I'll meet you at 2 a.m. at the Dunkin' Donuts in Natick," I said.

"Two in the morning? I must be nuts—but OK, I'll see you then," Tommy replied.

On my way back from Plainfield, I was involved in a car accident in Webster, Massachusetts, and had to be hospitalized overnight for minor injuries. I asked the Webster police to care for the dog, who was unharmed, and to call Tommy at his home and ask him to pick up the pooch. When the cops called Tommy, he was just a tad cranky. "I waited for two fucking hours at Dunkin' Donuts for Johnny, and now you guys are telling me that Most wants me to drive all the way from Natick to Webster just to pick up this animal?" Tommy said. "All right, I'll be there by 5 a.m."

When Tommy finally arrived at the Webster police station, he found "Little Tommy Heinsohn" resting comfortably on a cot in a locked jail cell. "Jesus, do I have to bail him out, too?" Tommy sarcastically asked. "I adopted this dog less than 10 hours ago, and already he's pissing on me."

Despite Tommy's protests, he ended up keeping "Little Tommy Heinsohn" and renaming him "Babe," who turned out to be the most lovable, obedient dog Tommy ever owned.

That summer I began hosting a weekend talk show on WROL. It gave me a chance to talk about the Red Sox and baseball, in general, as well as the Celtics. For each show, I would bring in a "special surprise guest." Being a boxing fan, my biggest thrill was reminiscing with such guests as my old friends Tony DeMarco, Joe DeNucci, and Paul Pender about their classic bouts. When callers began to ask questions of me and the guests by imitating my voice and expressions, it really planted a seed in my mind for what would become the "Johnny Most Sound-Alike Contests," which were held throughout New England in the mid-'80s.

Following the 32-50 season of '77-'78, there wasn't much hope for the future of the Celtics franchise. The media was attacking not only the players but also Red. Fans were hostile and pessimistic. With Havlicek retired and Cowens candidly voicing his frustration, the Celtics were, simply put, on death row awaiting execution.

Red's hands appeared to be tied. There weren't any major deals to be made, because Auerbach wasn't about to panic and trade either Cowens or Maxwell. And there wasn't anyone available in the draft who could immediately change the bleak outlook for Boston.

Auerbach had a plan, though. It would take some luck and finesse, but if he could pull it off, Red knew he would have at least a fighting chance to bring the franchise back to respectability in a relatively short period of time. He hoped to draft Indiana State forward Larry Bird, who had a year of college eligibility remaining and had told everyone he intended to stay in school rather than turn pro.

The problem Red faced was that the Celtics had only the sixth and eighth picks in the draft. Would Bird still be available that late in the draft? The draft certainly wasn't particularly deep in talent. The big names were UNC point guard Phil Ford, power forward Mychal Thompson of Minnesota, NCAA champion Kentucky's center Rick Robey, guard Ron Brewer of Arkansas, Montana's 6'5" point guard Michael Ray Richardson, underclassman Reggie Theus of UNLV and two-time NCAA scoring leader Freeman Williams of Portland State.

The teams drafting ahead of Boston were Portland, Kansas City, Indiana, New York and Golden State, respectively. Although it appeared that Bird would be an ideal choice for the Pacers, word was that Indiana wasn't interested in him for several reasons. Like the Celtics, Indiana's club needed help immediately because their attendance figures were the lowest in the NBA. Secondly, the Pacers were well aware that if they drafted Bird, they would have to pay him a huge salary, even as a rookie. Fact was, the Pacers, a limited partnership with limited funds and an extremely small fan base, didn't think they could afford Bird.

A few days before the draft, I talked to Celtics guard Kevin Stacom about the possibility that Red would draft Bird if he was still available at the sixth spot in the draft. "It'll take a lot of balls," said Kevin. "The fans are fed up that we've struggled so badly, and the media has been taking a lot of potshots at Red. The average fan wants to see the team make changes that will produce more wins right away, not a year from now. If Red does get Bird, I don't know what the reaction will be. You know Red, though, he doesn't give two shits about the opinions of the media, the fans or his critics.

"There are a lot of NBA coaches and general managers who have openly questioned Bird's potential. Some say he's too slow defensively. I've heard coaches say his lack of quickness will make it almost impossible for him to get his shot off against good defenders. Then there's also the fact that Indiana State's competition isn't exactly on a par with teams like North Carolina, Kentucky, Indiana, and so on. Personally, I think Bird will be a hell of a pro because he's so smart and does so many things well. I've watched him make incredible passes, hit 25-foot shots consistently, and even outrebound centers. As a player, I'd love to have a guy like him on the court with me."

I had more than a hunch Red was praying Bird would be available. Sure, he knew that if he did end up drafting Bird, it would mean another frustrating season for the Celtics because Larry would still be 1,000 miles away at Indiana State. However, by now I had learned that Red never panics and was always a long-term planner.

An hour before the draft, Auerbach privately confirmed my prediction. "If Bird's still available when we pick [in the sixth position], I won't have a choice to make. I've got to take him," he told me. "I know that he can shoot, pass and rebound. Plus, anyone can tell that the kid knows how to play the game. He's going to be a good one, absolutely."

As the draft got under way, Red was still concerned that the Pacers or perhaps Golden State might select Bird. Fortunately for the Celtics, the five teams drafting ahead of Boston all took a pass on Larry. Portland took Thompson as the first overall pick of the draft. Then Kansas City selected Ford. When the Pacers announced they were selecting Robey, Red was relieved but still not reaching into his jacket pocket for a victory cigar. The Knicks followed by taking Richardson, who reminded me of Clyde Frazier because of his defensive skills and his passing game. In my mind, the biggest surprise of the draft came when the Warriors opted to take Purvis Short of Jackson State. I knew he had a reputation of being an excellent shooting forward, but I never thought he'd be taken ahead of Bird or even Theus.

Needless to say, Red had a sly smile on his face as soon as Golden State's choice was announced. Then, taking his time, he leaned back in his chair and slowly declared, "Boston selects Larry Joe Bird of Indiana State."

To me, it was almost miraculous how Larry ended up just falling into Boston's lap, especially after all the times Red had snookered the entire league with his wise draft picks and his free agent acquisitions.

Just look at the Hall of Fame-caliber players Red had managed to "steal" from all the NBA's GMs over the years, either through the draft or by way of free agency: Bill Russell, Bill Sharman, Cliff Hagan, Andy Phillip, KC Jones, Sam Jones, Dave Cowens (chosen fourth in the 1970 draft behind Bob Lanier, Rudy Tomjanovich and Pete Maravich), John Havlicek (chosen seventh in the '62 draft). That's not even mentioning such great acquisitions as Arnie Risen, Jim Loscutoff, Satch Sanders, Don Nelson, Paul Silas, JoJo White, Wayne Embry and Charlie Scott.

And now the "Hick from French Lick" had joined the list of Auerbach coups.

After the draft, I interviewed Red and he admitted he had never seen Bird play in person. "But I watched him enough on television to know that he's going to be an excellent pro."

Then I asked Red if he had a contingency plan in case Bird had been chosen in the top five. "You always have to have a 'Plan B.' If another team had grabbed him before us, I was prepared to offer the sixth and eighth pick for him or the sixth pick and a player other than Cowens or Maxwell from our roster. I liked Bird a lot, but given our situation, I wasn't going to give up the store to get him.

"All these guys who claim he's too slow don't know what they're talking about. Nellie was slow, but he knew how to use a pick to get open. He knew how to fake. He knew how to get position on defense. I'll take a real smart, slow guy over a dumb, quick guy every time. I don't even think Bird is all that slow. He's got sneaky moves on offense and great anticipation when it comes to rebounding and defense."

The similarities between the drafting of Bird and the drafting of Russell were numerous: other teams had to pass on drafting both players in order for the Celtics to draft them; both players were not going to be available to play for Boston immediately; both players, according to many so-called experts, were not considered automatic future MVPs.

Many years later, Red looked back on his drafting of Bird. "All I definitely was a hundred percent sure of was that he could shoot, pass and rebound. What I didn't know was how great a rebounder he would be or how great a passing forward he would become. And I had no way of knowing that he would have the greatest work ethic of anyone who ever played the game," he said. "In a way, drafting Larry was like drafting Russell. I knew Russell could rebound and start the fast break for us. Basically, that's what I expected of him. I never could have anticipated that Russ would be the greatest rebounder, team player and shot blocker of any center I've ever seen."

Along with Bird, Red chose Freeman Williams with the eighth overall pick. As the draft was taking place, the Celtics were also busy finalizing the contract of free agent center Kevin Kunnert, whom Red envisioned as a capable backup for Cowens.

While the moves were good cause for long-term optimism, the bottom line was that I, along with the Celtics and fans, were still faced with another boring year of losing.

The utter turmoil surrounding the team entered the "Twilight Zone" when Celtics owner Irv Levin and Buffalo Braves owner John Y. Brown, who previously owned the now-defunct ABA's Kentucky Colonels, decided to swap franchises at the league meetings held in early July. Levin moved the Braves to San Diego and renamed them the Clippers. Brown, who would keep the Celtics in Boston, also negotiated a multiplayer trade as part of the franchise swap. In the trade, which didn't become official until a month later, San Diego received forward Kermit Washington, Kunnert, Freeman Williams, and Sidney Wicks. In turn, Boston received forward Marvin "News" Barnes, shooting guard Billy Knight, and former All-Star guard Tiny Archibald, who had sat out the entire '77-'78 season due to a torn Achilles tendon.

Red was stunned, because prior to the public announcement, neither Brown, whose principal claim to fame was being a co-owner of Kentucky Fried Chicken, nor Levin had the courtesy to inform him of the franchise exchange or the multiplayer trade. One week after the deal was made, Red, irate and embarrassed, accepted a long-standing invitation from Knicks owner Sonny Werblin to come to New York and discuss the possibility of becoming president of his club.

I called Red when I heard he was going to meet with Werblin. "You can't do this," I said. "You *are* the Celtics. If you leave, I couldn't stay in Boston. Do you think Cowens would stay if you left? Do you think Havlicek or Heinsohn or Sam or KC or any of your players would ever want to be associated in any fucking way with this organization again? Red, do you honestly believe Satch, a man of principles, would stay on as head coach if you quit? This team is in trouble. You're the only one who can rebuild it. Your former players know it, and most importantly, the fans know it. If you leave, all those championship banners will mean zilch."

"Do you think that deep down I want to go to the fucking Knicks? I've been their enemy for more than 30 years. But I can't put up with this amount of pure bullshit," Red replied. "I don't mind taking criticism—but only if I'm the guy making the decisions. I'm not going to be a stooge for John Y. Brown, a guy who obviously thinks he knows more about basketball than I do. I respect Werblin. I know he'll give me the power to run his team my way, without any interference. I don't want to leave, but under these conditions, I can't stay here and be humiliated any further."

Werblin offered Red a four-year deal worth more money than any pro basketball executive had ever been offered. The *New York Post* reported that Auerbach would sign a contract within three days. I immediately called Marty Glickman and asked him for help in finding another job, preferably in New York. "If Red goes, I'd lose every bit of enthusiasm for working for this fucking train wreck of a team," I said. "At least with Red here, I know he'd find a way to rebuild the Celtics into winners—in spite of that ass, John Y. Brown."

"I know it's a bad situation. I'll talk to Werblin and a few other people for you," Glickman said very calmly. "But for now just sit tight and keep your mouth shut about leaving, because I still think Red may change his mind. It's not a done deal yet."

Havlicek called Red and told him that he wouldn't allow his uniform number to be retired if Red left Boston. Heinsohn, who himself had been dismissed by Auerbach less than a year earlier, called for a fan boycott if Red left. Even Bill Russell phoned John Y. Brown and advised him, in no uncertain terms, to show Red the respect he deserved. The support from fans and players made Red hedge on whether to abandon ship. A stern pep talk from his wife, Dorothy, convinced him to rethink the pros and cons of joining the Knicks.

Auerbach met once more with Werblin in New York—but not before he got together with Marty, who told Red that coming back to New York 42 years after leaving his parents' home in Brooklyn wasn't going to bring him happiness. "You're a Boston institution. You'll always be perceived as the enemy here, even if you run the Knicks organization," Marty said. "The fans here not only won't accept you, they'll be rooting for you to fail. Lay down the law to this Brown guy. He can't be so stupid he doesn't know by now that he's about to lose you, his number one asset."

Red followed Marty's advice and sat down with Brown, who agreed to consult with Red on all Celtics personnel moves. While John Y. refused to give Red total control of all personnel moves, the new arrangement was enough to convince Auerbach to attempt to ride out the storm in Boston.

While my professional situation had stabilized, my personal life was falling apart. I had moved out of the house in Wayland for good. My greatest regret about the separation and eventual divorce was the fact that now I wouldn't be able to spend as much time with my children as I had in the past. No matter whether you're a player, coach, trainer, writer or broadcaster, the constant travel and hectic game schedule takes its toll on many marriages. During my marriage, Sandra received little help from me in taking care of the children. When I did get a rare break in my broadcasting schedule or during the summers, I spent all of my time playing with the children, taking them to movies or parties or other events. There's no question, Sandra handled all the tough tasks of the day-to-day raising of our children. Eventually, our relationship was not a good one for the two of us or our kids.

As the '78-'79 season began, Brown, who had decided when he became owner of the Buffalo Braves that he was an "instant expert" in the art of deal making, continued to wheel and deal as the owner of the Celtics. I don't know if John Y. actually kept his word by consulting with Red, but I am sure the stupid SOB must have ignored almost every single one of Red's opinions. For instance, one of Brown's first moves was to "pull off" an off-season trade with Indiana for 6'4" shooting guard Earl Tatum, a good guy but a mediocre player. The price tag for obtaining Tatum: $50,000 and a first-round draft choice. Needless to say, Red was not doing cartwheels after being informed of the acquisition. (Luckily for Boston, Red was able to quickly unload Tatum, who played only three games as a Celtic, to Detroit for a smart veteran guard by the name of Chris Ford and a second-round draft pick.)

After the Celtics lost 12 of their first 14 games, Red reluctantly dismissed Satch as head coach. Always a true gentleman, a disappointed Sanders told me, "I can't say I'm shocked. We weren't winning, and obviously Mr. Brown doesn't have much patience. I just wish that I had some say in who I wanted on this team. There were just so many changes in personnel over the 10-month span I was head coach that I couldn't establish specific roles for my players. I didn't know who would be on the team from week to week. Every trade we made forced me to alter my coaching strategy. Every trade meant players' roles had to change.

"A coach's strategy has to revolve around the strengths and weaknesses of his players. Those strengths and weaknesses would change with each personnel move that was made. All the moves confused the players. Each young man on this team started to believe he'd be the next to go. Worse, I couldn't reassure any of them they wouldn't be next. When you make so many moves, it makes the coach's job impossible, because one can't make instant evaluations and instant lineup changes and still expect to achieve immediate positive results."

Much more surprising than Satch's firing was Red's decision to name David Cowens, at age 30, as player-coach. As a player, David gave his entire heart and soul to the Celtics. He demanded so much of himself that I questioned whether he could handle the challenge of motivating players who didn't possess his will to win or his work ethic.

Cowens attempted to convince me (and probably himself) that he was realistic about assuming the added responsibilities of being head coach. "I'm not taking this job with the notion that I can perform miracles. I'm as frustrated as anybody about our situation. I don't have a bunch of solutions," he said to me privately. "You and I know this team has a few guys who just don't give a crap. Well, at least by taking this job, I can sit their butts at the end of the bench and use players whom I know will work hard. To me, that's a good first step. I'm not sure at all about my ability to coach. I'm taking the job because it gives me more of a say in how we can become more competitive. I'm going to be in a position now to change things I know are wrong with this team. I'm not a dreamer. I know I'll make mistakes, plenty of them. I know there are no easy answers to the problems we have."

If there was one thing I was sure of, it was that David would lead by example when he was on the court. How the players would respond to his new authority was a major question in my mind. David unquestionably deserved the players' respect, but would he get it? Would John Y. Brown stop meddling with the personnel? Doubtful. Could Red coexist with a know-it-all phony of an owner? No way.

When it became apparent by mid-December that the Celtics were going nowhere in '78-'79, Red began what he thought would be a systematic long-range rebuilding plan. First, he sent Dennis Awtrey, a hard-nosed backup center whom he had acquired in October, to Seattle for cash and a first-round draft pick. A month later, Red provided Cowens with rebounding help when he traded Billy Knight for Indiana's 22-year-old rookie center Rick Robey. Shortly before the trading deadline, John Y. Brown, ignoring Red's wishes to trade JoJo White to a contender, unceremoniously sent the veteran guard to Golden State for a draft pick.

At that point I was at least somewhat encouraged about the future, because Boston would, in all likelihood, have Larry Bird, Robey and three first-round draft picks to give Cowens, Maxwell and Co. some desperately needed help.

By March, the Celtics had made six trades and signed three free agents. The team was floundering, and I was now wondering if Larry Bird, knowing how utterly chaotic things were in Boston, would want to play here. After all, Red had to sign him before the '79 draft or lose his rights.

Right around that time Cedric Maxwell and I had a very candid, very private conversation concerning Cowens as coach and the future of the Celtics. Although only a second-year player, Max was wise beyond his years. "There's no stability. I don't know if I'll be here tomorrow, and a guy like Dave Cowens probably doesn't care if he coaches one more day, given the circumstances," Max said. "Dave is being Dave. He's working as hard as a coach as he does as a player. He doesn't sugarcoat things. He's very blunt, very opinionated. Guys know where they stand with him. He doesn't cater to anybody. He's inexperienced as a coach, and he's anything but a diplomat. Sometimes I think a coach has to hold in his emotions and frustrations. Still, I admire how he won't give up on himself or this team.

"The bottom line is you can't even expect a great jockey to win a race if he's riding a lame horse. And as a team, we're as lame as you can get. There's guys who have closed the books and given up, there's guys partying every night, there's even one or two guys using drugs. It's no secret. Drugs are a problem throughout the league. I survive because I'm my own man. I've never tried drugs, and I never will. I've never been a guy who follows the crowd. I go out of my way to stay out of trouble. I have my own circle of friends outside of basketball. I'd rather read or relax than go to some wild party."

Max, who lived in Framingham, then told me about the night he was watching TV in his apartment when a downstairs neighbor knocked on his door. "The guy was with an Atlanta Hawks player, Tom Henderson, and a Celtics player whom I won't name. We had a game the next night against the Hawks at the Garden, so I didn't think that much of seeing Henderson and one of my teammates at my door. First, they asked me for baking soda. I was so naive that I thought they must be baking a cake or something. Then they asked me if I had any ammonia. Damn, I thought to myself, why would three guys be cleaning at 11 o'clock at night? I was just a sheltered 22-year-old who had no idea that baking soda and ammonia were two ingredients used in freebasing. Here it was the night before a game and two opposing players are busy making drugs." Cedric's revelations didn't startle me. I knew the use of drugs was a growing concern around the league.

As Marvin Barnes admitted months after the fact, he was one Celtic who had used drugs during the '78-'79 season. What a waste of talent. I really liked Marvin as a person and a player. In fact, it's my opinion that had he not used drugs, he could have become one of the most popular and most exciting players in Celtics history. He had that much talent and charisma. Although he was constantly late and had a history of personal problems and run-ins with the law, his Celtics teammates, with the exception of Cowens, tolerated Marvin because he was a great guy to have on your side. Barnes' outgoing, charming personality also made him a favorite of John Y. Brown, for whom he had played as a Buffalo Brave.

"Marvin is basically a very lovable guy. He's a friend to everyone, from the ballboys, to the equipment manager, to the trainers. His teammates appreciate him because he always has their back," Kevin Stacom, who played with Barnes at Providence College, told me when Barnes first came to the Celtics. "He's very protective of everyone. He's a competitor who'll rebound, run the break, and score. I've known him for eight years, and I know him as a kind-hearted, generous person. His problem is that he sometimes listens to and trusts the wrong people. He thinks everyone is his friend, and because of that, people have led him down the wrong path in the past."

During his first two months as a Celtic, Marvin put up some impressive numbers. I, for one, thought he was going to have a positive impact on the team. Interviewing him was always enjoyable. "I'm gonna get a double-double tonight," he would say. "No, make that a triple-double. I'm in one of my shot-blocking moods. If we win— and we will—I'll pay for all the kids' ice cream next game. You can tell the Garden right now they can send me the bill. You get free ice cream, too, Johnny. Have a couple of popsicles on me. They're better for you than all those cigarettes."

By late January, though, Marvin's ice-cream giveaways had melted away. He had been missing planes, skipping practices and acting irrationally. I, along with Stacom, attempted to warn him that Red and David were fed up with his antics. "You're throwing away your opportunity here," I told him. "If I can see that you're using drugs, then everybody on the team knows it, too. You're only fooling yourself if you think people don't know you have a bad problem. If you want my help, I'm here for you. I care about you. So do a lot of your teammates. I bet even John Y. Brown will help you if you ask him."

"Thanks, Johnny, but I'll be all right," Barnes said. "I'm not perfect. I've slipped a little, that's all. I'm fine now, though."

However, less than two weeks later Marvin missed the team's plane flight from Detroit to Boston and failed to show up that night

Johnny, at age 14, standing in front
of his Bronx apartment building.
Photo courtesy of the Most family

Johnny gives his John Wayne
imitation with both guns drawn.
Photo courtesy of the Most family

A young Johnny during his high
school graduation.
Photo courtesy of the Friedman family

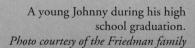

Johnny (second from left, bottom row) with his fellow
crew members in a photo taken in Canosa, Italy, in 1945.
Photo courtesy of the Most family

With son Jamie behind him, Johnny
plays with two-year-old Rob in 1965.
Photo courtesy of the Most family

Behind the microphone during
Brooklyn Baseball Corporation's
broadcast of a Dodgers game at
Ebbets Field in 1950. *Photo
courtesy of the Most family*

Red Auerbach pays tribute during a ceremony celebrating Johnny's 20th anniversary with the Celtics. *Photo courtesy of the Most family*

Coach Most delivers instructions to his Pop Warner players during a timeout. For eight years, Johnny not only coached but was president of the Wayland Pop Warner League. *Republished with permission of The Globe Newspaper Company, Inc.*

In 1972, Johnny and his dad. *Photo courtesy of the Most family*

Expert commentator Al Grenert
and Johnny pose for the camera.
Photo courtesy of the Grenert family

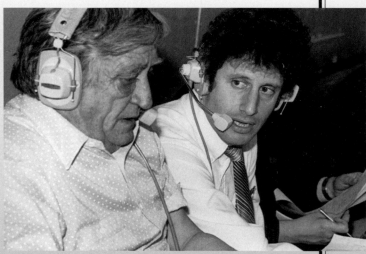

Johnny with color commentator Rick Weitzman, shortly
after their verbal battle with McFilthy and McNasty.
Photo courtesy of Noreen A. Murphy

Johnny and Lakers radio voice Chick
Hearn mug it up for the camera. The
two broadcasters were, in actuality,
good friends. © *Steve Lipofsky*

Jim Pansullo, color commentator for "Havlicek Stole the Ball," and Johnny pose for a photo. *Photo courtesy of Richard R. Maclone*

High above courtside with young color commentator Bob Lobel when Johnny's voice gave out. *Photo courtesy of the Most family*

Johnny with color commentator Glenn Ordway in 1985. © *Steve Lipofsky*

Always obliging to every fan, Johnny signs autographs at courtside. © *Steve Lipofsky*

Danny Ainge, Larry Bird, Johnny and Red relax during a break for filming of Red's instructional video, "Winning Basketball with Red Auerbach and Larry Bird." *Photo courtesy of the Most family*

Posing with Kevin McHale, dressed as the Statue of Liberty, Johnny relaxes on a Celtics summer cruise in 1985. *Photo courtesy of Jan Volk*

Kevin McHale cracks a joke during a roast for Johnny. © *Steve Lipofsky*

Larry Bird congratulates Johnny during a ceremony in which a piece of the Garden's parquet floor is presented by Bird to Johnny. © *Steve Lipofsky*

Responding with a raised fist to a standing ovation after his return to the broadcast booth following recuperation from a stroke, Johnny salutes the Garden crowd. *Republished with permission of The Globe Newspaper Company, Inc.*

Red Auerbach fondly greets Johnny Most during a ceremony honoring the Celtics broadcaster as Tommy Heinsohn looks on. *Republished with permission of The Globe Newspaper Company, Inc.*

An emotional Johnny wipes a tear from his eye during his retirement ceremony. *Photo courtesy of the Patriot Ledger*

A proud Johnny Most displays a microphone lapel pin presented to him by WEEI. The ring he is wearing represents the 16 Boston championships. It was presented to him by Red Auerbach at Most's retirement ceremony. *© Steve Lipofsky*

for a game at the Garden. He was promptly waived by Red, who, by the way, had warned John Y. Brown during preseason that Barnes would eventually be a disruptive influence on the team.

Years later, Bill Walton, who is also one of Barnes' friends, would tell me, "If it hadn't been for the drugs, Marvin could have been an All-Star, maybe even an MVP of this league. He had that much ability. Marvin was the second pick of the NBA draft in '74 and the first pick of the ABA draft. He was as dominating a college player as I ever saw. His problems really began when he chose to play in the ABA instead of the NBA. The ABA needed big-name players, so they let Marvin get away with breaking every team rule that existed. All they cared about was that he showed up for the games. They never disciplined him. From that point on, Marvin just self-destructed."

Walton also told me that during the summer of '79 he allowed Marvin to stay at his home in San Diego for three weeks while he was on a vacation in Mexico. Marvin was working out with some of the Clippers, and Bill was happy to provide him with a place to stay. However, when Walton returned home, he received a call from the local liquor store. It seemed Marvin had charged more than $2,000 for booze and put it all on Bill's tab. "I wasn't angry about the bill. I could afford the cost," Walton told me. "I was angry that Marvin wasn't serious about getting back into the league. I thought he was finished with the drugs and the booze. He told me he would pay me back, and I know he really meant it. Being a realist, though, I knew my two grand was lost money. I also knew Marvin just wasn't mentally strong enough to salvage his career. It was a shame, because he had so many good people willing to help him. He just wouldn't let them."

Five days after Red had gotten rid of Marvin, almost his entire rebuilding plan was sabotaged. John Y. Brown's wife and former Miss America, Phyllis George, convinced her henpecked hubby that the Celtics should attempt to acquire Knicks center Bob McAdoo, a player she admired. Phyllis unfortunately made her pitch to John Y. during a dinner in New York with Knicks GM Eddie Donovan and owner

Sonny Werblin, who were like two sharks circling their victims. Two days later, a deal was formally announced. The 28-year-old McAdoo went to the Celtics in exchange for three first-round draft picks. For the second time in two years, Red, who was kept in the dark about the trade, was ready to submit his resignation.

Publicly, Red held his temper. Privately, he was ready to punch John Y. right in his pearly whites.

"What a goddamned joke," Red said to me. "If I was going to have a legitimate shot at rebuilding this franchise, I needed those draft picks to do it. I have absolutely nothing against Bob McAdoo, but how the hell is he going to help Cowens' game? David's still going to have to do most of the rebounding. McAdoo's smooth, but he's not the effort-type player David is. He's an excellent jump shooter and scorer, but David gives us those things, too. Plus, David likes the contact inside. McAdoo is a finesse player. This clown [Brown] makes it impossible for me to do my job. Either he leaves or I do. And I don't see him going. He loves strutting up to the microphone and playing the big shot at all those goddamn press conferences."

By the time I got a chance to talk to Red about his situation, Auerbach had already discreetly phoned Brown's silent partner, Harry Mangurian, a successful Florida horse breeder and businessman, and given him an ultimatum. According to Red, he bluntly told Mangurian, "Harry, I can work for you, but I can't work for your partner. If you buy out his share of the ownership and give me complete control of the personnel moves, I can still save this franchise, as well as your investment. If you don't, I'm leaving. I hate to put you on the spot, but I have to start planning for whatever job I'm going to be doing next season. I'd appreciate it if you can let me know your intentions within a couple weeks. I know I'm putting you on the spot, but that's just the way it has to be. I'm fed up."

The fact that the Celtics' attendance had plummeted and the team was about to finish with its worst record in history enabled Mangurian, an astute, soft-spoken businessman, to entice Brown into giving up his share of the Celtics and head back to his home in Kentucky, where he would quickly con the good people of the Bluegrass State into electing him governor.

My very first interview with Harry convinced me that Red was once again in complete charge. "I am a huge Celtics fan and a huge Red Auerbach fan. I've been a silent partner of this team for a good reason—I don't know a thing about judging basketball talent. That's all going to be in Red's hands," Mangurian said. "I'll be around a lot more now, but just to handle the business side of the team and as a fan. Red Auerbach doesn't need my help; I need his."

Following a 29-53 season, Cowens announced that he would give up the coaching duties and return to strictly being a player, a decision he had reached shortly after the McAdoo deal. "With all the players coming and going, it felt like I was coaching an expansion team. After my experience, I don't think anyone can do a good job as player-coach. Each job is demanding. Playing takes a certain physical toll; coaching takes a toll on you mentally. You find out that there aren't enough hours in a day to do both jobs the way you'd like to," David told me. "I don't regret the experience, though. I learned a lot about myself and my emotions."

With Brown out of the picture, Red was back to being his old gruff but efficient, savvy self. He could now concentrate on just two things: hiring a head coach and signing Bird.

Auerbach didn't have to conduct a search for a coach. The day after Bill Fitch, who had been the league's Coach of the Year in '75-'76, resigned as head coach of the Cavs after nine seasons with that club, Red phoned him and all but offered him the job on the spot. "There weren't any long negotiations," Fitch told me. "Red and I knew each other for years. I had been to Japan with him twice for exhibitions and teaching clinics. We knew each other's styles. He wanted me, and I wanted to rejuvenate the Celtics. It was a dream job for someone who enjoys almost starting from scratch and building a contender."

While it was the first time in team history that Auerbach had sought anyone outside the "Celtics family" as head coach, Bill was, in my opinion, the perfect fit for this team's needs. He was tough, thorough and totally dedicated to his work. There's no question he had a drill sergeant's mentality, but that's just what the Celtics needed. They needed a rigid system in which each player knew precisely what his role would be. They needed a coach who meant it when he said: "It's my way or the highway." Preseason practices under Fitch would be as close as you could get to marine boot camp conditions. One of his favorite sayings was, "I don't get ulcers, I give them." Bill wasn't kidding around, either.

"I'm not here to win a popularity contest. I don't want my players to love me, just respect me. I had plenty of players in Cleveland who hated my guts, guys like Campy Russell, Bingo Smith and Jim Chones. Today, I know those same individuals would tell you they now realize I made them better players."

Could Red and Bill coexist? After all, they both were opinionated, with strong convictions on how a team can succeed. Bill quickly answered my doubts when he said to me in one of our first interviews, "If Auerbach wanted a 'yes man' for his head coach, he would have been making a huge mistake when he hired me. And Red doesn't make mistakes."

With Fitch on board, Red, who had been negotiating with Bird's agent, Bob Woolf, since February, now was totally focused on signing the Indiana State All-American. Woolf insisted that Bird had to become the highest-paid rookie in sports history. Red balked. A week before the draft, Mangurian, at the request of Red, joined the negotiations, Within a day, the two sides agreed to a deal that paid Bird a record $3.25 million over five years.

"Signing that contract was a big relief, because only a few days before I thought Mr. Woolf and Auerbach were at a total stalemate. The other really scary thing for me was that as I waited for a deal to be reached all I heard was the fans and the media talking about how

I was going to be the *savior* of this team," Bird told me when he arrived at vets camp. "Dang, I've never minded pressure, but I sure didn't like to hear that the Celtics' hopes rested almost entirely on one rookie's shoulders—mine."

11

THE BIRD ERA BEGINS

Combine the intelligence of Bill Russell, the inventiveness of Bob Cousy, the scoring knack of Heinsohn, the perpetual motion of Jarrin' John Havlicek, the aggressiveness of Dave Cowens, and you have an idea of the scope of Larry Bird's talents. What I have come to know is that he can rise to any height he wants, any height that's necessary to win.

When Bird officially joined the Celtics in '79, it was clear from day one that the Celtics were back on the right path to championship seasons. Larry did things that I hadn't seen for years—no-look passes, step-back three-point shots from 30 feet, on-target, fullcourt outlet passes, and head-first dives for loose balls. Fitch was immediately impressed with not only Larry's talents but, just as importantly, with his sheer hustle and work ethic.

"No rookie I've ever met had Bird's poise and ability to excel when the game would be on the line. Usually rookies try to blend in; Larry wants to be the team leader," Fitch said. Off the court, Bird was very unassuming during his first year. He'd say, "Yes sir" and "No sir" to everybody. He was very shy when he talked to the media. Almost every time a reporter would ask him a question about his individual play, he'd respond, "I'm just doing my job like everyone else. It's just a great honor being a Celtic, being around Red Auerbach,

Coach Fitch and players like Dave Cowens." It was obvious he chose his words very carefully in order to avoid saying anything that might be construed as being controversial. I quickly found out through my private conversations with Larry and his handling of media questions that this kid was no dummy.

Bird found out firsthand how mentally prepared Fitch was for each game. "One night during the first two weeks of my rookie season I was watching a movie in my room around ten o'clock when Bill called. "Hey, Larry, come on up to my room and watch some video with me. There's a few plays I think we can use against the Pistons [the next night's opponents]."

"Sure, Coach, I'll be right up," Larry replied.

For the next three hours Larry was trapped in Bill's room as Fitch went through two complete game tapes of old Detroit-Boston games. "Johnny," Larry said to me, "Coach made me suffer through two of the worst NBA games I've ever seen. Then he started reaching for another game tape. Shit, it was nearly 2 a.m. and I wasn't about to sit there one minute longer. As Coach was loading the new tape into the video machine, I made my move. I ran out the door, down the hallway and into the elevator.

The next day Bird was telling all his teammates about his late-night video sessions with Bill. "It'll never happen to me again," Bird stated flatly. "Fitch probably kept watching tapes until the sun came up. Hell, Bill's so intense when he watches all those game tapes, I doubt if he even realized it when I sneaked out of his room."

Bill's habit of regularly watching video tapes into the early morning hours earned him the title of "Captain Video," coined by the *Globe's* Dan Shaughnessy. Needless to say, that nickname was quickly adopted by all the Celtics players.

Even as a rookie, Larry was the cockiest player I'd ever seen play the game. His favorite pastime was talking trash all night. Unlike many players who'd yell, curse and berate their opponent to throw them off their games, Bird playfully tormented the poor saps who guarded him with humorous remarks about their inability to stop him from scoring. He'd always have a smile on his face as he chattered away. Rarely did he ever raise his voice above a normal conversational tone as he kidded his man. In fact, you'd have to be sitting at courtside to really hear how Larry would bait his opponent.

"He's not obnoxious about it. He doesn't really taunt players," referee Earl Strom told me. "In fact, he just sort of teases the poor guy who's guarding him. There have been times his remarks to opponents are so damned funny that even I have a tough time keeping a straight face."

His favorite target as a rookie was, of course, Magic Johnson. After his Indiana State team had lost to Magic's Michigan State squad in the '79 NCAA championship, Larry lived for the rematches against Magic when the Celtics and Lakers clashed. Magic has his own method for handling Bird's trash talking. He tries to completely tune it out. "I hear what he says. I just totally ignore him," Magic told me. "I think that bothers Larry, because he wants to get a reaction from me and I never give him the satisfaction of letting him think he's playing mind games with me."

From the opening tipoff, Larry's mouth can move faster than his legs. Like Sam Jones used to do to Chamberlain, he'd call his shots before he even released the ball. I remember one night in Phoenix in 1984 when the Celtics were trailing by a point with three seconds left in regulation. Larry was being guarded by Alvin Scott. As Bird prepared to receive the ball on an inbounds play 25 feet from the basket, he calmly warned Scott, "Better guard me closer or I'm gonna hit this three-pointer." Scott, who obviously believed Larry would be looking to get open for a higher-percentage shot, ignored Larry's banter and even backed off him a little. The ball came into Larry's hands, and he stepped back and buried a three-pointer to win the game. As he walked past the dejected Scott, he winked at him and said, "See, I told you to guard me closer. I was just trying to help you out...broke your heart, didn't I?"

That's the kind of supreme self-confidence Larry exuded.

If there is one characteristic of Bird's that stands out in my mind, it is the fact that he just does not accept the concept of losing—no matter whether it's in a playoff game or simply in a game of H-O-R-S-E. A loss is a loss. He's not a pouter or a whiner. But from the second he has been beaten, you can tell he wants revenge, the chance to redeem himself.

Yet I have noticed over the years that he is most cooperative with the media after a defeat. He's frank, even overly self-critical. For example, I'm sure you recall that after the Lakers had beaten the Celtics in Game 3 of the '84 playoffs, he told the press: "We played like a bunch of sissies."

One day I asked him why he would usually hide in the trainer's room after a victory yet always make a point of answering a lot of tough questions following a loss. "It's easy to talk big when you've just beaten somebody," he said to me. "Anyone can do that. But for me, a guy's real character comes across after he loses. That's when you see who makes the excuses, who the crybabies are, and who are big enough to admit that they just weren't as good as the other guy. The way I feel is that if you can't face the public, you won't be able to face yourself."

And let me tell you, Bird was a quick learner about dealing with the media. He knew which people he could trust and which people he couldn't.

I happened to be with him one day in the final weeks of his rookie year when a reporter he didn't respect approached him, looking for a story. "Johnny, this guy's bad news. He's just hoping I'll say something controversial, so he can make something really big out of it," Larry whispered to me. "Listen to the kind of the questions he asks and listen to how I answer 'em."

Well, Bird and the reporter talked for almost 15 minutes, and I swear Larry didn't say one thing worth printing. He simply double-talked the guy to death. When it was over, the reporter took off, and

Bird turned to me, grinned, and said, "Ain't going to make any headlines off what I told him. Mrs. Bird didn't raise no fools."

So much for his being a dumb hick. Yet I'm sure he enjoys maintaining that image because he is able to sort of hide behind it. His accent, that Midwestern twang of his, may make him sound like a bumpkin, but his mind works very quickly and efficiently. What he lacks in "sophistication," he makes up in common sense.

What Larry's done is to declare from his first day in Boston that he is what he is. He is determined to be his own person. He won't put on any airs. No Mercedes Benz for him; he's one person who would really rather drive a pickup truck.

No tie and jacket, either; just give him a comfortable pair of jeans, a lumberjack shirt, white socks and boat shoes. And if you demand that he be something other than himself, he'll tell you where to go in no uncertain terms.

Not surprisingly, he has little patience for phonies and hangers-on. "I'll never understand what makes those kind of people tick," he said to me once. "Usually I can spot them right away. They want to bend your ear for hours just so they can tell their friends that they are buddies with Larry Bird. I guess somehow that makes them feel important, but all they're really doing is making asses of themselves.

"If I acted like they do, I'd be embarrassed. Sometimes, when a guy is totally obnoxious, the only way to get him away is to tell him point blank that he's not wanted. With those people, sometimes that doesn't even work. When adults ask for an autograph, they always have to try and strike up a long-winded conversation. When a kid asks for an autograph, they usually just say 'thank you' and leave. Most of the adults don't even say thanks. They *expect* you to sign."

I don't think Larry will ever get used to being a celebrity—or as he likes to call it, a big shot. "Like everybody else, when I go out, I want to relax. Trouble is there aren't too many places I go where I can do that," he's complained to me. "It's funny, but I get the most privacy when I'm in some small restaurant or in a dumpy bar with sawdust on the floor. Even if some people recognize me at those places, they seem to understand that I want to be treated like everyone else in the joint."

That's why he looks forward to his summers in French Lick where he can just be himself. "The people back home treat me entirely differently," he told me. "They understand that I'm the same person I was 10 years ago. Nothing's changed. I still hang out with my high school friends, I still fish and golf, I still sit around the house and bug the hell out of my mom. The people in my hometown couldn't care less if I ever played another game of basketball. They like me as a person, not as some damn star."

One summer Larry invited me to French Lick to be master of ceremonies at a dinner honoring his first coach at Indiana State, Bob King, who was retiring. When I arrived at the hotel, he asked me if he could fix me up with a date. "Sure," I replied.

"Well, what would you like?" he asked.

"Blonde, maybe about 38, with a good sense of humor," I said.

Within an hour, Larry knocked on my door and said, "Johnny, I want you to meet Mary and Sue. Have fun."

I was stunned because Mary and Sue looked like they were college students. I pulled Larry aside and said, "Larry, they're not anywhere near 38."

"Yes, they are. Mary's 19 and Sue's 19. Nineteen and 19 is 38. Just what you asked for." Then he winked at me and walked out the door.

Because Larry's such a down-to-earth guy, his teammates genuinely respect him in every way. He blends in. He's just one of the guys. Yet I know they don't like the idea of facing him if they have screwed up. There's no doubt they don't like the idea of being in his presence, of feeling his wrath, when it's been obvious they've given less than a hundred percent. He has that kind of influence, that kind of respect.

As he was quoted as saying in one magazine article, "I'd rather be on the court with four guys who aren't that talented but are willing to hustle all the time than with four guys who have all the talent in the world but waste it by not caring." In his mind, there's no excuse for not diving for a loose ball, sacrificing your body to get a rebound or working your tail off on defense. That's simply how the game is supposed to be played.

Bird takes good care of his teammates. For instance, early on in his career Larry did several commercials that required "extras" to play the parts of either his teammates or opposition players. He insisted that those parts be given to his end-of-the bench teammates so they could make a little extra cash.

And Larry always backs up his teammates when they happen to get involved in a fight or shoving match. The first time I witnessed Bird's protective nature was when Dave Cowens became involved in an altercation with a group of Houston fans.

Cowens had been taunted by the crowd until he finally had to say something to a young woman who was particularly obnoxious. At that point, the crowd became even more unruly.

Bird was just coming out of the building and got involved in order to help Dave get onto the bus. A guy named Johnny Merla started to swear at Bird, and Bird swung a small duffel bag at the guy, barely grazing him on the side of the head. But the guy, seeing the chance to make some money in a phony lawsuit, went down like he had been hit by a rifle shot. Fortunately, there was a policeman who witnessed it all and filed an incident report that stated that the guy was "drunk, loud and boisterous." Although Merla sued Dave and Larry for $1.8 million, he didn't get a penny. In fact, he ended up looking very much like the fool that he was.

What the public doesn't realize is that Larry is a very funny and very warm person. They see him on the court, cocky and feisty, and assume that he must be the same way in private. Not so. To me, he's an impish prankster.

In fact, the whole Celtics team during the Bird years consisted of players who loved practical jokes, even if it was at their own expense. In my opinion, nearly all the laughs were inspired by Bird's sense of humor.

Over the years, Larry has pulled a million practical jokes on me.

As a rookie, he'd do anything to prevent me from smoking. One time he came up to me as we were waiting for the team bus to arrive. "Hey, Johnny, what kind of cigarettes do you smoke?" he asked me.

"Merits. Why do you ask?" I said.

"Let me see the pack. I want to see how much nicotine is in them."

Being unfamiliar with his gags, I handed him my pack of butts. Before I could do anything about it, Larry casually strolled across the street and gave away my pack of butts to a total stranger who thanked him and pocketed the "free sample."

I thought I had a way of getting back at him. Auerbach occasionally accompanies the team on road trips. When Red gets on the team bus, he immediately lights up a cigar. Even though Bill Fitch banned smoking on the bus, I figured if Red could smoke his cigars, then I could light up a cigarette or two without worrying about anyone complaining about my smoking. Bird wasn't about to let me get away with it. He walked up to Fitch and complained that my cigarettes (but not Red's cigars) were making him nauseous. Fitch knew what Larry was up to and played along. "Johnny, you know the rules," Bill said sternly. "You'll have to put that cigarette out right now." I grudgingly complied as Larry, Red, Bill and the whole team yukked it up at my expense.

Bird would also steal my cigarettes when I fell asleep on a plane. As I was snoozing back in the smoking section, he'd walk back from his first-class seat, "pickpocket" my cigarettes and then take eight or nine butts out of the pack. Then he would put the "stolen" cigarettes into his mouth and light all of them at once. As soon as he had them all lit, he'd wake me up and pretend to be enjoying the flavor as he puffed away without inhaling. I'd pretend to be angry, but he'd always manage to get me to laugh as he made faces as he puffed away on the smokes that were stuffed from one side of his mouth to the other.

Finally, after enduring two full years of his "dirty tricks" campaign against me, I made a truce with him. I wouldn't smoke more than two packs a day if he didn't drink more than two beers after games.

Both of us found ways to cheat. When we were at a party or a bar, I'd go to the bathroom, disappear for 10 minutes and smoke three or four cigarettes in record time; he'd have his two-beer limit and then proceed to hide his "over-the-limit" beer cans under his chair or put them in front of his drinking buddy, Rick Robey, or even give them to some non-drinker like Danny Ainge or Greg Kite to hold. We each knew what the other guy was doing. The object simply was not to get caught outright.

There was another gag I believe Bird played on me, although I never could get him to confess. We were at a hotel in Pontiac, Michigan, and I had gone out to a late dinner with some friends. I didn't get back to the hotel until 2 a.m. Bird also was out late and spotted me coming into the hotel lobby. The team had a 6:30 a.m. wake-up call, so I figured I'd go to my room and at least catch a few hours of sleep. Bird (or one of his accomplices) went up to the front desk and told the desk clerk that "Mr. Most wants to change his wakeup call to 4 a.m." (In those days, wake-up calls weren't done electronically. Instead, the desk clerk called your room and informed you personally that it was your wake-up time.) After receiving the call, I quickly showered, dressed and went down to the lobby. After sitting alone for about a half-hour, I began to wonder why it was still pitch-dark outside. Then I spotted a clock and realized that someone had really put one over on me. As I got on the bus two hours later, I could hear muffled laughter as Larry casually asked me, "Did you get a good night's rest, Johnny?"

"Larry," I replied, "I slept like a baby. Thanks for asking, you little wiseass."

Bird's constant sidekick during his first three years in the league was Robey. I called them "Frick and Frack" because I never saw one of them without the other being less than a couple steps away. Yet they had completely different personalities. Rick was the type of guy who walks into a bar and buys everyone a drink. He's a perpetual host, a Kentucky gentleman who loves to entertain people no matter what the cost. Larry, on the other hand, was very "thrifty" with his money when he first came into the league. In fact, Bird was the type of guy who'd enter a bar and nurse a beer while waiting for Robey to show up because he knew once Rick arrived, Robey would buy all the drinks.

Rick and Larry must have had 1,000 meals together, and I bet Robey paid for 999 of them. Rick didn't mind, though, because he loved to tease Bird about being so tight with a buck. "Larry, you're the only guy I know who's had the same wallet for 10 years and never has found out what the inside of it looks like," Rick would say. To which Bird would respond, "Yeah, but at least my wallet still has something in it."

Bird still tells of the time he and Robey went to a bar and Rick started buying drinks for a few people. After an hour had gone by, Bird turned to Robey and said, "Hey, you'd better cut this out. You haven't let anyone else buy a round. Right now your bar tab has to be at least a couple hundred bucks." Robey just shrugged his shoulder and replied, "Don't worry about it. I'm not paying for it. I'm putting it on my American Express card."

"Rick was so funny," Larry told me. "As long as he didn't actually have to use cash, it was like he figured it didn't cost anything to just sign a credit card slip."

Getting Robey into trouble was one of Bird's favorite pastimes. For instance, I remember a game in which the Celtics were playing at New Jersey. Guard Micheal Ray Richardson was destroying the Celtics singlehandedly, so Bird devised a plan to to stop the Nets' playmaker. During a timeout, Larry sat next to Robey and began to shout at him. "Damn it, Rick, you're not going to let Richardson get away with all that cheap shit he's doing, are you?"

"What's he doing?" responded Robey.

"Didn't you see what he tried to do to you?" said Bird, pretending to be angry. "The guy threw a vicious elbow that just missed the back of your head." (Richardson, in fact, hadn't done any such thing.)

"Oh, yeah? Well, I'll get him next time down the court," vowed Robey, who now had been convinced by Larry that he had been the intended victim of a "sucker shot" by Richardson.

"You'd better, or he's going to cheapshot you every chance he gets," Bird said, displaying some very credible acting ability. With that, Larry patted Rick on the behind and pushed him out onto the court. Within 30 seconds, Robey flattened Michael Ray with a three-step moving pick. Naturally, the startled Richardson took offense at Robey's unprovoked body block. Picking himself off the court, Michael Ray hurled the basketball at Robey's head and then cursed him out. As the refs quickly moved in and ejected both players, Bird just sat on the Boston bench roaring with laughter at the melee he had just instigated.

Larry and Rick loved to exchange little barbs at each other. Larry would tell people that he always invites Rick to his camp for kids just so the youngsters can see how *not* to play the game. Rick, in turn, came up with a classic line when a picture of Larry appeared on the cover of *Time* magazine. "I'm just glad *Time* didn't decide to use a profile shot of Larry, because if it did then the magazine would have had to clip off half of Larry's huge beak in order to fit his face on the cover."

Some of Rick's other lines:

"They shouldn't count any of Larry's free throws because when he's standing at the foul line, his nose is actually two feet into the lane."

"Given the size of Larry's nose, when he comes down with a cold, it's a major injury."

Bird, of course, had a few comebacks:

On one occasion, Bird saw Robey shaking hands with a guy who went to the University of Kentucky with Rick. "I bet that's the first time Rick has shook the hand of a Kentucky alumnus without plucking a fifty dollar bill from the guy's palm."

"Rick is the only player I know who could go one for five from the foul line and have his free throw percentage go up."

The back-and-forth joking between Robey and Bird got so much attention in the press that Kareem Abdul-Jabbar went up to Larry before a Celtics-Lakers game and asked if the two of them hated each other. "I love reading those remarks you guys toss at each other," Kareem told Larry. "They're really funny, but sometimes it sounds like you two are ready to fight each other. Are you actually friends or is there a problem between you?"

Bird explained that the remarks were just jokes. But because of Kareem's reaction, Larry and Rick made a pact to stop the friendly insults.

Although Rick, being fun-loving and somewhat gullible, was an easy target for pranks by his teammates, he was a physical player who didn't mind mixing it up with opponents. He set some of the most devastating, legal body-jarring picks I've ever seen—and he smiled as he watched the opponent crumble. When you ran into one of Robey's picks, you hit the deck and you didn't get up before a 10 count.

With Bird, Cowens, Maxwell and Robey, Fitch had plenty of talent in the frontcourt. Plus, he knew David would provide on-the-court leadership and inspiration for the younger players. Bill also had a plan for revamping his backcourt revolving around Nate "Tiny" Archibald.

As a member of the Buffalo Braves, Tiny had sat out the entire '77-'78 season after suffering a torn Achilles tendon in an exhibition game. The previous season with the Nets, Tiny played only 34 games due to a broken foot. After coming to Boston in the fall of '78 as part of the John Y. Brown franchise swap, Archibald was frustrated with all the infighting and chaos taking place. "I tried to focus on my job, but I just couldn't ignore all the turmoil," he told me. "Everywhere I looked there were major problems from the ownership, to Red's frustrations, to the coaching staff, right down to the players. No one was on the same page, and every day there was a new crisis. I tried to stay out of all the controversy, but eventually I got swallowed up by all the infighting. At first, I wanted to be traded. Later, I just wanted to quit because playing the game had become absolutely no fun."

The result was that Tiny averaged only 11 points and slightly more than four assists a game, far below his career averages. The media, as well as many NBA coaches and general managers, suggested that Archibald was washed up. Fitch, however, was a true believer in Tiny's abilities.

"Tiny's my starting point guard. It's his job, period. As long as Nate stays healthy, he'll be running the show. I don't care about what anyone says, he's still the best in the league," Bill said. "This is the same player who led the league in scoring and assists in the same season ['72-'73]. Sure, he's lost a step with age, but never underestimate the value of experience. I've learned that you can't judge a great player on just statistics. His knowledge of the game, his poise, his leadership are all things which will help us."

One player who definitely didn't fit into Bill's plans was Curtis Rowe. On the opening day of training camp, Curtis was going at three-quarter speed during fullcourt sprint drills. Bill, wanting to make a point to the entire team, pointed at Rowe and then barked out: "You want to jog instead of run? Well, jog your way back to the locker room, take a relaxing shower, pack your bags, and jog your butt out of the building. You've just been cut."

I soon also learned that Fitch had absolutely no patience for any player, including Tiny, who didn't follow his instructions. We were playing the 76ers in one of the first exhibition games of '79, and Tiny had missed a last-second shot that resulted in a Boston loss.

Afterward, Bill and I sat in a coffee shop discussing the game. "Damn it, Tiny wasn't supposed to shoot," he told me. "The ball was supposed to have been swung around to Bird. I guess Tiny had a better plan. It used to be that a coach would say 'do it' and it was done. Nowadays, if players don't like your thinking, they're going to run the play their way. They're all making big money. They're constantly being told by their friends about how great they are. That's when they start thinking that just maybe they know more than their coach. I'm not saying Tiny's shot was a bad one, but when I call for a certain set play to be run, it damn well better be. I'm never going to let the inmates run the asylum."

Backing up Tiny was Gerald Henderson, a quick, accurate-shooting free agent rookie whom Fitch had recommended to Red. "Signing him is like getting an extra first-round pick," Bill said when Boston announced on draft day of '79 that Gerald had agreed to a contract.

Henderson was a quiet kid who could hit the pull-up jumper, handle the ball well, and play solid defense. Fitch knew that as long as Tiny stayed healthy, he could afford the luxury of slowly bringing along Gerald as the backup point guard.

In July the Celtics signed free agent former All-Defensive swingman M.L. Carr, who had led the NBA in steals in '78-'79 while playing for Detroit. M.L. wasn't a scorer, but he was one of the league's most intimidating defenders. In fact, when he played for the Pistons, I used to call him "a common thug, a street brawler who is out there on the court with the sole purpose of maiming his opponent." Now, as a Celtic, I saw him in a different light. Playing for Boston, his quick hands and toughness became a valuable weapon. He was just what Boston needed, a player who would never back down to anyone, a type of person you almost have to have on a winning ball club. He never lost gracefully nor believed in moral victories. As Red used to tell me, "Show me a good loser and I'll show you a guy I'm going to get rid of."

M.L. Carr's restricted free agent signing, in the end, allowed Red to pull of one of his absolutely greatest swindles. As compensation for signing Carr, Red negotiated with the Pistons and agreed to give them Bob McAdoo. The "kicker" to the deal was that the Pistons had to also surrender two 1980 first-round draft choices to Boston to complete the transaction. Gaining those two picks would allow Auerbach to pull off another great trade following the '79-'80 season.

I remember the night M.L. challenged Atlanta's seven-foot center, Tree Rollins, to a fight during the game and then waited for a half-hour after the game in the hallway to challenge him again. (Rollins claimed M.L. was brandishing a straight razor; M.L. told me he was merely holding a set of car keys.)

M.L. also told me about the time he was playing for the Pistons and was ejected by official Jake O'Donnell for throwing an elbow at Pacer forward George McGinnis' head. As Carr was about to leave the court, he walked over to O'Donnell and said, "Hey, Jake, do you mind if I go over to McGinnis and shake his hand just to show him there's no hard feelings?

"Go ahead," said O'Donnell. "That would be a good gesture."

So M.L., right hand outstretched, approached McGinnis, who reached out to shake hands. At that instant, M.L. threw a looping left hook that caught George on the side of the head. "No hard feelings," M.L. yelled at McGinnis. "I just wanted to get in the last word."

When he first arrived in Boston, M.L. told me that he wanted opponents to always think he was stark raving mad. "I'll do anything to make my man wonder what I'm going to do next. Am I going to all of a sudden start a fight? Am I going to purposely run over my man when I have the ball just to show him he'd better give me room? Things like that, Johnny," he said. "Everything I do on the court is for a purpose. I'm not a dirty player. But if I have that reputation, that's OK with me.

"I'd been cut three times in 1973 when I came out of college, first by the Kentucky Colonels of the ABA, who had drafted me in the third round, then by the Kansas City Kings, who had drafted me in the seventh round, and finally by the Celtics, who had signed me after the Kings waived me. I don't think I spent more than two weeks with any of those teams before they more or less told me to find another profession. I actually did give up basketball for awhile and became a prison guard.

"When I finally gave basketball another chance with the Spirits of St. Louis in the old ABA, I knew I had to play a physical game. If I didn't intimidate people and hustle my butt off, I didn't have a prayer making the pros," he said. "I didn't have a great offensive game. I had to want to win more than the next guy. I had to capitalize on my greatest assets, my toughness and my defense. By acting 'crazy' at times, I caught people's attention."

Another key player in Fitch's rebuilding plans was Chris Ford, the guy I always say "was able to make chicken salad out of chicken shit." On the surface, Chris appeared to be a mediocre player. He had all the speed of a crippled turtle. Lack of quickness wasn't Chris' only liability. His vertical leap could be measured with a 12-inch ruler. As a shooter, he was good, consistent, but not great. Yet he was a pro's pro. He worked as hard as anyone in practice, he was unselfish, he knew his teammates' strengths and his opponents' weaknesses. Above all, he was a winner who understood the game.

Ford's smarts enabled him to maximize his effectiveness. On defense, he'd establish a position that would force his man either to shoot an off-balance jumper or drive into an area where one of the Celtics' frontcourt players could easily move over to provide help. As

Fitch told me, "You'll never see Chris make a mental error on defense. He knows each player's tendencies. He always plays the percentages. If he's going to get beat on a play, it's going to take a real difficult shot to do it."

Offensively, Ford's most reliable weapon was a one-handed push shot that he'd take while standing flat-footed. Although he was very accurate using it from long range, it took Chris a little bit of extra time to set up, find the seam and then release the ball. In order to free himself for those bombs, Ford became an expert at running his defender into picks set by one of Boston's big men, who would slide out to provide a screen.

"Chris loves that play," Bird told me once. "It's his way of getting even with an opponent who's faster than himself. After running into a few of those picks, pretty soon the guy guarding Chris becomes a little gun-shy. Next thing you know, Ford has his man slowing down just enough so that he can get an open shot without having to use those screens."

Chris wanted to be on the court at least 25 to 30 minutes a game. Fitch, realizing that Ford was a valuable bench contributor, would frustrate Ford by playing him for only six or seven minutes at a time. One night in San Antonio, Ford was hitting every shot he took. In a span of about half a quarter, he had knocked down a pair of three-pointers and two 18-foot jumpers without a single miss. Just then, Bill substituted for Chris to give him a rest. As he passed Bill on the bench, Chris was muttering to himself and to his teammates. "I guess I must be too hot. Just too hot. Boys, if you're too hot, you get yanked." The whole bench was laughing as Chris plopped himself down and continued to mutter to himself.

When Fitch called a timeout a minute or so later, there was Chris, pacing around the perimeter of the huddle. "I'm too hot. He's not going to put me back in 'cause I'm too hot. I guess Bill thinks I've made my quota of shots for the night."

Did Fitch hear Ford's sarcastic comments? "Of course I did," Bill said to me right after the Celtics had beaten the Spurs that night. "But, you know, sometimes us coaches pretend our hearing isn't real good. To be honest, I was laughing to myself at Chris' remarks, but I couldn't show any emotion. If I reacted to something like that, then I'd be hearing little comments from other guys when I pulled them out of the lineup. All it proved is Chris is a competitor. I don't want guys to be happy when I take them out of a game."

As the '79-'80 season began, both the Celtics and I were rejuvenated. Fitch's no-rest-for-the-weary approach to training camp produced positive results as Boston won 10 of its first 12 regular-season games. When I interviewed Max a month into the season, he got right to the point: "Everyone on this team knew the 'Larry Bird effect' was going to make us much better. Maybe the rest of the league had some doubts about his talent, but we knew right away he was a unique player, an instant All-Star. But that's just half of the story. The rest of us know our roles. For the past two years, we really didn't have any roles. Boston had 12 guys who each had their own idea of how to win. Now we have just one system, one plan for winning. Everyone's on the same page. That's why Fitch deserves a lot of credit."

Only once during the '78-'79 season was there the slightest hint of an internal problem. It came late in March following a game in New York when M.L. asked Bill if he could go straight to dinner with some friends rather than riding with the team back to our hotel. Bill refused M.L.'s request, telling him, "We go to the arena as a team and we leave the arena as a team." M.L. thought Bill was nitpicking and made his feelings known to everyone on the bus ride. While there wasn't a major dispute, it proved to be a precursor of long-term future personal disagreements between the two.

Despite David Cowens being hampered by foot problems throughout the year and missing 16 games, the Celtics finished the regular season with a 61-21 record. The 32-win improvement from

'78-'79 was the greatest turnaround in NBA history, earning Fitch Coach of the Year honors for the second time in his career.

If there had been a Comeback of the Year award at that time in the NBA, it would have been a unanimous vote for Tiny Archibald, who averaged 14.3 points and 8.4 assists.

Bird, beating out Magic Johnson, was named Rookie of the Year and first-team All-NBA. It took me and the rest of New England just one year to realize that he was definitely the best passing forward in the history of the game.

When the Celtics swept Houston 4-0 in the Eastern Division semifinals, Boston fans allowed themselves to dream of a championship for the first time in three long years. However, Boston proved to be no match for the Sixers, their division finals opponents. Philly had experience, depth at every position and the leadership of Julius Erving. Even their younger players—Mo Cheeks and Darryl Dawkins—played with poise against us. The series ended quickly, with the Celtics managing just a single win in five games. "It's a lesson learned," said Fitch. "They fried us to a crisp. We couldn't match their scoring power or their depth up front. We're a good team, not a great one. We've still got work to do."

During the closing moments of Philly's victory in Game 4 at the Spectrum, I engaged in a classic verbal confrontation with a group of rude, mental midgets. With less than a minute to go, about a dozen 76ers "fans" managed to find their way to an empty row of seats about 15 feet below my broadcast location. There was not a so-called security guard or usher in sight as these drunks attempted to interrupt my play-by-play by screaming at the top of their lungs, "Hey, Most, how do you like it? Hey, Johnny, your Celtics suck. Hey, Most, we kicked your ass."

After listening to the Philly fans' insults for about a minute, I stood up and responded on the air to their third-grade-level taunts, "You'll have to excuse me, boys, but I'm having a very private conversation with the people of New England and you're not invited to participate. I'd appreciate it very much if you'd shut the hell up."

12

LARRY GETS SOME REINFORCEMENTS

Thanks to the Bob McAdoo deal with Detroit, the Celtics owned the first and 12th first-round picks of the 1980 draft. Red and Bill, though, were looking to make a trade or two.

A week before the draft, I sat down with Bill for lunch. "I think we'll do something with Golden State because they want Joe Barry Carroll in the worst way. There's a kid in Minnesota, Kevin McHale, who I've followed for four years who has more potential than Carroll. He's livelier, he's got tremendous offensive moves and he's one hell of a defensive player. Red sort of likes Darrell Griffith, a damn good shooter. But my philosophy has always been to take a good big man over a good small man. If we can pull off the trade with Golden State, I'd like to convince Red that McHale would be a great player to have standing next to Bird for the next 10 years so so."

When the trade talks heated up, Warriors general manager Al Attles hinted that the team wouldn't object to packaging the team's center, Robert Parish, if the deal could allow Golden State to acquire Carroll, along with another mid-first-round draft pick. JoJo White, who played with Robert at Golden State, called Red and raved about the seven-footer's potential. "Parish is a big-time talent who's not appreciated by the Warriors. He's quick, he can block shots, and he's unselfish. He only shoots when he has a high-percentage opportunity. All he needs is good coaching to be an All-Star."

Red, after huddling with Fitch, who had also urged Red to make a trade offer for Robert, came up with an offer that, if accepted, might give Boston the tallest, deepest and most talented frontcourt in the league. The Warriors took the bait and received the 12th and first pick of the draft in exchange for center Robert Parish and the third overall choice. The deal was announced on June 9, 1980.

"Griffith is a great player," Fitch said to me, "but McHale has inside moves I have never seen from a college kid. He's also got these long arms and quickness that will make him an excellent defensive player. As for Parish, he's a very smooth center who can shoot both inside and outside. Now we've got Bird, Cowens, Maxwell, Parish and McHale up front. Teams are going to have a tough time matching up with that lineup."

My first meeting with McHale gave me a clear indication that here was a kid who could make you laugh. The day after the draft, Kevin came into Boston to meet with the media and get acquainted with Red and Bill. I bumped into him outside the Garden on Causeway Street and introduced myself. "I listened to you on many nights up in Hibbing, Minnesota, when I was a kid," Kevin said. "Now I can put a face to that voice I used to hear." Walking with him toward Red's office, I noticed he was hobbling badly on his right foot. "Are you OK?" I asked him.

Kevin looked embarrassed. "Not really," he said. "Some of my friends up in Hibbing and I did just a little too much celebrating last night out by one of the mining pits. By mistake, one of my drunken buddies got into his pickup truck, backed it up, and ran over my right foot. It just throbs. Feels like I crushed every damned ligament on the top of the foot. I'm trying not to limp too badly, because I don't want Red to think he drafted a guy who's damaged goods—and stupid, too."

"Gotcha, babe," I replied. "Just take small steps and nobody will notice. You'll be sitting down for most of the press conference, so that should help."

It became evident, right from his initial chat with the media, that McHale was definitely a guy who loved to talk. A reporter would ask him a question and he'd give a 10-minute answer. Still, he was very well-spoken and spontaneously funny. With M.L. Carr, another non-stop yapper, as his new teammate, it was guaranteed that Celtics practices would be enthusiastic and boisterous.

When the 1980 training camp opened, Bill described his coaching methods as "patting and kicking" at the same time. "At this level, players don't want to hear about their weaknesses," he said. "When you criticize, you have to sneak up on them. Praise 'em first, then sort of casually mention how they can improve. If you do it that way, sometimes they don't even realize you're telling them they're doing something the wrong way. It's what you call coaching with diplomacy."

However, with Parish and McHale in attendance, Fitch would employ a lot more kicking than patting throughout his second year as Celtics head coach.

Only 10 days into training camp, "Pistol Pete" Maravich, whom the Celtics had acquired in February of 1980, packed his bags and simply walked out of Hellenic College in Brookline, the Celtics' practice facility. He told the media he had lost his enthusiasm. However, there was more to the story than what Pete let on. He had come to Boston because he felt the team, with Bird, Maxwell, and Cowens as its nucleus, had a shot at contending for a title within a year or so.

"I wanted to be a part of that," Pete, who had never come close to winning a championship ring, told me a day after he left camp. "I passed up an opportunity to play for Philadelphia because Red and Coach Fitch convinced me that I would have a significant role with the Celtics. I wanted to play for a contender, but I also felt I had to be in the regular rotation. It was important to me that I would be able to make a legitimate contribution every night.

"Things just didn't work out that way. My knees and ankles were aching every day in practice, and it became apparent to me that Tiny [Archibald], Chris [Ford] and M.L. [Carr] were going to get most of the minutes. I don't mind playing with some pain, but I saw the handwriting on the wall. If I was only going to get five minutes here and five minutes there, then it just wasn't going to be worth it. I wouldn't be happy in that situation. I'm 32 and I've had a good career. I think I've made the right decision. There's no hard feelings on my part."

Nor should there have been. Pete, who was honest enough to admit he drank excessively as a younger player, was not as quick or resilient as he had been in the mid-'70s. He looked and ran the court as if he was much older than 32. My feelings are that Fitch's grueling preseason practices took too much of a toll on Pete, both physically and psychologically. Unfortunately, he simply was no longer the supremely self-confident "Pistol."

It was a sad ending for such a talented player. Throughout his career, his coaches—for some totally inexplicable reason—always used Pete more as a shooting guard than at the point guard position. I never understood that strategy. I'll even go so far as this: Had Pete been solely a point guard, he would have been as unstoppable and spectacular as Magic Johnson. In my opinion, as a point guard, Pete could have led the league in both points and assists, just as Tiny did when he accomplished the feat in 1973.

As training camp continued, Bill ran Robert to death in practice, day in and day out. If Robert let up for a few seconds during a drill, Fitch would be there to let him have it full blast in front of all his teammates and sometimes in front of the print and TV media. "I know it may seem like I'm singling him out," Fitch said, in response to a question I asked him about his criticism of Robert. "But it's the only way to get him to realize that he could be the best fast-break big man in the league.

"I see him beat Cowens, Bird, Robey, and even Max up and down the court when he makes his mind up to go all out. He may not have all the power moves and rebounding strength of some opponents, but none of them has his speed and endurance. He can outrun them all for an entire game. It's my job to make him understand that. Robert had it too easy at Golden State. He ran at half-speed, like Kareem does. I'm going to do whatever it takes to break him of that habit as quickly as I can."

Robert handled the criticism well, but deep down resented the fact that Fitch would embarrass him in front of his teammates. "I respect the man for his basketball knowledge and how he can teach the game," the Chief said to me. "Too often, though, he treats people like dirt. He wants perfection, period. Somebody should inform Mr. Fitch that humans aren't perfect. I can take his negative comments, but sooner or later, someone's gonna get fed up and then…well, we'll see what happens. It won't be pretty. All I know is I want to be there for it."

When McHale, who had been holding out and threatening to sign in Italy, finally signed with Boston and showed up at training camp, Fitch dished out an extra portion of torture to the happy-go-lucky rookie. "You're so far behind us," Fitch would yell at him, "that you'll be dragging your butt straight through training camp and into the regular season. Hope you enjoyed all that wine and pasta you ate over in Italy, because now you're going to pay for all that high living." And Bill was only half-kidding.

Near the end of camp, the Celtics were aboard a bus headed for a game in Terre Haute, Indiana, when a very somber David Cowens asked Fitch for permission to address the team. David then began to give an emotional speech to his teammates, announcing that, like his buddy Maravich, he had decided to retire. When David couldn't find the precise words to say and began talk about his appreciation of

Celtics' tradition and pride, M.L. Carr interrupted with this wisecrack: "Listen, Dave, we get the idea. You're hanging them up. You're leaving...now can we get this bus moving? The rest of us have a game to play tonight."

Right from the start of preseason, McHale was so self-confident that he decided he was going to stand up to Bill when he criticized Kevin for being too "chatty" on the court. "Basketball is something that's supposed to be fun," Kevin said to me. "To hear and see Bill, you'd think we're preparing for World War III. Whether or not we have a good practice is not going to determine the fate of the free world. Basketball just isn't a life-or-death struggle, and I'm not going to pretend it is—not to please Coach Fitch, not to please anybody. It's just a game, that's all. And I know I always play as hard as I can."

To a degree, Kevin was absolutely correct. If McHale saw a chance to irritate Bill or challenge him, he'd do it—mainly to get attention from his teammates. He was going to be the class clown, the class rebel. If Bill called for silence, Kevin would immediately put a finger over his lips to indicate to all his teammates that no one should dare say a word.

Fitch, I believe, handled Kevin very well. "If this nonsense came from somebody else, then I might be upset. But you've got to understand that McHale's just a big, overgrown kid who likes to make his teammates laugh. I can tell already just from our scrimmages that there really isn't anyone, except perhaps Larry, who cares more about winning." As the season progressed, Fitch's analysis proved to be right on track.

Even as a rookie, McHale was the perfect sixth man. He could play either the center or power forward spots. And as Fitch pointed out to me, "He studies how the game is going until I call on him. If we need offense, that's what he concentrates on: if we need rebounding, he'll go to the boards; if we need defense, he's all over his man while helping out on drives towards the baskets. I don't have to tell him what to do. He knows instinctively what it'll take to give us a lift."

McHale was, like Bird, another comical but slightly louder trash talker. He and Maxwell immediately established a running communication during games. "Hey, Max, I've got a big fish on the line. Time to reel him in." Max would feed the ball into McHale, who'd make a quick move for a score.

Before long, Maxwell coined a phrase to describe how McHale could absolutely torment the player guarding him. He called it simply the "torture chamber." Said Max, "When Kev gets a guy down low, four or five times in a row, the guy is virtually defenseless, and his legs become all tied up in knots. In a matter of five minutes, McHale's got eight points and his man is yelling, 'Help, help!' to his teammates every time we set up our offense."

There was no doubt Boston's strength was its frontcourt. The big question was could Tiny Archibald, at age 32, stay healthy for the entire season, because although Gerald Henderson was an excellent backup, he was only a second-year man who still lacked the poise of a true playmaker. "Gerald's going to make mistakes that you'd never see Tiny make," Fitch admitted. "Yet he's a good ball handler and passer who can come in off the bench and keep us running, which is our game."

Adding to concerns about Tiny's health and age was the fact that he missed the entire exhibition season due to a salary dispute. When Tiny settled his problems with management, it was clear he wasn't in game shape. Fitch was going to have to play Henderson as a starter whether he wanted to or not.

Minimizing Gerald's mistakes became Fitch's focus of attention. As a result, his play was scrutinized by Fitch after almost every loss. "No question," Parish said to me, "Henderson is the guy who Fitch always picks on. I know the reason why Fitch gets on him, but it's still tough to watch Gerald take so much grief for little things. Just once, I'd like to see Fitch tear into Larry or even Max the same way he does with Gerald. I'd pay to see that happen."

Henderson was one of those guys—and the Celtics had many over the years—who was the "perfect teammate." Quiet, enthusiastic, always in shape, a kid who just appreciated being in the NBA. Only two seasons before, Gerald, who had played both the point and shooting guard at Virginia Commonwealth, was the 64th choice in the draft and had been the final cut of the San Antonio Spurs. He ended up playing all of the '78-'79 season with the Tucson Gunners of the Western League, leading that club to the championship.

"A season of long bus rides, a season of playing in empty arenas, a season of staying in crummy hotels, a season of surviving on $10 a day meal money, it all has a way of motivating you every second you're on the court," Gerald said to me in my first interview with him back in September of '79. "My biggest adjustment will be learning how to be the point guard for this team. I've always had a scorer's mentality. Here with Boston, I know I'll be the last option, the guy who shoots only because I'm not being guarded or because we're desperate."

During the first two months of the regular season, the Celtics showed their potential by starting the season with an 18-8 record. Still, they trailed Philly by two games in the Atlantic Division standings. However, I just *knew* this was a team that was destined to win a title because this team had both supreme confidence and near-perfect chemistry. Tiny had taken over as the starting point guard and was intent on showing his doubters that he had regained All-Star status. On the fast breaks, he always made the perfect lead pass; in Boston's set offense, he was knocking down the 15-foot open jumpers whenever his man left him to double-team Bird or Parish down low. When Tiny rested on the bench, Henderson, having gained valuable experience as a starter, came in to reenergize the Celtics' relentless running game.

Larry, even in the early stages of the season, was by far the league's most complete player. No other forward in the NBA possessed his ability to gain rebounding position; no other player, with the possible exception of Magic Johnson, could match his imaginative "no-look" passes; and most impressively, nobody in the NBA was as capable of sticking a dagger in the opposition's heart by draining almost effortless-looking, rainbow step-backs in win-or-lose situations.

Robert had become what Fitch envisioned him as—the best running center in the game. In addition, his soft, accurate jumper from the foul line was an extremely effective weapon for the Celtics because it forced the opponents' center to move away from the basket to guard him. With Bird nearly always double-teamed, Maxwell was able to use his quickness to score inside with rebound baskets and tough post-up moves. On the perimeter, Ford kept the opposition guards honest with his long-range accuracy. Carr was the intimidating, physical and hostile example setter for Boston's defense.

If you asked me to name a weakness in the Celtics' game, I couldn't name one. This team was that solid.

There were a couple of funny moments during my broadcasts that season. The one that still makes me shudder a little occurred at the Hartford Civic Center during a game against the Knicks. Referee Jake O'Donnell had just made an horrendous call against the Celtics in the final minute of overtime. Just as he came over to the scorer's table, my broadcast partner, former Celtic Rick Weitzman, tapped me repeatedly on the shoulder. I was in the middle of calling Jake a "clown" and a "disgrace to the game of basketball," so I brushed Rick's hand off my shoulder and kept on talking. When O'Donnell signaled that his foul was on Bird, I became so irate that I slammed my hand down on the press table. I heard a squishing sound and immediately looked down at my fist, which now was covered by a disgusting, slimy layer of black goo. It seemed I had just killed the biggest, ugliest cockroach in history when I pounded the table. It was such a repulsive sight that I couldn't talk for a minute. Rick, trying to control his laughter, took over for me while I searched for a Kleenex to wipe away the insect's oozing remains.

During the next commercial break, Rick was in hysterics. "Johnny, you really nailed that sucker," he said to me. "I tried to warn you that the cockroach was crawling right in front of us."

"I didn't even see the fucking thing," I replied. "When we come back on the air, I'm going to explain what happened. I'm going to name that cockroach 'Jake' because I'd like to do to O'Donnell what I just did to that bug."

At a game played in Detroit, O'Donnell was again officiating. Again, he made a horrendous, erroneous call against Boston, this time in the third quarter. It just so happened the play took place right in front of my broadcasting location. I raised myself out of my seat and yelled in Weitzman's direction, "O'Donnell's lost his mind. He just called Robey for setting an illegal pick and Robey was standing completely still. I mean a statue moves more than Rick just did. The man just fabricated a call because the Celtics are winning the game."

O'Donnell, who had been heading toward the scorer's table, couldn't help but overhear my comments and did an about-face. For the next two minutes—and I'm not exaggerating—he and I stared each other down. Weitzman attempted to continue with the broadcast. "Johnny and O'Donnell are about two feet apart," Rick reported. "Neither is moving, neither is flinching. Even the cigarette in Johnny's mouth is perfectly still. It's a test of wills...OK, Jake has finally turned away and Johnny is now leaning over the table watching him go over to the scorer. Johnny won the stare-down."

"Stare-downs" between Jake and me became a regular event whenever I sat courtside, which was our broadcasting location at many arenas. I have to admit I'd purposely try to bait him into these eye-to-eye battles. I'd wait until he got within 10 feet of me, and then I would begin my verbal assault on his officiating skills.

O'Donnell rarely showed any emotion, except that his face would turn a bright shade of crimson. Once, though, he actually verbally responded to me. "Keep it up, and next game you'll be broadcasting from the last row of the balcony, Johnny. I'm not taking your crap every time I ref a Celtics game."

"Jake," I answered while still on the air, "Even if they moved me to the balcony, I could still see what's happening on the court a lot clearer than you do."

Even absurd officiating couldn't prevent the Celtics from systematically wearing down opponents as they won 25 of 26 games during one stretch. On the final day of season, the Celtics beat Philly, 98-94, at the Garden to tie the Sixers for the league's best record at 62-20 and give Boston a 3-2 series edge over the Sixers and the Atlantic Division title.

I still was having some voice problems, but this team was so much fun to broadcast that I was able to grunt my way through 90 percent of the games. When my voice became so scratchy that I couldn't handle the non-stop play-by-play, I switched jobs with Weitzman, who, for a newcomer to the business, sounded like an old pro. As his color commentator, I'd slip in a few comments during breaks in the game and also interrupt him quite a bit during his play-by-play, which I always told *my* partners in the booth never to do to me.

"Sorry if I screwed you up with all my interruptions," I told him. "I just get far too emotional watching these guys."

"I'm just along for the ride. I think the audience really wants to hear from you, not me," Rick responded. "They don't mind it one bit when you start barking into the microphone. It's gotta get them revved up."

The Celtics, who had a bye in the first round, swept the Chicago Bulls, 4-0, in the Eastern Division semifinals. It was no contest, just a mere preliminary bout compared to the all-out war Boston expected against Philly in the division finals. Along with having the home-court advantage, the Celtics, in my view, also would be seeking revenge, having been embarrassed by the Sixers, 4-1, in the 1980 playoffs.

The '81 series against Philly was one of my favorites of all time, because this Celtics team displayed as much determination and will to win as any Boston club I had ever covered.

Even when Philly, led by the uncanny streak shooting of rookie guard Andrew Toney, who would rightly earn the nickname "the Boston Strangler," and body-twisting, gliding moves of Julius Erving, took a 3-1 series lead, I was still optimistic the Celtics would come all the way back and win three straight and advance to the championship round. It had happened only once before in NBA history—and I had witnessed it—when the '67-'68 Celtics shocked Wilt Chamberlain's 76ers.

Red hadn't given up, either. "Just remember one thing," he told the team immediately after Philadelphia had gone up 3-1. "Until they beat you one more time, they can't win the series. They've got to beat you. And if you don't allow them to beat you one more time, then you win the series and they're all through. That should be the only thought in your mind."

In Game 5 at the Garden, the Celtics, who trailed 59-49 at halftime, were still down 109-103 with less than two minutes remaining. Boston dug in, though, and held Philly scoreless the rest of the way to pull out a 111-109 victory. As the game ended, I was once again totally hoarse. "This team refused to give up," I said. "I'm looking at Erving, [Bobby] Jones and Toney and they're all shell-shocked. They're all shaking their heads in disbelief. This one has crushed their confidence."

Now the series headed back to the Spectrum, where we had lost 11 straight. Early in the third quarter, Philadelphia was cruising with a 57-42 lead when Fitch called timeout. "I tried to be calm. I had a plan," Bill told me later. "I just told the guys that I wanted every play to go through Larry. I didn't have to be a rocket scientist to know that was the only way we could come back and beat them."

The Celtics began to play what I called "gang-tackling defense" from that moment. And when Maxwell, taunted by an obnoxious fan behind the basket, dove into the stands to physically confront the loudmouth, Boston suddenly had all the motivation to go to war against the 76ers.

Bird proceeded to score 11 points and grab three rebounds as the Celtics trailed by only three entering the fourth quarter. The two teams battled back and forth until Boston led by three with a minute and a half remaining. When Toney followed his own jumper from downtown with a steal, Philly had its chance to regain the lead with 30 seconds to go. As he drove to the basket for what appeared to be an easy layup, McHale, coming in from the left side of the lane, blocked the shot and grabbed his own deflection.

"Toney is just standing under the basket, looking up at the rim, looking at McHale, now looking up again at the basket," I said. "It's like he's thinking to himself, 'Hey, that just can't be done.' Incredible play. I haven't seen that kind of timing and poise from a rookie since Russell first put on his No. 6 green uniform." Two Maxwell free throws sealed the win and sent the series back to Boston for a deciding seventh game.

As was the pattern in this series, we fell behind early in Game 7. With a little more than five minutes remaining in the fourth, the 76ers took an 89-82 lead when Doctor J grabbed his own miss and flipped in a reverse layup.

Philadelphia would not score another basket the rest of the way as the Celtics made three steals by double-teaming the ball. "The Sixers are in a state of sheer chaos," I told the audience. "They're playing scared. They're in panic mode."

With 1:20 left and the scored tied, Darryl Dawkins barreled towards the basket. Three Celtics—Bird, Parish, and McHale—all converged on him. There was what I called "just enough incidental contact" to force Dawkins to miss his shot. Bird then grabbed the rebound, stumbled out of the pack, and dribbled upcourt. As he crossed the three-point line on the left side of the court, he made a shoulder and arm fake as if he was going to make a cross-court pass.

His defender bit for a split second, giving Larry just enough room to bank in a 17-foot pull-up.

When Mo Cheeks was fouled with 29 seconds on the clock, Philly had a chance to tie the game. As Cheeks prepared for his free throws, M.L. walked by him and barked at him, "Don't choke." When Cheeks could convert only one of two free throws, the Celtics were able to hold on and advance into the finals, having won the last three games of their series versus Philly by margins of two, two and one points.

"I could never understand why Bill would almost invent reasons to get all over us when we were in the middle of a long winning streak during the regular season," said McHale. "Now I know what he was doing. He was preparing us for being down 3-1 to Philly."

"The Sixers kept giving us chances to come back," Bird said to me after the series ended. "None of us gave up. Too many people in life give up. We just proved that if you keep thinking positive, you'll get the opportunities to succeed."

Afterwards I happened to bump into referee Darrell Garretson in the Garden hallway. "You know, Bird is so smart in every aspect of the game. He's even clever when he argues a call because it's difficult to give the guy a technical because he doesn't curse or yell or try to show up an official. He just mutters that you made a crappy call. He never waves or flails his arms. Unless you're standing right next to him, you can't even tell that he's really giving an official an earful."

The championship series against the Houston Rockets, who had only managed a 40-42 record in the regular season, was not the cakewalk everyone in the media had predicted. In fact, the Sixers series seemed to drain the Celtics of all their energy and intensity.

After Houston had tied the series at 2-2, Fitch seemed disgusted when I interviewed him. "Now I think we realize were not playing the Sisters of the Poor. The Rockets aren't patsies," he said. "They're playing with more emotion than we are. We're trying to win by letting our offense carry us. In a few short days, we've managed to forget that it was our defensive effort which saved us against Philadelphia."

Before Game 5, Houston's star, Moses Malone, whom I referred to as "Mumbles" for obvious reasons, made the monumental mistake of attacking the Celtics verbally with this nonsensical statement: "They're not that good. They just get a lot of write-ups. I didn't even have much respect for them after they beat us 14 straight times. A lot of their wins were nothing but luck."

Malone had just unwittingly succeeded in awakening a sleeping giant. A 109-80 win by Boston at the Garden was followed by a 102-91 victory at the Summit. Game, set, match. Championship number 14 was ours.

The championship series MVP honors went to Max, who shot 57 percent while averaging 17.7 points and 9.2 rebounds. When I interviewed Rockets coach Del Harris after Boston's clinching win in Game 6, he paid tribute to Cedric's play. "Our defense did a great job. Malone had twice as many rebounds as Parish; we held McHale to 38 percent shooting," he said. "Hell, if anyone had told me before the series that Bird would shoot just 41 percent and we still would get beat 4-2, I'd have told them to go straight to the Funny Farm. The truth is that even if we could have shut Bird down completely, the outcome would have been the same—because of Maxwell. We put four different guys on him and he was too quick for all of them. He'd sneak inside, get perfect position, and just kill us with rebound baskets. He did it every game and we couldn't do a thing about it."

The victory celebration in Houston had a few comical moments, such as a hungover, sound-asleep McHale being wheeled out of his hotel room on a long iron baggage cart and then taken down the service elevator out to the team bus the next morning.

"Here comes my prize rookie," Fitch said to me as he stood over Kevin while he was carted to the bus. "I want a picture of this so I can present it to him on the first day of training camp in front of the whole team."

As the 1981 draft approached, there didn't seem to be any "steals" available for Boston. Red chose Wyoming's 6'5" swingman Charles Bradley with the 23rd pick of the first round. Charles was an excellent defender and a power leaper, but he didn't possess much of a shooting touch. He certainly was going to have a tough time earning playing time at shooting guard, which was his natural position in the NBA.

But the Celtics would surprise the entire league about 45 minutes after the first round of the draft had concluded. Auerbach, Fitch and owner Harry Mangurian were casually discussing the draft in Red's office when they all agreed that it was at least worth a gamble to draft Toronto Blue Jays infielder/outfielder Danny Ainge with their second pick of the second round.

Danny would later tell me that he had watched the draft from the back row of the fan section at the Chicago Bulls' draft headquarters. "Not one person recognized me," he said. "I wore a big floppy hat and kept my head down every minute I was there. As soon as the Celtics chose me, I ducked out."

Ainge, a 6'5" All-American at BYU, had won both the Wooden and Eastman Awards as the top college basketball player in '81. However, he was under contract to play for Toronto, which would not give him permission to play pro basketball during the baseball off season. Ainge, in fact, had hinted to Red prior to the draft that he would consider playing pro basketball, but only if the Celtics drafted him.

"We all knew that by choosing Ainge in the second round we might be wasting a draft pick," Fitch told me. "Red was a good friend of Buzz Bavasi, the Dodger GM who was the father of Blue Jays GM Peter Bavasi. He wasn't anxious to start trouble by attempting to steal away one of Toronto's players. Still, had Ainge not been under contract to play baseball, he would have definitely been one of the top two picks in the NBA draft. Harry kept insisting we should draft him."

After Red announced that the Celtics had chosen Ainge with the 31st pick of the draft, the initial public reaction was that Red had outfoxed the entire league once again. But the cost of paying the Blue Jays for his rights was going to be close to a million dollars. In addition, Ainge, who would have a lot of leverage, would undoubtedly want a good chunk of change to sign a multiyear contract with Boston. Auerbach and Fitch were not optimistic at all about the chances of reaching an agreement with both Toronto and Ainge.

"Harry, Red and myself were watching a tape of Ainge playing in the NCAA tournament about two weeks after the draft had taken place," Fitch told me. "All of a sudden, Mangurian pounded his fist on the table and said, 'We're going to sign the kid. I'll spend whatever we have to to get him. I know it's going to cost at least two or three million to get the deal done, but I want to go for it. Let's get started.'"

The Blue Jays' asking price for the release of Ainge, as expected, was steep ($900,000). Fearing that Red might come up with a scheme to avoid paying for Ainge's rights, Toronto filed suit in federal court seeking to prevent the Celtics and Danny from having any further contact. Mangurian, true to his word, didn't hesitate to spend big bucks to hire one of Boston's most prestigious law firms, Hale and Dorr, to fight the Blue Jays in court. When Toronto prevailed in the case, Red and Bavasi began four months of intense, sometimes heated negotiations.

By then, Ainge was making it abundantly clear to the Blue Jays' management and to the public that, under no circumstances, would he return to his baseball career. Danny even went so far as to announce that he was becoming an assistant basketball coach at BYU and would recruit prospects in the off season. It was an obvious ploy that didn't fool the Blue Jays. Finally, on November 27 in a suite at the Ritz Carlton in Boston, the Celtics and Blue Jays agreed on a deal that would allow Ainge to join the Celtics. Before the deal could be finalized, however, Red had to reach a contract agreement with Danny, who had considerable leverage because Mangurian was about to fork over more than $800,000 to Toronto for his release. In a matter of five hours, Auerbach and Ainge reached an agreement that would pay the now ex-Blue Jay singles hitter $1.7 million over five years. The long-shot drafting of Ainge had paid off.

The drafting and subsequent signing of Danny is one example of why I consider Harry to be among the best Celtics owners in team history. He wanted a championship-caliber team, and he was always willing to pay for quality players such as Bird, McHale and now Ainge.

Danny is my all-time favorite pest/prankster. His principal hobby when he was a Celtic was thinking of practical jokes he could spring on me. In fact, he got me good the very first time I sat next to him on a plane ride. My initial impression of him was that he was very polite, very friendly. He just seemed like a nice, quiet, respectful Mormon youngster. I soon discovered I had made an error in judgment. As the team exited the plane, Danny patted me on the back several times and said, "It's been great talking to you." Then I started walking through the airport. I noticed that quite a few people were giggling and smiling as they glanced at me. Finally, a gentleman tapped me on the shoulder and said, "Sir, you have a sign stuck to the back of your jacket. I'll remove it for you."

The man then handed the handwritten sign to me. Let's just say it was a very unflattering note questioning my manhood. It took me all of two seconds to realize that Ainge had taped that sign on my back.

Within a couple weeks, Danny struck again. We were in a hotel out in Denver. At night, the room service staff would put a breakfast menu order card on each guest's doorknob. Danny found out what room I was in, sneaked up to my room, and filled out my breakfast order card. The next morning at 5 a.m., room service delivered five hard-boiled eggs, a double order of pancakes, side orders of bacon and sausage, two English muffins, an order of French toast, and four containers of buttermilk to my room. Am I sure it was Ainge? Yes, because only his little devious mind could have thought up such a crazy stunt.

As a rookie, Danny was himself the target of some teasing, especially from McHale. Ainge's shooting during his first year was way off, and McHale would really give him the business. "I put a jinx on you, Danny. I can control your brain waves. I can simply will you to miss all your shots."

Danny's struggles meant he came under fire from Fitch quite often. For the first few months, Ainge accepted the fact that Bill was going to give him a stern lecture every time he made a mistake in a game. I felt sorry for him, because he was really an effort-type player who wanted so badly to contribute to the Celtics' success. He also was a great role model for kids. Since he joined the team, no one had ever heard him curse. He didn't drink, and he read a religious book on a daily basis.

On the court, he would occasionally frustrate Bird and McHale. "Watch out, Danny's running wild again. He just comes down on a fast break and yanks up a three-pointer," Larry would kiddingly tell the entire team. "We can have a four-on-one, and Danny's going to shoot a 25-foot jumper even if Kevin or me are standing all alone under the basket."

McHale would pick up where Bird left off. "I think I'm shooting about 55 percent. Ainge is going along at around 36 percent," Kevin said. "That doesn't stop Danny from faking a pass to me inside the lane and then heaving up a brick. I guess BYU didn't offer a class in basic statistical probabilities."

Late in February, Danny no longer was able to remain silent when Fitch kept pointing out his errors in front of the entire team. Ainge's frustration with Bill's lectures came to a head while the team was playing the Sonics in Seattle. Danny was paired with Tiny Archibald in the backcourt. On a Boston fast break, Tiny threw an errant pass to Ainge, who managed to get a hand on the ball but lost control of it. Bill immediately called timeout and told Danny he was being benched for mishandling the pass. To everyone's surprise, Danny exploded: "Fuck you. That turnover wasn't my fault. You just don't have the balls to yell at Tiny for throwing a bad pass."

Gerald Henderson and Robert Parish, with their mouths wide open, glanced over at me with a look of mock shock on their faces. Robert then went over to Danny, gave him a wink and a thumbs up signal and said, "Ainge, dinner's on me tonight."

The regular-season play of the Celtics in '81-'82 gave me every reason to believe they would be the first team to repeat as champions since Russell guided Boston to the '68 and '69 titles. Led by All-Star Game MVP Bird and the inside scoring of McHale, Maxwell, and Parish, who were combining for 48 points a game, Boston never lost more than two games in a row the entire season and put together a club-record 18 straight wins as the playoffs were approaching.

This was the season I began calling Washington's Jeff Ruland, a rookie power-forward center, and Rick Mahorn, the Bullets' 240-pound enforcer, "McFilthy" and "McDirty." As I explained on the air, "Those two are doing everything short of raping the Celtics' big men. They want to start a brutal bloodbath. That's their goal every game they play against Boston."

When the Celtics faced the Bullets in the division semifinals, my color commentator, Rick Weitzman, approached Ruland before the opening game and asked him if he would do a five-minute pregame interview.

"You work with that guy Most, don't you?" Ruland said. "Well, my mother listens from Long Island to your broadcasts and she says you guys are assholes. She tells me Most's play-by-play is nothing but happy horseshit. Forget about me doing any interview for you stiffs. And tell him to go screw himself."

Weitzman told me about his conversation with Ruland. I didn't say a word. (Rick ended up interviewing Mahorn, who was funny and courteous.) When I went on the air, I gave my standard introduction: "Hello everybody. This is Johnny Most courtside at the Capital Center where the Boston Celtics are preparing to do basketball battle with the Washington Bullets." Then, without pausing, I added, "By the way, Mrs. Ruland, if you're listening to this broadcast in New York, you'd better turn off the radio, because you're not going to like what you hear."

That series was proof enough for me to say that Ruland and Mahorn led the league in both cheap shots and vicious elbow blows. In Game 3, Mahorn gunned a basketball directly at the back of Gerald Henderson's head, and Ruland threw a kidney punch that sent Parish to the floor in tremendous pain. All through the series, McHale and Maxwell received well-aimed elbows to the ribs almost every time they went up for a rebound. When Bullets reserve center Jim Chones gave Robey a shove and then acted like he was going to start throwing punches, Rick responded by grabbing Chones' throat with one hand and chest-bumping the aging veteran until he retreated toward the sideline.

McFilthy and McDirty also were better actors than most pro wrestling tag-team partners. Both would flop as soon as they felt the slightest bit of contact. For all his tough facial expressions, Ruland was a chronic whiner. I'll say this for Mahorn, he had at least one effective defensive move that occasionally tricked McHale. As Kevin would back in and bump Mahorn for position in the lane, McDirty would simply jump backwards, causing Kevin to lose his balance, stumble, and be called for a walk.

Despite the physical, sneak-attack tactics of the "Gruesome Twosome" and their teammates, the Celtics eliminated Washington in five games. Then Boston faced Philly for the third straight time in the division finals. After splitting the first two games, the Celtics saw their chances of advancing to the championship round diminish when Tiny suffered a dislocated left shoulder while diving for a loose ball in the opening minute of Game 3. Until that point, I was a hundred percent sure the Maxwell-Parish-Robey-Bird-McHale quintet would have no trouble overpowering Philadelphia's frontcourt personnel, which consisted of Erving, Dawkins, Caldwell Jones and "The Hatchet Brothers," Bobby Jones and Steve Mix.

Although Tiny, a lefty, would spend entire practices attempting to shoot free throws and short jumpers right-handed, it was a sad sight to watch him stand alone at one end of the court while the rest of the team practiced its set offense at the other end. It was obvious that Archibald was out at least for the remainder of the series, if not longer. "The media is sounding like it's the end of the world for us," Fitch said during my interview with him prior to Game 4. "It's my job to make sure my guys don't start believing it's true. We still have the horses to win if we're patient and execute."

A Cheeks' steal from Maxwell in the final five seconds of Game 4 preserved a 99-97 Philly win. Then the Sixers, behind the 6'3" Toney's "unconscious" long-range shooting (39 points), beat Boston by 25 points at the Spectrum to take a 3-1 series advantage.

"I guarantee this team is not through, not after the courage and confidence it showed last year," I told my audience in my postgame wrap-up. "The 76ers were dancing and celebrating on the court as if the series was over. [Philadelphia coach] Billy Cunningham was jumping up and down and hugging his players. It was totally unprofessional. Just bush league behavior from a bush league coach. Believe me, every Celtic will remember that uncalled-for, obnoxious display."

Back at the Garden for Game 5, the Celtics predictably showed their character by pressuring Toney and Cheeks for 48 minutes and forcing the 76ers to rush their shots. The result: a 114-85 Boston rout.

When the series returned to the Spectrum, Boston's defense again dominated as Philly managed to score only 27 points in the second half. The Celtics, with their 88-75 win, were going home for Game 7. Even the 76ers fans were fearing the worst as they booed and even chanted "Chokers" as Cunningham and his club walked off the court.

McHale, much to Fitch's displeasure, told the media, "Now we've got both legs out of the coffin and they [the 76ers] are climbing in."

"Shit, we don't need to have the 76ers read that quote," an upset Fitch said to me when we arrived back in Boston. "I want our actions on the court to do all the talking for us."

Unfortunately, the 76ers showed more poise in Game 7 than they had during the entire series. When the "Boston Strangler" began the game by nailing five of his first eight shots, it opened things up for Erving, who drove to the basket at every opportunity and finished off four Cheeks-led fast breaks with dunks or layups. There would be no comeback repeat for the Celtics as Philly took control by the end of the third quarter and won easily, 120-106.

"I'm not going to blame this on Tiny's injury," Fitch said. "Henderson and Ainge did a good job for us filling in for him. We should have known Philly wasn't going to forget last year, especially in a Game 7 situation. I actually think playing the deciding game in our place gave them extra motivation. We didn't match their intensity."

A candid Maxwell agreed. "Basically," he said to me afterward in the eerily quiet Celtics locker room, "we started celebrating one game too early."

There were changes in the Celtics personnel during the offseason.

Boston drafted 6'11" Darren Tillis with the 23rd pick of the first round. Tillis, who had played at Cleveland State, was a nice kid who never really had much of a shot of getting any playing time with Boston, given Fitch's talented and deep frontcourt. In late August, Cowens, then 34 years old, told me he had decided to make a comeback, not with Boston but with the Bucks, who were coached by his old Celtics teammate Don Nelson. Naturally Red wanted compensation from Milwaukee since Boston still held David's rights. When Auerbach suddenly became ill and required hospitalization in early September, it was up to Harry Mangurian and Fitch to negotiate the compensation deal.

Late one night, I received a phone call from Bill. "Hey, I'm going to set up a conference call with me, Harry, and you because we have something we want to discuss." I had absolutely no idea what the subject matter was going to be. Once the conference call began, Bill said, "Johnny, the Bucks have offered us our choice of three players for the rights to Cowens. We can have Brian Winters or Quinn Buckner or Junior Bridgeman. Harry and I have different opinions on who we should take, so we've agreed to go along with whoever you think is the best guy for us to take." I was flattered that they thought so highly of my opinion. "Well, I don't even have to think about who I would take if I were you guys. I'd grab Buckner because he always kills us," I told them. "He's smart, he's a tough defender and he's one of Milwaukee's leaders."

"That's what I wanted to hear you say," Fitch responded. "He was my choice, because I can have him back up Tiny at point and use Henderson as both a shooting guard and as our third point man."

Then Harry spoke up. "OK, you two win. Personally, I was leaning towards taking Winters over Buckner. I'll call Nelson tomorrow and make the deal. I just don't want Red going berserk when he recovers and I have to tell him about the deal."

During the annual referees' training camp, which is usually held in early September, McHale's twisting, up-and-under move in the lane was one of the principal topics. Kevin had been getting called for walking because the officials thought he *had* to be moving his pivot foot in order to beat his defender so consistently. Referee Earl Strom told me about the discussion among all the officials. "There were about five of us [not me, though] who were convinced McHale occasionally dragged his pivot foot in the middle of his spin to the hoop. Finally, we picked out 10 games in which McHale had been called for traveling and watched his move in slow motion on tape. We found only one time where he actually was guilty of walking,"

Earl told me. "The bottom line is that McHale moves so quickly and effectively that we got fooled. I can understand after watching the tape why he was always so upset when he'd get called for walking when he, in fact, had practically invented a perfectly legitimate method of spinning and then flipping in what amounted to an underhanded layup. We screwed up that call on a regular basis, John. I admit it. Now we know what to look for. I doubt he'll get a third as many calls going against him as long as he sticks to the exact same move."

Strom's explanation is one reason why I respect him. He is one guy who's not afraid to say, "My error. I blew the call." Some refs just refuse to admit they aren't perfect. Those are the refs I go after when I'm broadcasting. With guys like Strom, I have a little more patience than with the know-it-all type of official.

In July, WRKO announced that Glenn Ordway, who had worked with me on a part-time basis during the '81-'82 season, would be my full-time color commentator. Glenn was young, ambitious and talented. He always did meticulous statistical preparation work before each game. He was an excellent interviewer who wasn't afraid to ask tough questions. On the air, though, Glenn and I occasionally wouldn't see eye to eye. He wanted to make his comments about key plays, but his detailed remarks would sometimes delay my play-by-play. I'd remind him in no uncertain terms that the most important part of the broadcast was making sure the listeners didn't miss hearing the live action. "Make your point quickly, and then shut up and let me do my job," I told him. It took a year or so, but we finally adjusted to each other's broadcasting styles.

Near the end of the exhibition season, Fitch made a tough decision, cutting 33-year-old Chris Ford. The principal reason why Chris became expendable was that Ainge had proven to Bill he could provide the Celtics with consistent outside shooting, along with quickness on defense. "Danny went to the L.A. Summer Pro League and just worked his butt off. He averaged 30 points a game and didn't miss many shots in doing it," Fitch told me. "When he came to camp, he was an entirely different player than last year. He was confident, even cocky. He wanted to show everyone, especially his teammates, that his rookie-year shooting jitters were a fluke. He's made a believer out of me."

Boston wasn't the only team to make off-season moves. The 76ers, in my opinion, swindled the Rockets when they sent Caldwell Jones and an '83 first-round draft choice to Houston in exchange for Moses Malone, who had led the league in rebounding the past two seasons. Malone was a perfect fit for Philly, which now had a physical, relentless banger to complement Erving's finesse game and jump start fast breaks with his outlet passes to Maurice Cheeks.

When the exhibition season ended, Fitch made a decision to start Buckner instead of Archibald at point guard. Tiny was irate at what he perceived as a demotion. "Nobody beat me out for my starter's spot," he said. "It was just taken away from me and handed to someone else for absolutely no reason. They can trade me if that's how things are done around here."

Fitch defended the lineup change by saying, "Tiny is now 34 years old. I don't want to wear him down by playing him 35 minutes a game. I'd rather bring him in for crucial situations when we really need his leadership and experience. I need him to be fresh when it's crunch time."

When I asked Tiny if he wanted to be interviewed, he simply shrugged his shoulders and said, "What good would that do? Coach is just making up an excuse for taking me out of the lineup. I have no choice but to do what the man tells me to do. I said all I'm going to say in private to Fitch." Personally, I agreed with Fitch's logic. Tiny had clearly lost a step, and as a result, he had difficulty covering younger point guards such as Cheeks and Isiah Thomas.

At the same time, I sympathized with Tiny, a proud man who was embarrassed and depressed about becoming a role player. I admired Archibald greatly as a person. I don't think I've ever met a more caring, giving NBA star when it comes to working with kids.

Each summer he spends hundreds of hours in his old South Bronx neighborhood coaching youngsters and running a basketball league. More importantly, he spends his nights during the off season counseling youngsters, emphasizing the value of an education. He's their teacher, adviser, and, above all, their friend. Why does Tiny give so much of himself? Here are the reasons he told me: "Two of my brothers had drug problems. One was an alcoholic, the other a heroin addict. If it wasn't for the influence of one man, I probably would have gone down that same route. What happened to my brothers can happen to any kid in an environment like the South Bronx. The street corners breed that type of situation. I know from my own experiences that just one man can change a lot of lives. That's why I spend my summers here."

Throughout the season, the mood of the team was upbeat despite the fact that the Sixers kept piling up the wins. This Celtics team was fun to be a part of. While Boston was "all business" on the court, humorous banter was part of the daily routine. The players on this team acted like a bunch of college fraternity brothers who enjoyed harmless hazing and all kinds of practical jokes.

Ainge, who was being booed in every arena around the league because of his "crybaby" facial expressions whenever a foul was called against him, became an easy target for McHale, who came up with a "boo-meter" hand gesture to measure the crowd's reaction when Danny was introduced before every game. "By my mathematical calculations," McHale joked in an interview with me, "Danny is hated most by the fans in Philadelphia, Detroit, New York, and L.A. And there's about 10 other places where fans are jumping on the anti-Ainge bandwagon."

In reality, Danny didn't mind the booing. "It psyches me up, Johnny," he said. "M.L. tells me all the time that if other team's fans don't boo you, it means you're not doing your job. They boo you because your play is hurting their team's chances of winning. That's why I laugh when McHale starts motioning for the crowds to boo me during the introductions."

There were also a few laughs at Kevin's expense.

Early in the season, two writers from *Inside Sports Magazine* came to Boston to do an article about McHale. They started asking questions of members of the media, including myself, about Kevin's lifestyle. One of the two writers asked me questions about whether Kevin did a lot of partying and drinking. They even asked a couple of reporters if they suspected McHale might use marijuana or other drugs. I, along with everyone they interviewed, told them McHale enjoyed having a couple beers after games or occasionally might go to a bar to socialize when the team had a day off. Not one single person they interviewed said Kevin was even capable of being tempted into trying marijuana or any other drug.

As soon as I had been questioned by one of the writers, I phoned Kevin and told him to beware of these "magazine assholes," because they were looking to damage his reputation. Despite my warning, Kevin allowed them to visit his home. They brought along a photographer to take some pictures of him at his house. At the time, Miller Beer was a sponsor of the Celtics, and the company gave each Celtic player a year's supply of their product. Kevin had asked the Miller truck driver to stack the cartons of beer against the back wall in his garage. When the writers and their photographer spotted the beer behind his pickup truck, they managed to con Kevin into posing for a picture next to his vehicle, which was parked in the garage. When the magazine hit the newspaper stands several months later, the article suggested (without the slightest bit of proof) that Kevin was a real-life "Bluto" from the movie *Animal House*.

When McHale's teammates saw the magazine photo of Kevin smiling away in his garage with all that Miller Beer in the background, they immediately started giving him the business. Even Robert Parish, who rarely was a participant in all the joking conversations, couldn't resist ribbing McHale.

"Now I know why you're always smiling and talking nonsense," Robert said. "You're already half in the bag by the time you come to morning practice."

Kevin's tendency to talk about every subject imaginable earned him the nickname "4-1-1" from Danny. "We call him that because he's always got an answer for any question you ask him. He's 'Mr. Information.' Even if he doesn't know an answer to a question, he'll just make one up," Ainge said. "I like his other nickname better, though. I call him Herman Munster because he looks exactly like Frankenstein."

When I interviewed McHale, I asked him why he enjoyed teasing Ainge at every opportunity. "Danny is an easy target because he claims he's such a great athlete. He calls himself 'The Natural.' The only thing that comes naturally to Danny is cheating. He'll do it playing chess, Monopoly, cards, Trivial Pursuit, golf, anything."

I could see Kevin was really enjoying talking about Danny's habit of "bending the rules" in just about every competitive game known to man. And I knew Kevin was telling the truth, so I asked him to tell my audience about Ainge's methods of getting an edge on the golf course. "Well, he's either the luckiest golfer in history or he cheats his ass off," Kevin responded. "Just to give you one example, at least once or twice a round he'll hit a ball deep into the woods and everyone in the foursome will hear the ball smack off two or three trees. It's amazing, but Danny always manages to find the ball sitting up nicely in a patch of short grass, with a clear shot to the green. What's more suspicious is that despite the fact that his golf balls really carom hard off at least a couple of trees, there's never even a tiny scratch mark on it. It's funny, but every one of Danny's golf balls he *claims* to have found looks brand-spanking new, almost as if they had come right out of his golf bag.

"There are other things Danny does on the golf course that I've noticed. For instance, he has a real odd way of marking his ball on the green. He picks the ball up first, then he takes a dime out of his pocket and flips the coin three or four feet closer to the pin than where his golf ball originally stopped."

Bird, who was listening in to McHale's remarks, pulled up a chair and joined the interview. "Hey, I can back up what Kevin is saying because Danny pulled one of his tricks on me," he said. "I was beating him by a stroke as we came to the 17th hole. Just as I'm starting my swing, Danny, who was no more than five feet away from me, unzips his fly and starts peeing in the direction of my teed-up golf ball. I got so rattled that I almost whiffed. I ended up topping the ball and watching it roll about 50 yards as he fell to the ground laughing. You can't trust that little weasel. I've told him the only way I'll ever play him for money on the golf course is if we both ride in the same cart. I guarantee I won't take my eyes off him the entire round. I guarantee he won't 'miraculously' find a golf ball that went 100 feet into the woods when I'm playing against him."

I didn't doubt Bird or McHale for a second, because Danny was always devising new practical jokes to spring on me, such as putting salt into my coffee, crushing my pack of cigarettes while I was sleeping on a plane, or sneaking tiny, white miniature firecrackers called "loads" into my cigarettes.

Believe it or not, the biggest laugh of the season came at Fitch's expense. Early in the season, the Celtics were staying in Kansas City, where they were scheduled to play the Kings the next night. Darren Tillis went to practice and returned to his room only to discover that his wallet had been stolen from a jacket he had hung up in a closet. When Fitch found out about Tillis being robbed, he lectured the player in front of the whole team, because Darren had made what Bill called a "dumb fucking rookie mistake." Three nights later, the team was in Seattle for two days. On the first night, Bill went to the bar, along with assistant coach Jimmy Rodgers, to have a couple of drinks. When he reached for his wallet to pay the check, Bill realized he had been the victim of a pickpocket.

As soon as the team learned the next day that a pickpocket had snatched Bill's wallet, Maxwell couldn't resist a chance to needle his coach. "Hey, Bill, I heard about you getting pickpocketed. Would you call that a dumb fucking rookie mistake?"

To Bill's credit, he came up with a quick answer. "Yeah, I guess you could say Tillis and myself are what you call 'easy marks' for petty thieves. Thank God for per diem money, or Darren and I would be eating at McDonald's for the rest of the trip."

Even on the court, the Celtics had a few laughs from time to time. In the second game of the season, Boston was crushing Atlanta at the Omni. During a Hawks timeout, Fitch told Ainge to substitute for Henderson. Gerald, however, didn't realize Bill was taking him out, so we ended up having one too many players on the court. When Atlanta inbounded the ball, Danny went to cover Hawks guard Mike Glenn, but Gerald was already guarding him. Then Danny sprinted over to cover Atlanta's point guard, Wes Matthews, only to find Tiny was defending that player. As Danny kept running from one Hawk player to the next, everyone in the arena, with the exception of the Hawks and the refs, began to notice that we had six men on the court.

"I was practically falling to the floor from laughing so hard as Danny just kept running in circles, trying to avoid getting spotted as our sixth player," Maxwell told me after the game. "Just to show you how dumb the Hawk players are, their bench players were standing up and yelling, 'Zone! Zone! Ainge isn't covering anyone. He's just playing a zone. Call a damn technical.' Not one of those freaks had the brains to figure out we had six guys playing." Only when Danny tried to sneak off the court and hide near our bench did the officials finally pick up on the fact we had an extra guy out there. By then, our whole team, including Bill Fitch, was absolutely roaring. As one of the Hawks shot the technical, Fitch called me over and said, 'Max, remind me never to make a trade for any of those dumb Hawk bastards. Not one of them knows how to count to six.'"

As the regular season progressed, Boston kept losing ground to Philly, which was on its way to 65 wins. While we were playing sound basketball, Red believed we could use an experienced small forward who could prevent the defense from collapsing inside on Parish and McHale. Cleveland's Scott Wedman fit the bill perfectly, so, at midseason, Auerbach dealt Tillis and a first-round draft pick to the Cavs in exchange for the nine-year deadly accurate outside shooting veteran.

The day after the trade was announced, I interviewed Carr and Ainge, asking them what effect the trade would have on the team. "Well, for one thing, Danny's not going to get as many shots," a grinning M.L. piped up. "Let's face it, who do you think Larry is going to pass the ball to? Is he going to be looking to get the ball into the hands of a guy like Scotty who's scored 10,000 points, or is he going to throw the ball to a guy like Danny, who is still struggling to reach the 500-point plateau?"

"What you're basically telling me is that Ainge's role is going to change from shooter to permanent decoy?" I replied, playing along with M.L.'s ribbing of Danny.

"If that happens, I know one other effect the trade for Wedman will have," Danny joked. "My assist total is going to be down because I'm going to shoot every time I get my hands on the ball."

One month after the Wedman trade, I suffered a stroke while at Logan Airport. My rehabilitation period would last more than a year before I was able to return to the broadcasting booth. While I was recuperating, though, I watched every game, kept in touch with the players on almost a daily basis, and even taped some interviews with Ordway, who now was taking my place doing the play-by-play.

13

REBOUNDING
FROM A STROKE

The most frightening hours of my life occurred on the morning of February 8, 1983. That's when I suffered a stroke. And that's when I figured the phrase "high above courtside" would be said only once more—in my obituary.

The Celtics were playing the Bullets that night in Landover, Maryland, which meant getting up at 6 a.m. in order to catch the 8 a.m. team flight from Logan Airport to Washington. The night before I had gotten very little sleep, so I decided to take a limousine to the airport rather than drive myself. The decision not to get behind the wheel of a car probably saved my life. On the way to the airport I began to feel sick. I thought maybe it was because I was overtired, maybe it was because I hadn't had anything to eat for nearly 12 hours. For whatever reason, I felt weak and exhausted, so I shut my eyes and fell asleep—only to wake up in a cold sweat and discover that my right hand was curled into a fist. What scared me even more was that I was unable to pry my hand open even slightly.

After the limo pulled up at the terminal, I ran to the men's room, dizzy and nauseated. I splashed cold water on my face, but it did nothing to relieve the jelly-like feeling that my whole body was experiencing. I walked to the boarding area for our plane and slumped into a chair, hoping that a five-minute rest might snap me out of it. I tried to convince myself that it just had a case of the flu, but deep down, I knew this was far more serious.

My engineer, Dave Whelan, was the first to arrive and he immediately came over to say hello. He could tell right away that I needed medical assistance. "Dave, I don't think I'm going to be able to make it today. Glenn is going to have to handle the whole thing by himself," I reluctantly told him. In reassuring me, Dave just made sure I would have no reason to worry. "Don't worry about the game. Just see a doctor and get some rest. You'll be all right by tomorrow. We need you healthy."

It didn't take much convincing for me to know he was right. When I tried to get up from my chair, though, I was too weak to raise my body up. It was then that I asked a Northwest Airline service representative to call the Celtics physician, Tom Silva. Fortunately Dr. Silva was home. After the airline representative told him of my symptoms, Tom, realizing the situation was critical, gave instructions: "Get Johnny to the medical aid station. Do it now."

Around that time, Mike Carey of the *Boston Herald* walked into the terminal and spotted me, as attendants were preparing to put me in a wheelchair and take me over to the airport aid station, which was about 500 yards away. Mike asked if everything was all right, but I couldn't reply. By then, the effects of the stroke were becoming more obvious. Knowing full well that I wouldn't voluntarily quit on a ballgame unless there was something radically wrong, Mike decided to go along with me. By the time I had been wheeled into the aid station, my power of speech was all but gone. A nurse met us at the door and asked what was wrong, but I couldn't get a syllable out of my mouth. I was talking in gibberish while everyone was attempting to calm me down. "Just try one word at a time, Mr. Most," said a nurse. "You're rushing your speech. You just go as slow as you want."

I tried, but all I kept repeating was a series of totally mumbled sentences that were unintelligible. Naturally, I was in a state of panic, yet my thought process hadn't been affected by the stroke. I could understand everything that was happening. I could grasp every sentence that was said to me or about me. But I had absolutely no way to respond. I rested on the examining table for about five minutes and then attempted once more to communicate. Finally I was able to spit out two fragmented sentences: "What's wrong with me? Having a stroke?" The nurse clutched my hand and answered, "Maybe. You'll be getting the best of care, so don't worry."

I won't try to fool you. I was not a cool customer during the ambulance ride. The sirens scared me, my sweating put me in a frenzied state, and the lack of control over my body made me (excuse the term) a basket case. I was unable to talk, and Mike didn't quite know what to say to me. So we sat silently, listening to the paramedics until we reached the hospital's emergency entrance.

On the way to the hospital, my first thoughts were about my job. For a few seconds, I actually started worrying about missing the Bullets game. Was I putting Glenn and Dave on the spot? Had I let down the station by getting sick at the last minute? Would the station executives be angry?

Then it finally hit me. The odds were I had already broadcast my last Celtics game. My mind raced on to an even more depressing thought. Perhaps I was indeed about to die. "Just make it to the hospital," I told myself. "Do that and you've got a chance."

I wondered what effect all of this would have on my kids, the most important part of my life. How was I going to look after them and have an influence on their day-to-day lives if I wasn't near them or if I couldn't be coherent? Who would counsel them? They needed me and I needed them. I had to recover. There was so much more I wanted to share with them.

Once more I tried to say a few words to Mike, but again I was unable to talk, which only added to my frustration and confusion. All Mike could say was, "We're getting closer. We're almost there. Just another couple minutes and then you can relax."

The truth is the ambulance ride to Massachussetts General lasted only 10 minutes, but it felt more like we had taken the grand tour of the Bay State. Finally the ambulance pulled up to the emergency door and I was rushed into the examining room, where I was immediately put under the care of Dr. Allan Ropper, a heart specialist whose work turned out to be nothing short of miraculous.

After a brief exam, Dr. Ropper, who knew I was the Celtics' broadcaster, informed Mike and me that I had suffered what he termed a mild stroke. He calmed me down by saying, "We're going to give you some medicine which will start working within minutes. You'll feel much more comfortable and relaxed. We'll be right here with you all the time. OK?" At last, I felt reassured. Just knowing what the exact problem was helped settle my mind. Plus, being at Massachussetts General, I knew I would definitely be getting top-quality care.

"There's some partial paralysis on his right side," Dr. Ropper told Mike. "There's been some damage to his speech. Normally this type of stroke is not considered severe. But in Mr. Most's case, the loss of speech could mean the end of his career. We have two ways to go. We can use standard methods of treatment or we can use another procedure which is still somewhat new and, to a degree, is experimental. There's more risk involved with the drugs we would use, but they have been shown to be very effective in reversing stroke damage." Mike didn't think twice about the choices. "If there's a drug that gives Johnny a better chance of regaining his speech, use it," he said. "Johnny's whole life revolves around two things: his kids and the Celtics. If he doesn't regain his speech, he'll be totally lost if he isn't able to do the games any more."

The treatment proved to be highly effective. My speech improved slightly within an hour or so and became noticeably better during the next two weeks. "It wasn't a major stroke in terms of the amount of area affected in the brain," Dr. Ropper told Mike later. "In the first six to eight hours some people do very well. In fact, 15 percent of the stroke victims have a complete reversal. In the majority of cases, however, the patients are left with a substantial problem with their speech."

While Mike and Dr. Ropper discussed the possibilities, my thoughts turned to my youngest daughter, Andrea, who was 12 at the time and lived with me in New Hampshire. I started worrying about who would take care of her for all the time I was going to be at Massachusetts General. How would she react to the news that I had suffered a stroke? With considerable effort, I was able to communicate one word at a time until Mike and the doctor realized my concerns. Despite being dazed and confused, I was somehow able to recall the phone number of my niece, Barbara Friedman, who also lived in New Hampshire. Through hand signals and head nodding, I was able to relay her phone number to the doctor. A few minutes later, he informed me that he had contacted my niece, who said she would be more than happy to look after Andrea for as long as needed. For a brief second, I smiled and relaxed.

But when I was moved into the intensive care unit, it was as if I had entered the Twilight Zone. My first seven hours there were the roughest of my life. I had numerous needles sticking into my arms as various medications flowed into the veins. There were always two or three doctors and nurses working over me. They'd talk to me, reassure me, ask questions, give me orders. I knew they were doing all in their power to help, but the constant frantic activity around me made me more nervous and scared. After a while, my brain became totally scrambled.

When my condition was finally stabilized, I was taken down the hallway for a CAT scan that would determine whether the stroke had caused any brain damage, and, if so, how much. The machine, which resembled a huge steel beehive, intimidated me. The technicians positioned me on a cold metal table and ordered me not to move. Then the table began to slide, in a series of jerks and jolts, toward the dark metal tunnel in the middle of the CAT scan machine. As the table moved, there was a tremendously loud banging sound. I felt as if I was going to be consumed and incinerated. I became desperate and hysterical. My panic became so intense that the nurses had to hold me down.

"Scream, yell, curse, do anything—but don't move an inch," they told me. "This will only take 10 minutes and there is no pain involved. Just some loud sounds, that's all."

"Sure," I was thinking. "Ten minutes in this monster of a machine and I'll be ready for the nuthouse."

The CAT scan ordeal finally ended, and by the next morning I felt more at ease than at any time since my stroke began. In fact, I even attempted to tell Dr. Ropper a dirty joke when he came into intensive care to examine me. You know doctors, though. They're all business. To them, a stroke is no laughing matter. My legs were weak, but I was able to move them ever so slightly. My right arm remained paralyzed. My speech was coming back, if only word by word. Everything I said was slurred, but at least my brain was functioning well enough to vocalize my thoughts.

The first person other than the hospital staff and my family to offer encouragement was none other than Phil Esposito, the former Bruins center who ranks as one of the greats to ever play the game. It just so happened that Phil's father had suffered a stroke and was also a patient at Massachusetts General. While Phil was visiting his dad, he heard about my condition and decided to visit me. For more than a hour, he talked about his years with the Bruins, the Celtics players he had become friends with during the years, his father's stroke and my stroke. Most of all, he wanted to make sure I had a positive attitude. Anyone who has ever been ill can tell the difference between someone who merely says, "Get well quick" and someone who, with emotion and caring, doesn't have to mention a word to let you know they're in your corner. Phil was one person who rooted for you all the way.

Sometime during day two in the hospital, I began to practice my opening for the broadcasts. For 33 years I had used the same one:

"Hello, everybody. This is Johnny Most, high above courtside, speaking to you from the Boston Garden." The first time I attempted these lines in my hospital bed, I couldn't even get the first three words out of my mouth without stumbling. But I was determined to make progress. Each day I would practice the opening until I had added a word, or maybe just a syllable, to my dialogue. Over the course of my stay at Massachusetts General, I repeated my opening lines perhaps four hundred times. It was my principal method of charting my progress. I'm sure every patient on my floor was hoping that either I'd shut up or come up with a slightly different speech.

I wasn't allowed any visitors until the second day of my stay in the ICU, which was fine with me. I really didn't want anyone, especially my kids, to see me in my weakened condition. Although the doctors were satisfied with my improvement, I still felt like I was on another planet. My mind was functioning, but my speech was sloppy and my right arm was totally limp.

My first visitor was Bob Fish, the general manager of my radio station, WRKO, whom I had seen only occasionally at the station and at a few Celtics games. We were business associates, barely acquaintances. He was a good boss—and, as I was to find out, a very loyal and very caring friend throughout the illness. On his first visit, he didn't stay more than 10 minutes. All he wanted to do was reassure me that I had no worries concerning my job or my paychecks. When he first entered the room, Bob was more serious than I had ever seen him. "We miss you," he said as he pulled a chair over toward my bed, "but we don't want you to rush things. Just do what the doctors tell you."

Then came more jokes. "Johnny, you know this means no more all-night TV watching, no more 40 cups of coffee a day. You'll even have to give up your daily carton of smokes," Fish said. "And leave the nurses alone. They don't have time to fool around with a dirty old man." With that, Bob got up, patted me on the shoulder, and left.

Glenn also stopped in to see me when he returned from the game in Washington. With the exception of my relatives, Fish was supposed to be the only person allowed to visit, but Ordway managed to sneak up to say hello. We talked for a few minutes, and then he said, "For a guy who just had a stroke, you look great. You sound fine, too." He was lying, of course, and we both knew it.

Several of the Celtics players also dropped by the hospital on their way home from Washington, but because I wasn't allowed any calls or visitors, they couldn't get further than the lobby. All I was told by one of the nurses was that "a few basketball players wanted you to know they tried to see you."

Only my relatives were permitted to call me on the phone. And because I wasn't allowed visitors, including team members and front office personnel, my only real contacts with the outside world were by TV, radio and the mail. To my surprise, the cards, telegrams and letters poured in as soon as news of my stroke was announced in the media. By the third day of my stay, I had received more than a thousand pieces of mail, which, hospital officials told me, broke the record set by Henry Kissinger during his stay in 1982 when he underwent triple-bypass heart surgery.

Throughout my stay at Massachussetts General, the mail continued to arrive by the sackful. I remember one get-well message from a lady who had experienced her share of problems throughout life. I'll never forget the words of encouragement she wrote at the end of her letter: "Let's face it, Johnny, we're both survivors." Survivors—I liked that term. To this day, when someone asks how I'm doing, I smile and reply, "Pretty damn good. I'm a survivor."

I also received cards from hundreds of kids. Their scribbled, sometimes misspelled, or illegible messages never failed to warm my heart and increase my determination to get back and enjoy life even more than before the stroke. One little boy wrote, "Get well real soon, Mr. Most. The Celtics don't sound the same without you.

They're not getting angry enough. They're letting the officials make bad calls against them. That wouldn't happen if you were there."

The cards that brought the most joy were the ones I received from boys, some now men, whom I had coached in Pop Warner, Little League, CYO basketball, and the Wayland town basketball program. Almost all their letters began with "Dear Coach." I had always tried to teach kids that you don't have to be a great athlete to gain a great deal from sports. Sitting in bed, I realized that these kids I once coached had each learned a great deal from sports—although very few of them even made it to the varsity level in high school. Their letters, complete with vivid recollections about my coaching relationships with them, were very precious to me. In fact, I still have them safely tucked away in a briefcase. Maybe none of them ended up as superstars, but their letters told me that each one of them had developed into the type of person I could be proud to have helped in my own little way.

When the Celtics traveled to the West Coast a week later, I heard from Barksdale, my old roommate, who lived in the San Francisco area and had gone to the Celtics game against the Warriors at Oakland Coliseum expecting to have a reunion with me. Discovering that I wasn't with the team, Don went to the locker room and asked Bill Fitch where I was. Bill explained about the stroke and gave Don my private number at the hospital. Less than five minutes later, Don placed a long-distance call and then began giving me hell for "smoking too many of those dumb cigarettes." As the emotion rose in his voice, he began to get serious. "And why didn't you let me know you were hurting?" he said, crying in between sentences. "I'd be in Boston now if I had known."

I also heard from a number of the other old Celtics. There was Cousy, whose greeting was simply, "Hi there. Number 14 here." There was Satch Sanders, who, in his professor-like lecturing voice, wanted to know whether I had finally learned the lesson that I wasn't a kid any longer. And, of course, there was my buddy, Tommy Heinsohn, who got off a plane from the West Coast and came straight over to the hospital. When Tommy walked into my room, he put on one of his better scowls and barked, "You're a piece of work, John. A fucking piece of work. I go away for a few days and when I come back, you're in intensive care. Forty-eight hours without supervision and you end up in the hospital."

The most surprising visit I received was from Eric Fernsten, who played for the Celtics for three years at the beginning of the Bird era and now was pursuing a career as a stock broker. What shocked me is that I really didn't know Eric all that well. When he was with the team, he was always very friendly, courteous, quiet, and reserved. He'd be sitting on the plane reading every article in the *Wall Street Journal* while the other guys on the team were looking at the sports pages, the box scores and the comics. In short, Eric was not your typical jock. I was one of those who primarily stuck to the sports pages, so seldom did the two of us really ever say more than "Hi, how ya doing?"

So when he walked into my hospital room carrying a huge floral display (which had a green Celtics sneaker as the centerpiece), it was totally unexpected. Here was a guy who hardly knew me, yet had knocked himself out to show me that he cared.

Auerbach and Glickman flew up together from New York and stopped in to say hello. Marty was quietly asking about my condition, when Red interrupted, "Nevermind that bull crap. The nurses tell me you're being a pain in the ass. I guess that means you're getting back to normal. Just don't do too much too fast. Understand?"

Can you believe Auerbach? The guy was actually ordering me to get better. It was his gruff way of encouraging me—and it worked perfectly. By the time he and Marty were ready to leave, I had made up my mind to be back on the air within two months. No later. I told Red that. He looked me straight in the eyes, nodded, got up from his chair, and said, "I believe you," as he walked out into the corridor.

Looking back on my stay at Massachussetts General, I can honestly say there never came a moment when I gave up hope of returning to my perch at the Garden. It just never occurred to me— or at least I wouldn't let it enter my mind. By the same token, I wasn't going to kid myself. I was very aware that recovering from a stroke was far tougher than battling the common cold. I knew I had my work cut out for me, but I also knew it wasn't an impossible task. My goal was simply to make some amount of progress each day. Putting two sentences together, moving my right arm a half-inch, making a fist with my right hand, taking two steps without stumbling, these were all ways in which I measured my recovery.

Even while still in ICU, I began to watch the Celtic games on TV by turning off the sound and practicing my own play-by-play as the game went along. The TV screen, however, was so small that I really could only recognize the Boston players, so I only "announced" when the Celtics were on offense. During the first two weeks, I could only do about one quarter before I'd tire. The first few times, all I wanted to do was say the player's last name and the type of shot he took. My speech problems made it impossible to keep up with the action. I'd start with, "Quickly, Danny in the corner, over to Larry..." But by that time, the ball would already have been shot. Still, it felt great being able to call the games—even if it was from a hospital bed.

The idea for doing my "TV broadcasts" came from my favorite nurse, Nancy O'Brien, who, after conferring with my speech therapist, urged me to try it. Not all the nurses, however, were made aware of this unique therapy treatments, which led to a rather funny incident.

One night while doing a game by using the TV as my monitor, O'Brien (I never called her by her first name) came up to me and started to roar with laughter. "What's so damn funny?" I demanded to know, half suspecting she might have been laughing at some mispronunciation I might have made.

"Well," replied O'Brien, "there's this one nurse who heard you doing your announcing and didn't understand what was going on.

She thought that perhaps you had lost your marbles. She came up to me and whispered, 'I think Mr. Most is losing it. He's talking to himself loudly and he's doing it non-stop.' The look on her face was priceless. She was convinced that you had flipped out. You haven't, have you?"

As I say, O'Brien was a great person and a real character. Whenever she was on duty, I never once used the "call" light near the bed. All I'd do is shout her name and she'd hear me no matter how far down the hall she was from my room.

My daughter Andrea visited me on the fifth day. I wasn't expecting her, nor was I prepared mentally or physically to see her. The doctors discovered that polyps were blocking my digestive system and had scheduled surgery for the next morning. In the meantime, I was in agony. Plus, I was still having a great deal of trouble talking. I didn't want my daughter seeing me in this condition. Maybe I'd be in better shape in a week or so, but certainly now was not the right time for her to visit. Fortunately she left the room for a brief second shortly after arriving. That gave me a chance to tell my nephew, Allan Friedman, who had brought her, to make up some excuse why they had to leave.

Later that same day, Dr. Silva came to see me. He had stopped at the nurses' station to find out the room number when all of a sudden he heard a booming voice coming from down the corridor. "I guess that tells me what room Johnny Most is in," he said to the head nurse. "I've just located the human public address system. Now all I have to do is follow the echo."

By the time Dr. Silva entered my room, he was chuckling to himself. "I was going to ask you how you were doing," he said, "but if your voice is that loud and piercing, there's no doubt in my mind that your recovery is coming along rapidly. In my medical opinion, the vocal cords are working as good as ever, and you're on your way back."

Several days later I was in the middle of one of my practice broadcasts when O'Brien entered my room. "Johnny," she said, "the patients are starting to complain about your announcing." At that point, I got defensive. "Sorry, O'Brien, but I really don't think I was talking too loud. At least I didn't mean to be."

"What I'm trying to tell you," O'Brien responded, "is that the patients are complaining that you're not loud enough. They want to hear what's going on in the game, too, you know. They can't hear you if you're whispering, so start announcing as if it were for real. You've got a captive audience here. We've got people on this floor who have to know what's going on with the Celtics." Then she turned on her heels and walked out into the hallway.

I would have thought that after a while the number of get-well cards would diminish. But I was lucky, because people kept thinking about me. Nearly every team in the NBA sent cards. The Bruins, Patriots and Red Sox all were thoughtful enough to wish me a speedy recovery. Actually the card I received from the Sox was quite a collector's item, because it was signed by both Haywood Sullivan and Buddy LeRoux. For all I know, it might have been one of the last pieces of paper they co-signed without getting into an argument.

After 10 days, I was transferred to the third floor of the Phillips House, where patients complete their recovery from major surgery. During my first day there, O'Brien came into my room and explained she was taking me up to the eighth floor. "Don't ask any questions. Just get in the wheelchair and let's get on the elevator," she ordered. When we got to the eighth floor, she brought me over to a large picture window and said, "OK, just look out the window and wave to the guy standing below us." I stared down, spotted a guy waving, and I waved back. Then I did a double-take. There on the ground, in huge 10-foot-long white letters, was painted, "GET WELL SOON, JOHNNY THE MOST."

I couldn't believe my eyes, which I admit had a few tears welling up in them. It must have taken this man hours of work to so neatly have printed the message. I tried to find out his name and thank him but I was never able to discover who he was. Just a good, kind friend. I was later informed this amateur artist was a fan of the Celtics who several years earlier had painted a similar message for John Wayne when he was at Massachussetts General for cancer tests.

As my speech gradually returned, I worked on ways I could improve my voice strength and word speed. I'd pick up the daily papers and pretend that each article was a radio script. It didn't matter whether I was reading editorials, recipes, sports, or even the classified ads. The little game I played was to make each sentence sound exciting by emphasizing a word or phrase, by dropping or raising my voice, by making my intonation reflect various emotions. "Johnny," O'Brien said to me one day as I "announced" the Dick Tracy comic, "that other nurse was right. You have flipped out."

On the 11th day, I had my first visit from the hospital's speech therapist. After I performed a half-dozen voice exercises, she gave her evaluation. "Your pronunciation is excellent. There's only a slight slurring of words—and that unquestionably will disappear with time," she told me. "As for your pace, you're about 20 words a minute slower than you were before the stroke."

My initial reaction was one of disappointment, frustration and worry. I admit there was a brief second when I questioned whether the damage could be undone. But the therapist managed to calm me down. "Remember, I said you were 20 words slower than before the stroke. When you compare your pace to the average person's, you're only about 10 words slower per minute than the norm. With some hard work, we'll be able to get you to the point where you'll be speaking much faster and with much more force. It'll come."

Also encouraging was that Dr. Ropper told me he had no doubts I'd make a full recovery. "The area of the brain associated with speech was damaged by the stroke. That's a fact," he said. "But because you've been in the broadcasting field all your life, because you speak so rapidly and extemporaneously, other areas of the brain have developed the ability to perform speech functions. In other words, there won't be any permanent problem, because you've gotten to the point where you can almost broadcast a game in your sleep."

Then Dr. Ropper paid me a compliment that meant a lot. "You've got a strong will and a style all your own. People such as you tend to be emotional, which can work two ways. Either the emotion can be used to create motivation, or it can result in the person saying, 'Oh, my God, I'm lost. I'm going to get depressed. Forget it.' In your case, Mr. Most, you've made your character, your mental make-up, work for you. It's a positive motivation."

My improvement continued steadily. On February 23, Dr. Ropper said he was sending me home. "You'll have to work with a therapist, have a nurse help you for a while, and make weekly check-up trips to see me," he said. "And you're going to have to watch your diet. For starters, no cigarettes, no salted foods, and only caffeine-free coffee. You'll also require a minimum of eight hours of sleep a night."

Before Dr. Ropper had even finished his instructions, I was ready to pack my bags and clear out. I felt relieved, because deep down, the thought always lurks in the back of your mind that you may never get well enough to leave the hospital. On my last night at Massachussetts General I decided (as usual) to sneak a cigarette in my bathroom at about 4 a.m. I lit the cigarette and for some reason put it in my right hand, which I still had been unable to move. Out of habit, I tried to raise my arm, and to my surprise, there was some slight movement. I was so excited that I opened my door and yelled out, "O'Brien!" She came running down the corridor, believing that something was wrong. When I showed her that I had gained some motion in the arm, she put her arms around me and held me for a few seconds like a mother would do with her baby. That was her way of saying goodbye.

The next morning, Andrea escorted me through the front doors of Massachussetts General, and I was driven to my nephew and niece's home in New Hampshire, where I could relax and start dreaming of resuming a normal life. I had only been home for about six hours when I decided it was time for me to see some more of the outside world. To my daughter's surprise, I announced that I wanted to go shopping at the local mall. So off we went. Since the stroke, I had lost more than 40 pounds. I had gone from a 36 waist to a 29; I had gone from a 16-inch neck to a 14 1/2. At the mall, I immediately started buying a new wardrobe. After about a half-hour, I was completely beat. The remainder of my shopping could wait for another day.

With Andrea in school and both my nephew and niece working, it was impossible for me to receive the round-the-clock care I needed at home. Luckily, I had a friend by the name of Rodney Gould who insisted I stay with him until I became more self-sufficient. Never have I met a more caring person than Rodney. He took me to the hospital three times a week for blood checks; he took me to see my therapist, Mayo Kahn, whose office was located a good hour away, another three times weekly. Rodney chauffeured me everywhere and never once gave a thought about himself or his own schedule.

Despite all the help I received from every direction, I still wasn't ready to return to work. That's where Mayo Kahn came in. He was my physical therapist and close friend long before I suffered the stroke. In addition to his reputation as an excellent therapist, Mayo was famous for having been the original model for the Superman comic books in 1936 while he was the physical therapist at a local country club. He once told me of a meeting he had with President Franklin Roosevelt shortly after getting the job as Superman. "I told FDR that I always wanted to talk to a President, and he told me that he had always wanted to talk to Superman."

Mayo devised a set of exercises for me to do at home while also treating me twice a week at his office. In a matter of a month, he had me back on the air—at least to a limited degree. "To be honest with you," Mayo said after I told him I was returning to the job, "I figured it would take you six or seven months, maybe even a year. But I had no doubt you'd make it all the way back."

When I was finally able to leave Rodney's house and come back to my own home, I received plenty of loving care from my children. Andrea was going to school and then coming home to assume the role of my personal nurse. Jamie flew in from San Diego, where he was going to school. Robbie came in from Indiana State, and Marjorie drove up from Florida. When all four got together, the first thing they did was hold an organizational meeting to make sure there would always be two of them in the house at the same time to watch over me and to pamper me.

Having the kids home was great, but not working was boring. It became frustrating to listen to the games and not be part of the action. It hurt so much that there were times I simply had to shut off the radio and TV. Finally, in the middle of March, I decided I couldn't sit around any longer.

My first taste of getting back to business came when Glenn would call me up at home and I'd go on the air for two or three minutes from my bed. Then Glenn drove up to New Hampshire and we did a 10-minute taped interview, which was later played on the air. Slowly but surely I was preparing myself for the real test. I will say this, though. Nobody rushed me. I could name the day I wanted to work and the amount of time I wanted to put in. Just as Bob Fish had been when I first suffered the stroke, he was totally supportive during my comeback. If he detected that I was getting a bit down, he'd kid me about being a "goof-off." If he thought I was pushing myself too hard, he'd joke about how I was trying to impress everyone just so I could get a raise. Truth is he watched over me like a mother hen.

On February 6, 1984, just two days less than a year after my stroke, I returned to the Boston Garden broadcast booth. While being driven in by Jamie, I was extremely nervous. I didn't have any idea how people would receive me. You think negatively when you have a stroke. You really do. It had been so long since I had done play-by-play that I felt unsure of myself.

Upon arriving at the Garden, I went into Red's office to say hello. "Can you raise your right arm?" he greeted me. "What can you do? Can you do anything? Show me, talk to me." So I gave him a sample of my play-by-play and he grinned, sat back in his banker's padded chair and took a puff on his cigar. "You're getting there, OK," he said. "Now for Christ's sake, take it easy."

I talked with the entire front office staff and waited for KC Jones, who was Fitch's assistant when I suffered my stroke, to come out of his head coach's office and up the steps that led to the Garden. When he walked toward me, he didn't recognize me. That's how thin I was. One hundred and forty-eight pounds of bones and skin. Finally KC did a double-take and then we embraced. "Just enjoy the game. Don't work," he cautioned me. But I had ants in my pants. I wasn't going to sit in the booth and do nothing. No way.

As I took my seat in the press box, it was announced over the public address system that I was making my return to the job. The sellout crowd gave me a standing ovation that lasted three minutes. There were tears coming down my face. There were tears in my son's eyes. I looked down at the Celtics bench area and saw every player looking up, waving towels and clapping. Then I happened to glance over at the Cleveland bench and noticed that all the Cavs were standing and applauding, with former Boston College star John Bagley leading the cheers. As the ovation continued, I sneaked a peek over at Red's box and felt overwhelmed when he raised a hand and waved it in the air. My tears kept flowing as I turned in every direction of the old, historic building.

My first few times behind the mic were tentative. Two things affected me: my confidence level and the fact that I got tired very quickly. On my first night back, I did three minutes of play-by-play in the first half and five minutes in the second. Gradually I increased my "playing time" to the point where I was able to do half the game during the playoffs. Still, I struggled to regain my confidence.

On my first road trip since the stroke, Bird used his sense of humor to make me feel I was back as "one of the gang." Knowing I had lost movement on my right side, Bird decided to pull a joke on me. As we were about to arrive at our hotel, Larry stood up and walked to the front of the bus. "OK, we're going to play a game of 'Simon Says.' The loser has to buy the first round of drinks. Here we go: Simon says raise your right arm. Oops, Johnny, you lose. I'll have a Miller. What does everybody else want?" I cracked up. His little gag made me feel like I was part of the team once again.

Before the stroke, I thought of myself as a hulk, a guy who was virtually indestructible. After the stroke, I saw myself as just a shell of what I had been. A stroke lays you low. It knocks out a lot of faculties— and you start doubting whether your "old self" will ever resurface. You either battle or quit. I was fortunate enough to have made the right choice. I was going to fight.

14

BACK IN THE
BROADCASTING BOOTH

Thanks to the support of so many friends, colleagues, and
the Celtics management and players, I was able to get back
to my old cantankerous self quicker than I expected. Within
weeks, I was growling at the referees, shouting at opponents for dirty,
dangerous, sneaky and vicious fouls, and lauding the efforts of the
heroes in green and white uniforms.

I had made it all the way back—and I couldn't have felt more
grateful to be behind the microphone.

As I mentioned, I followed the team closely during my recovery
period. The trade for Scotty Wedman helped the Celtics end up with
a 56-26 record, third best in the NBA behind Philly and L.A. Boston
eliminated Atlanta 2-1 in the opening playoff series and then faced
Milwaukee in the division semifinals. Despite having the home-court
advantage, the Celtics lost the first two games of the series in Boston,
with Bird sidelined by illness in Game 2. When the team arrived in
Milwaukee, Ainge picked up a newspaper and was shocked by the
headline of the top story in the sports section. It read: "Nelson Says
Ainge Is a Cheapshot Artist." The article quoted Nellie as saying
Ainge undercuts players when they drive to the basket. Nellie went
on to say Danny would eventually cause a major injury if he didn't
change his tactics.

Naturally, Danny (who, just *coincidentally*, had scored a career-high 25 points in Game 2 at the Garden) was upset and shaken by Nellie's remarks. From home, I called Ainge to see how he was reacting to Nellie's comments. "Johnny, I guarantee none of the Buck guards think I'm a dirty player," Danny said. "I'm not a guy who cheapshots anybody. I'm getting a reputation as a guy who gets into fights, a guy who tries to hurt players. Nelson's remarks are B. S. The truth is I've been in two or three fights and I lost them all. I play aggressively, not dirty. Nelson knows better than to say something like that. He's trying to copy Red by being controversial."

Right after I had returned from my stroke, I finally got my chance to sit down with Nellie for the first time since he had "ambushed" Danny. Before he could even say hello to me, I gave him my opinion of his stunt. "I've always had total respect for you until I read that article about Ainge," I shouted at him. "As far as I'm concerned you're the fucking cheapshot artist. Danny's a hard-nosed, tough kid, but he's definitely not a dirty player. Right now you're on my shit list because that story was pure, unadulterated crap and you know it. You just wanted to throw Ainge off his game. Well, that wasn't the way to do it. You owe Danny an apology."

"I already sent Ainge a letter and I've talked with Red about my statements," Nellie replied. "Look, Ainge had this habit of racing in front of a guy as he would go up for a fast-break layup," Nelson replied. "I thought it was dangerous. That's the only point I was trying to make."

"Aw, you're full of it. I read that apology letter and it was only a half-hearted, phony explanation. You screwed up and now you can't admit it," I told him.

In Games 3 and 4, it was apparent to me, as I watched my TV, that Tiny simply wasn't playing his game. He'd come across halfcourt and take a 20-foot jumper instead of looking first to set up Bird or McHale by penetrating and dishing the ball off. Ainge was also not playing with his usual self-confidence. Clearly, Nelson's remarks had taken a toll on Danny's aggressiveness.

As a result of the Celtics' problems, the Bucks had no resistance in sweeping the series with two relatively easy victories in Milwaukee. "I know Tiny thought he should have been a starter all year," said Fitch. "But Tiny, being the pro he is, never gave us less than a hundred percent effort. The media are putting a lot of blame on him for our loss to the Bucks. I don't blame him. We just didn't play well as a team. Nobody had a particularly good series."

I had no doubts that Red was about to make some drastic changes, including parting company with Tiny, who would be waived on July 11, 1983.

But Auerbach's first move came as a total shock to me. He met with Fitch in late May, and they agreed it would be in everybody's best interest if Bill moved on. Just a day earlier, I had phoned Fitch and we had discussed possible ways to improve the team. We both concluded that if the Celtics could either draft or trade for a defensive-minded guard, it would give Boston depth and versatility at every position. During our conversation, Fitch hinted that he was troubled by the loss to Milwaukee. "Harry's told a few reporters that my job is safe. That was good to hear. But I have to do some soul searching. I have to believe that if I continue coaching here, I'm the best guy for the job. I have to know that Red believes that, too."

Ten days after Bill departed and subsequently became head coach of the Rockets, Red introduced KC Jones, who had been Fitch's assistant, as the new Celtics head coach. I was elated because KC was one of my closest friends and a very competent coach who was respected by the players. His relationship with Bill was always strained. On one occasion, KC had a physical encounter with Bill. "I was wrong when I went after Fitch," KC told me. "But I have my pride, and I think the fact that Bill wouldn't even allow me to give advice to players during practices, along with other factors, finally made me snap. We both apologized, but I never could understand why he didn't respect my knowledge of the game or my ability to teach. I think I'm a loyal person and a good communicator. All I wanted was to help Bill. He didn't want my input at any time. Even good coaches like him can benefit from their assistants' opinions."

KC was fortunate enough to retain Fitch's top assistant, Jimmy Rodgers, who would have been my second choice to be Boston's head coach. Jimmy was loyal, a student of the game, and another coach who had earned the respect of the players. In a move that pleased the players, KC named Chris Ford as his second assistant. Chris would be the most openly enthusiastic, emotional, and vocal member of the staff.

A day before the '83 draft, Auerbach dealt Rick Robey and two second-round draft choices to Phoenix in exchange for Dennis "Mr. Mean" Johnson and a first-round draft pick. Although DJ had been a first-team All-Defense selection five straight years, I wasn't initially thrilled with the trade. After all, Seattle coach Lenny Wilkens had called Dennis "a cancer," even though the Sonics had won the '79 championship with DJ being MVP of the championship series. Phoenix, making the trade, obviously believed DJ was not a positive influence on the Suns.

However, when I finally met Dennis in December of '83, I discovered that he was a down-to-earth, candid person who didn't make excuses about his past experiences. "I think Lenny got a little carried away when he called me 'a cancer,'" DJ said with a smile. "I was immature and could be a royal pain in the ass at times. I don't think Lenny would ever say I gave him any problems when I was out on the court playing. I'm here to win a championship. I'll accept any role KC gives me. All I ask is don't judge me until you get to know what I'm all about."

There were several reasons why Robey had been expendable. McHale had developed into such a versatile, effective player that KC needed to find a way of getting him more playing time. With Robey gone, McHale could play 25 minutes at power forward and another

10 to 15 minutes as the backup to Parish at center. Bird and Robey were known to do a lot of "celebrating" on the road with their friends and teammates. "It won't be as much fun without Rick here," Larry said to the media, with a wink, "but I think I'll be able to get more rest and concentrate more on basketball. I know one thing: all those bars we went to are going to suffer financially now that Rick and I won't be hanging around together."

DJ was welcomed by Ainge with typical Celtics team humor. "Hey Dennis, I'm not buying into the idea that you're black," Danny said. "Whoever heard of a black guy who has red hair and a face full of freckles?"

Max, who loves to do imitations, was thrilled to have DJ around because he was such an easy guy to mock. "Dennis has the biggest butt of any guard in the league," Cedric said when I phoned him one day. "I can either stick a pillow under my shorts or just stick my backside out. I guarantee that one of these imitations will have McHale, Bird, Chief, and Ainge in stitches." Of course, Max enjoyed imitating me. "Johnny, I can hear you now barking into the mic, 'DJ is in his shirt, now he's in his jock, now he's in his socks, he's completing suffocating him...oh, no, Jake has called a phantom foul on DJ. It's disgraceful, despicable, vicious, and ridiculous.' Does that sound like something you'd say?"

Among some of Max's other targets were: Ainge making faces, throwing a tantrum, and flailing his arms in disgust after being called for a foul; M.L. shooting a 25-foot jumper with his legs kicking out to the side like a frog; Robey shooting, then praying, then tossing an air ball from the free throw line; Dave Zinkoff introducing Philly's starting lineup; and, my favorite, Bird repeatedly struggling not to mess up his lines in a simple, three-word, one-sentence TV commercial for 7-Up. His repertoire was endless, and he never failed to get a laugh from the very person he was mocking.

Cedric could also laugh at himself. After Atlanta's Tree Rollins bit Ainge on the middle finger of his shooting hand during an '83 playoff game, the Celtics were watching video replays of the brawl that occurred as Danny and Rollins wrestled on the court. All of a sudden the TV camera zoomed in on Max, who was on his belly trying desperately to crawl his way out from the pile of bodies as players threw wild punches at each other. The look of absolute panic on Cedric's face was priceless.

Fitch told me that following the incident, Ainge had Max squirming in his chair for a solid 10 minutes as the Celtics watched the replay of the incident. With Ainge controlling the remote switch, Cedric's moment of utter panic was replayed perhaps a dozen times for the benefit of every Celtic Maxwell had ever imitated. In Ordway's postgame interview, he was prompted by Parish to ask Max to give his account of how he retreated from danger. "I know Danny or Chief put you up to this. I've never seen Chief or Larry laugh so hard," Cedric told Glenn. "All I'm going to say in my own defense is that I never claimed to be the second coming of Audie Murphy, did I?"

Occasionally Maxwell would even joke around with the fans at the Garden. "There's one guy who sits in the first row across from our bench and spends the whole game yelling at me," Cedric said. He never changes his routine. 'Hey, Maxwell, you're the invisible man out there.' 'Hey, Maxwell, get a real job.' One night he screamed at me another of his standard lines, 'Hey, Maxwell, if all you're going to do out there is watch, then why don't you just take my seat.' So, as soon as a foul call was made, I went over to the guy, helped him up from his seat, and then sat down and grabbed a handful of popcorn from the guy sitting next to me. The fans sitting in his section gave me a standing ovation, because I guess they were bored of hearing him screaming out the same old, stale lines game after game.

"As long as my teammates respect me and realize I make sacrifices, that's all that matters. Fans can say whatever they want and it won't bother me. My role is to hit the boards, run the court, pass the ball to Larry or Kevin, and just try and do the little things that give opportunities to everyone else. In other words, I might seem to go unnoticed out there, but I'm still working hard."

But I noticed Max's contributions, especially on the defensive end. Was he ever adept at putting the clamps on some of the league's premiere shooters, guys like Bernard King, Julius Erving, Adrian Dantley, Dominique Wilkins and Alex English. His offensive game wasn't shabby, either. He was too big to be guarded by a small forward, so he usually was covered by the "muscle-tussle" type of players. And he would give them fits, because he could twist and turn so quickly that they were never able to put a body on him. As soon as he felt contact when he was in the lane, he would spin and slide away so fast that his defender couldn't catch up to him as he went up for a layup.

Cedric seemed to thrive on controversy. One year he said in an interview that Boston was a racist city. "The atmosphere doesn't affect me because I happen to play for the Celtics," he said. "But I'm not blind or deaf. I see how blacks are treated here. There are certain sections of Boston where blacks just aren't welcome. I can go there because of my profession. To be honest, though, I don't feel comfortable doing that. If people want to criticize me because I'm just being honest, then so be it."

If I had to put a label on the '83-'84 Celtics, I'd call them a team of character and characters. They had tremendous talent, as well as great team chemistry. Individually, their personalities blended perfectly, which led to them having a lot of laughs off the court and unbeatable teamwork on the court.

KC was able to recognize that he had a unique group of veteran players to coach. "I treat them with respect and they appreciate that. I don't think I ever have to yell or scream, because every one of these players are self-motivated. If they have a bad game, they are their own toughest critics. There's never any finger pointing," he told me in mid-December when the Celtics had already taken a four-game lead in the Atlantic Division while owning the best record in the league. "I've never had more fun, either as a player or a coach, being around these guys."

There was one particular "boys will be boys" incident on the road that illustrated KC's patience and his calm manner of handling his players. It occurred in January of '84 after the Celtics had arrived in Milwaukee on a Saturday afternoon, a day before they were to play the Bucks on national TV in a noontime game. A group of McHale's friends had driven down from Hibbing, Minnesota to tip a few beers with Kevin. Buckner, who had played six seasons with the Bucks before being traded to Boston, hosted Bird as they visited several of Quinn's favorite hangouts. With two of McHale's buddies, "Big Joe" and "Bones," buying rounds, Kevin, along with Buckner and Bird, was feeling no pain by the time the bars closed for the evening.

The next morning, the Celtics threesome looked as if they didn't get more than an hour or two of sleep. KC obviously knew his team was in deep trouble even before tipoff. "I thought celebrating usually occurs *after* a game," KC said to me as he watched McHale, Buckner and Bird struggle as they went through layup drills. "Our best hope is that the Bucks were out on the town too last night."

The final result was an easy Milwaukee win, 108-87, with Kevin missing all eight of his field goal attempts. Bird didn't fare much better, making just three of 13 shots, while Quinn managed to convert one of five shots. Boarding the team bus, McHale carefully avoided eye contact with KC, who sat across from me. Bird and Buckner were also very quiet as they walked past their coach and headed to the rear of the bus. As the bus left the hotel, even KC had to laugh at the sight of "Big Joe," Kevin's brother, John, his cousin, "Jimbo," and his friend, "Bones," raising their bottles of beer in a toast to their drinking companions.

I had met "Big Joe," a former University of Minnesota lineman who now weighs 350 pounds, once before at a restaurant across from the Garden on Causeway Street. He was sitting with McHale and his wife, Lynn, and had a pitcher of what appeared to be ice water in front of him. When I saw him take a drink straight from the pitcher, I asked him why he wasn't using a glass. "Well, this pitcher is holding a giant martini, and it would take too long to down it if I used a glass. Using the pitcher is just a more convenient, faster way of getting bombed."

When Don Nelson heard about Kevin going out on the town with "Big Joe" and "The Minnesota Crew" the night before the game, the Bucks coach told the media to relay a message to "Big Joe." "Tell him that any time we're playing the Celtics in Milwaukee and he wants to do a little drinking with his buddies and McHale, I'll not only pick up the entire tab, I'll get him a suite at the Hyatt, complete with a fully stocked bar."

Most coaches would have at least given a stern lecture to the team about such a disastrous game. Not KC. "The whole team knows why we lost so badly. Every player is aware that I know some of them screwed up," he said to me privately. "It's a lesson learned. I think they're embarrassed and feel badly for me because we played like garbage on national TV." That kind of thinking is why the players wanted to win a title for KC as much as for themselves.

As I've mentioned, McHale never missed a chance to tease Ainge at every opportunity. When Danny, who was in a four-game shooting slump, took his four-year-old son, Austin, on a West Coast road trip in February, Kevin asked Austin to search the team bus because, in Kevin's words, "Your daddy's lost his jump shot. We've got to find it for him. Austin, go check under all the seats and see if you can find it." It was a hilarious scene watching little Austin crawl under all the bus seats looking for his dad's "lost jumper."

Whenever Danny's older brother, Doug, who coached high school basketball in Oregon, visited Boston, Kevin would give Ainge the business. "Oh, oh, Danny must believe he's starting to struggle with his jumper. He's made an emergency call to the 'Shot Doctor.' Never fails. As soon as Danny has two or three bad shooting games, all of a sudden Doug shows up. Wonder what the Shot Doctor charges for house calls?"

Robert Parish, in my opinion, was a silent leader of the team. He was quiet but observant. On the rare occasions when he did speak up, everyone listened. By now, his running game was his trademark. His play with the Celtics was totally unselfish, which made him the perfect frontcourt partner for Bird and McHale. Chief was one of those players who never cared about his individual stats. If he didn't take a shot all game, it wouldn't bother him as long as the Celtics won. If Boston was having trouble on the boards, Parish would pick up the slack and end up with 15, 18, or even 20 rebounds. He didn't get the headlines, which, at least outwardly, didn't bother him in the slightest. The media seldom gathered around him in the locker room, even after many of his best efforts. "I let Larry, Danny, and Kevin do all the talking. They love to yap and yap and yap," Robert would tell me. "I like to do my talking with my play on the court."

Despite their one minor slip-up in Milwaukee, Bird and McHale were enjoying their best seasons. Larry was easily on his way to MVP honors, leading the team in scoring average, rebounding, steals, assists, and free-throw percentage. Meanwhile, Kevin was running away with the Sixth Man of the Year honors by utilizing his assortment of inside moves and fallaways to shoot 56 percent from the field, while also earning the reputation as one of the league's best defenders. In fact, McHale was almost always given the assignment of guarding the opponents' best shooting forward and was holding so-called scoring machines such as Dominique Wilkins, George Gervin, and Kelly Tripucka to almost 10 points below their season average.

As the Celtics continued to win, Boston players were in demand for endorsements, commercials and promotional appearances. Yet for some unknown reason, Parish never got involved in these events. Finally, I asked him why he didn't try to cash in a little on his success. "One reason: I've got the wrong paint job in this town to be a big attraction." Like Maxwell, Robert believed that Boston's chain stores, auto dealerships and corporate leaders preferred to have white players as spokesmen. To a great degree, he was correct, although Robert's "shy" image also hurt what the public perceived as a guy who "never smiled."

I saw Chief on a daily basis, and I couldn't disagree more with the public's perception of his personality. Robert loved the camaraderie, the laughter, and the interaction among his teammates. No one smiled and laughed more than he did from his "observer's seat" in the back of the team bus. If some joke tickled his funny bone, his deep-voiced belly laugh would last five or 10 minutes. Guys loved to watch Robert react to a joke, because his whole body would shake and he'd stamp his foot on the floor as he went into hysterics.

Later in his career, he did receive a number of offers to do personal appearances. I'd bump into someone who attended one of Parish's autograph signings, and they'd inevitably say to me, "I can't believe he's so outgoing and personable. He takes the time to talk and joke with everyone, especially kids. He's not the stone-faced robot that we see during the games. He's really a genuinely nice guy, isn't he?" And I'd reply, "I'm glad you got to see the real Robert Parish. Now you know why his teammates think so highly of him."

During the season, I came up with a new descriptive phrase, "fiddlin' and diddlin'." I used it originally as a description for how Philly point guard Maurice Cheeks dribbled the ball for four or five seconds as he waited for the Sixers to set their offense. But I ended up applying that same expression to the guard play of the Celtics. Because DJ and Ainge weren't true fast break-style point guards, they'd be very patient in bringing the ball upcourt and then waiting to set up the offense. They'd dribble the ball to one side of the court and then dribble the ball back to the middle.

Rather than describe all the ball handling for five or six seconds at a time, I decided to use the phrase "fiddlin' and diddlin'." (Later, I added, "He daddles and doodles.") It caught on with my audience. It also gave me extra time to describe the action away from the ball where Bird, McHale or Parish were working to get into position for their favorite shots. Larry would be running off picks, looking for three-point opportunities or to get past his man for a drive to the basket; Kevin would be battling in the low post, calling for the ball when he had his defender off balance; and Robert would maneuver near the foul line, waiting to get open when his man would attempt to help out on either Bird or McHale.

I began having some fun calling Atlanta's young star, Dominique Wilkins, "The Princess," because if he was so much as touched by one of the Celtics, he'd start complaining about being manhandled. What I detested was that the officials' calls usually favored Wilkins. He'd drive to the basket and McHale would just tap him with his pinky, and "The Princess" would go into his crying act. Wilkins loved making spectacular moves that resulted in slam dunks, yet he felt it was his absolute right to drive the lane without any defender blocking his path. He was definitely not a believer in physical play. His defense was pathetic. He'd put on a good act of fake hustle, but "The Princess" would never think of sacrificing his body to prevent Bird, for instance, from driving for a layup. I would say on the air, "The Princess has the agility of a ballet star. I'm surprised he's wearing basketball shoes instead of dainty, pink little slippers."

This was the season when many arenas instituted a no-smoking policy. At least once or twice each half I would sneak a few puffs of a cigarette. Immediately a security guard or two would swoop down and order me to put the cigarette out. These paper cops acted as if I was Public Enemy No. 1. I found a way to get even, though. I'd make sure the security people were watching me, then I'd light a match and hold it a sixteenth of an inch in front of my cigarette. I didn't actually light the cigarette, but I pretended to be inhaling. When the ever-vigilant security guards would move in on me, I'd hide the unlit cigarette under the press table. They'd insist that I immediately cease smoking. That's when I'd hold the cigarette up, show them it hadn't been lit, and then told them to "go find one of the many drunken fans in this fucking dump and pick on them." They were trying to make my life miserable, so I gave them a little dose of their own medicine.

The Celtics finished the '83-'84 season with a 62-20 record, 10 full games better than Philadelphia, which was runner-up in the East. Boston eliminated the Bullets, 3-1, in the opening playoff round and then barely escaped being upset in seven games by the Knicks, who were carried by the red-hot Bernard King. Before the Knicks series, Maxwell, goaded on by M.L. Carr, kiddingly told his teammates, "No way that bitch is going to score 40 against me." Unfortunately for Max, his remarks were quoted in the papers. King responded by averaging 29 points in the series, including scoring 44 and 43 in two of the games. Game 7 was, however, dominated by Bird's triple-double effort, which included a career playoff-high 39 points.

Advancing to the Eastern Division finals, the Celtics now had their chance to gain revenge for the humiliating 4-0 sweep by the Bucks in the '83 playoffs. With six Celtics averaging double figures while Parish and Bird controlled the boards, Boston disposed of Milwaukee in five games to move on to the championship series against the Lakers.

It was "Larry vs. Magic" as far as the vast majority of the media was concerned. I knew differently. These were two deep, talented teams. You had Parish vs. Abdul-Jabbar, McHale and Maxwell going against James Worthy, DJ and Ainge defending Magic, and Michael Cooper guarding Bird. No two players were going to dictate the storyline of this series.

In Game 1 at the Garden, Kareem's 32 points and Magic's fast-break brilliance enabled the Lakers to hold off a late Boston surge and take a 115-109 decision.

Game 2 ranks as the fourth most exciting game I've ever broadcast. It appeared that the Lakers would win the first two games of the series at the Garden when McHale missed two free throws with 20 seconds remaining in regulation, allowing L.A. to grab the rebound, call timeout and maintain its 113-111 lead. It definitely wasn't the slightest bit funny at the time, but the Celtics players enjoyed a long laugh after the game watching a replay of Kevin's knees knocking together and his legs shaking as he attempted his second free throw. "Kevin was so wobbly at the line, I wonder how he even managed to get the ball up to the rim," Bird told me in the locker room.

Maxwell was also on a roll, talking trash to Kevin. "Hey," Cedric yelled as the team watched the replay, "if you're that damned scared, you'd better go and buy yourself a Doberman [for protection] right now."

As the Lakers celebrated McHale's missed free throws, L.A. celebrity fan Jack Nicholson pointed to his Adam's apple and gave the choke sign to the Garden fans. When play resumed, Magic inbounded the ball to James Worthy, who was guarded by McHale as Ainge moved in for a double-team. The Lakers forward tossed a cross-court lob in the direction of Byron Scott. Gerald Henderson, anticipating the pass, cut in front of Scott and raced in for the tying layup as Worthy tried in vain to catch him from the side.

The play didn't win the game, but it sure as hell put Boston in position to pull out an absolutely miraculous win. I was almost as emotional on the air that day as I was when Johnny Havlicek intercepted Hal Greer's pass. The call differed slightly because I didn't actually use a "Henderson stole the ball" description and because the play didn't decide the outcome of the game. Instead I began very calmly when Magic Johnson received the inbounds pass from Worthy. "All right, Magic gets the ball back to Worthy...AND IT'S PICKED OFF...GOES TO HENDERSON AND HE LAYS IT UP AND IN." I eventually did use the phrase, "Gerald Henderson stole the ball!" but only after the Lakers had called timeout following Gerald's tying basket. My call went from a conversational tone, to my Sani-Flush shout, to, as the *Boston Globe's* Bob Ryan calls it, my "dog-whistle voice."

Still, there were 13 ticks on the clock and the Lakers had the ball at midcourt. Worthy had no problem inbounding the ball to Scott, who immediately gave the ball to Magic as the clock went down to 11 seconds. Magic slowly backed his way down the left side of the court to the three-point line but lost track of the time remaining. "OK, Magic's got the ball. He's trying to work on Maxwell. Now the clock is down to two seconds...one second...He's going to have to shoot it...HE DOESN'T GET IT OFF," I screamed into the mic. It was such an unusual play that I didn't even have time to mention that Magic, out of sheer desperation, passed the ball to Bob McAdoo just before the buzzer went off.

While Max had done an excellent job distracting Magic with his pressure defense, I couldn't believe such a normally smart player as Magic had not so much as an inkling as to how much time remained from the time he received the ball until the final two seconds when he went into panic mode. I also mentioned that even if Magic had managed to realize he had to shoot, Max was in his shirt and would have blocked the attempt easily.

Thanks in large part to Magic's mental lapse, the Celtics battled to take a 123-121 lead in overtime on a Scotty Wedman baseline jumper from the left side with 14 seconds remaining. Magic then inbounded the ball to Bob McAdoo, who took one step and had the ball stripped by Parish, which sealed the Celtics' victory. Following the game, I headed down to the locker room where I was bear-hugged by Henderson. "Johnny, I swear I could hear your call the instant I made the steal," he said to me. Then Gerald, doing his best impression of my grunt and groan play-by-play, told me how he envisioned my description: "Henderson stole the ball! HE LAYS IT IN...it's all tied up...it's all tied up...Henderson stole the ball!"

A few years later when Gerald was with Seattle, I interviewed him and he admitted that he's never heard a tape of how I called his most famous steal. "I've never actually heard the call or listened to a tape of it. I have my own mental picture of you getting all excited and calling the play with a cigarette in your mouth. That's how I want to remember it."

Three days later when the series resumed in L.A., I knew the Lakers would be intent on erasing memories of their numerous mental mistakes during Game 2. Scoring 80 points in the second half and a record-setting 47 in the third quarter alone, Magic and Company left the Celtics questioning themselves following a 137-104 loss. Larry, in particular, was disgusted. "We played like sissies," he told the media. Then, on the bus ride back to the hotel, Bird was a little more blunt when he talked to me, "That was a fucking disgrace. We let them get layup after layup on the break. Not one time did we even give them a hard foul just to let them know we were pissed and we hadn't given up. But that's just what we did—we fucking quit. Every one of us just stopped being aggressive. You can't let the other team know you're throwing in the towel and surrendering. We're the team who's supposed to make opponents believe they can't beat us on their best day. Now we've got to prove to them [the Lakers] we still believe in our hearts we're the better team. That's going to be hard to do after a crap game like we just played."

After two days off, I thought we were going to take command early in Game 4. It didn't turn out that way. At halftime the Lakers had a 10-point lead and, as in Game 3, ran the break to near-perfection, putting 68 points on the scoreboard. In the Forum hallway I bumped into an elated Jack Nicholson. "Are you telling everyone back in Boston that your guys are getting an old-fashioned ass-kicking?"

"No, Jack," I answered, "I'm telling them not to worry because Magic or Worthy will find a way to screw things up for the Lakers—again."

Jack is one of the few Hollywood hotshots I actually like. He loves the game and enjoys joking with players from his seat next to the visitors' bench. Veteran referee Wally Rooney once told me a story after a Celtics-Lakers game about Nicholson that I thought was hilarious.

Rooney had whistled Kareem for a foul, and as the teams lined up at the free throw line, Rooney stood near the sideline right in front of Nicholson. "Hey, W-A-A-L-L-Y," Jack said. "I really didn't care all that much for that last call of yours."

"That's all right, Jack," said Rooney. "I really didn't care all that much for that last movie of yours."

Nicholson wasn't going to find much to cheer about in the second half of this game as Boston suddenly came alive by succeeding in turning the game into a down-and-dirty "muscle tussle." Up until that point, the Lakers were getting away with pushes, shoves, cheap shots, and even muggings. L.A.'s hit-and-run defense had been led by Michael Cooper, who was constantly getting away with sneaky quick shoves, slaps, and bumps while guarding Bird, and by Kurt Rambis, whom I described as a dirty, elbow-throwing, ratty-looking animal. "Here in L.A., fans liken Rambis to Clark Kent. Well, he might look like Clark Kent with those glasses of his," I said on the air. "But Clark Kent comes out of a phone booth; Kurt Rambis comes out of a sewer."

It was Bird who told the team at halftime, "We have to start putting guys on their asses. Kareem doesn't like contact and neither does Magic or Worthy. Let's start knocking some guys around. It's only gonna cost us a foul. We've got five a quarter to use. Let's make them all hard fouls."

I should mention that in my conversation with Rooney, we also talked about Bird's non-stop talking on the court. "Whenever Larry says something to an opponent, he has a definite purpose. He's pretty clever in the way he gets under a guy's skin. He starts out by flatly telling his man, 'There's nothing you can do to stop me, so don't worry when I start hitting five or six in a row.' Then, once he gets into the second quarter, Larry will remind the player that the guy is incapable of stopping him. 'Look, you're playing hard, you're working your ass off, but I'm feeling really good. It's not your fault that you can't guard me.' By the time the second half starts, I can just look into Bird's opponent's eyes and know he is starting to say to himself, 'I think Bird's right. I don't think I can guard the guy.' Larry's that good an amateur psychologist. He knows how to break players' spirits."

Bird set the tone early in the third quarter by sending Cooper flying ass over tea kettle on an inbounds play. But the crucial play was when McHale prevented a Rambis fast break layup attempt by extending his arm and "clotheslining" L.A.'s power forward. It was not your typical McHale foul, but I loved it. "McHale just flattened Rambis, and Henderson is also trying to commit a hard foul," I was yelling. "Now Rambis is back on his feet and wants [to go after] McHale...Worthy accidentally shoves Rambis, his own teammate, into a photographer...Buckner just tackled Cooper, who's trying to punch Henderson from behind. It's a war, and the Lakers now can be sure the Celtics have sent an emphatic message. I guarantee neither team is going to get a single easy layup," I said. "The Celtics are fighting mad, which is just what KC Jones wanted to see."

When Kareem grabbed an offensive rebound and then jerked a sharp, deliberate elbow that hit Bird on the temple, Larry got right into Kareem's face and was ready to exchange punches. But as has always been the case, Kareem was more a debater than a boxer. He looked like giant-sized Don Knotts trying to act tough as he stalled for time and backpedaled, waiting for the refs to step in and save him from Bird's wrath. If there are two things every player, coach and GM in the NBA should know about Larry, they are 1) don't get him angry; 2) don't challenge him. The Lakers, Kareem in particular, had done both.

The Celtics came all the way back to tie the score at 113-113 in the final minute after Bird hit a pair of free throws, thanks to a frustrated Abdul-Jabbar's sixth foul. With six seconds remaining, Magic made another major blunder when he made an all-too-casual entry pass into Worthy. Parish easily intercepted the gift pass and immediately called timeout. Boston had four seconds to score and win. Bird missed a 20-foot runner off an inbounds pass, but McHale grabbed the rebound and got off a six-foot jumper before the buzzer. The shot hit the back of the rim and bounced off, forcing overtime for the second time in the series.

In overtime, the Lakers had a chance to go up by two with 35 seconds on the clock, when Magic was fouled as he began to lead a three-on-one break. His personal nightmare continued as he missed both ends of the free throw situation. On Boston's ensuing possession, everybody in the building knew the ball was going to Larry. When Cooper slipped in the lane trying to keep up with Bird, Magic moved in to guard Larry, who was begging for the ball. Finally he broke to the outside, surprising Magic just enough to get off an open 15-foot fallaway swish.

Down by two, the Lakers had a chance to tie when Worthy was fouled, but he missed the first foul shot. As the ball hit the court, Max casually walked across the lane, smiled, and gave the choke sign to Worthy. The second free throw was good, cutting Boston's lead to 125-124. Now L.A. had no choice but to foul with only 12 seconds remaining. When DJ converted two free throws, the Lakers called time and set up for a three-point shot to tie the game. Worthy, looking for Magic, inbounded the ball, but M.L. Carr sniffed out the play, stole the ball, and went in for a dunk to give us a 129-125 victory, tying the series at 2-2.

On the plane ride back to Boston, KC jokingly talked to me about his strategy before Bird hit his crucial shot. "I was diagramming a play for Larry when he interrupted me and told his teammates, 'I'll find a way to get free. Just get me the ball. I'll make the shot.' End of conversation. I'd like to take credit for great coaching. But the truth is great players can make their coaches look like geniuses."

Bird didn't act thrilled with the win. "We still didn't play well," he told me. "The only two things I liked were the win and the way we made them play our [physical] style in the second half."

Back at a sauna-like Boston Garden for Game 5, Bird was frustrating L.A. at both ends of the court. Hitting 15 of 20 shots, including two for two from downtown, he also helped limit L.A. to one shot each possession by collecting 15 defensive rebounds. The entire fourth quarter was extended garbage time as the Celtics took a 121-103 decision.

On the plane ride back to Los Angeles, the Celtics got a chance to mockingly boo Nicholson, who sat in first class near the team, when the attendant announced that the movie on that flight would be Jack's own *Terms of Endearment*, which no one watched.

Needing one more win, the Celtics were a relaxed team as they headed to the shootaround before Game 6 in L.A. Equipment manager Wayne Lebeaux decided to play a joke on Quinn Buckner. Lebeaux had spotted a huge, plump stuffed gorilla outside a store near the Forum a day before the game. An hour before the team was to board the bus for the Forum, Wayne, along with an unnamed accomplice whose initials I suspect were L.B., drove to the store and put Quinn's No. 28 Celtics jersey on the gorilla. The bus driver was given instructions to take a route to the Forum that would take the team right past the gorilla. When the players and coaches spotted the gorilla, the bus actually shook from the laughter.

"For a few minutes, I didn't appreciate the humor one bit. On other teams, someone might take offense and label it a racist joke. On this team, though, anything goes," Buckner told me once we returned to the hotel. "Religion, race, personal habits, physical features, you name it, they are all fair game for jokes. After a few minutes, I heard Chief stomping his feet and laughing uncontrollably. When Max said something about that damn gorilla weighing a lot less than I did, I gave in and started chuckling, because that gorilla was so fat and ugly. It was a good joke, but I'll find a way to get revenge."

All the laughter stopped when the Lakers outscored us by 22 points in the final 16 minutes of the game to even the series at three apiece with a 119-108 victory. "What's really disappointing," said Maxwell in the postgame interview, "was that they beat us in the halfcourt game, not with their fast break. Kareem was hitting his skyhook, and that forced us to double him. That opened up room for their outside shooting. We just couldn't rotate fast enough."

I had a good feeling before the deciding game at the "tropical" Garden. Before warmups, Ainge kept the players loose by grabbing a stethoscope from the training room and checking the heartbeat of M.L. Carr. "I've got to make sure we don't have any 'tin men' or 'cowardly lions' in this locker room. Everybody's got to have heart and courage today, baby. M.L., your heart's pumping hard. You're OK...Johnny Most, you're next. On second thought, I'd better not. I wouldn't want to jinx us if I can't find your pulse."

Carr, one of the Celtics' poker-playing regulars on the plane rides, compared the upcoming battle to a no-bluff card game. "This is a hand of showdown, boys," he announced, "and the pot is huge. No folding allowed. There's thousands of dollars on the table and we're either going to rake it in or go home flat broke." Shortly before game time, it was Maxwell who stood up before the team left the locker room and loudly said, "Climb on my back, fellas, and I'll take you all in."

And Cedric followed through on his pledge, scoring 24 points, grabbing eight rebounds and also assisting on eight baskets. By the end of the third quarter, we led by 13. High above courtside, I knew the Lakers were running on an empty tank. "Kareem's got his face buried in a wet towel...Riley's hair is so sweaty that all that grease he uses on it is dripping on his $1,000 suit...Magic is just sitting silently," I commented. "The Fakers are ready to wave the white flag...but there's still 12 minutes remaining, and KC is not about to let anyone start celebrating."

Although the Lakers made a run in the final five minutes to close to within three, a Dennis Johnson steal and two free throws by Bird sealed the Celtics' victory and gave Boston championship number 15. "This is the sweetest," said Buckner, who had just earned his first championship ring. "After we fell behind 2-1, everyone jumped on the Lakers' bandwagon except the guys in this room and our fans."

I was elated for KC because he had worked so hard to prove to everyone in the league that you don't have to be a high-profile, know-it-all, public relations-oriented, slick coach to motivate players and earn their respect. "KC was always so relaxed in the locker room. He didn't yell or show any signs of panic during the entire series. He set the tone for us," said Parish. "He showed confidence in us even when we might have been doubting ourselves. He doesn't lecture us or show his emotions. He just calmly treats us as men and explains what we need to do to win. He doesn't look for or want credit. He'd rather see his players getting the accolades."

While Larry earned his first regular-season MVP and Playoff Finals MVP, McHale captured his first Sixth Man of the Year Award. For me, the ultimate disgrace was that KC, whose team had the best regular-season record en route to winning a title, wasn't the runaway winner as Coach of the Year. In one of the greatest robberies since the Brinks case, that award went to Utah's roly-poly funny man, Frank Layden, whose team barely managed a plus-.500 (45-37) regular-season record and was eliminated in the Western Division semifinals by a mediocre Phoenix club. I guess it pays to be a quotable comic who provides the media with their "Fat Joke of the Day." If I were Layden, in good conscience I couldn't have accepted the award.

In July of '84 the Celtics named Jan Volk, Red's longtime right-hand man, as the team's general manager. Regarded as the league's top expert on salary cap rules, Jan knew how to manage the Celtics' team payroll to take the greatest advantage of the rules to help improve the Celtics through trades and free agent signings. Auerbach hated all the salary cap restrictions. It was through Jan's hard work and knowledge that Red, despite dealing with what he called a "bunch of salary cap bullshit," was able to come up with ways of obtaining players he considered to be excellent additions to the team.

In the off season I began what was to be a fun gig, hosting the Johnny Most Sound-Alike contests for Sportschannel. Ainge, of course, found a way to give me the business. "All I can say," he said to me, with a big wink, "is that the greatest fear in my life would be to be invited as a participant in a Johnny Most look-alike contest."

The sound-alike contests, which lasted three years, took place all over New England, with local celebrities serving as judges. The regional winners were invited to the finals, which were held in Boston. I was constantly amazed at the imagination of the competitors. Some would bring scripts in which they used all of my favorite phrases and nicknames. Others would just ad-lib my descriptions of fights between Celtic players and opposition players, such as Laimbeer, Mahorn, Ruland, and Abdul-Jabbar. The contestants ranged from 10-year-old children to 70-year-old women. One fan even prepared himself for one of the contests by going outside into a parking lot and yelling at the top of his lungs until he became as hoarse as I sometimes sounded on the air. The contests became so popular that Sportschannel televised each year's finals.

There was a major move made by the Celtics two weeks into the '84 training camp. Auerbach traded Gerald Henderson, who had just been signed after a salary holdout, to Seattle for an unconditional '86 first-round draft choice. I understood why the team was willing to part with Gerald, who had been a valuable contributor to two NBA championships. Obviously, KC believed that Ainge was ready to become an effective full-time starter, giving Boston a backcourt rotation of DJ, Danny, and Buckner, with M.L. Carr and rookie Rick Carlisle in reserve roles.

However, I totally disagreed with Red, who said he "got rid" of Gerald because the guard had come into training camp "out of shape." Why Red would say anything negative about such a hard-working, well-liked player who never was so much as a pound overweight is beyond me. Hell, getting an unconditional first-rounder for Henderson was an excellent move. But why would Red then go out of his way to criticize a player who gave his heart and soul to the Celtics? I thought it was unfair, and I told Red privately about my opinion. Since Auerbach didn't argue with me or tell me I was full of shit, I guess he knew I had a valid point.

There seemed to be numerous omens that this team was on its way to a second straight championship. Bird showed his fiery spirit early in the '84-'85 season when he scored 42 points against an aging and frustrated Julius Erving. That was the game (see All-Opponents chapter) in which Julius and Larry exchanged punches as Malone and Charles Barkley held Larry's arms while Erving got in an extra shot, an act of a frightened coward.

By December, the Celtics were 15-1 and executing their offense to perfection. Boston's frontcourt regulars were combining for better than 75 points a game while the Ainge-DJ backcourt was coming up with crucial steals and reliable outside shooting. Ainge, as a starter, was much more aggressive than he had ever been. He was shooting better than 53 percent from the field and knocking down 87 percent of his free throws.

One funny story I have to mention involved Bird and referee Joey Crawford. Crawford had been the lead official in a game at Houston against the Spurs in late December of '84. During a timeout in the second quarter, Crawford was handed a note by an usher that said his two guests were waiting outside the Summit because the ref's complimentary tickets could not be found at the box office. Crawford was irate and went over to the Rockets' equipment manager, David Nordstrom, and began screaming at him.

"Where the hell are my tickets? I gave them to you to bring up to the box office and they never got there," Crawford yelled. "I've got two guests who have been waiting for more than an hour." For the remainder of the game, Crawford was so steamed that he called 18 fouls against the Rockets while only signaling two fouls against the visiting Spurs. Needless to say, the Rockets lost the game, and Crawford was reprimanded by the league.

About a week later, the Celtics were taking a flight out west when none other than Joe Crawford boarded the plane. As Crawford passed by Bird, who was sitting in the second row of first class, Larry yelled out, "Hey, Joe, if you ever need five or six tickets or even a dozen for a game in Boston, here's my home phone number. Just call me and tell me how many you need. I'll make sure they're at the box office—and they'll be there on time, too." Crawford couldn't help but laugh as he sheepishly made his way to his seat without saying a word.

As the season entered February, Boston looked all but invincible. Then Maxwell injured his knee in a loss to the Lakers. The injury required arthroscopic surgery, which meant McHale moved into a starter's role.

On February 12 in Utah, Larry had what I consider one of the best all-around games of his career, recording a triple-double by the end of the third quarter. At that point in the game, he also had come up with nine steals. With the Celtics coasting to an easy victory, Bird told KC he wanted to sit out the fourth quarter rather than playing for the sole purpose of recording a quadruple-double by snatching one more steal. Afterwards he told me, "I've never played for stats. I play for wins. We still have a tough game in Denver to end this West Coast trip. We always seem to struggle there, so I thought getting some extra rest was the right thing to do." (As Larry predicted, the Nuggets gave us a really tough time, winning by three.)

Two weeks later, McHale scored a team-record 56 points against the Pistons, with Larry setting up Kevin for his final six points. Pistons defenders Bill "Flopper" Laimbeer, Earl Cureton, Kent Benson and Major Jones weren't just in what Maxwell called McHale's "torture chamber;" they were in an execution chamber, with Kevin hitting 22 of 29 field goal attempts, along with grabbing seven offensive rebounds. McHale loved playing the Pistons ever since "Cry, Kelly, Cry" Tripucka, a chronic and totally obnoxious whiner, said that Kevin "wasn't an athlete. He's just got real long arms and some good moves. That's all." McHale took offense and half-joked, "Well, I never looked at Tripucka as being a [world-record track star and 49ers wide receiver] Renaldo Nehemiah."

Only 14 days later, Bird, with McHale feeding the ball to Larry at every opportunity in the final quarter, topped Kevin's effort, scoring 60 against the Hawks in a game played in New Orleans. Bird's shooting display was so amazing that the Atlanta bench went wild while rooting for Larry to hit a couple off-balance shots from downtown during the final two minutes. When Bird nailed a shot from downtown while falling out of bounds near the Hawks' bench, Atlanta's Antoine Carr, Cliff Levingston and Eddie Johnson just leaned into each other while sitting on the bench and toppled like a row of dominoes. And when Larry put in a jumper from just beyond the foul line at the buzzer for point number 60, four Hawks stood up and cheered him for his amazing performance. (After viewing the video tape of the Atlanta bench players' actions, the NBA actually fined those guys for cheering an opponent.)

These two games illustrated why I always have maintained that McHale and Bird were teammates who had mutual respect for each other and wanted each other to play at their highest levels. Many fans have asked me about Kevin's and Larry's relationship. Were they "best friends" off the court? No, but they played golf together, shared a few beers together, and joked with each other often. For two true superstars, they got along well and shared many unforgettable moments and memories. Did they root for one another to succeed? Unquestionably, yes.

There were a few reporters who wrote articles hinting of a few major arguments between the two. Those stories were exaggerations. I'm not saying they didn't have disagreements. I don't know any two teammates in the history of the team who *didn't* have occasional spats.

However, those rare instances when Larry and Kevin verbally sparred with each other were minor, especially when you consider they were teammates for more than a decade. Anyone who has played a team sport knows individuals are going to have differing opinions and sometimes a war of words or even minor physical confrontations. What you had in those two were great team players with vastly different personalities. One thing I know for sure is that their little spats were never caused by jealousy. End of story.

Throughout the '84-'85 season, there had been some rumors that Maxwell was on the trading block. One day a reporter asked Cedric about a report that he might be heading to Cleveland. Max laughed off the story and said, "Well, they've got two guys—Mel Turpin and Lonnie Shelton—who both weigh at least 280. If I go to the Cavs, at least I'm sure no one will ever accuse me of being out of shape—not with those two guys on the team." That comment came back to haunt Max when he faced the Cavs for the first time since his injury. He was just standing near the foul line when Shelton popped him with an elbow. "Hey, what was that for?" a startled Maxwell asked the portly Cleveland center. "That's for making a joke about my weight, you wiseass. Your remark was printed in the Cleveland paper, and I've had to listen to a lot of crap about it."

In one of the final games of the regular season, McHale got a chance to play a prank on journeyman center Chris Engler, Kevin's close friend whom he had roomed with for a year while at the University of Minnesota. At the time, the 6'11" Engler was a member of the Nets. With the Celtics up by 25 points with four or five minutes remaining, McHale went over to Engler and said, "Hey, Chris, I want to make you look good to your coach. Next time you get the ball, you make a fake, and I'll pretend to go for it. Then just drive past me to the basket and dunk the ball."

"Sounds good to me," replied Engler. "With the little playing time I get, I can use every point."

About a minute later, Engler got the ball at the foul line and faked taking a shot. Kevin took a step in Engler's direction and Chris made his move to the hoop. McHale's "plan" seemed to work perfectly for Engler until he went up for the dunk. At that point, McHale came up from behind and cleanly swatted the ball into the stands. "What the hell are you doing?" a puzzled Engler asked McHale. "You told me you'd let me go by you for an easy basket."

Kevin looked his old friend in the eyes, paused, and then, with a wink, said, "I lied."

"You bastard," said Engler. "I should have known you'd do something like that."

"That's right," said Kevin. "You should have."

Boston finished the regular season with a league-best 63-19 record. Larry won his second consecutive MVP Award and Kevin was voted Sixth Man of the Year for the second straight year. The Celtics breezed through the Eastern Division in the playoffs, beating Cleveland, Detroit and Philly. But when the Celtics faced the Lakers in the finals, L.A. used their fast break effectively and relied on Kareem in the halfcourt game to beat the Celtics twice at the Garden and go on to prevent Boston from repeating as NBA champs with a 4-2 final series victory.

The Lakers really rubbed it in with Magic and Kareem mugging for the cameras, pointing fingers at each other and giving each other high-fives during the closing moments of the series. L.A. coach Pat Riley, whom I referred to as "The Imported Suit," also was taking part in the Lakers' little party. Bird, for one, took notice. "Let 'em celebrate," Larry told me. "It just motivates me more than ever. I'm going to work my tail off this summer, because I never want to have to watch another team taunting us in our own building. It just won't happen again. That's a freaking guarantee."

In the off season, Bill Walton called Red and asked him for the chance to play for the Celtics. "I literally begged him," Bill said to me later. "I wanted a shot at one more championship and I wanted to play with Larry Bird, the absolutely best player I had ever seen. I would have played in Boston for free—and I told Red that." Despite the fact that the injury-plagued Walton had only played a total of 169 out of a possible 328 games over the course of the previous four years, Bill convinced Red he was sufficiently healthy to make a major contribution to the Celtics.

"Red knew I could never pass a physical, but he still wanted me. Heck, an 80-year-man would have had a better chance of passing a physical than I would have. At that point in my career I already had undergone a total of 27 operations," Bill told me.

Believing Maxwell did not push himself hard enough to rehabilitate his knee following his surgery, Red was able to obtain Walton from the Clippers in exchange for Cedric. While I thought Walton was a tremendous addition, I disagreed with Red's assessment of Cedric's knee rehabilitation, because no one but Cedric knew how much pain he was experiencing. Watching Max walk with a slight limp for months was proof to me that his knee was not responding well to treatment.

I also want to say this: Max deserves to eventually have his number hanging from the Garden rafters for a number of reasons. He was a stabilizing force during his first three years in the league when the Celtics first began their climb back to respectability after the John Y. Brown years. He was clearly the MVP of the championship series in '81 and he was one of the heroes of the '84 championship team. Cedric, as far as I'm concerned, was always willing to sacrifice personal stats. He was a contributor who seldom received the praise given Larry, Kevin or Robert. In my mind, his attitude was similar to that of the key role players during the Russell years.

While I hated to see Maxwell leave, I was elated that Walton was going to be wearing the green and white uniform. Without a doubt, with the lone exception of Russell, he was the greatest outlet passer in NBA history. He also was the best high-post passer I've ever seen. Had he not been plagued by countless major injuries throughout his career, I know a debate would rage as to who was the best center in history—Russ, Walton, or Chamberlain.

In addition to handling my talk show on Sportschannel and judging the Johnny Most Sound-Alike contests in the off season, I began a venture with Glenn called "The Johnny Most Fiddlin' and Diddlin' Fantasy Tapes" in which I announced play-by-play of key moments in Celtics history and inserted the name of a fan as the player taking and making the game-winning shot. The tapes were well received, so much so that they became a very popular gift for birthdays and holidays. The ages of the fans who received fantasy tapes ran from newborn babies to men and women celebrating their 100th birthdays.

Over a span of three years we sold approximately 4,000 fantasy tapes. Some were special requests, such as a fan wanting me to have him punch "McFilthy" or "McNasty." Another tape request I received came from a Celtics supporter who was only 5'6". He asked me to create a play-by-play scenario in which he would leap five feet in the air to block one of Dr. J's dunk attempts. Most of the tapes, though, involved Bird throwing a no-look pass to the "fan/player" who would bury a jumper from downtown at the final buzzer to give the Celtics a one-point win. We also produced a tape that was a takeoff on my "Havlicek Stole the Ball" call. Instead of having John steal the ball, I would insert the fan's last name for that particular historical play.

Even celebrities wanted to buy the fantasy tapes. We did a comical one for Jack Nicholson in which the Boston players all throw towels at him as the Celtics beat the Lakers to win the title. Other celebrities who requested tapes included Heather Locklear, Ted Danson and George Wendt of *Cheers*, Bird's golfing buddy Greg Norman, The E Street Band's Nils Lofgrin, Bon Jovi band member Richie Sambora, Boston mayor Ray Flynn, and pro wrestler Big John Studd.

The fantasy tape business was a fun, sometimes nutty, project that proved to be very profitable. Based on their success in New

England, Glenn and I eventually helped Chick Hearn start producing fantasy tapes for Lakers fans.

In September of '85 the Celtics sent Quinn Buckner to Indiana for a second-round draft choice and a month later acquired feisty 6'1" point guard Jerry Sichting from the Pacers in exchange for two future second-round draft picks. Bird immediately tagged him with the nickname of "The Chicken Farmer" because he and his family lived in the rural Indiana town of Martinsville.

As preseason play began, Walton not only assumed the role of a veteran leader, but he was also absolutely delighted to be in Boston. "This is paradise," he told me. "Red gave me my career back, he gave me my life back. I had forgotten that basketball was fun. With the Clippers, there was no joy in either basketball or in life."

I knew Bill was going to be very popular among his teammates, not only because of his talent and attitude, but because McHale and Bird loved to tease him about his past. "Hey, Bill, I heard you hid Patty Hearst in your garage when she was robbing banks. C'mon, you can tell me all about it," Kevin said. With a straight face, Bill jokingly replied. "Not the garage, the basement. As usual, you've got your facts wrong."

Ainge was busy getting laughs at the expense of newcomer David Thirdkill, who wore basketball shoes that had his college nickname, "The Sheriff," imprinted on them because he was noted for his jailhouse defense while playing at Bradley University. Since Thirdkill rarely received playing time, Ainge wisecracked, "I'm not going call you the sheriff; I'm calling you Deputy Dawg." The new nickname stuck, much to David's displeasure.

Danny also stuck second-year guard Rick Carlisle with the nickname "Flipper," because of his narrow, size 16 1/2 basketball shoes. "With those feet, you probably swim faster than you run," Ainge said.

As the '85-'86 season got underway, I found myself involved in a verbal battle with Philadelphia's young rising star, Charles Barkley.

For an undersized (6'6" maximum) and pudgy (230 pounds minimum) power forward, the so-called "Round Mound of Rebound" was quick, strong and clever, especially under the offensive boards. The officials constantly allowed him get away with charges, walks, pushes and elbowing. I began to inform my audience that refs such as Jake O'Donnell, Earl Strom and Joey Crawford would refuse to call fouls on him simply because he was "The Great Sir Charles" in their minds. There was no doubt in my mind that Barkley was being treated by the officials as if he were NBA royalty—and I made sure the Boston fans knew he was getting away with murder, courtesy of the refs.

When Barkley heard about my comments, he told the media, "Johnny Most is just a fucking old man who knows absolutely nothing about basketball. Like I care about what some short, prune-faced guy says." When I heard about his remarks, the war was officially on. I wasn't about to let some 22-year-old fat bag of wind whom I had never even interviewed make a wiseass statement like that without retaliating. Every time he ran into McHale, who usually guarded him, I went wild. Every time he shoved and pushed to get position for a rebound, I criticized the officials for allowing such a blatant foul to go uncalled. "He gets away with those cheap, dirty tactics because the refs are afraid to offend Barkley because he's SIR CHARLES. It's out-and-out favoritism, because this guy is a con man who charms the pants off the refs even while he's grabbing, shoving and even punching our players."

My beef with Barkley continued for two years until McHale, whom Charles acknowledged was the toughest opponent he ever faced, invited him to attend Kevin's charity golf tournament at Ocean's Edge on Cape Cod. Only then did Barkley and I sit down and talk to each other face to face. I hated to admit it, but I found him to be a genuinely humorous and friendly kid.

By the conclusion of the tournament, Charles was sitting down with me and imitating my descriptions of his play. He was damn good at it, too. He might have even won one of my sound-alike contests. From that point on, Charles would always come over to me before the game and say something like, "Sir Charles is going to be on his best behavior tonight, so don't rip me too bad." Or he'd walk over to Ordway and me and greet us by saying, "Well, it's the pear and the prune." I'd laugh, but I still ripped him anyway, because he was one of the bad guys who loved to see how much he could get away with without getting called for absolutely beating up Kevin or any Celtic who dared to box out "Saintly Sir Charles."

The '85-'86 Celtics team had no weaknesses. We had four Hall of Fame-caliber frontcourt players—Bird, McHale, Parish and Walton. Then there was a starting backcourt of DJ, another potential Hall of Famer, and Ainge, who was by now one of the most accurate outside shooters in the league. From the experience of playing together since '84, DJ and Bird could read each other's minds. If Larry was open, DJ would get him the ball with perfect timing. With Sichting and Wedman coming in off the bench, our outside shooting had to be respected all 48 minutes. The opposition clearly had a defensive dilemma. Should they double-team Bird or McHale and dare Ainge, Sichting or Wedman to bury wide-open, 18-foot jumpers, or should they attempt to guard Kevin and Larry on a one-on-one basis? There were no easy answers. The only thing, in my opinion, that could prevent Boston from dominating the East this season would be a major injury.

Although the Celtics were atop the Eastern standings in December, they hadn't been winning as easily or as often as I predicted. When we blew a 25-point lead in New York on Christmas Day and lost in double overtime, KC uncharacteristically chewed out the entire team. "I told them they were getting too cocky," he told me after the game. "I told them that they can't rely on talent rather than effort. I let them know I was embarrassed, because there's no excuse for playing without intensity, no matter what the score."

The players responded by winning 17 of their next 18 games. Even an Achilles tendon injury to McHale, which forced him to miss 11 games, didn't slow the team down as Wedman stepped into a starter's role and averaged 16 points during Kevin's absence.

"Before each and every game, Big Bill Walton is like a TV evangelist," I commented during one of my late-season broadcasts. "He delivers his sermon and doesn't get down from his pulpit until he's sure his 'congregation' gets his message. His face gets red, and he yells, screams, and marches around the locker room to make sure everyone is ready to shout 'Hallelujah.'"

DJ agreed with me, sort of. "He's like a high school kid getting ready to play against a big rival. It doesn't matter whether we're playing the Clippers or Philly," said DJ. "Bill wants us to go out and rip apart teams. The only problem is guys sometimes crack up at the way he makes these weird faces and starts getting so angry and loud. Shoot, we haven't even gone through warmups and Bill is ready to explode. I think Larry especially gets a kick out of Bill's pregame wild-man act."

Whether Bill's fire-and-brimstone speeches actually motivated the players or just served to give them a little laugh before each game, his attitude seemed to keep everyone focused. When the regular season ended, Boston had achieved a 67-15 record, losing only once at home, a defeat against Portland.

During that season, I almost missed a game against the Mavs because I became involved in a verbal altercation with two Dallas policemen. My problem began when I decided to sneak out into a back hallway of Reunion Arena to smoke a cigarette. I wasn't within a hundred yards of anyone, but these two cops spotted me and started threatening to arrest me for the "high crime" of inhaling a cigarette in a public building. Naturally, I told them they were poor excuses for law enforcement officers. Because I managed to sprinkle in a few curse words as I argued with them, they overreacted and pushed me against a wall. Then they started lecturing me for not giving them respect. As I exchanged words with them, the national anthem began playing, and then the tipoff took place. Finally Mavs public relations director Kevin Sullivan rescued me. I got to my broadcasting position three minutes into the game.

Glenn, who already knew why I was late, immediately asked me on the air why I was "detained." I was still irate, so I decided to tell my audience just how ridiculous the police had been. "Two Dallas cops threatened to arrest me for smoking in the stadium...right now in Dallas there are 6,346 robberies taking place, 243 stabbings and shootings are being reported, and there's probably a dozen rapes taking place. And here's these two cops who think Johnny Most having a cigarette makes me public enemy number one."

The classic moment of the Celtics' season came during the final game of the season against the Nets at the Garden. It seemed Larry had a $100,000 bonus if he won the free throw percentage title, and the only player who had even a remote chance of beating him out was Ainge. However, Danny needed to make 14 of 15 free throws if he was to officially qualify for the honor of beating Bird and thus depriving Larry of the extra hundred grand. To be candid, I wasn't aware of the situation, and not many fans were, either. Since Ainge rarely shot more than a few foul shots a game, it seemed Bird had the free throw title locked up. As the game got under way, though, Danny drove to the basket every time he touched the ball and just hurled himself into the opposition's defenders, drawing foul after foul.

By the middle of fourth quarter he had hit 12 of 13 free throws as he purposely got the crap kicked out of him by Buck Williams, Mike Gminski and Darryl Dawkins. Danny looked like a human pinball as he bounced off the Nets' big men and crashed to the court. With every foul, he'd jump right up with a huge grin on his face. By now, everyone in the building realized he was trying to beat out Larry for the best foul-shooting percentage in the NBA.

When KC was made aware that Larry could quite possibly lose $100,000 because Ainge, ever the competitor, needed to make only two more free throws to edge Bird while busting Larry's balls in the process, he pulled Danny out of the game.

"If Danny had gotten to the line one more time, I would have stepped into the lane to cause a violation just to make sure he didn't cost Larry all that dough," said McHale. "Larry was laughing about what Danny was trying to do, but I think he might have killed Danny afterward if Ainge had succeeded in qualifying. In the end, Ainge, who didn't have a bonus clause in his contract for winning the free-throw title, finished with an "unofficial" .904 mark, while Bird ended up with .896. Still, as Bird said afterward, "Danny went to the free throw line less than two times a game. I shot 492 foul shots for the season. He wasn't just trying beat me for best free throw accuracy. He cared more about being able to go around bragging to everyone on the team about how he stole all that money from me."

The Celtics swept the Bulls in the opening round of the playoffs—despite Michael Jordan scoring an NBA-record 63 points in Chicago's double-overtime loss to Boston in Game 2. Then the Celtics methodically destroyed the Hawks in five games in the Eastern Division semifinals. The Celtics swept Milwaukee 4-0 in what was particularly sweet revenge for Ainge, who shot better than 50 percent from the field and went 16 for 16 from the foul line while averaging 16.5 points in the series against Nellie's team.

Then we faced Bill Fitch's Houston Rockets, who finished the regular season with only a 51-31 record but had upset the always cocky Lakers, 4-1, in the Western Division finals, for the NBA title.

Boston's depth and the shooting touch of Bird, Parish and McHale put Houston in a 3-1 hole. Then in Game 5 at the Summit, I witnessed one of the most cowardly, despicable and downright ugly incidents I have ever seen. It was all caused by Houston's 7-4 center Ralph Sampson, who had been getting his butt kicked throughout the series by McHale, Parish and Walton. Early in the second quarter, fearless Ralphie decided to take his frustrations out on little Jerry Sichting, who happened to find himself guarding Sampson in transition.

When Sichting "dared" to put his hands on Sampson's back, the Houston center threw an elbow that caught Jerry on the side of the head. Sampson was immediately called for a foul, and Sichting took a step toward the Rockets' center to tell him to knock off the cheap shots. At that point, Sampson began throwing wild roundhouse punches down at the Celtics guard's head. When Dennis Johnson tried to break things up, Sampson hit DJ with a sneak punch and then started backpedaling. Walton tackled Sampson, but somehow Ralphie escaped and once again "bravely" decided to go after Jerry. "I'm Ralph Sampson. I have the right to break your head," I said on the air. "He's shown his true colors. He's nothing but a gutless big guy who picks on the little people."

With Greg Kite holding Ralph from behind, Sampson attempted to kick Sichting, who was being held from behind by a member of Houston's police department. Finally, when Kite had Sampson in a bear hug, Ralphie and Sichting, whose only crime was defending himself from an embarrassingly inept bully, were ejected from the game.

"I guess he [Sampson] didn't like the fact that I wasn't going to let him go right over me to the basket," Jerry told me afterward. "He threw punches like a little girl does, so I really didn't feel the one little slap he landed. I just wanted to get one good shot in at him after he tried to kick me, but I was being held by a cop. I'm six foot nothing and Sampson's seven foot four, and here's this cop—on the court—grabbing me. I couldn't believe it. As I was walking toward the locker room, I saw the cop again, and he apologized. I guess he must have known beforehand that Sampson was such a weakling, even someone my size could outbox him. Anyway, I guess that fight is going to go down as my 15 minutes of fame."

Without Sampson, the Rockets actually played much better as a team and went on to win that game 111-106, forcing a Game 6 at the Garden. With Bird and McHale each scoring 29 points while combining for 21 rebounds, we easily captured NBA championship number 16 with a 114-97 victory. (For the series, "Slugger" Sampson shot 43 percent and put up little resistance against the frontcourt offense of Bird, McHale, Parish and Walton, who combined for 61 offensive rebounds. Larry was voted the playoff MVP, with Kevin a close second. For the third straight year, Bird was the league's MVP, while Walton earned Sixth Man of the Year honors.

The question I'm asked most frequently is whether the '85-'86 Celtics team was the best Boston team, the best NBA team, in history. I can't give an honest answer, because several of the Russell-led teams also completely dominated the league. You can't compare teams from two different eras. I will say this: the '85-'86 Celtics had as much depth as any of the Auerbach-coached championship teams. This team, though, played a different style of basketball than some of Red's title teams during the late '50s and '60s. The combination of Russell's rebounding and outlet passing, along with Cousy's relentless on-the-run passing skills, made the Auerbach-coached teams uniquely effective. While the '86 Celtics did not have the same fast break capabilities, they did, in my opinion, have a more productive half-court offense.

The two characteristics all the Celtics' title teams shared was "chemistry" and self-sacrifice. The '86 Celtics were as close a group of players as any coach could desire. Each player knew and accepted his role. The credit for that belongs to KC Jones. What really was a travesty was that for the second time, KC led the Celtics to an NBA championship, and for the second time he was overlooked in the voting for Coach of the Year. In '86 that honor went to Atlanta's Mike Fratello, whose Hawks won only 50 games in the regular season and then were eliminated 4-1 by Boston in the Eastern Division semis. Figure that one out, because I—along with every Celtics player— will never be able to come up with a reason why KC was snubbed.

On draft day, Boston, using the choice it had obtained from Seattle in the Gerald Henderson trade, selected Len Bias, the talented 6'8" forward from Maryland, as the second overall choice behind

UNC center Brad Daugherty, who was taken by the Cavs. Even though Daugherty came from a great program, had a nice scoring touch and good rebounding skills, I honestly believed Bias had far greater potential to be a superstar.

I had known Len since he was a sophomore, and I had followed his career closely. As an underclassman, he had been a counselor at Red's summer camp in Marshfield, Massachusetts. During the nightly scrimmages, Len actually outplayed many of the veteran Celtics who participated as a way of staying in shape in the off season. It was very obvious to not only the Celtics staff but also the fans that he was a quick learner and a player who would be able to contribute a productive 15 to 20 minutes a game once Len entered the NBA.

On two occasions, he, Red, Jan Volk and I shared a meal together at a restaurant near Red's camp. Len was polite, articulate, and intelligent. The Celtics players at the camp, without exception, raved about his skills and potential. "When he becomes a pro, no one will want to guard him, because he's so quick and so skilled," M.L. Carr told me. "He can shoot the jumper or go right by you, because he handles the ball like a guard."

The day after the draft, he attended a Reebok party where Ainge, then the father of a daughter and two sons, joked with him about how a rookie occasionally has to babysit a veteran's children. "Hey, I'll be happy to, if you need me," Len replied. "All I want to know is how much does a babysitter make."

The next morning I was watching TV when a news bulletin interrupted whatever program I was watching. Len Bias, the report claimed, had died of a heart attack in his dorm room after returning from Boston to the University of Maryland campus. My first reaction was that it could not be true. Then, as the TV feed from a Washington station showed friends, teammates and family gathering at a hospital, I began to cry as I tried to comprehend the sad news. When a Boston station cited unnamed sources as saying the cause of death was a cocaine overdose, I became angry, because knowing Len, this was an impossibility. I called Red and he confirmed the report. "Yeah, it's true," he said to me. "I don't know any details, and I still don't believe Bias would use any type of drugs. I mean this kid was a straight arrow all the way."

It took me months to come to the realization that a person as intelligent as Len could possibly not understand the dangers of using drugs. I firmly believe that Len Bias had never used drugs before that tragic night. I believe peer pressure during a dorm room celebration resulted in him deciding to try cocaine "just one time." Whether I'm right or wrong in my beliefs, doctors who spoke of Len's death emphasized that "just one time" can be fatal. It's a message that his mother, Lonise, now delivers on a regular basis to kids from grade school to college across the country. In my opinion, she's a courageous woman who wants to make sure something positive comes out of such a personal loss. To quote her, "Len has done more in death than he ever could in life. Had he lived, he would have entertained. But in death, he fought for life."

In the off season, I continued with my talk show and the sound-alike contests. I also was asked to play the part of a broadcaster in a movie entitled *Amazing Grace and Chuck*, which was shot in Bozeman, Montana. The plot of the film, which starred Denver Nuggets scorer Alex English, Gregory Peck and Jamie Lee Curtis, was that a star Little League pitcher refuses to pitch as a protest against nuclear weapons. Before long, pro athletes from Russia and the U.S. join in the protest, putting pressure on the two countries to hold a summit meeting. The two countries eventually agree to a summit, which results in a commitment to total nuclear disarmament. My role was small, but I thought the movie sent a worthwhile message, so I accepted the opportunity. It was a great experience, even though the production was not exactly a box office blockbuster.

During filming I developed a friendship with Gregory Peck, and I'm quite sure I fell in love with Jamie Lee Curtis, who not only is beautiful but also has a tremendous, outgoing personality. The real bonus was that I discovered makeup can do wonders for just about anyone, including me. The wardrobe people dressed me up in a sharp-looking camel hair sports jacket, and my "personal assistant" put so much pancake makeup on my wrinkled old face that I looked as if I were 45 rather than 63. When the movie came out in '87, so many Celtics fans commented on how good I looked that I kiddingly told them that from now on I would be hiring a "personal assistant" to dress me up and apply makeup before every Celtics game.

Despite the Bias tragedy, I still believed that Boston, with its depth and talent, would be champion again in '87. However, injuries would deal the Celtics one setback after another, beginning with a foot injury to Walton during training camp. Bill told me off the record that he was positive his right foot, the foot that had held up reasonably well throughout his career, was broken. "There's just constant pain and throbbing. It's real major." Although he consulted with numerous specialists, it wasn't until mid-December that a conclusive diagnosis was made that he had suffered broken bones and required surgery.

"Now I have two options," he sadly told me. "I can undergo more operations, or I can retire and try to be happy with my memories of two championships. Quitting just isn't in my nature, though. I know this team can win back-to-back titles. And if it takes me all of the regular season to recover from surgery and be able to play, then I'm going for it. This team, the coaches, and the players are all special, and I'm going do everything in my power to play an *active, productive* role in winning the title again."

The Celtics also went through the year without the services of Scotty Wedman, who had undergone off-season surgery to remove bone spurs from his left heel. The operation left him with a deep bruise that never healed, forcing him to miss all but six regular-season games as well as the entire playoffs.

A week before the regular season was to begin, Ainge suffered a fractured transverse process in his back that forced him to miss the first eight games of the season. Still, with Sichting and Greg Kite getting increased playing time, the Celtics got off to an 8-2 start.

When Ainge returned, he began to use his three-point shot more frequently than ever before. By season's end he had connected on 85 of 192 shots. But Danny's long-range, off-target bombs drove Cooz, the TV color commentator, nuts. "Cripes, we'll have a four-on-three break, and Ainge will pull up and take a three-pointer. Why not take advantage of the break and pass the ball? When you have a fast-break advantage, you should be ending up with layups, not 25-foot jumpers."

Ainge, hearing from family and friends about Cousy's on-air comments, defended his shot selection. "I'm shooting better than 40 percent with my three-pointers. Figure out the math, Johnny," he said privately to me. "My three-point percentage is really better than a guy who's shooting 60 percent with two-point shots."

I thought the "feud" was comical, because Bob and Danny respected and liked each other but strongly disagreed on the value of the three-pointer.

Cooz would point out that when Danny missed a three-pointer, the ball would rebound over the heads of the Celtics' big men and give the opposition far too many fast-break opportunities. "I agree there are certain times when the three-point shot is the right play. Danny, though, just fires up those threes without thinking about the game situation," Cooz said.

In response, Ainge would get a little testy. "I'm hitting them, and as long as the shots are going in, I'm gonna keep on taking them," he said to me. "Cooz makes it sound like I shoot them every time I get the ball. Cooz may have been one of the greatest passers and ball handlers, but he wasn't a deadly shooter by any means. I don't think his 38 percent lifetime shooting percentage gives him much ammunition to knock my three-point accuracy."

They never argued about the pros and cons of the three-point shot face to face. However, it was amusing for me to hear them both complain to me about the other's opinion. Personally, I thought each had some valid points. Missed three-point shots do create a number of easy-basket opportunities for the opposition. However, with a team like the Celtics, a Bird or Ainge three-pointer can be the type of basket that completely demoralizes the enemy. I can't count the number of times a Bird three-pointer in the final minute has won games for us. What I can say is that it is a mind-boggling number that either put the game out of reach or won the game outright in the closing seconds.

This was the season when Chuck "The Rifleman" Person entered the league as a rookie, a trash-talking one at that. For some delusional reason, Person decided he could both outplay and outtalk Bird. Those were two monumental errors in judgment. Before each Celtics-Pacers game, Person would boast that he was going to outscore Larry. Bird absolutely savored the scoring duels with Person, who usually took more shots and ended up with 10 fewer points. But those results failed to keep Person humble. Because of his consistent losing battles with Larry, I would occasionally question why he called himself "The Rifleman," when all he ever shot against Boston were blanks.

I think Chuck, who is always an interesting player to interview, enjoyed all the media attention. But there's no way he could have gotten any pleasure whatsoever from Bird's scoring exhibitions and Larry's not-so-subtle, yet humorous, verbal abuse.

Speaking of taking abuse, I've got to tell the story of the night my pants caught on fire. Glenn and I were preparing to do our postgame wrap-up following a game against the Bucks at the Garden. I had put a lit cigarette on the edge of the table while I was reading the final stats. I also was busy finishing a lukewarm cup of coffee when we went on the air following a couple of commercials. Forgetting I already had a cigarette burning, I lit up another one and put it in my mouth as Glenn and I began to talk about the game. The cigarette I had put on the table fell into my lap as the two of us were talking. Suddenly Glenn yelled out, "*Oh my God, Johnny, your pants are on fire!*" I started sprinkling the coffee in the direction of my crotch area to extinguish the fire, which had burned a 10-inch hole. Throughout this whole incident, Glenn and I were still on the air, trying to ignore my mini-crisis. "I've been broadcasting Celtic games for 34 years, and nothing like this has ever happened to me," I explained to the listeners.

At that point, Glenn was laughing so hard, he couldn't speak. There was dead silence for at least five seconds. Then Ordway composed himself and said, "Well, Johnny, I have to do a commercial for our good friends at Eastern Clothing of Watertown. Maybe one of them will deliver you a new pair of pants in a hurry."

"I'd better go over there. Maybe they have fireproof pants," I told Glenn just before we went to a commercial break.

Off the air, I remarked, "Maybe that hole in my pants will help me get lucky tonight." Now Glenn was totally overcome with the giggles. He knew he wasn't going to be able to recover from my one-liner, so he just said, "Well, that's it from the Garden. Our final score from the Garden: Boston 123, Milwaukee 104."

"If you think the Celtics were hot," I said, "you should have felt what I felt."

When I walked into the locker room, the entire team gave me a standing ovation, which I acknowledged by taking a bow while displaying the damaged area of my pants.

Less than a week later, I was sneaking a cigarette at the Richfield Coliseum. After I had taken a few puffs, I threw the cigarette towards the floor. Unfortunately for me, the still-lit butt landed in my shoe and started burning a huge hole in my sock. I jumped up and started stomping my foot and doing a little dance to put out the cigarette. Our producer, Doug Lane, was looking at me like I had gone mad. Glenn, realizing what had happened, told the audience I had set myself on fire—again. "That's back-to-back games in which you burned an item of clothing," Ordway cracked. "That has to be a record."

Although the team maintained its first-place position throughout the regular season, the one danger sign was that Boston did not have a winning record on the road. In an interview with KC, he told me, "That bothers me. I don't want teams to start feeling too comfortable when they're playing us in their own building. It's not a big deal now, but it could become one once the playoff starts."

Then in early March, McHale suffered what was at first believed to be a severely sprained right ankle when his foot was stepped on in a game against Phoenix. For the next month and a half, he missed only five games despite the obvious pain and the daily swelling he suffered from the injury. Late in March, when the team was playing in Chicago, the pain became almost unbearable.

"I've played almost a month with this injury. I'm not going to stop when we have a good chance of repeating as champions. 'Iron Rangers' [Minnesota miners] don't miss work unless they're dying," he joked with me. "I'm an Iron Ranger, babe. As the song goes, 'The Sun Hasn't Set on This Boy Yet.'"

Not only did McHale continue to play, but he set an NBA record that I believe will stand for years to come. When the regular season concluded, he became the only player in league history to shoot better than 60 percent from the field and better than 80 percent from the foul line in one year. I don't emphasize individual stats, but in Kevin's case, I'll make an exception. He averaged 26 points and 9.9 rebounds, along with 2.2 blocks. To me, his effort took both guts and pride, not to mention the hours of physical therapy he endured every day following his injury.

Walton was determined to overcome his never-ending severe bone problems in both feet. On March 11, after missing the first 61 games of the season, he was activated and received a three-minute standing ovation from the Garden crowd when he came off the bench and entered the game against Phoenix. But the foot injury hadn't really healed. "The bones are brittle," he told me. "They heal with rest, but then they crack again after they get pounded for a while."

Bill was working as hard as ever, but he just was hobbling up and down the court. After playing just seven games, he sat out the next 11. "If I can just be a help for five, or hopefully 10, minutes a game in the playoffs, maybe it can make a difference between winning and losing," he told me. "Whether that's realistic, I have no clue." It was going to have to be a case of mind over matter, because even walking wasn't an easy task for Bill at that point.

Despite the long list of injuries, the Celtics finished the regular season with the second best record in the NBA at 59-23, second only to the Lakers, who won 65 games. In order to win the Eastern division, though, Boston had to beat Atlanta at the Garden in the final game of the season.

McHale had no trouble getting up for the game because the Hawks' Kevin Willis had made the following statement: "I can stop McHale. You just have to know how to play him." I don't know what possessed Willis, whose "alligator arms" are about half as short as Kevin's, to make such an outrageous claim. After all, in the five previous Celtics-Hawks games, Kevin had scored an average of 26 points against Atlanta while shooting better than 60 percent. Even though Willis did "limit" McHale to 18 points in that decisive final game, Kevin outrebounded him 14-5, while Bird torched the Hawks for 32 points in a relatively easy 118-107 win.

Then, as the playoffs began, the Celtics suffered a string of major injuries that would have meant instantaneous disaster for any other team. In the opening round, Boston swept Chicago, 3-0, but there was a major casualty. McHale's right ankle became so swollen that he had X-rays taken, which revealed that he had been playing since March with a broken navicular bone and probably had suffered additional damage when he twisted his foot in the second game of the Bulls series. Such a major injury would have ended the season for 99 percent of all players. McHale, however, wasn't about to miss out on an opportunity for another title. "I've played a month on this bum ankle. I can keep going another month. I'll worry about surgery once the playoffs end."

McHale sat out the final game of the Chicago series and the opener against Milwaukee in the Eastern division semifinals, which the Celtics won easily, 111-98, at the Garden, as a limping Walton came off the bench to provide Boston with a huge lift. With Ainge hitting for 30 points, Boston took a 2-0 lead in the series. However, the next day at practice Walton heard a cracking sound in his right foot. "I knew what that sound meant. The foot was broken again," he said. Although Bill continued to play, he just didn't have any mobility or power to jump for the remainder of the playoffs.

After splitting the next two games, the Celtics and Bucks battled into double OT in Milwaukee. Two clutch three-pointers by Larry and reserve forward Darren Daye's four points in the final minute enabled the Celtics to edge the Bucks 138-137. What I focused on in my postgame show was that McHale, despite his swollen, black-and-blue ankle injury, played 56 minutes as Boston took a 3-1 series lead heading back to the Garden. "I kept telling Kevin to come out for a rest, but he pretended he didn't hear me," KC told me. "I couldn't yank him, because I couldn't do that to someone who was showing so much heart."

Game 5 was a disaster, as Parish, who had been the Celtics' most durable player all year, came down awkwardly on a rebound attempt and sprained his left ankle. After Robert was helped to the locker room, the Bucks took control of the game and handed us a 129-124 defeat. Robert would sit out Game 6, and this time Walton was just in too much pain to provide help.

The result: Milwaukee forced a seventh game with a 10-point win in their building.

Even I didn't think we had a shot at beating the Bucks despite having the home-court advantage for the deciding game. KC was equally depressed. "Robert can hardly walk; Kevin is limping, and Bill should be on crutches. We've got to find a way of climbing out of some very deep doo-doo," he said to me. "I've never seen anything like this. [Trainer] Ray Melchiorre is putting in 18-hour work days."

Milwaukee, using the fast break to take advantage of the hobbled Celtics, led most of the game. And when Ainge twisted his right knee in the fourth quarter and had to be taken to the locker room, I commented, "Well, we're down to only two healthy starters, DJ and Larry. It's going to take a miracle finish." Down by eight, KC called on Sichting. Jerry immediately nailed his first two shots. With a minute and a half to go, Sichting found Bird coming off a pick, and Larry buried a jumper to put this hustling, proud, wounded team ahead. On the Bucks' next possession, their bid for a series win all but ended when Parish blocked a shot by Bucks center Jack Sikma and DJ hurled himself into the Bucks' bench to knock the ball out of bounds off Sikma's leg. Celtic free throws during the closing minute gave them an improbable 119-113 comeback victory.

Now the Celtics had to face the Pistons in the division finals. Ainge would miss the first three games of the series, and Walton was, for all practical purposes, finished for the playoffs—although he stubbornly kept on hoping his broken foot could stand the pain for one or two minutes a game.

The Celtics took the first two games at home. Sichting, replacing the injured Ainge in the starting lineup, outplayed Isiah Thomas in Game 1, limiting the Pistons guard to just 16 points, while Parish embarrassed Laimbeer by scoring 31 points. Bird's shooting touch, along with Parish's rebounding, dominated Game 2. However, Detroit came right back with two convincing wins at the Silverdome.

The Pistons' strategy, devised by Detroit's coach, Chuck Daly, and his floor leader, "Trash Mouth" Isiah Thomas, was obvious right from the tipoff: use every dirty tactic to cause an injury to Larry and Robert. On one play, Dennis Rodman threw a cross-body on Bird. When Bird somehow managed to duck, Laimbeer deliberately threw a punch at Larry's face and then used a headlock to slam him to the court. There was no question in my mind that Laimbeer was not making any attempt to block Larry's shot. He just had one goal: to cause a serious injury. I was surprised he chose to sucker-punch Bird, mainly because he usually picked fights against guards.

"Laimbeer's a violent, vicious coward," I yelled. "And Bird just smacked him. A completely unnecessary foul by Laimbeer and Laimbeer got walloped...now Rodman wants Bird and Larry throws Rodman away...now Thomas is coming over...oh, the yellow, gutless way they do things here. This is a typical disgusting display by Rodman, Laimbeer and Thomas."

When Detroit somehow got a tape of my broadcast, Thomas, another dirty and sneaky player, and Laimbeer told their teammates to refuse to do any interviews with either me or Glenn. They were going to stage a boycott to protest my remarks about their vicious, dangerous style of play. My initial reaction: Big fucking deal. Who needs them?

Before Game 5, Glenn at least attempted to coax a Piston into joining us for our pregame show. No dice. Instead, Glenn and I decided to fake an interview, with Glenn playing the part of Laimbeer. I'd ask Glenn (as Laimbeer) why he was such a fraud and a dirty player, and Glenn would answer, "Because I'm fat, insecure and a big baby who just enjoys the pleasure of hitting people from behind when they're not looking." It was a pure cornball routine, but it was fun anyway.

I have to rate Game 5 as the third most exciting Celtics game I have ever broadcast. Parish, who, as usual, always refused to shake Laimbeer's hand before tipoffs, went up for a rebound, and Laimbeer elbowed him right in the gut as Robert was in midair. The Chief responded with a punch and a karate chop that sent Detroit's hit-and-run "enforcer" down to the court, curled up in a fetal position. (The refs, who didn't call a foul on the play, later said they didn't see Robert's attack on Laimbeer. I suspect that even if they had seen it, they would have viewed Chief's actions as justifiable self-defense.)

The teams battled back and forth, with the Celtics being led by DJ's uncanny passing to an always-on-the-move Bird for spectacular baskets. I could never compare DJ's passing abilities to Cousy's, because Rapid Robert's passing skills were all consistently accurate, spectacular and unsurpassed. Yet DJ and Bird did have the unique ability to read each other's minds. They instinctively knew each other's actions and they knew how to time their plays to perfection.

With 17 seconds remaining in regulation, Boston had the ball, but the Pistons had a one-point lead. When Bird drove to the basket for a layup attempt, the ball was batted away toward the sidelines. Rick Mahorn managed to knock the ball out of bounds off Sichting. The Pistons—with only five seconds on the clock—had the game all but locked up.

Fortunately, Thomas then suffered a severe case of "total brainlock," as Ainge said to me following the game. Apparently no one with the Pistons noticed Detroit coach Chuck Daly frantically yelling and signaling for timeout. Instead, Thomas immediately went to the sideline to inbound the ball. All he had to do was throw the ball upcourt. Even if it was intercepted, Boston would only have a few seconds for a desperation shot.

Instead, Thomas lobbed a pass in the direction of Laimbeer, who was standing just outside the left side of the lane. The pass was a lazy one, enabling Bird to cut in front of Laimbeer and snatch it away from him. Before the play began, I was resigned to the fact that Detroit was going to take command of the series. My play-by-play started in a rather subdued tone that lasted for all of a mini-second: "And...THERE'S A STEAL BY BIRD...UNDERNEATH TO DJ...HE LAYS IT IN...RIGHT AT ONE SECOND LEFT." Then I went into my high-pitched voice, "OH MY, THIS CROWD IS GOING CRAZY."

The Celtics had pulled off a miracle. Afterward Bird told me he wasn't thinking about making a steal until he saw Thomas lob the ball. "I just was hoping to foul Laimbeer immediately," Larry told me. "Then I saw the pass was a soft one, because Thomas had to loft it over Sichting's arms. That's when I actually thought I might have a chance to get to the ball before Laimbeer did. Once I got it, I was facing the endline. I just turned around and saw a white jersey heading towards the basket. I had no idea it was DJ. His layup wasn't easy, either, because Joe Dumars was right there defending him."

In the locker room, Ainge was smiling and shaking his head in disbelief. "They [the Pistons] had that game all wrapped up. Isiah made one tiny mistake, though," Danny said, winking at me. "He forgot about a guy named Larry Bird."

After Detroit won Game 6 at the Silverdome, the Pistons decided to end their boycott and "allow" us to interview them. Isiah Thomas was the first Detroit player to talk to us. The little weasel was so ultra-polite and well-mannered that I almost threw up. Then Laimbeer came out of the dressing room and headed towards us.

"Oh my God, look at this," I said to Glenn. "If he takes a swing at me, you'd better back me up."

Well, I refused to even look at Laimbeer as Glenn asked him about his reputation as a sneaky, dirty player. As I stared straight ahead, Laimbeer looked in my direction and said in a sing-song style, "I'm really a nice guy. I really am. I'm a happy guy who likes to smile and joke around." As he taunted me, I kept on thinking, "What a complete jerkoff. Maybe I should just take my chances and call him what he is—a guy who throws sucker punches and then runs and hides."

Despite all their injuries, the Celtics dominated Detroit on the boards in the deciding seventh game of the series, winning 117-114 to move on to face the Lakers in the finals.

At the Forum, the Celtics were outrun in the series' first two games. KC refused to use Boston's injuries as an excuse. "I had devised a brilliant master plan," he jokingly told the media after the Celtics had lost the opening two games. "It just didn't work."

There was a little comic relief before Game 2 in L.A. I was feeling some pain in my right ear, and I could barely hear any sounds. I told Dr. Silva that I must be suffering from an earache. He examined the ear with a tiny flashlight and spotted a small chunk of plastic blocking my ear canal. It was then I remembered that about a year before while I was doing my Sportschannel show, my earpiece cracked and I couldn't find the part that had chipped off. "I bet that's the plastic chip that broke off my ear piece a year ago," I told him. "I guess it fell into my ear without me realizing it." Using a pair of tweezers, Dr. Silva managed to pull out the small but sharp piece of material. Reserve center Greg Kite, who had been watching Dr. Silva extract the chip, then came up with a line I'll never forget. With a straight face, Greg commented, "With ears that size, I wouldn't be surprised if Doc Silva found a '57 Chevy in the other ear."

A clutch three-pointer by Bird in Game 3 at the Garden gave the Celtics new life, enabling Boston to trail by only 2-1 in the series. When the Celtics took a 16-point lead early in the third quarter of Game 4, I thought we might just be able to pull off a miracle and come back to win championship number 17—despite all the injuries. But then L.A. responded with an all-out fast break blitz that put them down by only a point with less than 30 seconds remaining.

During one of Boston's timeouts, the crowd began shouting, "WALTON, WALTON, WALTON." Bill stood in the huddle, wanting desperately to enter the game to help the Celtics hold off L.A. As he told me after the game, "As the Garden crowd was chanting my name, DJ came over to me. He was with the Sonics on the night they were playing the Trail Blazers when a bone in my right foot broke in half back in '78. I was about to tell KC that I wanted to go into the game when DJ put his arm around my shoulders and begged me, 'Don't do it, Bill. Don't do it.' That's when I knew I couldn't help, even though I desperately wanted that chance to try and make a difference."

When Abdul-Jabbar missed the second of two free throws that would have tied the game at 106, the rebound went out of bounds off the hands of McHale, who was battling L.A.'s Mychal Thompson. On L.A.'s ensuing possession, McHale guarded Magic tightly and forced him to drive from the left side into the lane, without allowing him to face the basket. With Kevin receiving help from Robert Parish, they both timed their jumps perfectly, leaving Magic with but one choice—a Kareem-type skyhook. How Magic managed to arch the ball over the outstretched hands of Robert and Kevin is still a mystery to me, but the shot was perfect, leaving the Celtics down by a point. When Bird missed a last-second three-pointer, L.A., with the next two games at the Forum, owned a commanding 3-1 series advantage.

Before Game 5, Bird told a hobbled and mentally drained McHale, "Kevin, you've given everything you've got. No one wants you to risk your career. It might be time for you to sit out the rest of the way."

Kevin just looked at Larry and said, "Can't quit now. We can still take this thing." Unfortunately, the battered Celtics frontcourt just couldn't match L.A.'s speed, and the Lakers simply used their fast break to easily win the title with a 106-93 win in Game 5.

"This Boston team makes me extremely proud," I emotionally told my audience in the closing minutes of L.A.'s win. "The '87 Celtics are truly a profile in courage. This group of Celtics are, to a man, true champions in my book."

In the '87 off season, Celtics assistant coach and player personnel director Jimmy Rogers received a long-term contract offer from the Knicks to become their head coach. Boston was paying Jimmy a very good salary and thought highly of his abilities. So Celtics general manager Jan Volk demanded that New York compensate Boston with a first-round choice. The Knicks refused. Jimmy became very bitter and refused to talk with Volk or Red for months. After all, after being an assistant coach for more than 17 years, he finally was given the opportunity to lead one of the league's premiere teams. "Johnny," he told me, "I had a signed contract in my jacket pocket when I flew back from the meeting with the Knicks. I was so excited. Never did I figure that the Celtics would stand in my way of a tremendous career move."

Volk, who had been a close friend of Jimmy's until the New York offer became a major issue, explained the Celtics' position to me. "Look, we value Jimmy's services. That's why we're paying him a salary which surpasses some head coaches in this league," he said. "I'm open to compromise, but the Knicks aren't offering anything close to a first-round pick. Between you and me, if New York counters with a second-round draft pick, we'll probably be able to get a deal done."

New York never made that proposal, and Jimmy was forced to remain in Boston. Within a couple weeks, the Knicks announced they had signed Providence College coach Rick Pitino to a multiyear deal as head coach.

Jimmy was crushed and felt betrayed. "You don't reward loyal people by standing in their way of a once-in-a-lifetime opportunity," he told me. "If I were the Knicks, I wouldn't give away a first-round draft choice for an assistant with no head coaching experience, either. If I were in the Celtics' shoes, I wouldn't have asked for a first-round choice in the first place. Their compensation demand wasn't fair to me, and it wasn't fair to New York. Now I have to go back to Boston, do my job, and forget about the fact that I was screwed."

In the draft, the Celtics picked up Northeastern's one-man offense in Reggie Lewis. I had known Reggie for a couple of years and, as the 22nd overall choice, I thought Boston had just selected a potential starter two or three years down the road.

Reggie was a quiet, respectful kid who was a quick learner. At 6'7", he was quick enough to play both small forward and big guard. KC couldn't have been more excited. "He's about as smooth a shooter as you'll find. He may only weigh 190 pounds, but he can rebound, because he has that instinct you look for when you're evaluating

players. We thought Reggie would be gone long before we could get
a shot at him. We tried to move up five or six spots just to make sure
we got him, but there were no takers. Here's a kid who wasn't a big
secret around the league. I mean he scored 30 points or more 19
times in his college career and he did it by moving without the ball,
using screens, and taking high-percentage attempts. I'm surprised
scouts didn't recognize all his skills and poise."

The addition of Lewis couldn't change the fact that the '88
Celtics were now an old and injury-prone club. Walton had retired.
McHale missed the first 17 games of the season recuperating from
ankle surgery that left him with a half-inch screw holding together
his navicular bone. Sichting played only 24 games due to an ankle
injury. Still, led by Bird, who finished second to the Bulls' Michael
Jordan in the MVP balloting, Boston won the Atlantic Division before
losing to Thomas' Pistons,4-2, in the conference finals.

"If there's two things I've learned from this group of players, it's
that they never make excuses and they never accept defeat," I said,
following Boston's final loss to Detroit in the playoffs. "Don't count
them out for next year."

(Editor's note: In July of 1988, Johnny, whose health was
beginning to decline, decided to take a break from continuing with
his autobiography.)

15

MY ALL-OPPONENT TEAM

I've been asked countless times to choose an all-time Celtics team. It's one request I cannot, will not, honor. For me to pick the five, 10 or even 20 best players to wear a Boston uniform would be a tremendous injustice to a lot of other guys I respect and love.

Emotionally and friendship-wise, I value the feelings of the players who might not be included on my list. In my opinion, each and every Celtic who played on any one of the 16 title teams can properly think of himself as a champion. Each of them has the right to feel he was as good as anyone who ever played the game. I'm simply respecting that right.

Besides, when it comes to Boston, you don't think in terms of great players, you think in terms of great teams. You look at what the players could do collectively, not as individuals. That's been the key to the Celtics' unparalleled success. Everyone sacrifices, everyone shares in the glory, everyone's role is important. Don't ask me to pick favorites.

I have, however, chosen an All-Opponent team, 15 players, all All-Stars, who had some of their finest moments playing against Boston. Some would have made great Celtics because of their unselfishness and desire; others probably were better off having never been a Celtic, because their individual talents, their attitude, their

willingness to accept a role that might not equal their skill level just
would have made it impossible for them to blend in with the character
of the Celtic teams.

Fact is I admire almost all of the players I have selected. So how
did I handle a broadcast when one of them destroyed the Celtics?
Well, I gave them credit—but in a very understated way. For instance,
if Dolph Schayes hit three set shots in a row, I might comment, "He's
doing a nice job out there despite Boston's defense covering him
tightly. When Schayes has that shot working, there's very little you
can do to stop it." I provided straight reporting, with no emotion.
Then I'd wait for one of the Celtics to score and my voice would rise
almost automatically. I wanted to let the audience know that Red's
teams could always handle adversity with poise and desire.

Here are my rankings, by position, of which players belong at
the top of Boston's All-Opponent team:

CENTERS

1: Wilt Chamberlain—A powerful force, a force unto himself.
One look at Wilt's muscular 7'2" frame and opponents instantly
became Chamberlain's victims for the evening. They were, in a word,
"fearful" of Wilt. You could see it on their faces, even during warmups.
Unfortunately for Wilt, there was one other guy in the league—by
the name of Russell—who was The Master of psyche jobs. Russ knew
every trick there was. He'd stare you down, occasionally talk you
down, do everything short of spitting in your face to get that little
extra edge.

One of his favorite tricks that he employed to begin a game
against Wilt was to simply allow Chamberlain to drive right by him
for a layup just for the purpose of luring Wilt into thinking that he
would be able to make that move successfully anytime he attempted
it. Then Russ would proceed to block Wilt's next two layup attempts.
Chamberlain would become so angry that he would not give up on
that particular move because he wanted to prove to everyone that
luck was the only reason Russell had managed to swat away his shots.

Which is exactly what Bill wanted Wilt to think. For the rest of the game, Russ would toy with Chamberlain by blocking his path, batting a few of Chamberlain's awkward layup attempts, and forcing him into settling for off-balance fade-away jumpers, one of Wilt's least accurate shots.

Another tactic Russ employed was to run at half-speed for five minutes at a time. Wilt would see Russ jogging and slowed down himself. Then when the Celtics had an opportunity to put on one of their classic spurts, Russ would turn on the jets. Before Wilt could realize what was happening and quicken his pace, the Celtics would have an insurmountable lead. "Usually," Heinsohn would say, "Russ would slow down to start the fourth quarter, then, maybe with six minutes to go and the game on the line, he'd start sprinting, outhustling Wilt for rebounds and setting up our fast break. I don't know how many times Wilt was fooled by Russell, but Bill won a lot of games for us by just outthinking Chamberlain."

Offensively, Russ might stand around out at the foul line and not take a shot for the entire first quarter of a game. Wilt would eventually ignore Russ and try to double-team Heinsohn or patrol the lane to prevent Cousy from penetrating to the basket. When Russ would spot Chamberlain being preoccupied, he'd immediately swoop in for a series of dunks or short, driving hooks, with Wilt always a step too late to catch up to him. "Whenever Wilt plays Russ, he looks so unsure of himself, so confused," KC Jones said to me immediately after Russell had led Boston to a 4-1 Eastern Division title win over Chamberlain's Warriors. "Wilt plays very hard, but he's always looking around nervously, wondering what Russell is going to try to do next. Almost always, Chamberlain seems to guess wrong, because Bill designs his play against Wilt to be unpredictable. We'll sometimes find ourselves standing around and watching Russ torment him."

Chamberlain never could understand that Russ did, in fact, abuse him with his mind games. In fact, Wilt spent more than a decade being victimized by Russell's constant trickery and never would admit that he was outsmarted even once in his whole career.

However, the record books tell the whole story. In the 10 years of Russell-Chamberlain confrontations, the Celtics won nine championships. During that time Russell held an 84-57 advantage over Chamberlain in head-to-head meetings. Of the five playoff showdowns between the two, Russ won four of them. Yet to this day, Wilt will tell anyone who is willing to listen that he was the better player. Which, of course, is pure cow chips.

Wilt's one shining moment against Russell came in the '67 playoffs when Philadelphia took the first three games of the Eastern Division finals against Boston and went on to win in five, with a convincing 140-116 victory in the last game when Chamberlain scored 29 points, grabbed 36 rebounds and also contributed 13 assists. Russell, who was in his first year as player-coach, offered no excuses. "They beat us at our own game. They outran us. And Wilt, he outplayed me," Russ admitted to me in the locker room after the Celtics' string of eight straight titles had been ended. "He was a leader. He wasn't going to let them lose. He never once let up or allowed any of his teammates to let up. We lost, but I think we learned from it. We'll be better next year because of this. That's the best you can get out of losing."

Afterward Wilt sounded like a death-row prisoner who had just received a pardon: "We did it, we finally did it. I'm happy now but not as happy as I'll be in July and August when I walk down the street and won't have all those people saying, 'How come you guys didn't beat Boston?' That's all in the past." But, boy, was Chamberlain mistaken. The Celtics would go on to win two more championships before Russell retired, forcing Wilt to make more excuses for losing.

I won't argue with those who claim that Wilt was every bit Russell's equal when it came to pure talent. As a scorer, there was no one better than Chamberlain. Among his individual accomplishments: he led the league in both scoring (37.6 points a game) and rebounding

(27.0) as a rookie for Philadelphia in 1960; scored 100 points (36 of 63 from the field and 28 of 32 from the free throw line) against the Knicks by overpowering New York's 6'9" center Darrall Imhoff on March 2, 1962 in Hershey, Pennsylvania; he maintained a 50.4 point average for the '61-'62 season; shot an astounding 72.7 percent for the'72-'73 season; and recorded 31 games of 60 points or better during his 14-year career with Philly, San Francisco and the L.A. Lakers. No question in my mind, Wilt was the original inspiration for the term "scoring machine." Funny thing is that Wilt did not like the slam dunk, because he thought that play didn't require any pure basketball talent. Instead he preferred to use a hook shot or a fallaway—even though a dunk would have been the easier, more efficient way for him to score. But Wilt's ego dictated that he wanted to be known as a pure basketball player rather than just another tall guy who could slam the ball through the net.

Wilt also won other individual honors. He led the NBA in rebounding 11 times, was chosen MVP four times, and was named a first-team All-Star seven times and a second-team All-Star three other seasons. He even managed to top the NBA in assists in 1968 when he averaged 8.6 a game for Philly.

Chamberlain, all 280-plus pounds of him, could also be just as awesome at the defensive end of the court. He'd send a loud, emphatic message when he'd swat away shots almost effortlessly. It was as if Wilt was telling opponents, "The lane is my private territory. Stay the hell away or pay the price, baby."

On the boards Wilt (with the exception of Russell) was the best I've ever seen. When you average more than 22 rebounds a game for a career, you must possess superhuman strength and great timing. (I used to taunt him by calling him "unhuman" whenever he was near my broadcasting location. He hated that term, so I used it every chance I got.) The difference between Russell and Chamberlain was that Bill was an under-control shot blocker who knew where his block would send the ball while Wilt just wanted to use his muscle to ram the basketball five rows up into the seats in order to draw a response from the crowd. Sure, his monster blocks would look ferocious and the fans would "ooh" and "aah" in appreciation of his effort. But there was just one major drawback to Chamberlain's shot blocking: his team's opponents always got the ball back, thanks to Wilt's desire to bat the ball into the stands.

If he and Kareem Abdul-Jabbar were both in their prime, Wilt would totally dominate because of his physical power and his willingness to fight for rebounds. No contest. I'd also be willing to bet that Moses Malone would need medical attention if he ever made the mistake of getting into a physical confrontation with Chamberlain. You might beat Wilt with finesse and smarts, but you'd never get the best of him through sheer brawn.

Just how strong was Chamberlain? Well, the guy could have been a world-class power lifter. I remember the time KC Jones, using a pick from Bill Russell, made the mistake of driving towards the basket—with Wilt standing directly in his path. As KC, who was rock solid at 210 pounds, hit high gear and went up in the air to shoot, Chamberlain reached out with one arm and caught him, just like you or I would catch a baseball. There was Wilt standing there expressionless as KC dangled like a rag doll. The guy had just caught a human missile without so much as a flinch.

Wilt was anything but a gentle giant on the court. Just ask Sam Jones, whose favorite pastime was to provoke Chamberlain. Sam would be open for a jumper, and rather than taking the easy shot, he'd simply stand there, daring Wilt to come out and stop him. When Chamberlain would finally make his move, Sam would quickly release the ball and taunt Wilt by yelling out, "Too late, baby!" as the ball sailed into the net. This went on for months, until one night Wilt decided he'd had enough of Jones' antics. Instead of pulling up short when Sam released his "too late" jumper, Wilt kept on charging. In fact, Chamberlain chased Sam around the court until Jones stopped and picked up a stool for protection. "If you're gonna fight me," said

Sam, who was a hundred pounds lighter and a foot shorter than Wilt, "this will even things up a little."

Although the Garden fans respected Wilt's abilities, they, too, loved to taunt him at every opportunity. His mistake was letting all the booing and razzing get to him and then showing his emotions outwardly. He quickly became the league's number one "cry baby," a term I used regularly on the air. The more the crowd yelled, the more upset Chamberlain became. The more upset Chamberlain became, the more the crowd made life miserable for him.

Wilt was an easy target because he was the world's worst free throw shooter. I'm convinced that when Chamberlain stepped to the foul line, he had absolutely no idea whether the ball would end up two feet short of the basket or bounce off the top of the backboard. He was that shaky. Throughout his career, Chamberlain experimented with every method of foul shooting known to man, from the underhand toss to the two-hand release to the one-hand push-and-pray shot. All of them produced the same result—a steady stream of bricks.

Because Wilt was such a pitiful free throw shooter, the Celtics employed a very logical and very effective defensive strategy—hack away at Chamberlain each time he got near the basket. Auerbach was more than willing to give Wilt two free throws as long as the foul prevented Chamberlain from using the "dipper dunk." Heinsohn, in particular, took special delight in coming in from the blind side to hammer Wilt across his shooting hand, a hand that had been broken several times. "I'm what you'd call a hit-and-run fouler," Tommy said to me after one Celtics win over Wilt and the Warriors. "I whack him hard on the hand and then head for the hills as soon as I see him grimace and shake his arm in pain."

I had my own method for driving Wilt nuts. Once I found out how much he hated to be called "Wilt the Stilt," I made it a point to use that nickname every time Chamberlain came within earshot of my voice. Why did I purposely try to infuriate him? Because he thought he was better than me and the rest of the world. I had known the guy since he was a shy, somewhat scared and insecure 17 year old. He was entering the University of Kansas and, along with a number of excellent college players, had been invited to participate in a summer league at Kutsher's, a resort in the Catskills. Red coached one of the teams, and I worked there as the public address announcer. One day I invited Wilt to lunch and talked to him as a friend. After putting him at ease by telling a few funny stories about Red and the Celtics, I ask him about his family background, because I knew he was one of 11 children. Then I told him just to enjoy life in college and have fun playing basketball. At the time, Wilt seemed willing to listen and grateful to have someone take an interest in him as a person rather than as a basketball player. Yet once he became an NBA pro, he thought he was too much of a star to say hello to just anyone, such as a mere radio announcer.

Personality aside, Wilt did have superstar qualities. But he lacked certain characteristics Russell possessed in abundance, the desire to win, the caring about the win. When Wilt was on the court, he thought in terms of "me." Russell was concerned with "us." That was the difference between the two, the reason why one is remembered as a frustrated loser and the other goes down in history as the consummate clutch player. And did Wilt ever despise being thought of as second best. As a result, he constantly moaned and groaned about how the media "always favored Russell."

He'd constantly compare his stats to Bill's. He'd claim that the Celtics would have won just as many titles if he had played for them instead of Russell. After a while, his begging and pleading became too much. "We may have won a couple, maybe three championships with Chamberlain as our center," Cousy said in an on-the-air interview with me a few years ago. "But we never would have become a dynasty that Russ created for us. Russell's unselfishness and desire was the inspiration for all of us. Without that kind of leadership, we wouldn't have dominated like we did—even with Chamberlain on our side.

Russ complemented our games. The genuine superstar makes his teammates play above their heads. Wilt, he was strictly an individualist. To this day, I don't think Wilt has a solid idea about what the game is all about."

To illustrate his point, Cousy talked about Wilt's "illogical" offensive game. "Almost everything he did offensively was directed away from the basket. He should have been exploiting his size and strength by bullying his way inside. Instead, Wilt would take the path of least resistance by shooting a fallaway jump shot," Cousy said. "The shot itself was decent, but if Chamberlain had been as determined as Russell, he never would have settled for anything less than a two-foot hook, a layup or a dunk."

Red bristles whenever he hears a reporter talk about Chamberlain's stats versus Russell's. "Anyone who looks at statistics involving those two just doesn't know basketball," he lectures. "Why, one of Russell's greatest tricks he used against Wilt was to actually let him score a few baskets and grab a handful of rebounds once we had the game all locked up. He'd give Wilt a dozen points and maybe eight rebounds on purpose, just so Chamberlain would walk off the court thinking he had played a good game. He'd let Wilt think he could get away with a certain move. Wilt would be satisfied that he had done his best, yet he'd also be that much more convinced that no matter what he did, he couldn't beat Russell and the rest of us. What Russ did was build up Wilt's ego but at the same time destroy his desire to beat us.

And when it came time for the next game, Russell would remember exactly what moves, what types of shots, what kinds of rebounds and blocks he had allowed Wilt to get the last time. Wilt naturally thought he had finally figured Russ out and would try these moves and shots and blocks again. Only this time Russ wasn't playing possum. He'd swat away a layup that Wilt thought was going to be easy, he'd outposition him under the boards, he'd put in a driving hook that Wilt couldn't come close to. All of this was Russell's way of psyching out Wilt. And it worked year after year. Wilt would get the stats, Russ would get the win. And Chamberlain never could grasp how it could possibly happen.

Ironically, Wilt did eventually acquire that all-important caring about the win—but only after Russell, proud owner of 11 championship rings, had retired. In his final four years, Chamberlain changed his entire style. He began to concentrate more on defensive rebounding; he also began to pass the ball when he was double- and triple-teamed rather than power his way through all the resistance between him and the basket. Individual stats, particularly scoring stats, became unimportant. Winning and being recognized as a team player were the things that mattered to him. Why the attitude change? I can only theorize that he had finally come to realize through the lessons Russell had taught him what the true meaning of being a champion was.

But by then, permanent damage had been done. He would always be viewed as second best, as the most talented loser in NBA history.

Wilt's reputation as a loser began in his college days. As a senior at Overbrook High in Philadelphia he had been the object of the greatest recruiting battle in history. After receiving scholarship offers from hundreds of colleges, Chamberlain finally chose the University of Kansas, known for its excellent basketball tradition. While he was clearly college basketball's most dominating player, Wilt failed to lead the Jayhawks to an NCAA championship in his two years on the varsity. Kansas came close in '57, losing the title game to North Carolina by a point in triple overtime. But that loss only served to promote Wilt's image as a player who couldn't make the big play at the crucial moment.

The criticism Chamberlain received prompted him to quit Kansas after his junior year and play a year for the Harlem Globetrotters while waiting to become eligible for the NBA. This decision only further subjected Wilt to some brutal treatment from the media. On top of being branded as a loser, he was now unfairly called a quitter and a money grabber for accepting a very lucrative contract from the Globetrotters. Chamberlain had very valid reasons for accepting the 'Trotters' offer while waiting a year to join the Philadelphia Warriors, who, through owner Eddie Gottlieb's clever maneuver, had the territorial rights to the nation's greatest young player.

First of all, his family needed the money. Secondly, the rules in college basketball actually discriminated against Wilt. He'd get the ball and five guys would go all out to surround him and not give him an inch to move. The NCAA even put through legislation to prevent Wilt from scoring on a play that was virtually automatic for him. It was the inbounds play where the ball was passed in from underneath the offensive basket. A Kansas teammate would lob the ball over the backboard and Chamberlain simply would outleap the opposition and end up with a dunk. So the NCAA outlawed the play to "make things fairer" for every other team.

I get a kick out of Chamberlain's once-a-year threats to come out of retirement and teach the current NBA stars a thing or two. That's unadulterated bilge, because today's quick, strong and tall centers would absolutely destroy him at both ends of the court. There are no Darrall Imhoffs in today's NBA. All of Chamberlain's comeback "threats" are pitiful. Here's a man living in the past, trying desperately to grab some attention because he's so fearful people will forget him. I will say this, though. If Wilt did go back to basketball, he could still be a holy terror for the first three minutes. After that, he'd be nothing more than dead meat for today's young bulls to feast on.

Even today, Wilt feels the indignities that were imposed on him by that Boston dynasty team so deeply that any time he gets a chance, he sticks a knife in members of the Celtics organization.

Look at his criticisms of both Heinsohn and Russell as national TV commentators. He would constantly complain that Tommy was biased in his comments about the Celtics. Well, I believe Heinsohn worked four years doing the national games in the early '80s, and Boston won two titles and played in three title series during that time span. It's difficult to be critical of a team that produces those results, yet Wilt would always find something to say—just to keep his name in the papers. As for Wilt's criticism of Russ, it was totally sour grapes. "Russell should go back to broadcasting school," he told one reporter. "Even I don't understand the points he tries to make." That remark didn't surprise me. Wilt couldn't understand Russell's tactics on the court, and he sure as hell didn't possess the same degree of knowledge of the game as Russ did. Which may be why network executives never knocked at Wilt's door to offer him a job in TV.

2: Kareem Abdul-Jabbar—I hate the skyhook—and for good reason. I can't tell you how many times that damn shot has ruined perfectly good endings to my broadcasts over the years. There I'd be, getting ready to celebrate a Celtic victory, and along would come Abdul-Jabbar to rewrite the script by catapulting the ball into the basket. So automatic, so predictable, so annoying.

Whether I look back at the Lew Alcindor era of the early '70s when he played for the Milwaukee Bucks or recall the more recent feats of Abdul-Jabbar as a Laker, I think it's fair to say he's proven to be at his best when he's played the best. In that sense, he's been very much like Russell, a guy who devours pressure, a guy who does not condone losing.

Overall, though, Russell was a far more complete player than Kareem. Russell's domination on the boards, electric sense of timing, and instinct for defense would have taken away from Kareem's effectiveness offensively. As a rookie, Abdul-Jabbar could not handle Chamberlain or Willis Reed, for that matter. If he couldn't handle them, he definitely would never have been able to handle Russ. Which is not to say Kareem isn't a great, tough competitor, especially against the Celtics. However, Kareem is, without a doubt, the captain of my All-Cry Baby team. If a defender so much as breathed on him, Jabbar would go into a five-minute, almost tearful temper tantrum if an official didn't make a foul call. And when Kareem was called for a foul, he'd moan and groan and pout until you could almost see a stream of tears starting to flow. On one occasion, his "poor little me" routine became so disgusting that I turned to my producer and said, "Kareem's still wailing. Will you please go and find me a bucket, because I'm about to throw up. He's been carrying on now for five minutes. You can pacify a one-year-old in less time."

Some of Abdul-Jabbar's greatest moments in his career came early on against Dave Cowens. Despite the aggressive, physical style of Cowens, Kareem was usually able to use his six-inch height advantage to launch his skyhooks from eight to 10 feet away from the basket with accuracy. But David was smart enough to know how to offset Kareem's moves. He'd simply outhustle him, toss a few elbow shots, and outrun him up and down the court. Today, Kareem is still capable of frustrating Robert Parish with the very same moves, the very same shots. I'm talking about 15 years' worth of those damn skyhooks. Like Cowens, Parish uses his running ability to wear down Kareem, because the one asset he definitely has never possessed is stamina.

And I enjoyed getting on his case about his habit of walking up the court while his teammates played "stall ball" in order to allow him extra time to set up in the low post. "Magic is fiddlin' and diddlin' because Kareem is a little slower than usual as he sleepwalks up the court," I'd tell my audience. "I've always known he has no endurance. Now it's doubtful he has much desire. You've got to wonder if there's any gas left in his tank. He looks like an aging giraffe leisurely grazing all by himself in a pasture. Somebody ought to remind him there's a basketball game going on."

Despite my frequent verbal jabs at him, I can only admire the fact that Kareem is very durable and has always tried to play through the pain of nagging injuries. What I like about watching this graceful 7'3" athlete is that it seems the more hair he loses, the more his game improves. When he goes completely bald, then I'll really worry. Year after year, I noticed little improvements in his competitive drive. I've seen it reflected in his will to win, his self-confidence, his leadership abilities, his pride.

Yet I rank Jabbar well below Chamberlain for several reasons. First of all, I've seen him play in crucial playoff games where he just doesn't seem to push himself. Because he has always been surrounded by extremely talented teammates—Magic, James Worthy, Jamaal Wilkes, Norm Nixon with the Lakers and Oscar Robertson, Bob Dandridge, Jon McGlocklin and Greg Smith with the Bucks— Kareem has always had the luxury of working at his own pace.

Abdul-Jabbar also will never be known as one of the great rebounders. He doesn't like a lot of contact, and he plays accordingly. He was particularly very tentative around Cowens. Like many other players in the league, Jabbar didn't really want to find out if David was as wild and totally unafraid as he appeared to be. One night Kareem was poked in the eye by Cowens. Not knowing who did the poking, he wheeled around and began to throw a punch—until he saw that his target was David. Quickly, Kareem changed his mind and punched the basket support instead, badly injuring his hand in the process.

I never have gotten to know Abdul-Jabbar as a person. He would never grant me any interviews. In many ways, he outwardly acted much like Russell. While his teammates liked him, Kareem always seemed to have a chip on his shoulder when it came to dealing with the media and the public. Even Lakers play-by-play man Chick Hearn, the one broadcaster whom Kareem would talk to on the air, told me Abdul-Jabbar usually was moody and somewhat difficult to deal with. "I don't think I'll ever know exactly what makes him tick," Chick explained to me.

3: George Mikan—Because this guy's career ended before the Russell-Chamberlain era, he's been underrated over the years by experts, many of whom never even saw him play. George was the single most powerful force in the early '50s when his team, the

Minneapolis Lakers, won five NBA championships in six years. He could rebound, he could score, and he could intimidate on defense. Sure, the guy could neither run well nor jump more than a few inches off the ground, but he would be a force today, because he was smart, knew how to get position both offensively and defensively, and wasn't afraid to throw around his weight, which at times reached 255 pounds. You could pretty much count on him to give the Lakers at least 20 points and 10 rebounds a night.

Voted "Greatest Player in the First Half-Century," George was so dominant under the boards that the NBA once decided that by raising the basket height to 12 feet, it might give the smaller players a better chance to compete against the Lakers and Mikan in particular. So on March 7, 1954, the NBA decided to play an official game, with the Lakers hosting the Milwaukee Hawks, using 12-foot-high baskets. The results were disastrous. The guards, in particular, had trouble adjusting their shots. Everyone's free throw shooting suffered. Mikan was the only one who seemed to benefit. "With the 12-foot basket, I had an extra quarter of a second to react when a missed shot came off the rim or the backboard. Hell, I must have had 35 [actually 32] rebounds tonight," he told reporters after the Lakers had beaten Milwaukee 65-63, despite shooting just 28 percent. "I hope this experiment stops all the talk about raising the basket, because all that does is make big men appear bigger. The fans hated watching it. That much I know for sure."

The NBA also created the 24-second clock rule specifically to prevent teams from attempting a game-long stall if they happened to be so lucky as to get an early lead on the then-almost unbeatable Lakers, led by Mikan. That rule change stuck, because it made the game more exciting by forcing teams to come up with run-and-gun type strategies—something Red Auerbach took full advantage of.

It wasn't the rule changes that forced Mikan into retirement. It was the amount of punishment inflicted upon him by teams whose primary strategy against Minneapolis was to physically gang up on

Mikan. "I'm getting shoved, punched and kicked, all at the same time," George said just before he retired. A list of his injuries during his career included two broken legs, three broken fingers, a broken wrist, two broken ribs and a fractured nose.

Many today see black and white film of George in his playing days and conclude that he was nothing but a big goon. They're dead wrong. Yes, he moved somewhat awkwardly. But he had huge, strong hands and a surprising soft touch with a hook shot that he could make with either hand. He also was well conditioned and coordinated.

Late in his career, I interviewed Mikan, and he told me about an interesting story that illustrated Red Auerbach's show-no-mercy mentality. "We were playing Red's Washington Caps team," Big George said. "Their center, a guy by the name of Kleggie Hermsen, body-blocked me into the first row of the stands, and I broke my left arm. I was rolling around on the court in utter agony when I saw Auerbach standing over me. Instead of asking if I was OK or asking if he could help, Red screamed at our bench, 'Drag the son of a bitch off, and let's get this game going.'"

In his book *Seasons to Remember*, Curt Gowdy recalled an interview he had with Ray Meyer about Mikan, who had played for the DePaul coach. "George was the hardest worker he had ever coached. Here's a kid who was six feet tall when he was only 11. When I first met him he actually called himself a freak. 'I'm like the fat lady in the circus or the tattooed man,' Meyer quoted Mikan as saying before his freshman season. 'At DePaul, I spent hour upon hour giving him drills to perform. He never complained, never bellyached about his practices lasting an hour longer than anyone else on the team. By the end of his second year, George was a different player and a different person. He was our MVP and he also had become very proud of his size. All his self-consciousness about his looks were past history.'"

And it's my opinion that Mikan wouldn't be outclassed in today's modern game, because he'd make his physical strength count, much like Moses Malone does against opponents who are more mobile than he is. Put Jabbar against George, and Mikan would manhandle him, beat him up, and outfight him for rebounds. Kareem might have no trouble scoring, but you can bet George would make him pay a physical toll for each point.

Cousy, for one, disagrees with my belief that George would be effective against today's players. "Mikan played for the right team at the right time," he said. "In his glory years there was no 24-second clock, so his lack of speed didn't matter. The Lakers would bring the ball upcourt and just wait for George to catch up. He was strong and tough. He also happened to play next to two other guys who were among the league's biggest and meanest players, Jim Pollard and Vern Mikkelson.

"Mikan would go up against a guy like Ed Macauley, who was a highly skilled player and had a big edge in agility, and even things up by just plain beating the hell out of him. The Lakers' whole front line played like that, and it worked well for years. By today's standards, though, I don't know if he could survive, whereas Russell, Chamberlain, Macauley, they'd have the quickness and stamina and pure athletic ability to do more than just be an average starter."

FORWARDS

*Maurice Stokes—I use an asterisk because Maurice only played three years for the Royals before being struck down at age 25 by encephalitis, a tragic illness that left him paralyzed for 12 years before the disease ultimately claimed his life on April 6, 1970. Stokes' achievements in his all-too-short NBA career were Magic Johnson-like. He could do it all.

If you examine the numbers the 6'7 1/2", 240-pound Stokes put up in his brief but spectacular career, you'll find they compare very favorably with those of all the great forwards, from Baylor to Erving to Bird. There's just no telling how great Mo might have become had he not suffered a blow on the head that produced massive swelling in the brain. In his final season, '57-'58, for example, he led the league in rebounding while averaging 16.9 points and 6.4 assists a game. He was another Magic—or rather Magic is another Maurice Stokes. My personal opinion: Maurice Stokes was the most complete player I had ever seen until Larry Bird entered the league.

The story of Maurice's medical struggle and the loving care he received afterward from teammate Jack Twyman is one of sports' most heartwarming situations. Shortly after Stokes was stricken on March 13, 1958, Twyman became his guardian. Paying his own expenses, Twyman would travel across the country during the off seasons raising money in order to ensure that Maurice's staggering hospital bills could be paid. Maurice required round-the-clock care because he couldn't speak, eat food by himself or use his arms and legs. With a great deal of effort, he was able to move his fingers ever so slightly. His goal became to learn how to use a typewriter to communicate, but even his own doctors doubted that Mo would achieve that goal, because all his muscles had deteriorated.

When I spoke to Twyman one summer at the Maurice Stokes benefit game held at Kutsher's, I asked him if the fundraising efforts and the time he spent away from his family was mentally draining. His answer brought me to tears. "Johnny, this is the most rewarding experience of my life, because every time I see Maurice, he manages to give me the biggest smile you could imagine. All I am doing is returning the love given to me by a dear friend."

Twyman's greatest reward for his efforts was a Christmas message from Stokes a year before he died in which Maurice had miraculously managed to type out, "Dear Jack. How can I ever thank you?"

1: Elgin Baylor—"All right, the ball comes in to Baylor. He takes the shot, misses the shot, gets the offensive rebound, puts it back in."

I must have spoken those words a hundred times. I had to say them in rapid-fire fashion, because Elgin was blindingly quick and explosive. The rebound basket was the trademark of the 6'5" Baylor. I knew it was coming, the fans knew it was coming, the Celtics knew it was coming. Yet nobody could stop him from scoring off a missed shot.

Red would go ballistic every time Baylor scored on a second-chance shot. "For Christ sakes, I've got Russell, the best center in the game; Heinsohn, a big, tough forward; and Satch, the best defensive forward in the league, and we look helpless. Can't any one of you box out and get us a rebound?"

The truth is that more often than not, Baylor's initial shot, usually a running one-hander, would go in. But Elgin was the type of player who never took any chances or any shortcuts to success. He was a blue-collar worker, a forerunner of Larry Bird.

Plagued by a nervous twitch, Baylor, who played his entire 14-year career with the Lakers, didn't let the affliction affect his performances or his athleticism on the court. Baylor was a player who defied description. He not only had a springboard-like jump shot that was usually on target, he also possessed the quickest first step to the basket in the game. And once he got by his defender, Baylor could twist his body in midair to avoid the opponent's center, who inevitably would be standing underneath the basket in a vain effort to block Elgin's shot.

"I give Baylor credit," Russell told me. "He has so many moves, so many speeds, it's difficult to time a block attempt against him. He is so smooth that there are times I'd swear he has the ability to suspend himself in midair until he has a clear shot at the basket." Not that Russ feared Elgin's penetration moves. "There's only one way to block his shot once he drives past whoever is guarding him. You just have to wait him out, let him make the first move and then react. The mistake most guys make against Baylor is trying to anticipate what he is going to do. Then Baylor has the complete advantage."

Anyone who witnessed the fifth game of the '62 championship series played at the Garden could never forget the most spectacular effort of Baylor's career. Playing the full 48 minutes and grabbing 22 rebounds, he took apart Boston's defense, scoring a record 61 points and singlehandedly giving the Lakers a 3-2 series lead. It left even me speechless. Well, practically speechless. Concluding my broadcast, all I could say was, "I guess the Celtics' leprechaun must have taken the night off. All I know is they sure could have used a little luck stopping Baylor tonight." Fortunately, Boston was able to bounce back and win the title with two straight wins.

The league's Rookie of the Year in '59 and a 10-time All-NBA first team member, Elgin averaged more than 27 points a game for his career. But his rebounding was even more amazing. For a player who was among the league's smallest forwards, Baylor's amazing sixth sense for the basketball, coupled with tremendous jumping ability, enabled him to average better than 13.5 rebounds for the Lakers.

"When it came to athleticism, he was among the top three in history," Knicks coach Red Holzman told me. "But he also was what I call 'sneaky smart.' Every coach in the league would put their best and quickest defender on him. Every night he'd go up against bigger and stronger guys and he'd make them look so bad and so awkward that sometimes they'd resort to purposely fouling out just to avoid being embarrassed by Elgin. It drove coaches crazy, because there was no way to stop him. You just hoped and prayed he'd have an off night."

2: Bob Pettit—One of the first true power forwards of the game, the 6'9" Pettit played 10 years for the Hawks and was an absolute expert at getting position underneath the basket and then holding it until he could get his hands on the rebound. He learned to fully take advantage of those huge shoulders, long arms and sharp elbows. If you were going to keep Pettit away from the boards, it was going to cost you more than a few black and blue marks.

Yet I hesitate to label Pettit strictly as a power forward, because he possessed a deadly outside shot from 18-20 feet. He was the Dave Cowens of the late '50s and early '60s, a guy who could kill you with power moves or burn you with smooth jumpers. And was he ever a master at setting his man up for a pick. He'd dribble and look confused until his center, Charlie Share, would sneak up behind Pettit's defender. All of a sudden, Pettit would take a step to the right and start to drive. His defender would crash into Share, allowing Bob all the time in the world to drill a soft 15-foot jumper. I loved to watch Pettit do his thing. It's just that I hated to see him doing it so well whenever he met up with the Celtics.

Bob, however, claimed Boston was the one team he hated to face. "They didn't psyche me out," he told me several years ago when I interviewed him before an exhibition game in Chicago, "but they had a lot of guys who could punish you physically. Satch Sanders was a tremendous defensive player who used smarts and finesse to keep you away from the basket. But they also used Loscutoff and Heinsohn to guard me, and they were both very physical players. Auerbach would keep switching assignments so there was always a fresh player coming at me with a shove in the back or an elbow in the chest. If that wasn't enough, they had KC Jones sneaking in for the steals or Russell waiting patiently under the basket, ready to pounce on you if you dared to drive the lane. It was a team without weakness."

In an interview I did with Bob during his final season, I asked him what his greatest asset was. "It's my mental approach to the game," he responded. "I'm always prepared to play my best game, and I am motivated to play the best I can every night. I'm not saying I didn't have more than a few terrible nights when I couldn't even get the ball to the rim, but those bad games didn't occur because I wasn't mentally prepared or because I gave less than a full effort. I always had a plan of how I was going to attack my opponent. I studied the guys who guarded me. I tried to know their strengths and weaknesses as well as I knew my own."

Which is why Bob Pettit was elected into the Hall of Fame in 1970 and was named to the NBA's 25th and 35th Anniversary All-Time teams. For his first 10 years, he was voted to the NBA first-team All-Star squad. Four times he was named MVP of the All-Star game. In 1956 Bob led the league in both scoring and rebounding, earning MVP honors. Then in 1958 he led the Hawks to the NBA title, scoring 50 points in the Hawks' 110-109 victory over Boston in the sixth and final game of the league's championship series. He won his second MVP award in '59 when he topped the league in scoring and finished second in rebounding to Russell.

Pettit may not have worn the green, but in my opinion, he was a Celtic-type player in every way.

3: Dolph Schayes—The craftiest forward of his day, the Syracuse Nats' perennial top scorer was a guy who appeared slow, mechanical, and a bit clumsy. Yet Dolph could pick a defense apart by taking his defender from one pick to another, making a semicircle around the court as he patiently looked for a small opening. For a player who stood 6'9", Schayes had an arsenal of accurate shots, all of which he could release in a split second.

People talk about the great three-point shooters of today's game. Well, I'm sure Schayes could have competed with them all using his 25-foot two-hand set shot. It was actually a push shot, and it appeared so difficult to aim that defenders would actually back off and dare him to take it. That sometimes was a huge mistake. "As long as Schayes has the time to set up, aim, and sort of heave it up, he's capable of making them," Tommy Heinsohn said to me. "It's just such a crazy-looking shot for a guy his size to take. But he has a great touch, so you can't just leave him alone out there if the game in on the line."

Not that his entire game came from the outside. Play him too tightly, and Dolph would drive right past you, dip his shoulder into you, and then go up for a soft runner that seldom missed its mark.

Schayes was a dogged competitor, a guy who refused to let anything slow him down, not even a broken right hand, his shooting hand. I remember the injury, because it occurred during one of the Nats' melees against the Celtics. I also remember that less than two weeks later he was back on the court against Boston, using his left hand almost as effectively as he had used his right one. "I didn't want to sit around and wait for my right hand to heal," he told me. "Since

I had to run to stay in shape anyway, I figured I might as well see if I could be effective in practice shooting with my off hand. I'd work on my lefty layups and hook shots for a couple hours a day until I felt comfortable enough to rely upon it in game situations. That broken right hand ended up helping make me a more complete player."

A 12-time All-Star, Schayes finished his 15-year NBA career with 18,438 points, leading the league in the free throw shooting percentage three times and in rebounding once. "You just don't find a big man with such a soft shot," Auerbach said to me. "Rebounders usually are guys who make their living by scoring on tip-ins or short little jumpers. Schayes is a very obvious exception."

Dolph had his comical moments, although the humor was strictly unintentional. Whenever he got upset at a call, he'd scrunch up his face, turn his huge body toward the official, and literally begin to whine and squeal. Fans at courtside could never quite figure out whether that high-pitched voice of his was a gag or whether he really spoke in such squeaky tones. Take it from me, it was no gag.

4: Julius Erving—I thought I had seen all the great moves until Dr. J arrived on the scene to invent a thousand new ones.

One of the great showmen in the game, Erving's ability to control his body in midair made him look like a ballet dancer as he would glide, hang, float, and twist his way to the basket. I've seen him go around, under and over defenders. I've seen him attack the basket from every imaginable angle. Once the ball was in his huge right hand, Julius would find a way to disrupt or completely break down an entire team's defense. In that respect, he was the most spectacular player the game has seen.

Did he get the so-called superstar calls? At times, yes. Did he walk with the ball on many of his moves to the basket? No question about it. But I don't blame the refs too much for not calling it. When the Doctor took off, he moved so quickly that an official at ground level had a tough time deciding whether he walked or not. This is one case where even I had to give the refs the benefit of the doubt.

Julius' defense was anything but spectacular. Because Erving was not as physically strong as many of his opponents, he never became a great rebounder. He also could be guilty of basket hanging, of cheating a little in covering his man. That was the difference between him and players such as Baylor or Pettit, who both gave a hundred percent at both ends of the court.

As a person, Erving always impresses me. He never refuses to do an interview, he signs autographs for kids before games, he never shows up a ref or an opponent.

He was always a strictly class act. That is, until his infamous fight with Larry Bird at the Garden. At the end of three quarters, Julius had six points while Bird had 42. Larry was doing a number on Julius and giving Julius the business in a comical sort of way. Dr. J didn't see the humor in Bird's remarks and became steamed. As they ran side by side, both threw elbows at each other. At that point, they both seemed to come unglued and started exchanging punches while grabbing each other's throats.

Those types of things happen now and then in games involving such intense rivals. But what disappointed me were Erving's actions while Bird was being held in a headlock by Moses Malone, who had grabbed Larry from behind. Three times Erving threw punches into Bird's face. If he hit him once, you could say the punch was on his way, and Julius couldn't check it. But three times? Thrown at someone who clearly was helpless? You've got to have more control than that. To me, it was clearly the despicable act of a frightened coward.

The day after Bird's fisticuffs with Erving, the Celtics played Washington in Landover, Maryland. While all the other Celtics players, along with the coaches, went out on the court for some early shooting practice, I sat in Boston's locker room with Larry as he watched the videotape of his fight with Julius. As the two of us sat in front of the TV, Larry kept rewinding the tape to the moment he was held by Malone as Erving continued to throw punches. "Johnny, I'll even the score with that guy sooner or later. I'm not going to forget what he did to me when I had no way to defend myself."

Eventually Larry forgave Erving for his cheap shots, but it took Bird a few years to come to the conclusion that Julius had simply been guilty of a moment of temporary insanity, a moment, Larry finally believed, Erving sincerely regretted.

5: Elvin Hayes—A member of my All-Cry Baby team, Elvin will never be remembered for his passing skills. In fact, I used to say that when the ball went into Elvin down low, it stopped there. But that wasn't a bad place to stop, considering Hayes' amazing accuracy 10 feet away from the basket. The "Big E" may not have had a reliable outside shot, but I would never call him a "limited" offensive player. That old-faithful reverse turnaround of his was responsible for burying many an opponent when the game was on the line. Just as Abdul-Jabbar perfected the skyhook, Hayes worked to make his turnaround virtually unstoppable. He'd establish position in the low post, let you know what was coming, and then go ahead and beat your brains in with deadly, rhythmic timing. Even if the defensive man was in his shirt, Hayes' quick release eliminated any chance of a block.

Contact didn't throw off Elvin, who played both center and power forward and was usually matched up against the muscle guys, such as Dave Cowens and Paul Silas. The only problem Hayes faced defensively was that he was foul-prone, which forced him to play a little too cautiously in the late stages of games. He could look tentative, but he really wasn't afraid to mix it up under the baskets. Believe me, Hayes was very capable of dishing out as much punishment as he received, even though he cried a thousand tears a night when the calls didn't go his way.

I remember the night Hayes started arguing and whining to referee Earl Strom. "I got the call right," Strom told him firmly. "Why can't you just play basketball?" At that exact moment, Cowens walked over to Hayes. "Listen to what Strom just told you. Elvin, you're just too great a player to be crying all the time about fouls. Let your game do your talking for you."

6: Rick Barry—This guy had all the right offensive instincts, much like a Larry Bird. He could pass magnificently, particularly on the pick and roll, where he'd sense the right moment, throw a perfect lead bounce pass and set up the layup before the defense could react.

Like Bird, he also possessed all the shots. Play him too closely, and he'd breeze right by you on a drive. Give him just that fraction of daylight, and he'd pull up for a 20-foot jumper that seldom missed its mark. Despite being only 6'6", Barry was no slouch in the rebounding department. He couldn't outmuscle anyone, but he managed to become very adept, very sneaky, at scooting into the lane and scooping up a loose rebound just as it hit the floor.

His underhand free throws looked like something a seven-year-old kid might try in order to make sure the ball at least reached the basket, but it was so reliable that it enabled Barry to become the most accurate foul shooter in history. Rick knew that if he could manage to draw a foul, it was an automatic two points, so he'd "flop" if a defender so much as breathed on him. In one game against the Celtics at the old Cow Palace in San Francisco, he tripped over his own feet and then started to complain to referee Richie Powers about how he had been pushed by John Havlicek. Powers glared at Barry and then yelled out, "That's pathetic. Havlicek wasn't even guarding you; Don Nelson was, and he didn't touch you." My broadcasting position was 10 feet away, so I proclaimed, "For once, Powers is absolutely correct." Powers overheard me and came over to the sidelines and scolded me, "Johnny, for once, *you* got it right."

Barry's weakness came at the defensive end, where opponents took advantage of his lack of size and strength. For a forward, he was light, almost to the point of being fragile. In fact, the slightest amount of contact would send him sprawling to the court.

Barry, whom I nicknamed "The Brat," is a starter on my All-Cry Baby team. In fact, I once sat next to him at a luncheon and leaned over towards him. "Hey, Rick," I began, "Could you please tell me when you first started falling in love with yourself?" To Rick's credit, he just started laughing at my remark.

Throughout the years, I have come to respect him very much as a person as well as a player. Off the court, I always found him to be very human, very caring. I found this out when I was recovering from my stroke and he was one of the first people to call me. Then when the Warriors visited the Celtics, Rick went out of his way to welcome me back. "It's great to see you looking so good, Johnny," he said. "Everybody's missed you. The game itself has missed you." And every time I'd see Rick after that conversation, he'd ask how I was doing and if there was anything he could do for me. I may have nicknamed him "The Brat" when he was on the court battling the Celtics, but he's never been anything but a gentleman to me once the game ends.

GUARDS

1: Oscar Robertson—He could do anything he desired on the court—rebound, pass, ball-handle, penetrate, shoot. No other guard in the NBA has rivaled his natural talents. In just his second season as a pro, '61-'62, Oscar averaged a triple-double for the season (30.8 points, 12.4 rebounds and 11.4 assists per game). And when it came to pressure situations, to making the big play, the Big O thrived on taking control. Defensively, Robertson could be equally brilliant. He'd make the critical steal, outmaneuver a bigger player for a rebound, block a shot from the blind side. Give him a challenge, and he'd respond.

As a collegian at Cincinnati, Robertson gave a preview of his pro potential. Hall of Famer Joe Lapchick, then the Knicks' coach, told me that Oscar possessed more potential that any player he had ever watched. "He's got the shot, the timing, the confidence, the speed. Most of all, he's got the greatest set of reflexes I've ever seen. His hands, feet, and body move as if he anticipates every play. Actually, he's just reacting to something he spotted on the court."

Talk about floor generals, no one was better than Oscar when it came to directing, deploying and motivating his "troops." Bill Russell, for one, couldn't get over Robertson's take-charge attitude. "Johnny, I swear the guy has a split personality," Russ said to me after one of Robertson's triple-double efforts had beaten the Celtics. "For three quarters he's just an average player. You don't even notice him. Then all of a sudden when the game is on the line, this same mild-mannered guy goes into his Red Auerbach act, yelling and cursing at his teammates until they respond to him. Some guys couldn't get away with it, but because Oscar backs up his words with actions, he gets everyone's respect."

Sharman agreed. In a talk the two of us had on a train ride from Chicago to Cincinnati, Bill talked about Oscar, who was just a rookie at the time. "You know, I've been one of the league's best scorers for the past nine years. My best year was around 22 points a game. Now along comes Robertson into the league, and he averages 30 in his first year. It kind of humbles you. It also kind of makes you wonder just how great he'll be."

Was Oscar better than Cousy? Talent-wise, yes. As a competitor, no way. I remember Dick McGuire, the Knicks' playmaker, making the bold statement that "Robertson is better than Cousy in every way." I remember Twyman, Oscar's teammate, commenting that, "Robertson does everything for us that Cousy does for Boston." Everything, that is, but help produce championship teams.

Yet in fairness to Oscar, I should point out that the Royals never did have the dominating big center so essential to win championships in the NBA. And when Oscar, at 31, finally did end up playing in Milwaukee with Kareem, he did lead the Bucks to a title in '71 by scoring better than 19 points a game while also averaging 8.2 assists and 5.2 rebounds.

You will never hear me say that Oscar was a Celtic-type player. He didn't hustle unless a game was close. He would only give an all-out defensive effort in crunch time. In other words, he relied on pure talent far too often. As KC Jones once said to me, "When the fourth quarter begins, that's when Oscar comes alive. In his mind, the first three quarters of a game are nothing more than extended warmups."

The other major difference between "The Big O" and players like Cousy, Bird and Magic Johnson is that when Oscar had the ball, his first option was himself. If he couldn't get a decent shot, then he would look for someone else. And he did so reluctantly. With Cousy, Bird, and Magic, they always looked for one of their four teammates first, then themselves.

Oscar's minor flaws may have cost the Royals a chance at winning one or two titles. For instance, he hated training camp so much that he made a habit out of holding out just to avoid all the preseason drudgery. As a result of his annual sabbaticals, he did not get into really good playing shape until the season was at least a month old. Since he was universally known as the "Big O," I decided to expand slightly on his nickname by occasionally referring to him as the "Really Big O—O for Oversized, that is." By the time Oscar had shed his excess weight, the Celtics had usually built themselves a four- or five-game lead. For the remainder of the season, Oscar and his Royals teammates tried without success to play catchup.

Only when Oscar was traded to Milwaukee, where Alcindor was beginning to dominate the league's centers did he finally earn a championship ring in '71 and come to understand all the hard work it takes to win an NBA title. But even his success that season failed to provide further motivation for him. As Kareem candidly told *L.A. Times* columnist Jim Murray, "After we beat the Bullets 4-0 in the finals, I personally don't think Oscar felt he had anything left to prove. The NCAA record book was filled with his name. The NBA record book showed he was the best guard in history. And he had won that title, which proved he was a winner. In his mind, there wasn't anything much left to fulfill."

My most vivid memory of Oscar was seeing him, at 36 years old, sitting alone and exhausted in the Milwaukee dressing room after the seventh game of the '74 Celtics-Bucks championship series when Boston had deprived him of a chance at another title. It was Robertson's final game as a pro. Only then was I 100 percent sure that, despite all his individual greatness, he could never look back on his career and have the same sense of accomplishment as any of the Celtics guards who participated in the Boston's dynasty years.

2: Jerry West—What can I tell you? It was because of this guy that I was forced to invent the "stop-and-pop" shot for my broadcasts. West was just so quick at driving, putting on the brakes, and then going straight up for an automatic jumper that my play-by-play vocabulary couldn't keep up with him. Finally, out of self-defense and semi-desperation, I came up with the "stop-and-pop" expression or a variation such as "stops, pops, bang."

In his 14-year NBA career, all spent with the Lakers, West averaged 27 points while shooting better than 47 percent. Among his honors: League MVP in 1969, selected to the All-NBA team 12 times, four-time NBA All-Defensive team member, member of L.A.'s '72 championship team, playoff MVP in 1969, NBA scoring leader in 1970, and NBA assist leader in 1972.

His scoring abilities were so immense that they overshadowed the fact that he probably was the best defensive guard in the NBA. He made you work for every basket, every shot. As a rookie, one of the few flaws in West's game was that he was a weak, tentative passer. He couldn't find the open man; he didn't know how to create scoring chances. Jerry changed all that through hard work. By the end of his second year, he had become a more than adequate playmaker, setting up his teammate, Elgin Baylor, at exactly the right spots.

Like Pettit and Baylor, there was absolutely no stigma attached to West's game. He didn't bitch, moan or cry when the calls went against him. He didn't loaf, didn't give anything less than a full effort. He didn't come just to play, he came to win. If he didn't succeed, it wasn't because of lack of effort. Auerbach recognized this and adopted a unique game plan for handling West and Baylor, whom he referred to as Mr. Outside and Mr. Inside respectively. "Look, I know that between them, those guys are going to get 60 or 65 points a night," Red told me during a pregame interview. "They're so damn steady that you can count on it. But I also know we're going to get somewhere around 110. So we just have to make sure the Lakers' other guys don't score more than 45. Do that, and you beat the Lakers."

While West was justifiably known for his great hustle, one of his most memorable plays against the Celtics required not only determination but superhuman speed as well. That play occurred in the final two seconds of the third game in the '62 championship series. Somehow Jerry managed to steal Sam Jones' inbounds pass at halfcourt and then race in to score the winning basket for the Lakers—all supposedly within a two-second span. The next day, with the press as witnesses, an irate Auerbach ordered Sam to reenact West's feat. Needless to say, Sam didn't come close to beating the buzzer. Either West was the world's fastest human, or the refs had made a terrible call.

"I guess if I had my choice of guarding West or Oscar," said Cousy, "I'd rather be up against West, because I was more vulnerable to Oscar's size and strength. Oscar would post me up every time if I were on him. Even though West was bigger than me, he'd just play his regular game. He was confident enough that if he just did his own thing, no one, including myself or Havlicek, could stop him. Frankly, I enjoyed playing against guards bigger than myself, because I could use my speed and quickness to better advantage than I could against a little point guard like St. Louis' Slater Martin, who was only 5'9 1/2"."

3: Magic Johnson—He creates havoc and will continue to do so for the near future. It's just unnatural for a 6'8 1/2" guy to be that quick, that explosive. When you talk about a guy who's all over the court, you're talking about Magic. I swear the guy sits up nights just thinking about new and different ways to burn you. He's got the creativity and penetration moves of an Archibald, the instincts of a Bird and rebounding talents of a Cedric Maxwell.

Still, I wouldn't put Magic in the same class as Bird. Obviously, he's a quicker, better fast-break leader than Larry, but you can't tell me that Magic is as good on the boards as Bird. Bird fights and claws for lunch-pail rebounds; Magic "steals" rebounds with timing and speed. Bird plays solid, if not spectacular, fundamental defense. He's clever about picking his spots when he gambles on making a steal. Magic needs help covering his man, because he gambles on defense all the time. Bird can score from 20 feet away from the basket while the defender is in his shirt; Magic's shooting range is more limited.

I will say this, though, Magic gets better with each season. For instance, he was a reluctant outside shooter when he first came into the league. Teams would dare him to shoot, and still he'd pass up the opportunity. It was a weakness he recognized and worked to correct. After watching him perform in the last two championship series, there's no question in my mind that you no longer can sit back on defense and allow him to casually set up for a three-pointer.

Magic still has a great deal of growing up to do, however. His complaints about the coaching of Paul Westhead resulted in the guy being fired. To me, that's a case of the tail wagging the dog. Magic's behind-the-scenes backstabbing was selfish, immature and inexcusable. Several of the Laker players disliked Westhead's coaching methods, but only Magic resorted to crying on Lakers owner Jerry Buss' shoulder and planting anonymous quotes in the media about Westhead being incompetent. Causing someone to lose his job is something I wouldn't like on my conscience. When the announcement of Westhead's firing finally came, all Magic managed to say was, "Well, it's always tough when a coach gets fired, but that's part of this business." My reaction: What a bunch of PR horse manure. Keep your mouth shut and don't be a complete hypocrite.

Magic's showboating routine during the '84 playoffs also made me sick to my stomach. When he and his Laker teammates had the

Celtics whipped in Game 6, he proceeded to rub it in by high-fiving and finger-pointing his way up and down the court. Hopefully, he learned a lasting lesson in humility when McHale and Maxwell turned the tables on him in the closing moments of Boston's seventh-game title victory.

4: Walt Frazier—A team leader for the Knicks, an out-and-out pest for the opposition. His specialty was defense, where he used his long arms and amazing reflexes to strip the ball from opponents in a matter of a heartbeat. Clever "Clyde," as he was universally called, would sit back, just waiting for his opponent to take the bait he tossed out. When his man finally made a move, he was always a couple of steps ahead of him to either take a charge or force a bad pass or shot.

As a playmaker, the 6'4" Frazier was superb. He'd milk the 24-second clock, direct traffic, and then calmly make the perfect pass to set up an easy basket just before the buzzer could sound. He made time his ally—which could be very frustrating for a team like the Celtics, who loved to run. Talk about controlling tempo, no one was better at doing that than Walt.

Even though he was a very capable scorer, especially on drives through the lane, Clyde was one of those players who was more than willing to sacrifice for the good of the team. For instance, when Earl "The Pearl" Monroe was traded by the Bullets to New York, Clyde enjoyed feeding Monroe for easy jumpers more than he did setting himself up for baskets. "I fully expected to be sort of an outsider on this team," Monroe told me. "Clyde owned New York City. The fans loved his grace and leadership on the court, and they also were admirers of his flamboyant lifestyle. It was Clyde's team to run, not mine. I thought I was the one who would have to make major adjustments in my game, but as things turned out, it was Clyde who changed his game to get me more shots. The championship we won in '73, my first full season in New York, was a credit to his unselfishness."

Personally, I thought Clyde's wardrobe was every bit as eye-catching as his basketball abilities. I'd make fun on the air of his fur coats, purple suits, and weird-colored huge floppy hats: "I wonder who picks out your wardrobe, Clyde. You can tell me. It's Liberace, isn't it? One day you're going to have to take me shopping with you. I have dreams about what I'd look like dressed in some of the things you wear. Those dreams are called nightmares." The next time the Celtics visited New York, Clyde walked up to me during warmups. "I waited for you all day, and you never showed," he said. "I had a nice full-length mink coat and a canary yellow suit all picked out for you. And I got you a discount, too."

"That's OK, babe," I responded. "I'll stick to my brown jacket and red tie for another couple of years."

5: Lenny Wilkens—Perhaps you might wonder just how this guy fits in with the rest of the names on my All-Opponent team. He certainly wasn't as flashy as Magic or Frazier. He also wasn't the offensive force that West and Robertson were. However, I respected Lenny's playing abilities and work ethic immeasurably. No, he wasn't spectacular—just incredibly sound in every regard. He was a thinking man's guard, a guy who believed there was never a valid excuse for a single turnover or a mental error on defense.

While his stats weren't eye-popping, they were more than respectable. In 15 seasons with four different clubs—St. Louis, Seattle, Cleveland and Portland—he averaged 16 points and seven assists. He led the NBA in assists in 1970 and was selected to play in the All-Star game nine times.

The bottom line on Wilkens was that he had guts. He was one guy who would consistently challenge Bill Russell with his drives, while also being able to shoot what I called a "rainbow floater" over Russell's perfectly timed leap. In addition, Wilkens could also beat Russell on a regular basis with a dish-off pass, something no other guard in the league could do as effectively. The fact that Lenny showed no fear of the greatest center this game has known tells you much about his confidence and his character. Lenny wasn't a cocky player, yet he displayed a quiet sense of confidence and intelligence in every game he played. If there is one guy who would echo Ernie Banks' old saying, "It's a great day. Let's play two," it was Lenny.

6: Bob Davies—Here was the first of the "tricky dribblers." Davies invented all the behind-the-back moves—at a time when Bob Cousy was still at Holy Cross. Davies was a true field general, very clever in finding the open man. The differences between Cooz and Davies are subtle. Cooz was more of an "ad libber." Even he didn't know what kind of pass he'd make until he saw where he had to throw the ball. And Cousy would make his passes while moving at full speed. Davies, on the other hand, made many of his fancy passes from a standstill position. Still, his over-the-shoulder, no-look passes managed to catch opponents off guard almost as consistently as Cooz.

Davies had All-American looks, with blonde hair, blue eyes, and an athlete's build. He didn't curse or drink alcohol. At every meal, including breakfast, he would drink a milkshake. In fact, Bob was such a role model that he was the inspiration for author Clair Bee's 25-volume *Chip Hilton* book series written in the '40s and '50s about a three-sport All-American who displayed outstanding character, leadership and talent.

You may not recall Davies' achievements as a Rochester Royal, but take my word for it, he, along with Cousy, set the stage for modern basketball. For four straight years, '49 through '52, Davies was named a first-team All-Star. In 1951, he led Rochester to the NBA championship. I wasn't broadcasting in the NBA at the time, but I saw enough of Bob to know he was a spectacular player and a definite future Hall of Famer. Had Cousy not appeared on the scene, there's no doubt Davies would have been known as the best playmaker in the first 25 years of the NBA.

"People tell me I was born 20 years too early," Cousy said to me at last year's Old-Timers' Game. "If that's true, then Bob Davies was born 30 years too soon. I think he would have been a superstar by today's standards. He was the first of the ball-handling guards who could drive both ways and also bury the [two-handed set] bomb. At 6'1", the only tool he lacked was size. Of all the guards who came before West and Robertson, he clearly was the most impressive.

"We didn't copy each other. I got credit for inventing the behind-the-back dribble and pass, but Davies had used those moves way before me. The midair transfer pass behind the back, that's a play I think I can claim as my own. Davies, though, was every bit as imaginative as I was. Maybe he wasn't quite the showman. There's a little ham in me that showed itself most when I was on the court."

Perhaps the player with the greatest insight on Davies' talents is none other than the "Rifleman," Chuck Connors, who played with Davies at Seton Hall when their team won a then-NCAA record 43 straight games. "In my mind," Chuck said, "Cousy and Davies were equals. Not taking anything away from Cousy, but Davies was the real inventor of those incredible passes behind the back or through the legs or over the shoulder. And he did those things in college back in the early '40s. Cousy's passes were every bit as awesome and accurate as Davies, but I've got to think that somewhere along the line, Cousy picked up a few of those tricks of his from watching Davies. A big difference between the two, though, was that Davies made a lot of his passes while almost standing still; Cousy always made his passes while running at a good clip."

Arnie Risen also played alongside both Cousy and Davies. "I guess I'm a little bit of a politician on who was better," he said. "Rochester played at a slower pace, so Davies had a little more time to work his magic. I happened to like Boston's fast-break brand of basketball, so I would rather play with Cousy. In my mind, it's a lot more difficult to make those fancy passes when you're going at full speed, and the man you're passing the ball to is also sprinting upcourt."

Even Bobby Wanzer, Davies' backcourt mate at Seton Hall and then with the Royals, told me, "Cousy is in a league of his own, but Davies wasn't far behind." Wanzer, a talented playmaker and shooter in his own right, recalled one example of Davies' speed. "We played in a very small gym at Seton Hall. There were only about five feet between the backboard and the two exit doors at the back of the gym, which were about 10 feet apart. Davies would drive to the basket with such speed that he'd have to literally run out of the gym through one exit and then race back onto the court through the other exit. The fans loved it. Despite all that extra running, Bob would always catch up to the play. He was that quick."

EPILOGUE

BY LARRY BIRD

Johnny Most was my friend. I loved the man and his spirit. He was an intriguing person and one of the most loyal, caring and passionate people I've ever known. My friends were his friends. I introduced him to my buddy, Tom Hill, an Indiana state trooper, and Lou Mies, a friend of mine who had always given me great advice. Both these guys were good judges of character. It didn't surprise me that they became pals with Johnny from the first time they were introduced to him. Johnny had no airs, no attitude of self-importance. He was just a fun-loving, regular guy. And my friends enjoyed his company, because he just was a "regular guy," like them.

When Johnny's health began to deteriorate rapidly in late 1989, it affected me emotionally—and I'm not the sentimental type. I remember asking Dr. Arnie Scheller, the Celtics' team physician, if it was possible that Johnny could make another miracle recovery, like he did following his stroke. When Arnie shook his head negatively, I said to him, "There must be something that can be done. The guy's not a quitter. He'll battle all the way. You tell him what to do, and he'll fight back. As Johnny always tells me, he's a survivor."

Arnie, knowing I wanted to hear anything that would be the slightest bit encouraging, looked me straight in the eyes and said, "Larry, the smoking has finally caught up to him. He's got major circulation problems. We're eventually going to have to amputate his legs. By doing that, it will lessen the strain of pumping blood on his heart. It will buy him some time, but it's not a long-term solution to all his problems. He has diabetes and he has emphysema, as well as the circulation issue."

As I walked out of Arnie's office I wasn't merely depressed; I was devastated. As I drove home, I thought of how many laughs Johnny and I shared together over the years, how he had been as close to me as any of my teammates, how proud he always was of his children and their accomplishments. Tears came to my eyes, and I'm not ashamed to admit it.

But I kept saying to myself, "At least I'm sure of one thing: Johnny won't give up and feel sorry for himself. He'll see it as a challenge, one of many he's faced head on in the past nine years."

On January 6, 1992, Johnny's legs were amputated. The next day I visited him in his room New England Baptist Hospital. At first, it was so sad to walk in and see him in his bed with no legs. All I wanted to do was to cheer him up, but I was too choked up to come up with the comforting words. Instead, he ended up cheering me up.

"Well, I guess this means I won't be doing any more wind sprints," he joked as I stood a few feet away from him, completely tongue-tied. "But I've asked the doctors to get me the fastest motorized wheelchair on the market. This operation isn't going to slow me down."

As always, he got me to smile at his wit and his optimism.

Then, becoming serious, he began to list his future plans. "As soon as I get out of here, I'm still going to do a talk show with Jim Tuberosa. The plans are already in the works. I'm hoping to do some halftime interviews from my home, and I'm going to start producing the fantasy tapes again.

"I'm set for another comeback. There are a lot of people out there who have problems as bad, if not worse, than mine," he said. "I feel like I have a duty to lead by example, to be seen in public, because people know me as a so-called celebrity, and they're aware of my medical problems. They'll see that I have no legs, but they'll also be able to understand I'm not going to allow myself to be filled with self-pity. That would be gutless—and that's not what I'm all about."

I recall the first time Johnny attended a Celtics game at the Garden after his legs had been amputated. As the crowd gave him a standing ovation while he sat in his wheelchair near the Celtics' bench, Johnny raised his left hand and bowed his head. The *Globe's* Bob Ryan echoed my feelings about Johnny when he wrote about Johnny's appearance the next day: "From now on, whenever I think of Johnny Most, I'll think of the word 'courage.'"

If there's one thing Johnny hated, it was someone who didn't possess a winning attitude.

I remember one time when I started talking about my quickness on the basketball court. "Hey, Birdie," he said, "When I was your age, I would have beaten you easily in the 100-yard dash."

I made the mistake of laughing at his statement and then saying, "I ran the 100 in less than 12 seconds in high school, so think again, Johnny."

The next day he came over to me, holding an old newspaper article that stated that he came in second in a high school 100-yard dash, with a time of 11 seconds flat.

Then he showed me a few newspaper stories about his football days. For a relatively small guy, he was always a scrapper. And he remained a ferocious competitor for his entire life. In that respect, I felt, right from the first time I got to know him, that Johnny was just like me when it came to heart and effort. He would constantly kid me by saying, "I'm the franchise, babe. Sixteen championships and I've been a part of them all. You've still got to win 13 more titles to catch up with me." And he had a valid point as far as I'm concerned.

Like the late Dave Gately, who for years operated the 24-second clock at our games, and the late Walter Randall, our longtime equipment manager, Johnny was our teammate in every sense of the word. He rooted for every player who ever wore the green and white uniform. If you didn't play well or gave less than a 100 percent effort, he'd try to motivate you by cussing you out. But despite his cussing, he left no doubt that he cared about you, not just as a player but as a friend.

No offense to Chick Hearn, a truly great announcer, but if Chick was voted into the Hall of Fame as a contributor to the game, then Johnny deserves the same honor. When the Hall of Fame decided to give Johnny one of its annual media awards, the voters gave him his full due because he was not only a legend in Celtics' history, but also in professional basketball. It was Johnny's enthusiasm that sparked the New England fans' support of pro basketball from his first days as the Celtics broadcaster right through the championship years of the '80s.

When Johnny passed away on January 3, 1993, I was overseas on a scouting trip. I didn't even learn of his death until two weeks after he passed away. I was upset and disappointed that I had not been able to attend his funeral and pay my respects, because his friendship meant so much to me.

When I returned to Boston, I read a few of the stories about his funeral. I think *Herald* columnist Joe Fitzgerald said it all about Johnny: "Life did quite a number on Johnny's body, but it never laid a glove on his spirit. Never. Never."

FRIENDS, COLLEAGUES, REFS AND FOES REFLECT ON JOHNNY

Celtics Hall of Famer Tommy Heinsohn:
Without the unabated enthusiasm of Johnny's play-by-play and the brilliance of a magician named Cousy, I doubt whether the Celtics would have financially survived long enough to capture that first championship in 1957. It was Johnny's flair for the dramatic and his tremendous ability to paint an exciting, nerve-wracking, fast-paced verbal picture of each Celtics game during his broadcasts that lured the majority of fans into the Garden to watch Cooz "do the impossible" with his passing. Pro basketball didn't take Boston by storm, especially when there was so much regional interest in Holy Cross, which won the national championship in 1947 and compiled a record of 213-40 from '47 through '56. It was Holy Cross who totally captured the hearts of New England while the Celtics struggled to gain acceptance.

And when Red was finally able to assemble a legitimate title contender by adding players like Russell, Ramsey, Sam Jones, KC Jones, Sharman, and me, Johnny started to capitalize on all the talent. Suddenly, the Garden crowds grew and so did the radio audience. He'd embellish, he'd exaggerate, he'd turn a shoving match into a all-out brawl, he'd call the refs "cheats" and the opponents "thugs." The result was that the fans became as emotionally involved in the team's fortunes as Johnny did himself.

Having played sports in high school and college, Johnny had that certain passion for winning. He related to each and every player. He was one of us, not just in his mind but in ours, too. For Johnny and the rest of the Celtics, it was truly "us against the world." When the Celtics were winning a game, Johnny would literally be shouting for joy during each moment of Celtics heroism. On those occasions when Boston would be losing, Johnny's voice would become belligerent and angry, because there were always villains "conspiring" to prevent a Boston victory. Each game John broadcast was a passion play. He had a great philosophy about his broadcasts. He would always say, "The most important game I'll ever broadcast is the one I'm doing tonight." That attitude kept him refreshed, emotional and always enthusiastic. It's why he had such a loyal audience game after game, year after year.

As great a broadcaster as Johnny was, he was an even better person. There was far more to Johnny Most than simply announcing basketball. I would have to say he's the most complex person I've ever known.

Why complex? Well, it probably all started when, as a young adult, Johnny was very insecure because he was homely-looking rather than handsome. As a result, he was painfully shy and always self-conscious and embarrassed about his appearance. He had a difficult time in every social setting except one: sports.

But Johnny found ways to cope. Even though he was constantly rebuffed by young ladies, he forced himself to talk with women until he developed a personality that appealed to them. He'd use his personality, his sense of humor and his sensitivity to attract women. Eventually Johnny, because of his own experiences of rejection, came to realize that inner beauty is far more important than what a person looks like. That's why he became very comfortable with the person that he was. That's why Johnny didn't care about what a woman looked like. While the average guy usually gets bowled over by seeing an attractive woman, Johnny wasn't that way. He was attracted to women who were beautiful on the inside. Looks were strictly secondary.

Johnny even came up with his own classic pickup routine. He'd meet a woman and ask her to pick a number from one to ten. The woman would say "six" and Johnny would shout, "That's it. You win. Take off your clothes." When she recovered from the shock of his statement, he'd say, "OK, OK, I was only kidding. Now pick a number from one to ten." This time she'd say "Four," and Johnny would reply, "You lose. Take off your clothes." Next thing you'd know Johnny would be walking off to his room with the woman clinging to his arm.

When I talk of how complex a person Johnny was, I have to also discuss how much he was affected by the trauma of his war experiences. There were dozens of times when Johnny would become strangely silent and distant for prolonged periods. When he would "space out," I didn't understand what was bothering him. One day I finally asked him if there was a problem in his life that was causing him to become depressed. "I can't really explain it," he responded. "There are just times when thoughts about my combat experiences creep into my mind and I can't find a way to push them aside. I can't rationalize why I survived so many dangerous missions while so many of the men I had trained with had died in battle. I want to live in the present, but these memories won't let me. It just takes me some time to regain a positive outlook on life. I don't expect people to understand." I may not have grasped the depth of Johnny's depression completely, but the pain he experienced was obvious to everyone.

For his entire life, Johnny's sensitivity and intelligence enabled him to appreciate the beautiful things in life—close relationships, poetry, music, art and even ballet. Had he not chosen broadcasting as a career, he would have ended up as a great character actor in the theater or in the movies. To me, he would have made a great gangster or Indian chief. He also could have done comedic roles, because he had Walter Matthau-type unforgettable facial features and expressions, plus that voice of his.

The only reason Johnny was never given an opportunity to be a television sportscaster was because of his looks. He certainly possessed great knowledge of the game, great interviewing skills and a tremendous personality. However, I'm personally glad he remained in radio, because Johnny's greatest talent is to create a picture of the events of a game through words, emotion, voice, imagination and embellishment. Had he gone into television work, it would have changed him. With a camera as his "partner," he'd have been limited in describing the action. Frankly, I think Johnny would have been bored beyond belief, because television would have forced him to practically follow a script dictated by what the cameras were showing. That certainly wouldn't have appealed to Johnny in the slightest. He wanted to be able to stir his audience's imagination, to allow their minds to be the camera. No one did it better.

While basketball broadcasting was the job of his dreams, his greatest loves were his children. His greatest regret is that his job required him to spend so much time away from his kids. If Marge was in a dance recital or Andrea had a school play, without fail he called from wherever he might have been to hear all about the performances. If Jamie had a basketball game or Rob was taking part in a track meet, Johnny would be on the phone for an hour getting every detail from them about how they did. He'd always end his conversations by offering encouragement and praise. I can remember when he coached Pop Warner football and actually spent an hour on the phone from Los Angeles giving his assistant coach a complete game plan.

Johnny was a man who thought of himself as a plain, ordinary guy. Thousands of Celtics fans viewed him as a celebrity, but Johnny certainly didn't see himself as a big shot. In fact, he never got bored with signing autographs for anyone who "flattered" him by asking for one. I never saw Johnny refuse to sign—even after his stroke cost him the use of his right hand, his writing hand. He still would always take the time (and a great deal of effort) to scribble his name for a fan.

When it came to giving his time to charities, Johnny was unrivaled. "Just tell me what you want me to do, when and where to be there, and I'll stay for as long as you need me, babe." That was his standard response.

The Johnny Most I knew was caring, sensitive, loyal, unselfish, humble and loving. He was the living example of what inner beauty is all about.

Celtics Hall of Famer Bill Walton:

When I played for Portland and the Clippers, Johnny called me every name in the book, short of curse words. I was the enemy, the devil. I—like every opposition player, coach or general manager— was pure evil. And that's the way it should have been. Johnny truly believed his play-by-play was helping the Celtics win. The Celtics players knew this and considered him a member of the team.

Johnny's unique style can't be copied. He never let anyone shape him. What his audience heard on the air is how Johnny genuinely felt about his team. If you weren't a Celtics fan, then you wouldn't want to hear Johnny call a game. Johnny wouldn't want anyone to listen to his broadcasts if they weren't a true believer like he was.

The older Johnny got, the more passionate he became. That's unusual, because age has a way of making almost everyone more skeptical, more critical, more negative. In Johnny's case, it was just the opposite, because he loved his job. Every game he seemed to be telling the lucky Celtics faithful: "Watch out, because here we come. We're going to win. We have to win."

When Larry Bird was performing his amazing feats, Johnny had to describe the impossible. Mere words couldn't do justice to Larry's talents, so Johnny used his emotional and magical voice to emphasize the truly great play-by-play phrases he had perfected to paint a picture that was nearly perfect. Only the lucky ones who were listening—the cabbies, the doormen, the truck drivers, the young kids in their beds—got to experience the joy Johnny conveyed so well when a great moment occurred on the court.

He was so genuinely proud of how the team performed and behaved. As I grow older, I see the pride my parents show for me. I saw that same pride a parent has for their children in Johnny. We were all his kids, and he wasn't about to let anyone say a bad word or an unkind thing about any one of us.

What I loved the best about my relationship with Johnny were the casual times we spent talking at the baggage claim area or in the hotel coffee shop or on the team bus. He knew basketball inside out, but he also knew so much about life in general. Basketball was his profession, but he had a million other loves, starting with his kids. There was his appreciation of poetry, opera and art. Besides those things, there was his delight in caring about the people who were fortunate enough to be his friends.

When Johnny left us, the one thing I was sure of was that no one will be able to come close to his popularity or his talent level. Bob Dylan wrote a song called "I Shall Be Released," which begins by stating that everyone is replaceable. Dylan then goes on to refute that statement throughout the rest of the song. You can't replace a Johnny Most, a Jerry Garcia, or a Larry Bird. They can't be imitated or duplicated. They're in a class by themselves. That's why I say this about Johnny to everyone, "Enjoy the moments he shared with you, because you were listening to the best."

Former Celtics Broadcaster Glenn Ordway:

There's one story about Johnny that sticks out in my mind. The Celtics were playing the Warriors on the road during the '87-'88 season. Johnny was supposed to interview KC Jones for the pregame show. However, no one could find him. I filled in for Johnny while our producer, Tom Carelli, hunted for Johnny. Just before tipoff, Tom found him chatting with his old roommate, Don Barksdale, in an unused locker room.

"Johnny," Don said to him, "you're going to miss the show."

"Remember one thing, kid," Johnny shouted at Carelli. "I am the fucking show. I'm the fucking show, got it?"

Carelli came running back to me and relayed Johnny's comments. Larry Bird happened to be standing next to me and overheard what Johnny had said. Larry then went out on the court and scored 41 points as Boston beat Golden State 115-110. When Bird stepped onto the bus, he tapped Johnny on the shoulder and kidded him, "Remember one thing, Johnny. I'm the fucking show. Got it?" Johnny nodded his head in agreement as he laughed uncontrollably.

Bird was constantly trying to get Johnny's goat. Larry would call him over to him before a game and whisper to him, "Hey, be careful of Ordway. He just told me he's getting tired of being your color commentator. I think he wants to push you out of your job. All I can say is that if you and Glenn are ever on the edge of a cliff, just make sure you're standing in back of him."

After Bird said things like that to Johnny for a solid year, Johnny actually started half-believing that I was trying to get him to retire. I had to actually sit down with Johnny and tell him that Larry was simply stirring up trouble as a joke. "Yeah, I know what he's up to. But I think it makes his day when I pretend to buy into his bullshit."

WEEI Broadcaster Ted Serandis:

In my opinion, the funniest Johnny Most broadcast was when the Celtics were playing a Yugoslavian team in the McDonald's Classic held in Madrid in 1988. Almost every Yugoslavian player had a long, multisyllabic name. Johnny knew right from the start, he wouldn't be able to pronounce the players' names correctly. He decided to improvise.

"Oh, boy," he told his audience, "I'm having trouble with the names...Now quickly it goes to the big guy with the beard, and now to the lefty. He lost the ball...but it's picked up by the little fellow...Oh, my, I'm having trouble with the names...Now the rebound goes to one of the big guys who gets the ball out to one of the little guards, who misses the shot."

But Johnny's sense of humor came through. "I wish just one of these Yugoslavians was named 'Smith' or Jones,'" he said.

Former Celtic Don Chaney:

During my second year, I was briefly hospitalized for a virus. As I started watching the Celtics play Chicago on TV, a nurse came into my room and began to lecture me. "What kind of Celtics fan are you?" she said. "How can you play for Boston and not listen to Johnny Most?" Then she turned off the volume on the TV and turned on a radio.

I was sitting up in bed, watching the TV, and enjoying Johnny's call of the game when he suddenly began screaming about a brawl breaking out on the court. All the TV screen was showing was a little pushing and shoving, nothing out of the ordinary. At first, I thought the camera must be focused on the wrong players. Then Johnny started describing how Havlicek was "leveled by a Chet Walker punch." It just so happened I had been watching Havlicek and saw with my own eyes that all Walker had done to him was to give him a one-handed push that caused John to slow down for a minisecond.

By the end of the game, Johnny was sounding angry and downright disgusted. "If the league allows these type of dirty, yellow, closed-fist attacks on the Celtics' stars to continue, it will undoubtedly lead to serious injury," he was yelling. "These officials are inept and bordering on corrupt."

That's how I found out how Johnny didn't mind stirring up a little trouble. The funniest thing was we won that game by 16 points. To hear Johnny lash out at the Bulls and the officials was something that still cracks me up when I think about it. I figure that during the course of the game, he "created" three brawls, two fistfights, and a bench-clearing bloodbath.

Legendary Broadcaster Marv Albert:

I first met Johnny when I was Marty Glickman's stat man for WMGM's *High School Game of the Week.* Marty assigned Johnny the job of handling the pregame show with former women's tennis player Gussie Moran, who was known more for her eye-catching skirts and blouses than for her tennis abilities. When I first saw him, he just didn't look like your typical broadcaster. His clothing was drab, wrinkled, and, well, messy. And then there were his looks. His hair wasn't combed, he barely stood 5-10, and he certainly didn't have "pretty boy" facial features. His voice was anything but smooth and polished. Our whole crew wondered aloud, "Who the heck is this misfit?"

But once I heard him on the air, I knew he was something special. On the occasions when Marty had a schedule conflict, Johnny filled in as the play-by-play man, and instantly I found myself saying, "Wow, this guy's good." Johnny got your attention, because he had at least four different voice changes. He was so good at changing voices, there were times you'd swear there were three or four different people sharing the play-by-play duties. No one else could ever duplicate his style. His enthusiasm, his knowledge, and his fast-paced descriptions made his broadcasts exciting. By the time he became the Celtics' broadcaster, he had perfected his formula for doing play-by-play. What his audience got was the game and some excellent entertainment. He didn't copy anyone. What you heard on the radio was Johnny being Johnny. Sure, he had his critics, but what the hell do they know? His thousands of fans loved him—and that's what counts in this business.

Celtics Hall of Famer Bob Cousy:

I think in a sense John was as recognizable in the Celtics' cult as any member of the team. In the old days he was the best ticket salesman the team had. What's remarkable about him is that through-out the years, his enthusiasm for the Celtics and the game itself never diminished. In 35 years he never changed. When it comes to who was responsible for selling the product, Johnny should be mentioned as prominently as Arnold or Walter Brown. He certainly had just as much effect on making professional basketball popular in New England.

I never realized just what a "subjective style" Johnny had while I was a player. Because I didn't miss a game until 1958, I wasn't aware that he might have been just a bit biased. Even when I was hurt and heard him do a complete broadcast for the first time, his bias didn't have an impact. You hear what you want to hear. I'd listen from my bed and say, "Yeah, John, go get 'em. Those officials are killing us—just like you're saying. They're picking on us for absolutely no justifiable reason." Once I retired and saw things from a different perspective, I was able to see that John had the unique ability to make a pushing match sound like a knife fight. But I'm sure Arnold always sees things Johnny's way. In fact, he probably yells at Johnny for underplaying things.

Jim Pansullo, Johnny's color commentator and friend, in an '88 interview with the **Boston Herald's** Joe Fitzgerald:

A lot of young guys in the broadcasting business tend to make jokes about John. If they stopped joking and started listening to him, they could learn a lot about the game of basketball. I'll never forget a night in St. Louis when Johnny mentioned that Hawks owner Ben Kerner had gone through 16 coaches in ten years. When someone questioned that, Johnny proceeded to reel off the names of all 16 coaches in order.

Celtics Hall of Famer Bill Russell:

I hate to admit this, but I never heard Johnny work a full game. I got hurt one game and tried to listen to Johnny's broadcast, but it was so nerve-wracking to hear his emotional, usually angry descriptions of plays that went against us that I actually got the hives from listening. I got so edgy that I had to turn the radio off.

Years before, I found out what kind of person and friend Johnny was. We were sitting in a coffee shop in Philadelphia and I was down in the dumps. Johnny knew something was wrong and he asked me if everything was all right. I told him, "A white guy couldn't understand my problem." Johnny looked me right in the eyes and said, "Try me. I know more about prejudice than you think." For the next three hours we talked about the many types of prejudice in the world. I still remember Johnny's advice: "Ignore ignorance. Be proud of who you are as a person. Never let the irrational concept of prejudice affect you. Above all, realize that prejudice is nothing more than people who are fearful, people who are cowards. If you can remember that, they can't hurt you as a person."

Because of Johnny's words, I began to realize that people from other backgrounds can understand your experiences. They don't have to walk the whole mile in your shoes. If they can walk just a few steps, they can understand a lot of things. Over the years, I've learned that it's far better to understand than to be understood. One of the things I gained from my friendship with Johnny is that you don't have to be perfect and you don't have to carry everything inside. You can let it all hang out so that you can exorcise some of the things that are bothering you.

Former Celtic Rick Carlisle:

Johnny rooted as hard for the guys at the end of the bench as he did for the stars of the team. In fact, he may have rooted harder for guys like me, Greg Kite, and Sam Vincent than he did for the guys who played big minutes. If I got in for a few minutes and scored on a breakaway layup, Johnny would come over and say something like, "Good anticipation." Even if I didn't score when I got in, he'd always make sure to come right over to my locker and praise me for playing great defense. After I left the Celtics and scored 21 points in my first game with the Knicks, he was one of the first guys to call me and offer his congratulations. When he finished praising my game, I said, "Hey, I thought I was the enemy now." Johnny paused and then replied, "In your case, I'll make an exception."

Former Celtic Don Barksdale:

Johnny wouldn't say a bad word about anybody on the team. Some guys would love to needle you about a mistake or a bad shot you might have made. Johnny would have a way of joking about your play in a kind way. He wouldn't laugh at you, he'd laugh with you. That was his style. He was such a happy-go-lucky guy. It was infectious to be around him. He was always a good person to be around, because he was truly in everyone's corner, from the starter's to the players at the end of the bench, to the people behind the scenes, like Howie McHugh and Walter Randall.

Having been his roommate, I can tell you prejudice upset Johnny more than it bothered us black players. I learned to roll with the punches. I told Johnny that I learned from Jackie Robinson that you can take anything they can dish out. If not, you don't have a chance. But Johnny would say, "That was a horseshit thing they did. It's not right. I can't stand here and pretend it's right." My only response was that things would change. And they have. Thanks in part to people like Johnny Most.

Not only did Johnny have a passion for the game, but he knew basketball damn near as well as any coach. He was excellent at analyzing a game. He knew all the necessary skills and how to teach them. I've watched him work with youngsters. He was just like Red. He taught the meaning of heart and desire first, then he talked of all the other things involved in the game.

Celtics Hall of Famer John Havlicek:

The Boston players loved having a broadcaster like him. The way he told it, we never took a bad shot, never made a bad pass, and never ever committed a foul. Johnny competed as hard in his broadcasts as the players did in the games. The players appreciated that fighting spirit in Johnny. For him to have totally maintained his enthusiasm as a broadcaster for all those years took incredible durability. When he left the booth, the Celtics just weren't the same. Players can come and go and the franchise can remain stable. But losing Johnny left a gap that I don't think will be bridged easily.

My favorite Johnny Most story happened at the Atlanta Airport, which was the team's destination, but not the plane's final stop. All the players and coaches got off the plane—but Johnny had fallen asleep. He awoke just as the plane was taxiing onto the runway for takeoff to New Orleans. Somehow Johnny managed to convince the flight crew to turn the plane around and head back to the terminal. When Red realized Johnny was still on board, he, along with the entire team, ran back to the gate and was relieved to hear the pilot had turned the plane around in order to let Johnny deplane. The embarrassed look on Johnny's face as he walked up to us was priceless.

I never got a chance to listen to him while I was playing. After I retired, though, I did what a lot of people did for years. I turned on the TV, turned off the volume, and switched on the radio to hear Johnny. After all, I wanted to listen to someone who was rooting for Boston as much as I was.

Referee Darrell Garretson:

What a fireball! I don't think anyone loved his job more than Johnny. Jake O'Donnell and I were his "enemies" whenever one or both of us reffed a Celtics game. Once the game ended, though, Johnny was a different person, a friendly guy who just loved talking about the game of basketball. When the Celtics were on the road back in the

'70s, Johnny's radio station had a reciprocal deal with the Sheraton hotels, which is where the referees usually stayed. We'd have breakfast with him or talk with him in the coffee shops. He'd tell us how dirty some of Boston's opponents were and then he'd talk about what wonderful, special people the Celtics were. I'm surprised he never tried to convince us that, deep down, Red was our pal.

However, we did enjoy talking basketball with him because he knew the game and he understood we had a tough job to do. His favorite line was "I wouldn't want your job for a million bucks." I'd reply, "Johnny, we don't make anything close to that, so don't expect me to pick up your check."

Johnny would often offer to pay for the check. We'd kid him by saying, "Oh, no, you don't. You're not going to buy us off with a Danish and a cup of coffee. We'll get your check—as long as you go easy on us tonight." He'd promptly shake his head negatively, grin, and reach into his wallet and pull out the cash for his food. "You can't buy me off, either," he'd joke.

I guess my favorite moment came at the Garden when a fan was becoming unruly. I had to walk behind the press table and give the guy a lecture. I could actually see Johnny yelling and screaming at me from his perch in the balcony press box. I knew he must have been telling his audience that I was "going after" a fan, which was not the case at all. I was just forced to tell the heckler to watch his language and stop being obnoxious, or I would have to have him thrown out. A day later, I received a call from the league headquarters telling me that Boston owner Don Gaston had reported me for "berating the crowd." I had to laugh because this protest was coming from the same guy who used to stand up, along with Auerbach, and give me holy hell (which is putting it charitably) at least three or four times a game. I saw Johnny after the game and he said, "Darrell, you did a good job. That fan verbally attacks every ref, so don't take it personally."

I couldn't believe my ears. Here was Johnny paying me a sincere compliment an hour or so after I had witnessed him condemning me for warning the fan about his behavior. Which just proved what I had always known: When the Celtics were battling on the court, you'd better be wearing green or rooting for Boston if you didn't want to face the wrath of Johnny Most.

Former Celtic Robert Parish:

Everyone with the Celtics knew that when Johnny was in between marriages, he would occasionally go find a hooker for companionship. He never tried to hide it. Many times we'd see him at a hotel bar having a drink with some young lady and then we'd watch him escort the young lady to his room. He even would joke about his adventures with "ladies of the evening" by calling himself "the original dirty old man."

One time we were staying at a hotel in Richfield, Ohio, and we spotted him leaving the bar with a middle-aged hooker. The next morning Johnny was pacing the lobby as we waited to board the team bus for a trip to the Cleveland airport where we were catching a flight to Atlanta. It was obvious that for some reason Johnny was very upset. Bill Fitch approached Johnny and very sympathetically asked Johnny if there was a problem.

"Yeah, I have a fucking problem," he said. "I've lost my brand new $500 hearing aid."

"Johnny, did you check with the hotel's lost and found department?" Bill asked in a comforting tone.

"Of course I checked the fucking lost and found," Johnny replied. "It's not there."

"Well, did you look in the coffee shop?" Fitch inquired.

"Yes, I looked in the fucking coffee shop and I also tore my fucking room apart looking for it. It's gone. Vanished. Now I'm going to have to spend another $500 to replace it," said Johnny.

Finally Bill said to Johnny, "I wish we could hunt for it some more, but if we don't get on the bus, we're going to miss our flight. If the hotel staff finds your hearing aid, we'll have them FedEx it to us."

Johnny sadly nodded and, with his head down, slowly got on the team bus.

After all of us had boarded the bus, Fitch got up from his seat and dramatically yelled out, "OK, I want total silence from everyone. I have a very important question to ask."

Well, we were all startled, because Bill had never sounded so serious. Every player was wondering if one of us had gotten into a fight the night before or caused some sort of damage in the hotel.

You could hear a pin drop as Fitch paused and then marched up the aisle of the bus until he stopped directly in front of Johnny. After staring down at Johnny for at least ten seconds, Bill finally addressed the team. "Men, we have a crisis. Johnny has lost his new hearing aid," he said. "I have just one question to ask. Has anyone seen a $15 hooker wearing a $500 hearing aid?"

The bus literally rocked with laughter as Johnny appeared ready to explode. "That's real fucking funny, Bill. Make fun of the handicapped," he grumbled. "I hope all you assholes get a good laugh at my expense. You don't see me smiling. I'm out five hundred bucks. There's nothing funny about that."

Johnny didn't say one more word to anyone until we arrived in Atlanta. When Fitch came over to him while we were waiting at the baggage area and put his arm around Johnny's shoulders, Johnny couldn't help but start laughing. Then he wagged his finger at Bill and said, "I have to admit that was a pretty good line. But now I owe you one, you bastard."

That was Johnny. He took a lot of abuse from us about his habits, his voice, his mannerisms. Guys like Larry and Danny could get him mad in a heartbeat. But Johnny couldn't stay angry at them for long, because you could tell he really got a kick out of all the joking around, even if a lot of it came at his own expense.

Bob Fish, Former General Manager at WRKO and friend of Johnny's:

Johnny was on a West Coast trip with the Celtics and was supposed to do a prerecorded five-minute halftime interview for each game. Before the trip, I bought him a state-of-the-art tape recorder to use for the interviews. I listened to the first few road games and realized that he was doing live halftime interviews rather than prerecording them. I didn't say anything to him, but I was stumped as to why he wasn't making use of his new tape recorder.

When the Celtics returned home, Johnny turned in an expense sheet which included a $200 "entertainment" entry and a $100 voucher for "new equipment." I phoned him and asked him to give me more details about his expenses. "You have to be more specific," I said. "Our accounting department won't pay $300 for items unless you have receipts or a very good explanation."

"Bob, I do have an explanation but it's too embarrassing to write down on an expense sheet," he said. "I invited this woman up to my room, and when I went to the bathroom to take a leak, she stole my wallet and the new tape recorder and then ran out the door. I had to borrow $200 from KC Jones just so I could have some meal money. I also had to pay $100 to buy a halfway decent tape recorder to replace the one that got clipped. I wasn't trying to cheat the radio station. I hope you don't think I was."

I was laughing so hard that I couldn't get angry with John. "What you're trying to tell me is that some woman from an escort service robbed you blind, right?" I said.

"You've got the fucking picture, babe," Johnny immediately replied.

"OK, knowing those particular circumstances, I'll tell accounting to issue you a check today. I guess you've suffered enough."

Former Celtic Rick Robey:

Even after Johnny had turned 55, he was still the life of the party. He loved to laugh and he loved to make people laugh. Johnny had one particular routine he used to get a woman's attention. When he would see a good-looking woman walking towards him, he'd take a twenty-dollar bill, put a dab of water on it, and stick it on his forehead. As soon as he was sure he had gotten her attention, he'd smile at her and say, "Want to get lucky tonight, honey?" I can't explain why, but that little gag always made women laugh and, right away, they'd start talking to him. I guess they thought that anyone who would do something that crazy and nutty must have a funny, outgoing personality. Which Johnny certainly possessed.

Former Celtic Paul Silas:

For all his ranting and raving on the air, even the opponents who knew Johnny found him to be one of the nicest guys in the basketball business. Heck, I liked him when I played for Phoenix and he referred to me as "The Butcher, The Ultimate Hatchetman."

When I became a Celtic, though, I became "Tall Paul" who teamed up with "Small Paul" Westphal. I don't think Johnny ever saw me make a mistake on the court. For that matter, I don't think he ever saw any Celtic make a mistake. At least he never said so on the air. He had his own patented way of smoothing things over when Boston wasn't performing at its best. Turnovers were "unfortunate bounces," according to Johnny. Not getting an easy rebound was always the result of "dirty, despicable plays" by the opposition. Missed shots were always caused by "obvious fouls" that the refs failed to call.

That was Johnny's view of things, and the fans of New England believed him and, in turn, they believed in us. He helped make playing for the Celtics and their fans a great experience. Every player understood and appreciated that fact.

Former Celtic Rick Weitzman:

I first met Johnny when I was 11 years old. I lived in Brookline on the same street as Johnny's future wife, Sandy, and her family. When Johnny would stop by for a visit, he'd come out on the street and play basketball with me and Sandy's younger brother, Lewis. He really was my first coach because he knew how to teach the fundamentals and would work with us for at least an hour each time he visited Sandy.

He was an idol of mine. In fact, years later, when I was playing for Northeastern, I would play his "Havlicek Stole the Ball" record the night before every big game to get myself psyched up.

When I became a rookie with the Celtics, Johnny had what I'd say was a "rooting interest" in how I performed. He wasn't blatant about it, but my friends would always tell me how Johnny would praise me for my defense or my hustle, or for a particular shot I might have made, even if it occurred during garbage time.

My funniest moment with Johnny occurred when we roomed together on the road. We both had gone to bed around midnight. Three hours later, I was jolted out of a deep sleep by what sounded like gunshots. I jumped out of bed and turned on the light to see what was happening. There was Johnny sitting at the end of his bed, engulfed in a cloud of cigarette smoke, holding an ashtray overflowing with butts, and watching a John Wayne shoot-'em-up Western on TV—with the volume turned up to full blast. "Sorry, is the noise bothering you, babe?" he said innocently. "I couldn't sleep, so I just wanted to watch a little TV to help me relax. I just can never sleep straight through the night."

Needless to say, I called the radio station the next day and begged the general manager to let me get my own room instead of rooming with Johnny. "I don't want to hurt Johnny's feelings," I told the GM, "but one more night of his smoking and I won't be able to stop coughing for the rest of the road trip. My voice will sound more scratchy than his."

Longtime Cleveland Cavs Play-by-Play Voice Joe Tait:

Having worked in Bloomington, Indiana, broadcasting Indiana University football before becoming the first Cavaliers radio play-by-play man, it really didn't dawn on me that I had actually achieved my dream of working on the NBA level until I met Johnny on the parquet floor of the Boston Garden. I was looking up at all the championship banners when he came over to me, stuck out his hand, and said, "Hi, Joe. My name is Johnny Most and I've heard some great things about your work. If I can ever be of any help to you, please call me. Here's my home phone number."

I was flattered and somewhat in awe that a guy who had been around since the early '50s and had called so many classic games would be so friendly to a stranger.

Our friendship just grew from there. He'd always sit down with me in the press room and BS. I kidded him about quitting smoking and he warned me about overeating. "You've got to get rid of that basketball that's under your shirt," he'd say. "I don't want to see you running into health problems."

He was genuinely concerned about my weight problem. But can you imagine anyone whose daily diet consisted of four or five packs of cigarettes, a half-dozen Danish, and a gallon of coffee giving advice on how to live healthy?

What I loved about the man was his passion for the game and the Celtics. He was antsy before every game. He couldn't wait to get behind the mike. That type of enthusiasm, in my opinion, was matched only perhaps by Chick Hearn. You would think after so many years of broadcasting there'd be a tendency to be complacent or relaxed every now and then. That never was the case with Johnny. He was nervous, excited, and highly emotional every time he performed his job. He was involved, he became part of the game itself, and that came through to his audience. It's what made him a one-of-a-kind broadcaster.

Power Forward Rick Mahorn (alias McDirty):

I learned as a rookie that unless you were hated by the opponents and their fans, you weren't doing a good job. I actually took

Johnny's nickname as a compliment. Because I grew up in Hartford, I have a lot of friends who would call me up and say, "Is this Mr. McDirty?" I heard that nickname so much I had to make a joke out of it. I'd tell my friends they had the wrong phone number. "You're talking to Mr. McFilthy" or "This is Mr. McNasty. Better check the phone book for the right number." Then I'd hang up on them."

I really was never quite sure whether I was McFilthy, McDirty or McNasty. It really didn't matter. I knew Johnny called me at least a couple of them.

You couldn't tell it by how he'd describe my play during games, but Johnny and I got along well off the court. He'd always say hello to me before games and I would always say hi to him. I always smiled to myself because I knew that as soon as play began, he was going to start accusing me of being the dirtiest, most bloodthirsty player in the league."

Center Jeff Ruland (alias McFilthy):

Johnny Most was a Boston institution. He was everything a coach or GM would want in a play-by-play man because he cared so much about *his* team. He was the ultimate homer.

When I had my famous run-in with him and his color commentator, I was a rookie. My mom, who lived in Lake Ronkonkomo on Long Island, couldn't pick up the radio signal for our games against Boston on our home radio. She discovered, however, she could listen to my games on her car radio, because the signal from the Celtics' radio station somehow came in clear. So every time Boston played the Bullets, she would grab a blanket, a thermos of coffee and some snacks and go out to the car and listen to Johnny describe how I was bullying and butchering all the poor Celtics.

After the games, she called me to tell me how Johnny was referring to me as "McFilthy" and she said he was really going out of his way to make it sound like I was out to hurt players. My mom would really get genuinely upset. So when Johnny's color commentator, Rick

Weitzman, a nice guy, asked me to do a pregame interview, I declined and told him my mom told me Johnny sucked.

The next year I bought my mom a satellite dish, which solved the problem, because she could watch how I played against Boston rather than hearing Johnny rip me.

Looking back, I can laugh about my mom's reaction to Johnny's broadcasts. Truth is I had to defend against both Robert Parish and Kevin McHale at times. Both of those guys were taller than me and played a physical game. There were times when they were the ones who dished out more physical punishment than I gave them. Johnny never saw it that way, though. And that's how it should have been. That's why all the Celtics players loved the guy. He portrayed the Celtics as heroes and everyone else were the villains.

Hall of Famer Rick Barry:

This may be difficult for New Englanders to believe, but Johnny was one of my favorite people in all of basketball. Why? Because he had a love for the game that many players couldn't match. Yes, I knew he constantly called me everything from a brat to a crybaby. Still, he understood my displays of temper stemmed from the fact that I wanted to beat the Celtics as much as he wanted Boston to beat us. He was as much a competitor as I was. That's why there was a mutual respect whenever we talked man to man off the court.

When Johnny became ill, I wanted to offer him encouragement because I knew he was a fighter and I knew the NBA needed him back. He was good for the game because he was the ultimate fan. He loved his team so much and knew the game so well that Boston fans learned from him and admired his endless enthusiasm. For the opposing teams, playing in the Garden was a nightmare. Johnny Most, in my opinion, was responsible for that. He was the fans' inspiration.

I wish more people connected with the NBA—from players, to coaches, to general managers—had his intense, boundless love for the game. The league owes Johnny a huge debt of gratitude for capturing the essence of NBA competition. He was a winner, just like his beloved Celtics.

Celtics TV Play-by-Play Man Mike Gorman:

When I first began my TV work with the Celtics, Johnny was a coach to me personally. He'd go out of his way to give me little tips. He did it in a very nice way, not as a know-it-all. He'd tell me I had a great knowledge of the game and that I had a natural casual style. "Now all you have to do is develop your own expressions for certain plays," he'd say. "Just be yourself on the air, and there's no doubt in my mind you're going to have one hell of a career." Coming from Johnny Most, that meant a lot to me.

Sportscaster Len Berman:

When I came to Boston to work for WBZ-TV, the station assigned me to handle the color commentary with Johnny. It was the '73-'74 season and it was the only season when the Celtics were simulcast on radio and TV. Once I got used to Johnny's style, I realized my comments had to be made quickly and briefly, because Johnny didn't believe in "discussions" between him and his color commentator. He didn't run a democracy when it came to the broadcasts. And I admit that there were times when I thought he and I were watching two different games, because he was pro-Celtic through and through. Still, for a relative novice like myself, I found him to be a great guy who tried to be a mentor. Right from the start, though, I realized he needed a partner about as much as he needed someone constantly poking him with sharp needles.

Our principal problem on the TV side of the simulcasts was that all our replays on the road originated back in Boston. This meant we couldn't even see the replays, yet I had to comment on them as if I was actually watching them on a monitor. If I missed something during the live action, then I was obviously going to miss it again during the replay. Johnny fought the station to spend extra money so we could use the opposition team's video equipment, but the station said it would cost extra money. At that time, WBZ was so cheap that originally it wouldn't pay Johnny extra money for doing the TV plus the radio. It took months, but Johnny eventually did get a little extra money for doing both the TV and radio. He had to go to war with the station to get that raise.

Looking back on my experience, it's just a great memory to have worked with Johnny. Not many broadcasters can say they worked with legends like him, Dick Enberg and Vin Scully, among others. Guys like that don't come along more than once in a lifetime, as Celtics fans well know.

Celtics Hall of Famer KC Jones:

People tell me I have a great sense of humor. Well, Johnny topped me in that department. He loved a good joke and he could laugh at himself. He knew he was a character, and he enjoyed living up to that image. "It makes life more fun for me when I can make others laugh," he would say.

Johnny was the victim of more practical jokes than anyone in the history of the Celtics. Yet, after he pretended to get angry at those pranks, he'd tell me, "If the day comes when wiseguys like Bird, McHale and Ainge don't make me their target, then I'll worry. They love teasing me, and I like the attention."

Being a first-class showman, Johnny didn't believe in scripting his broadcasts. Every word he used was spontaneous. "Just put me behind a mic, toss the ball up, and let me go crazy," he would say. I just hope New Englanders realize what a treasure he was both as a person and a play-by-play man.

Celtics Hall of Famer Sam Jones:

In my opinion and the opinion of many other Boston players, he deserved a championship ring for each title we won. He was our spokesman, our defender, our friend, and, in our hearts, a teammate.

He probably didn't view himself as a contributor to our success, but we certainly thought of him as one of the team's greatest assets.

I know this: Not one player would have resented it if Johnny had been awarded a championship ring every year we won a title. He was one of us, a guy who always stood up for us, a guy who was willing to fight for us.

As an example, Don Barksdale, Johnny, and I went to the movies one night in St. Louis. An usher told Barksdale and me we'd have to sit in the "blacks only" section of the balcony because the theater was segregated. Well, Johnny became so enraged and visibly upset that the manager came out of his office and threatened to call the police and have him arrested.

Celtics Hall of Famer Bill Sharman:

If there's one person who deserves to be in the Hall of Fame as a contributor to the game, it's Johnny Most. He was more popular among Boston fans than many of the players. It was his broadcasts that drew people into Boston Garden at a time when the team was on the verge of financial ruin. If we drew 5,000 fans to a game in the mid-'50s, a third of them were there thanks to the enthusiasm generated by Johnny's play-by-play. He made us all heroes, and the fans of New England followed his lead.

Why the Hall of Fame continues to ignore the fact that Johnny did so much to create interest in the Celtics and the NBA in general is something I don't comprehend. It's got to be politics or ignorance. Whatever the reason, it's an injustice that should be corrected, because he was one of the NBA's true pioneers.

Former Celtics Coach Bill Fitch:

When I first became Celtics coach, Johnny asked me if I could come up to his perch in the balcony to do a pregame interview. I climbed the sixth flights of stairs and sat down for what I thought would be a five- or ten-minute chat. Well, Johnny asked me two quick questions and then abruptly ended the interview. When he went to a commercial, I asked him why the interview was so short. He explained that the engineer had told him he was running behind schedule and that there wasn't time for more conversation.

"Johnny," I said as I left, "I have two words for you—Peggy Lee."

Well, he just looked at me quizzically, wondering why I would mention the name of a pop singer out of the blue. Then, just before tipoff, I saw him frantically waving to me, giving me a thumbs-up signal, and laughing hysterically.

He had just gotten my little joke. It had dawned on him that Peggy Lee's trademark song was "Is That All There Is?" and he realized that my reference to her was my way of letting him know I didn't expect to climb all those stairs just to answer two measly questions.

Former Celtics Coach and Player Chris Ford:

My favorite story about Johnny was when he was honored at a banquet at the Park Plaza Hotel. As the guests filed in, the first thing they saw was a huge ice sculpture of his face right in the middle of the room. The sculpture made Johnny look young and even distinguished.

"Damn," Johnny joked, "I never looked so good."

As the dinner began, the ice sculpture began to melt. By the end of meal, the "art work" had changed dramatically. There were a million cracks all over Johnny's face, water was dripping from his nose, and his ears were sort of drooping as water dropped off them.

Kevin McHale had snuck over to the sculpture and placed a cigarette in Johnny's mouth and Tommy Heinsohn placed a cup of coffee under Johnny's chin.

As people gathered around the sculpture, a photographer asked Johnny to pose next to it. "OK, but the thing really doesn't look much like me. There's still not enough wrinkles on my face, my ears aren't big enough, there's no circles under my eyes, and I'm not smoking my usual brand of cigarettes."

Former Celtic Gerald Henderson:

Ask any player and they'll tell you Johnny was a member of the Celtics. He was so supportive, not just on the air but when he talked to you in the hotel lobby or while you were waiting to board a plane. "Everything OK, babe?" he always asked. And you could tell he meant it. If something was bothering a player, Johnny had a way of sniffing it out. I think he viewed himself as an "unofficial assistant coach." He knew a guy might not be able to talk candidly to Red or Bill Fitch or other players. He knew everyone trusted him to keep a conversation confidential. And he gave good, straightforward advice. He was a funny guy with oddball habits, but the bottom line is that he was respected by the entire team.

To be honest, I couldn't spend too much time with Johnny, because I hated the smell of those cigarettes he always had hanging from his mouth. Because of his non-stop smoking, I tried to avoid eating too many meals with Johnny, because his cigarettes made my meal taste like tobacco.

Every once in a while, though, we'd have breakfast together. He'd see me come into the coffee shop and he'd wave for me to come over and join him. All I could see was this hand gesturing to me through a gigantic, thick, white cloud of smoke. He's the only guy I know who could mess up a table completely just by having coffee and pastry. By the time Johnny would leave the table, the ashtray would be overflowing with butts, there'd be crumbs and ashes all over the place, and in front of him would be a dozen little puddles of spilt coffee.

Lakers Broadcaster Chick Hearn:

Johnny and I shared a few things in common: we both wanted to see our teams win; both of us invented our own phrases and nicknames; both of us had a lot of fun doing our respective jobs.

When it comes to broadcasting styles, we were worlds apart. I get angry when someone with the Lakers makes a mental mistake. On the air I get frustrated if the Lakers aren't playing up to a certain standard of excellence they've set for themselves. However, when my team is playing well, I can be as enthusiastic as the most diehard Laker fan. Johnny, on the other hand, always emphasized the good and ignored the bad.

By nature, I'm just more critical than Johnny was. That's the biggest difference between us. A broadcaster's job is to entertain and inform. I think we both accomplished that even though our styles were quite different.

In all the years we knew each other, we always respected one another's work. In contrast to the Celtics-Lakers rivalry, there's never been any jealousy, feuds or arguments between Johnny and me. I've told aspiring broadcasters that the key to success is being true to yourself. Don't imitate anyone else. Don't be a fake. Be creative, be enthusiastic, be spontaneous. That was Johnny.

Jim Tuberosa, Reporter and Friend:

Johnny and I co-hosted a nightly sports talk show on WLYN in 1992. Even after his legs were amputated, he worked another two months without missing a single show. Then his health problems forced him, as he explained, "to take a little vacation." Unfortunately, he just never regained his strength.

I happened to visit him the day before he passed away. He told me there was one thing he wanted more than anything. "Getting into the Hall of Fame for my contributions to the game would be wonderful, but that's a very minor thing compared to getting my name or even my initials up to the rafters—with all my boys. Please work on that for me, will you, babe?"

Former Rockets Guard Mike Newlin:

I was proud to have him as a friend. I consider it a great compliment that he told a reporter in one of his last interviews that he had always wished I had been a Celtic. Who wouldn't appreciate a statement like that? The Celtics were considered champions and winners by the entire basketball world. It was like getting Johnny's imprimatur on my attitude and abilities as a player.

Celtics Director of Basketball Operations Danny Ainge:

I used to spend my spare time thinking of new practical jokes I could play on Johnny. Each time he fell victim to one of my pranks, Johnny would grumble, call me "a young Mormon punk," curse me out, and then finally scowl at me. What he couldn't do was hide the fact that he loved being teased by all the players, especially me.

Johnny had a great sense of humor. I remember shortly after he had suffered the stroke that took away all feeling in his right arm, he told me he could beat me at any board game ever invented. "No way, Johnny. I know at least one game that I would win easily."

"Oh yeah, what game is that?" he asked.

"Twister," I replied.

"Ainge, only your warped mind would come up with something like that," he said. "I bet you'd just love to see me fall flat on my face."

Despite the fact that Johnny would always pretend he detested what he called my "childish antics," he was a great friend, a guy who really cared. When I was a rookie and every player was giving me the business about shooting 35 percent in field goals, it was Johnny who always would be there to boost my ego. "Danny, just keep shooting. Don't let anyone discourage you, because your shooting form is damn near perfect."

Then I'd tell him, "Johnny, don't worry about me not getting my fair share of shots. You know what the most important individual stat in basketball is, don't you? It's FGAs—field goals attempted. And my goal is to lead the league in that category."

"Just keep thinking like that, babe," he'd say, with a big grin.

And when Bill Fitch would yell at me during my first year, Johnny would come up to me and give me a pat on the back. After one game when Atlanta's Eddie Johnson had scored the winning basket after I got caught by a pick, Bill chewed me out pretty good.

Johnny noticed that I had tears in my eyes. "Danny, don't let Bill get to you. So what if you got beat on a well-designed play? It could've happened to anyone. It could have happened to [Larry] Bird. Just learn from it, and remember that Bill wouldn't have had you out on the court in crunch time unless he believed in your abilities. One play isn't going to shake Bill's faith in you."

He was always a Celtic player's biggest supporter. After I was traded, I never forgot his friendship while I was with the Celtics. Which is why when I came back to the Garden for the first time after being traded to the Sacramento Kings, I made sure the first thing I did when I was introduced to the crowd was to wave to Johnny and point my finger at him as an expression of my admiration for him. I always believed we had 13 guys on the active roster—12 wore uniforms and the 13th was high above courtside.

Former Celtic Quinn Buckner:

Johnny was not just considered a member of the team; he was part of the fabric of the team. As a player, you knew he was rooting for you. You knew he cared about you as a person.

When I was with the Bucks, he said repeatedly that I was "nothing more than an overgrown football player, a linebacker who bumped and banged into people." I was, in his words, "the NBA's version of a hockey goon." On the day I arrived in Boston, he came up to me and said, "It'll be great having you in a green uniform. I was tired of being angry at you because you've been killing us these past couple of years. I love how hard you play the game. You're going to fit in great here."

I couldn't believe these words were coming from the same guy who loved to hate me when I was with Milwaukee.

Former Celtics TV Play-by-Play Man Gil Santos:

In Johnny's mind, the Celtics never lost a game; they just ran out of time.

Former Celtic Togo Palazzi:

Johnny was a frustrated coach. I know this from firsthand experience.

When I was 28, I was practicing with the Celtics as a member of Boston's "taxi squad." One day Walter Brown called me and told me that the Babson College coach, Tom Smith, had been seriously injured in a hit-and-run accident. Walter then asked me if I would mind doing him a personal favor and taking over the head coaching position at Babson.

I still wanted to play basketball, but out of respect to Walter, I became the Babson coach. A day before my second game as a college coach, Johnny called and said he would be coming to Babson to watch me coach. I thanked him for his support and told him I looked forward to seeing him.

Well, when Johnny walked into the Babson gym, he didn't head toward the stands. Much to my surprise, he walked straight to our bench and sat down near me. Five minutes into the first half, the refs made a call against us. Johnny jumps up off the bench and proceeds to start screaming and cursing at the call. One of the officials quickly called a technical on him. About three minutes later, there was another questionable call. This time Johnny storms out onto the court and starts berating the officials, much like Red might have done. The result: he got a second "T" and was escorted out of the gym by a campus policeman. The game wasn't ten minutes old and Johnny had cost us a bundle of points.

Somehow we managed to win, and afterward Johnny waited for me in the parking lot. He was still fuming. "God damn it, Togo," he said. "Those guys were out to get *us*. I had to let them know that *we* weren't going to let them call the game so one-sided," he told me.

"Johnny," I told him, "You acted just like Red might have. However, these college officials have never dealt with someone like you or Red."

"I know, I know," Johnny said. "I won't be as tough on the officials next time I come to one of your games."

Thankfully for Babson's team and the officials, Johnny's schedule prevented him from "helping" me on the bench again that year.

Former Celtic M.L. Carr:

As you know, almost all hotels have non-smoking floors. As we used to joke, though, if your room happened to be on the same floor as Johnny's, you were on a non-sleeping floor, because he was an insomniac who would take out his hearing aid and watch TV all night with the volume at full blast. If your room was within 100 feet of Johnny's, the racket from his room was going to keep you up until dawn.

The noise from Johnny's TV was always so loud that the first thing all the players did when we checked into a hotel was to look at the team's rooming list to make sure their rooms were as far away as possible from Johnny's. When a hotel we were staying at happened to be completely booked and you were assigned a room on Johnny's floor, you had two choices: either buy a set of ear plugs or resign yourself to getting no sleep.

Former Celtic Hank Finkel:

Johnny had a way of making legends out of everyone who wore the Celtics' green uniform. I'm still amazed that I get recognized by so many strangers who call out, "How's it going, High Henry?" I was just a role player for most of my years with Boston, but Johnny, through his play-by-play, made sure the average fan appreciated guys who worked hard and did what was asked of them. There would be games when I'd play five minutes and maybe get a basket and a couple rebounds. Johnny would enter the locker room after the game, and the first thing he'd do would be congratulate me.

After I retired, every time I attended a game at the Garden Johnny would invite me to be the halftime guest. Eventually I sat in from time to time as his color commentator. I loved sitting next to him and watching him pour out his emotions. The way he was as a broadcaster was the way he lived life. He was a passionate, loyal, stand-up friend.

Patriots Great Ron Burton:
I first met Johnny when I was coaching the Charlestown Pop Warner football team and he was coaching Wayland's team. He was so darn competitive that his playbook was bigger than the one the Patriots used. He absolutely loved working with the kids and they loved having him as their coach. I think he viewed himself as the Vince Lombardi of the Pop Warner League. He'd chew out the referees, pace the sidelines, and give his players pep talks after every change of possession. When the game was over, whether his team won or lost, Johnny would shake every opposition player's hand and tell each one of the boys how well they had played. It was obvious to everyone that he hated to lose, but it was just as obvious that his primary goal was to teach the meaning of sportsmanship.

Steve Holman, Radio Voice of the Atlanta Hawks:
In 1972, when I was 20 years old, I met Johnny and told him I wanted to be a sports broadcaster. He was kind enough to let me sit with him in the radio booth. I would hand him a few notes during the game that I thought might be helpful to him. When the game ended, Johnny invited me back to sit in with him again. Soon he allowed me to be his regular stat man.

"All I want are stats which tell the story of the game. Most stats mean very little. There's only one stat a play-by-play man has to make sure your audience is kept up to date with—the score and the time, Steve. People getting into their cars or just arriving home or just turning on their portable radios may have missed most of the game. The first thing they want to hear is who's ahead and how much time is left in the game. You've got to give them the basics every five minutes." It was simple but excellent advice that I've never forgotten.

When Johnny's voice gave out on him during a broadcast back in 1977, he handed me the microphone and told his audience, "Bear with me while I try to regain my voice. Now here's my partner in the booth, Steve Holman, to take over for a few minutes." I guess I did a decent job filling in for him while he was sidelined due to his laryngitis, because the next year the Celtics offered me the public address announcer's job. At the same time, I also was offered the chance to host WEEI's *Sports Final* show. It was sheer luck that the station's general manager, Gene Lothery, sat in the first row of the balcony right behind Johnny and me.

"Kid, you did a hell of a job filling in for Johnny," he said to me. "You just stepped right in and acted like you'd been doing play-by-play for years. I've got a show where I need someone who's a quick thinker. You're the guy I want to host it."

Johnny was genuinely thrilled for me. "You're on your way, babe," he said. "You've got all the tools. The only thing that bothers me is that it's going to be difficult to find anyone who can come close to being as good and as professional as you are."

When Gene took over the Atlanta Hawks' radio station, he asked me to join the Hawks' broadcast team and host a sports talk show. Since 1988, I've been the Hawks' broadcaster, and I haven't missed a game yet. I owe so much to Johnny Most, who taught me so much and had confidence in my abilities.

About a year before Johnny passed away, I was fortunate enough to meet him at the Garden and spend a few private moments with him. "I've got a big favor to ask of you," I told him. "I would like to honor you by using your signature opening for my Hawks broadcasts. It would be my tribute to the man responsible for giving me the biggest break of my entire career. I won't do it, though, if you have any objections." As tears fell from Johnny's eyes, he said, "Thanks, babe. If you used my opening, it would mean so much to me."

Ever since, I begin my broadcasts by saying, "Hello again, everybody. This is Steve Holman from courtside at so-and-so Arena where the Atlanta Hawks prepare to do basketball battle against..." And each time I use that opening, I think of all the advice and encouragement Johnny gave to me when I was just a young, eager and very inexperienced kid.

Former Celtics General Manager Jan Volk:

One of my jobs was to select the hotels where we would stay when we were on the road. There were a number of factors in choosing which hotel would be best suited for us.

I always tried to choose hotels that were close to both the practice facilities and the arenas. Of course, I also wanted to pick modern, clean hotels that had large rooms with oversized beds for the players. There was another very important factor in selecting our hotels. Because of Johnny's insomnia, it was, in his opinion, imperative that we stayed at a hotel that had a coffee shop that either was open all night or stayed open until at least 2 a.m.

If the hotel I selected didn't have an all-night coffee shop, Johnny wouldn't speak to me for days. "Don't tell me about hotels which have all-night room service. That's nothing special," he'd lecture me. "I like to meet people in the coffee shop and talk with them casually as they come in. I don't need fancy room service meals. All I want is a pot of coffee, plenty of Danish, and a place to meet people. Is that too much to ask for, Jan?"

Former Celtic Bob Brannum:

In 1966 I worked part-time as Johnny's color commentator. I didn't know much about broadcasting, but with Johnny doing the play-by-play, I really only had to say a few words every now and then.

Johnny usually handled the halftime interviews, so I would just take a little break. However, on one occasion the producer informed Johnny that his halftime guest would be Boston mayor John Collins. "I want to talk basketball, not politics," Johnny screamed. "I know as much about Collins as I do about farming."

A minute before halftime, Johnny turned to me and said, "Bob, I'm going to the bathroom. You interview the mayor for five minutes."

"But what will I ask him? I'm new to this interviewing stuff," I stammered.

"Ah, it's easy. You won't have any problems," Johnny said as the halftime buzzer sounded. And off he went.

For the next five minutes, I quizzed Mayor Collins on every subject that popped into my mind: "Who's your favorite player?" "What restaurants do you like?" "How many people work for the city of Boston?" "Do you think the Celtics will win the game?"

Finally, Johnny joined us and said, "Well, Mayor, it's been great having you as our guest. Now we know how great a Celtics fan you are. Please stop in again."

I looked at Johnny, who hadn't heard a single word of my interview, and told him, "Well, we probably just lost half of our listeners, thanks to my dumb questions."

"Believe me, Bob," he said. "As soon as I said a fucking politician was going to be our halftime guest, every single listener did the same thing I did—they went to the bathroom and took a nice, long five-minute leak."

Former Celtic Cedric Maxwell:

I remember asking Johnny what he planned to do when he retired. "I've never even given that a thought," he replied. "I still get pimples, I still chase women, I still have a love for my job. My face may have withered, but my talent has grown with experience and my mind is still clear."

My funniest moment with Johnny occurred when he and I went into the men's room at the same time. As we were relieving ourselves, Johnny, totally out of the blue, said, "You know, Cedric, you can never tell a man a lie when you're standing beside him at the urinals because you *have* to look him straight in the eye."

Broadcaster Jimmy Myers:

In 1978, Johnny lost his voice during the second quarter of a game against the Lakers. I happened to be watching the game from press row when I was asked if I would mind going upstairs to work with Johnny for the rest of the game. When I sat down next to him, Johnny gave me a wave and a wink. Without saying anything to me beforehand, he told the audience, "I apologize, but I can't continue. WBZ-TV sportscaster Jimmy Myers will be providing you with the play-by-play the rest of the way."

When the game ended, Johnny praised my work on the air and then said, "You'll be hearing Jimmy a lot more in the future, because he knows the game of basketball as well as anybody."

I'll never forget the advice he gave me. "When you do a game, any game, always do your play-by-play as if the game is Game 7 of the NBA finals. If you do that, your audience will know you believe the game has excitement and importance."

I still laugh when I think of sitting next to Johnny as he stood up and bent over his perch while broadcasting high above courtside. The poor fans below him were showered at least once a game with cigarette ashes and little drops of coffee that spilled out from his cup whenever he got excited.

Celtics Hall of Famer David Cowens:

I mean this is in a fond way, but Johnny was "a piece of work."

When Tommy Heinsohn was coaching, he and Johnny were inseparable when we were on the road. They both drank a ton of coffee, they both chain-smoked, they both would hang out at night in the hotel coffee shops. When they would go to a movie or something, the two of them wore identical long, London Fog trenchcoats with the collars turned up. Because we hardly ever saw one of them without the other, we nicknamed them "Batman and Robin." They'd walk by and one of us players would start humming the theme song from the *Batman* TV show.

Then there was the time I walked into a birthday party thrown for Johnny when he first was required to breathe into his nose through a small tube connected to an oxygen tank. There were quite a few people at the party, but they all seemed to be ignoring Johnny, who was sitting alone in one corner of this huge room. My first reaction was to wonder why all his friends and family were being rude to Johnny. I immediately decided I'd cheer him up and keep him company for awhile. As I pulled up a chair and sat down next to him, I glanced down at his hand and realized that he was holding a lit cigarette— about an inch away from the oxygen tank. It took me about a minisecond to sprint across the room and join all the other guests. Once I made it to "relative safety," I looked over at Johnny, who stared back at me with that impish grin of his. I could read his mind. It was like he was thinking, "Boy, did I just scare the crap out of you."

(Editor's note from Jamie Most: Dave would never mention this himself, but he visited my dad in the hospital so that my father wouldn't be alone on the night he missed his first Celtics opener. The two of them watched the game together and shared their thoughts about how the refs' calls were all going against Boston. Dave, in my father's opinion, was a truly loyal and caring friend.)

Former Celtic Dennis Johnson:

During my final year as a player, the team was about to leave on a bus from our hotel in Indianapolis to go to the airport. Suddenly, Wayne Lebeaux, our travel coordinator and equipment manager, yelled out, "Johnny's missing. Has anybody seen Johnny this morning?" No one replied. A few players went to check the coffee shop and the restaurant. (Coach) Jimmy Rodgers went to speak with the hotel manager. Wayne rushed back into the hotel lobby and placed a call to Johnny's room. When Johnny failed to answer, Wayne asked a member of the hotel security staff to accompany him to Johnny's room. By now, everyone on the bus was worried about Johnny.

The security man and Wayne both knocked loudly on Johnny's door, but there was no response. Finally, fearing the worst, the security man used his master key and unlocked Johnny's door. As they rushed into the room, Johnny, who was sitting up in bed while lighting up his fifth cigarette of the morning, seemed both startled and grumpy. "What the hell is going on?" he demanded. "Well," said Wayne, "you didn't answer your wake-up call and we got worried when you didn't show up for the bus. We've been banging on your door for two minutes straight. We thought you might have had a heart attack or something."

"Hate to disappoint everybody," Johnny said sarcastically. "I'm alive and fucking kicking. I took my hearing aid out last night and forgot to put in back in when I woke up. I didn't hear my phone ring and I didn't hear you guys knocking on my door. Big deal...It's like you guys are rooting for me to croak. I'm fine. I wish people would stop thinking of me as a goddamned invalid. Now if everyone will excuse me, I'll be down in five minutes."

When Johnny finally boarded the team bus, he received a loud mock ovation from the players. "What a bunch of children! I'm dealing with nothing but a bunch of infantile brats," he mumbled to himself as he took his seat. "I'm ten fucking minutes late and everyone just presumes I'm on death's door."

From the back of the bus, McHale yelled out, "You tell 'em, babe. Hey, boys, we've got to go easy on Johnny. He's a little on the grouchy side. Must be because he didn't get a chance to swig down his usual gallon of morning coffee."

Former Celtic Larry Siegfried:

Johnny never had an enemy on the team. Every single player considered him a close friend. He wasn't just an announcer. He knew basketball and wouldn't hesitate to tell you privately when you were playing poorly. However, his criticism was always constructive because he'd tell you how you could correct your mistakes. If you listened, you'd learn from him because he was an observer of the Celtics' style of basketball and a true student of Red's coaching methods.

I remember Johnny teasing me about my most embarrassing moment. It came in a game against the Warriors at the old Cow Palace. The arena's scoreboard and game clock were located directly above the halfcourt line. We were down by a point late in the fourth quarter and John Havlicek passed me the ball. I quickly glanced upwards and thought I saw :05 on the clock. There was just enough time for one dribble, and then I heaved the ball from 40 feet, missing badly. I hung my head, thinking we had lost the game. To my surprise, the buzzer didn't sound and play continued. Havlicek raced over to me and basically asked me if I had lost my mind.

"The clock showed only five seconds left," I told him.

"You dummy, you obviously couldn't see the entire game clock. The clock was at 1:05, not :05," John said. As Red began yelling at me, I was looking for a place to hide. Fortunately we came back and won the game. Afterward Johnny came into the locker room. "Siggy, that was one crazy play. I've never heard of a desperation shot with more than a minute left in a one-point game," he joked. "When we get back to Boston, I'm taking you to my eye doctor."

Former Celtic Kevin Stacom:

If there was one topic Johnny could talk about for hours at a time, it was his children. You could always detect an overwhelming sense of pride in his voice as he spoke of his kids' achievements, from Jamie winning a football game, to Rob finishing second to the state champ in the 100-yard dash, to Margie being the star of her class play, to Andrea taking fourth place in a grade school spelling bee.

The older players devised a standard gag they'd play on rookies involving Johnny's never-ending stories about the kids. A veteran like Steve Kuberski, who had heard countless accounts of the Most children's adventures, would be standing next to Johnny in a hotel lobby when some innocent rookie would walk up and join the conversation. Casually, Steve would say to Johnny, "Hey, by the way, what's going on these days with your kids?" As Johnny began what usually would be at least an hour's worth of stories, Steve would immediately excuse himself from the conversation by saying something like, "I'll be right back. I forgot something in my room." Now the rookie was caught in a trap, totally alone with Johnny as he bragged and bragged about each and every event in his children's lives. Even if the rookie were smart enough to attempt to change subjects, Johnny would continue his rambling commentaries on the kids' day-to-day lives. I have to admit that Kuberski suckered me into an hour's worth of "The Adventures of the Most Children." I learned from the experience, though. I never again used the words "kids," "children," "sons" or "daughters" in Johnny presence.

Former Celtic JoJo White:

In December of 1978 when the Celtics were in turmoil, Johnny sensed that I was really depressed. He came up to me one night and said, "Let's talk. You look like you're carrying the weight of the world on your shoulders. Tell me what's wrong. Maybe I can help. I'll never repeat what you have to say."

That was Johnny. He cared about people. He was a confidant to everyone because he was a man you could trust completely.

I began by saying, "You're not going to like hearing this and you won't agree with what I've done, but I've asked to be traded. Red has told me he's close to completing a deal with the Lakers. I think they have a chance of going all the way."

To my surprise, Johnny, looked me right in the eyes and said, "I understand. You want to play for a contender. You're frustrated about how John Y. Brown has tore apart this team with his meddling. Don't feel guilty."

"There's nothing more I wanted than to play my entire career as a Celtic. But things are going from bad to worse here. There just comes a time when you either become part of the solution or part of the problem. I'm at that crossroad right now. We've got no chemistry, no teamwork," I told Johnny. "There's a few guys who came here from other teams who feel they should be the focus of the offense. Each one of them wants to score 25 points a game. You could put any one of them in a gym all by themselves and not one of them could score 25 points. And they're blaming me for not getting them the ball every time we're on offense. I don't have the power to change attitudes."

"I'm with ya, JoJo," Johnny told me. "I hate to say this, but unless Red can regain control of personnel moves, these players wearing the green uniform are just Celtics in name only."

When I was traded, I found out John Y. Brown had gone behind Red's back and sent me to Golden State, a team that was at the bottom in the Pacific Division. I was devastated, because I wanted to contribute in some small way to a team that had a chance for a championship. To add insult to injury, I was notified of the trade by a secretary in the Celtics office. Red, I'm sure, hadn't even been told yet that John Y. had vetoed Red's plan to get me to L.A.

As soon as Johnny heard about my being dealt to Golden State, he phoned me. "This is a disgrace. I'm going to rip the owner on the

air. JoJo, I just want you to know I'll miss you. If you ever need someone to talk to, I'm always there for you."

Johnny Most was not only the best broadcaster in NBA history
because he made you feel like you were actually at the Garden watching the game, but he was also a great friend and, for all practically
purposes, a teammate. I still can hear his voice as he rooted for us
from his broadcasting perch "high above courtside."

JOHNNY'S CHILDREN
TALK ABOUT "DAD"

Jamie Most:

My dad's love for the Celtics was second only to his love for his children. He would take me to Celtics games from the time I was four years old. I became such a regular that the players, Garden personnel and even some fans would refer to me as "Johnny Junior," which, of course, I loved.

One of my great joys came after Fleetwood Records released "Havlicek Stole the Ball." Fans would mob my father and ask him to sign their albums. I'd be at his side as he obliged each and every person. Over the years, I was so proud of the manner in which he treated the public and the public's huge affection for him.

What a way to grow up. There are so many great memories: attending the Celtics' family Christmas parties; being kiddingly called "Little Most" by Bill Russell after games; staying up late to hear my dad say "Happy Birthday, Jamie" over the air during the Celtics' annual February road trip; having John Havlicek and Satch Sanders as guests at my Bar Mitzvah; growing up with the Heinsohn family and becoming lifelong friends with Paul Heinsohn, Tommy's son; becoming one of my dad's statisticians when I turned 14 years old.

I especially recall standing at center court as my dad was honored in halftime ceremonies for his tenth and 20th anniversaries as the Celtics broadcaster. At age five, I didn't comprehend the tenth anniversary's significance, but I sure realized my pop must have been very special to all those fans who stood and cheered for him as he stepped to the microphone to thank everyone.

In retrospect, what I admire most about my dad was all the time he spent coaching my brother and I and our peers in Pop Warner football, Little League, and CYO basketball. He was so dedicated, so competitive, so encouraging to every single player.

Later, when I played varsity basketball at Wayland High, my dad would attend the games and often end up screaming at the top of his lungs at the refs. Believe me, that bellowing voice of his didn't help in my desire for anonymity.

As a teenager, I didn't want the permanent label of being "Johnny Most's son." Despite my dad's hope that I would follow in his footsteps, I was determined to be independent. I moved to California and graduated from UC-San Diego, where I majored in film and production. After my father's stroke, I moved back to Boston and witnessed the peak of my dad's career.

In 1991 when I received an offer to work for NBA Entertainment's production department in New York, my dad, despite his poor health, told me, "You can't pass up this opportunity. Go carry the torch, babe. Marge and I will be all right."

(Marge would never say this, but I can speak for the rest of the family when I state that for the final two years of my dad's life, she willingly devoted her entire life to caring for him. It was a huge and stressful responsibility, yet she never complained. Her love for our dad was unlimited.)

At my dad's funeral, I read what he had written five years earlier for his own father's funeral:

"Good night, dear Dad, sweet friend. You have finished a long, full journey. You have brought warmth and joy into every life you touched. You gave me the strength and courage to face the challenge of living. You showed me compassion and adoration. I love you, dear Dad, and I miss you."

Margery Most:

My dad could be difficult and stubborn at times. Yet I, along with my brothers and sister, knew that beneath that "tough" exterior was a teddy bear, a father who took such great pride and interest in our every achievement, no matter how small or insignificant. His support helped us become self-confident, both in adolescence and adulthood. If there was one thing my father displayed for everyone to see, it was his love for us.

When my father began his fantasy tapes business, he asked me to work for him. It was during that time when we became very close. He trusted me to run the day-to-day business, because he was not "a businessman" per se, but rather a broadcaster who used his professional skills to advantage in a business. The trust he placed in me in running a project that meant a great deal to him was the ultimate compliment to me. The Celtics had just won a championship, and what began as a small fantasy tapes business was taking off like a rocket. He was really proud of both the tapes' success and my management of the business.

At the same time, I felt sad because I could notice that my dad was hiding, even denying, that he was developing some serious health problems. He would visit the business for an hour, be in an upbeat mood, and then leave. As I watched him walk back to his car, I could see he was suffering physically just by the way he was carrying himself. He just didn't have his usual bounce and swagger. I knew he didn't have much more time. Despite my worries, I felt I had to be strong for him. Otherwise, he would have worried about me. I couldn't let him down, because he had always been there for me. And now it was my turn to be there for him.

Rob Most:

At an early age, I became aware of my father's celebrity status. Wherever we went, total strangers would approach us and start imitating his voice. Then they would turn to me and ask me to imitate him. I'd oblige by doing the "Havlicek Stole the Ball" call—even though I had absolutely no idea of its significance.

My dad was bigger than life. For years, I thought he was the original Fred Flintstone and that someone had created the cartoon by using him, with his booming voice, as the model for Fred.

Although my father was the roughest, toughest man I've ever known, I recall the day when he returned from a road trip to discover my mom had packed up and moved out of our house. I'll never forget watching this "rock of a man" leaning against a wall, his head in his arms, and crying uncontrollably. That moment taught me how difficult life can be, even for a person who seemed so invincible and strong.

My dad lived life on his own terms. He had two favorite sayings: "Mean what you say, and say what you mean" and "Winners never quit, and quitters never win." Even in his final days on earth, he was true to those words.

Andrea Most Gottschall:

Daddy was larger than life. He'd enter a room and immediately create an air of energy and excitement simply by his laughter, voice and presence. As the youngest child, I was always daddy's "little girl." And I was proud to have that distinction. All of us knew he loved us with every ounce of his being.

I never excelled at sports. Still, my father beamed with pride because he knew I always attempted to do my best. I remember one meaningless CYO softball game when I took my turn at bat. As I walked to home plate, I happened to glance out toward the outfield.

There, standing far away from all the other parents, was my father. He stood alone because he didn't want his presence in the stands to be a distraction from my moment in the spotlight.

When I left home to attend orientation at C. W. Post College in Brookville, N.Y., my father was not in good health. Still, he drove more than four hours to visit me just to make sure I was adjusting well and had someone with me for support. He spent three hours walking the campus with me before making the long drive back to Boston. Such a gesture was typical of my father's love and caring.

A sadness will always exist for me because my dad passed away before I married and began raising a family. Fortunately, I have so many photos, tapes and awards of my dad's that enable me to show my children what an amazing person my father was.

I know I speak for my sister and brothers when I say my father was a man who constantly found ways to express his love, and, thus, make all of us feel so secure, proud and special.

Celebrate the Heroes of Basketball and National Sports
in These Other 2003 Releases from Sports Publishing!

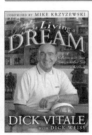

Dick Vitale's Living a Dream: Reflections on 25 Years Sitting in the Best Seat in the House
by Dick Vitale with Dick Weiss

- 6 x 9 hardcover
- 275 pages
- 16-page color photo insert
- $24.95

Tyrone Willingham: The Meaning of Victory
by Fred Mitchell

- 8.5 x 11 hardcover
- 144 pages
- color photos throughout
- $24.95

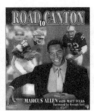

Marcus Allen: Road to Canton
by Marcus Allen and Matt Fulks

- 8.5 x 11 hardcover
- 128 pages
- color and b/w photos throughout
- $24.95

Ain't No Sense Worryin': The Wit and Wisdom of "Mick the Quick" Rivers
by Mickey Rivers and Michael DeMarco

- 6 x 9 hardcover
- 164 pages
- photos throughout
- $19.95

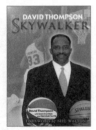

David Thompson: Skywalker
by David Thompson with Sean Stormes and Marshall Terrill

- 6 x 9 hardcover
- 279 pages
- eight-page photo section
- $22.95

Tales of the Magical Spartans
by Fred Stabley, Jr. and Tim Staudt

- 5.5 x 8.25 hardcover
- 200 pages
- 25 photos throughout
- $19.95

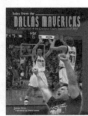

Tales of the Dallas Mavericks
by Jaime Aron

- 5.5 x 8.25 hardcover
- 200 pages
- caricatures throughout
- $19.95

Tales from the Boston Bruins
by Kerry Keene

- 5.5 x 8.25 hardcover
- 169 pages
- 29 photos throughout
- $19.95

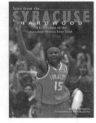

Tales from the Syracuse Hardwood
by Bud Poliquin

- 5.5 x 8.25 hardcover
- 200 pages
- 25 photos throughout
- $19.95

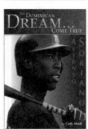

Alfonso Soriano: The Dominican Dream Come True
by Cody Monk

- 8.5 x 11 hardcover
- 160 pages
- color photos throughout
- $29.95

 To order at any time, please call toll-free **877-424-BOOK (2665)**.
For fast service and quick delivery, order on-line at **www.SportsPublishingLLC.com**.